Law and Happiness

Edited by

Eric A. Posner and Cass R. Sunstein

The University of Chicago Press | *Chicago & London*

The essays in this volume originally appeared in *The Journal of Legal Studies*.

The University of Chicago Press, Chicago, 60637
The University of Chicago Press, Ltd., London
© 2010 The University of Chicago
All rights reserved. Published in 2010
Printed in the United States of America
ISBN-13: 978-0-226-67600-5 (cloth)
ISBN-13: 978-0-226-67601-2 (paper)
ISBN-10: 0-226-67600-5 (cloth)
ISBN-10: 0-226-67601-3 (paper)

14   13   12   11   10   5   4   3   2   1

Library of Congress Cataloging in Publication Data

Law and happiness / Eric A. Posner and Cass R. Sunstein, editors
    p. cm.
    Includes bibliographical references and index.
    Summary: This book explores the rapidly developing area of research called he-
donics or "happiness studies." Researchers from fields such as philosophy, law, economics, and psychology explore the bases of happiness and what factors can increase
or decrease it. The results have implications for both law and public policy.
    ISBN-13: 978-0-226-67600-5 (cloth : alk. paper)
    ISBN-10: 0-226-67600-5 (cloth : alk. paper)
    ISBN-13: 978-0-226-67601-2 (pbk. : alk. paper)
    ISBN-10: 0-226-67601-3 (pbk. : alk. paper)
1. Happiness—Congresses.   2. Happiness—Economic aspects—Congresses.   3.
Well-being—Government policy—Congresses.   4. Compensation (Law)—Congresses.
I. Posner, Eric A.   II. Sunstein, Cass R.
BJ1481.L275 2010
340′.11—dc22   2009042195

Law and Happiness

DATE DUE

DEMCO 38-297

Contents

Introduction to the Conference on Law and Happiness / 1
Eric A. Posner and Cass R. Sunstein

Measuring Well-Being for Public Policy: Preferences or Experiences? / 5
Paul Dolan and Tessa Peasgood

Happiness Inequality in the United States / 33
Betsey Stevenson and Justin Wolfers

Who Is the Happy Warrior? Philosophy Poses Questions to Psychology / 81
Martha C. Nussbaum

Two Recommendations on the Pursuit of Happiness / 115
Christopher K. Hsee, Fei Xu, and Ningyu Tang

Hive Psychology, Happiness, and Public Policy / 133
Jonathan Haidt, J. Patrick Seder, and Selin Kesebir

Illusory Losses / 157
Cass R. Sunstein

Pain and Suffering Awards: They Shouldn't Be (Just) about Pain and
Suffering / 195
Peter A. Ubel and George Loewenstein

Death, Happiness, and the Calculation of Compensatory Damages / 217
Andrew J. Oswald and Nattavudh Powdthavee

Happiness Research and Cost-Benefit Analysis / 253
Matthew Adler and Eric A. Posner

What Does Happiness Research Tell Us About Taxation? / 293
David A. Weisbach

The Effect of Crime on Life Satisfaction / 325
Mark A. Cohen

Index / 355

Introduction to the Conference on Law and Happiness

Eric A. Posner and Cass R. Sunstein[*]

Economists who make normative proposals traditionally assume that policy should advance "efficiency," usually in the Kaldor or Hicks sense, which defines efficiency in terms of whether the project's winners can hypothetically compensate the project's losers. A compensation criterion is used because it can be based on ordinal utilities, which puts a smaller information burden on the decision maker than cardinal utilities do. Ordinal utilities, unlike cardinal utilities, can (in principle) be inferred from observations of consumer behavior. By seeing how people trade off goods, willingness-to-pay (or willingness-to-accept) amounts can be derived and summed, so that alternative policy outcomes can be easily compared.

This approach has received a great deal of criticism over the decades, but it has survived mainly because no alternative method has commanded widespread agreement. In recent years, however, a small group of economists and psychologists have argued that an alternative method is available. This method, often called the "happiness approach," relies on surveys that ask people to rate their happiness on a scale. Econometric analysis then finds correlations between ratings on the scale and various characteristics or experiences of the survey respondents—wealth, income, family relationships, and so forth. Though still regarded with

ERIC A. POSNER is the Kirkland and Ellis Professor of Law at the University of Chicago Law School. CASS R. SUNSTEIN is the Felix Frankfurter Professor of Law at Harvard Law School.

* After this book was completed, Sunstein began work for the United States government in the Office of Management and Budget; nothing said here represents in any way an official position of the United States.

[*Journal of Legal Studies*, vol. XXXVII (June 2008)]

skepticism in many quarters, the happiness approach has scored some notable successes. The various factors that are correlated with happiness appear to be robust: they recur in different surveys and are correlated with other factors that are plausibly linked to happiness such as physical well-being as measured with clinical tests.

In addition, many of the findings have a certain plausibility, while at the same time deviating from the results of willingness-to-pay and willingness-to-accept measures. Happiness improves with wealth but only to a point, and people are less happy when their neighbors are wealthier than they are. Happiness is correlated with health, but the happiness levels of people who suffer grievous injuries rebound with the passage of time. Happy people have friends and families, but adults with teenagers are less happy than adults with younger or older children. Educated and politically engaged people are happier.

The idea that policy should focus on happiness rather than preference orderings is hardly new. Indeed, the happiness view predates the preference-orderings view. Jeremy Bentham advocated a form of utilitarianism that maximized pleasures and minimized pains, an idea that is similar, though not identical, to the premise that self-reported happiness measures should be used. Economists subsequently abandoned this view in favor of ordinal utility functions. But the Benthamite approach never really went away. It has lurked at the margins of mainstream economic thought for decades. The most famous example is the Easterlin paradox. Richard Easterlin (1973) was the first to observe that self-reported happiness is correlated with wealth at the individual level but not, above a threshold, at the aggregate level: he found that happiness does not appear to increase with gross domestic product in wealthy countries (this finding has been challenged; see Stevenson and Wolfers 2008).

More recent work has exploited improved data sets; much of it is oriented toward public policy. Much work continues to investigate the methodological foundations of happiness research, with some authors (for example, Kahneman 2000) expressing concerns about the reliability or accuracy of the happiness surveys and proposing alternatives. Most of the public-policy-oriented work has focused on the implications of the research for structuring political institutions (for example, Frey and Stutzer 2002), for evaluating government projects (for example, Van Praag and Baarsma 2005), and for determining legal damages for various types of injuries (for example, Clark and Oswald 2002).[1]

---

1. Applications in the legal literature have been sparse. See, for example, Bagenstos

The current issue of the *Journal of Legal Studies* contains papers delivered at a conference on the new happiness research and its implications for law and public policy, which was held at the University of Chicago Law School on June 1 and 2, 2007. The purpose of the conference was to encourage greater collaboration across disciplines and reflection on the implications of happiness research for law and public policy. Several of the papers (Haidt, Seder, and Kesebir; Hsee, Xu and Tang; Nussbaum; Dolan and Peasgood; Stevenson and Wolfers) explore continuing methodological challenges to the happiness approach, the empirical data, and the implications for public policy in a general sense. The other papers address the implications of happiness research for specific areas of the law, including the determination of damages (Oswald and Powdthavee; Sunstein; Ubel and Loewenstein), crime (Cohen), tax (Weisbach), and cost-benefit analysis (Adler and Posner).

We thank the John M. Olin Progam in Law and Economics at the University of Chicago Law School for providing financial support for this conference.

REFERENCES

Bagenstos, Samuel R., and Margo Schlanger. 2007. Hedonic Damages, Hedonic Adaptation, and Disability. *Vanderbilt Law Review* 60:745–97.

Bronsteen, John, Christopher Buccafusco, and Jonathan S. Masur. 2008. Hedonic Adaptation and the Settlement of Civil Lawsuits. *Columbia Law Review* 108: 1516–49.

Clark, Andrew E., and Andrew J. Oswald. 2002. A Simple Statistical Method for Measuring How Life Events Affect Happiness. *International Journal of Epidemiology* 31:1139–44.

Easterlin, Richard A. 1973. Does Money Buy Happiness? *Public Interest* 30: 3–10.

Frey, Bruno S., and Alois Stutzer. 2002. *Happiness and Economics: How the Economy and Institutions Affect Human Well-Being.* Princeton, N.J.: Princeton University Press.

Huang, Peter H., and Rick Swedloff. 2008. Authentic Happiness and Meaning at Law Firms. *Syracuse Law Review* 58:335–50.

Kahneman, Daniel. 2000. Experienced Utility and Objective Happiness: A Moment-Based Approach. Pp. 673–92 in *Choices, Values, and Frames*, edited

and Schlanger (2007), Bronsteen, Buccafusco, and Masur (2008), Huang and Swedloff (2008), Posner and Sunstein (2005), and Warner (2008).

by Daniel Kahneman and Amos Tversky. Cambridge: Cambridge University Press.

Posner, Eric A., and Cass R. Sunstein. 2005. Dollars and Death. *University of Chicago Law Review* 72:537–98.

Stevenson, Betsey, and Justin Wolfers. 2008. Economic Growth and Happiness: Reassessing the Easterlin Paradox. *Brookings Papers on Economic Activity*, spring, pp. 1–102.

Van Praag, Bernard M. S., and Barbara E. Baarsma. 2005. Using Happiness Surveys to Value Intangibles: The Case of Airport Noise. *Economic Journal* 115:224–46.

Warner, Daniel M. 2008. Uses of Subjective Well-Being in Local Economic and Land Use Policy. *Journal of Land Use and Environmental Law* 23:263–303.

Measuring Well-Being for Public Policy: Preferences or Experiences?

Paul Dolan and Tessa Peasgood

ABSTRACT

Policy makers seeking to enhance well-being are faced with a choice of possible measures that may offer contrasting views about how well an individual's life is going. We suggest that choice of well-being measure should be based on three general criteria: (1) the measure must be conceptually appropriate (that is, are we measuring the right sort of concept for public policy?), (2) it must be valid (that is, is it a good measure of that concept?), and (3) it must be empirically useful (that is, does it provide information in a format that can be readily used by policy makers?). Preference-based measures (as represented by income) are compared to experience-based measures (as represented by subjective evaluations of life) according to these criteria. Neither set of measures meets ideal standards, but experiences do fare at least as well as preferences, and subjective evaluations perform much better than income alone as a measure of well-being.

1. INTRODUCTION

In various ways, policy makers seek to improve of the well-being of the populations they serve. The question is, do they have a clear idea about what constitutes well-being? Economists have for some time framed this in terms of utility, as represented by preferences (Fisher 1918). The degree to which preferences are fulfilled is determined primarily by an

PAUL DOLAN is Professor of Economics at Tanaka Business School, Imperial College, London. TESSA PEASGOOD is a Ph.D. student at Imperial College, London. The British Household Panel Survey data were made available through the Economic and Social Research Council (ESRC) Data Archive. The data were originally collected by the ESRC Institute for Social and Economic Research at the University of Essex. Neither the original collectors of the data nor the archive bear any responsibility for the analyses or interpretations presented here.

[*Journal of Legal Studies*, vol. XXXVII (June 2008)]

individual's budget constraint, which is determined by her income and prevailing prices. It is not surprising, then, that economists have paid so much attention to national income as a proxy for well-being. More recently, some economists have sought to improve the use of income as a proxy for well-being by focusing only on those aspects of income that are deemed to bring genuine improvements in well-being. Examples of this approach include adjusted income accounts, such as the Index of Economic Well-Being (Osberg 1985). A preference satisfaction (or desire fulfillment) account of well-being has also been at the heart of philosophical discourse.

Many alternative approaches in philosophy adopt mental-state accounts of well-being. These accounts view well-being as a psychological phenomenon characterized by feelings of pleasure and displeasure, happiness and sadness, and satisfaction and dissatisfaction. Such accounts of well-being are generally grounded in hedonistic philosophies (Kahneman 2000), but we use the term "subjective evaluation" to refer to a more general account that considers how people evaluate their lives, as well as how they feel in a strict hedonic sense. Direct measures of subjective evaluation—usually asking people how satisfied they are with their lives overall—have been used by psychologists for 50 years, and they are now becoming popular among economists (Dolan, Peasgood, and White 2006). Subjective evaluation is also making its way up the policy agenda, particularly in the United Kingdom (see, for example, Defra 2005).

Of course, the debate about what constitutes well-being is longstanding.[1] Despite a lack of theoretical agreement, policy decisions reflect judgments, at some level, about the well-being of those who may be affected by the decisions. Moreover, the choice of well-being measure may have very different implications for which people we judge to have high and low levels of well-being. Consider the following data from the British Household Panel Survey (BHPS) in the United Kingdom. The BHPS is an annual survey of about 5,000 households (about 10,000

---

1. Another prominent account is one that takes the view that well-being can be represented as an objective list of social and economic attainments or that well-being is usefully correlated to such attainments as measured by, for example, the Human Development Index, which is a weighted average of longevity, educational attainment, and real gross domestic product per capita (United Nations Development Programme 2006). We do not consider this approach further in this paper and concentrate instead on the preference satisfaction and subjective-evaluation accounts of well-being.

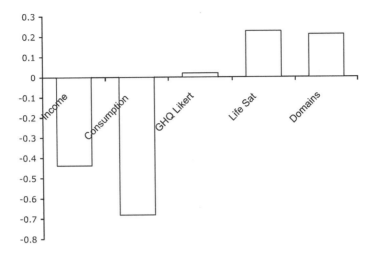

Figure 1. Average standardized scores of well-being for those over age 70

individuals), has been running since 1991, and is broadly representative of the British population (Nathan 1999).

For subgroups of respondents in 2004/2005 (wave 14), Figures 1–4 show average standardized scores of income (net current household income controlling for household size), consumption (for a limited range of consumption items and controlling for household size), a General Health Questionnaire (GHQ) measure of anxiety and depression (12 questions with four possible responses, giving a score out of 36), life satisfaction (scored from 1 to 7), and weighted responses to satisfaction in eight domains. The domains are health, household income, house or flat, spouse or partner, job, social life, amount of leisure time, and use of leisure time. Weights are derived from a regression model predicting overall life satisfaction.

It is clear that different groups have different levels of well-being based whether preference satisfaction (income or consumption) or subjective evaluation (GHQ, life satisfaction, or domain satisfaction scores) is used. In the case of people over age 70, the difference between consumption and life satisfaction is close to 1 standard deviation. Given that the choice of well-being measure is important, it is necessary to decide which measure is most appropriate to use in resource allocation decisions.

It is important that the choice of well-being measure be based on

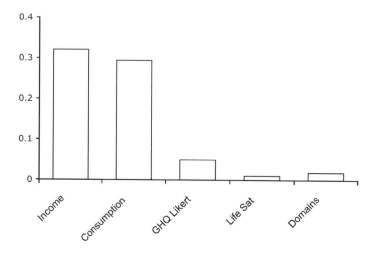

Figure 2. Average standardized scores of well-being for those with a degree or equivalent

clear criteria that are relevant to the policy context. It is surprising that there has been very little consideration given to precisely what conditions a well-being measure for policy purposes should satisfy. Sumner (1996) does set out criteria for a theory of welfare of "descriptive adequacy," which, among other things, requires compatibility with widely held intuitions about well-being and shares many of the features we consider here. However, our emphasis is on the need for a measure of well-being that can actively be used for policy rather than to establish criteria for an account of well-being for philosophical dialogue.

In this paper, we consider three general criteria that any measure for policy should be evaluated against: (1) the measure must be conceptually appropriate, (2) it must be valid, and (3) it must be empirically useful. We suggest that a conceptually appropriate measure is one that is a complete measure of prudential value (that is, what is good for the individual rather than what might be considered to be the good life). An appropriate measure will measure what it purports to, but validity is problematic in the absence of a gold standard for well-being. Nonetheless, the measure should allow for comparisons across time and people and should converge with and predict things (such as health) commonly thought to be associated with well-being. A measure of well-being will be empirically useful if it is cardinal, unbiased, sensitive to changes in well-being, and practical to collect.

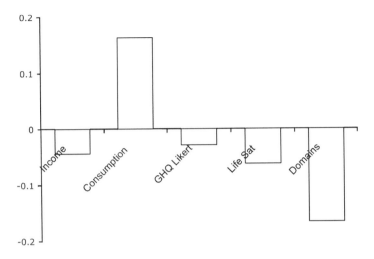

Figure 3. Average standardized scores of well-being for those ages 25–50 with children

We evaluate the preference satisfaction account (as largely proxied by income) and the subjective-evaluation account against these criteria as measures of individual (rather than social) well-being.

Subjective evaluation is usually identified through survey questions, which vary from single questions (for example, "All things considered, how satisfied are you with your life as a whole these days?" [World Values Survey 2000]) to multiple questions (for example, Satisfaction with Life Scale [Diener et al. 1985]). Questions may also use the terminology of "happiness" (for example, "Taking all things together, would you say you are . . . Very happy, Quite happy, Not very happy, Not at all happy" [World Values Survey 2000]). Responses to questions using the language of satisfaction generally correlate highly with those asking about happiness (van den Berg and Ferrer-i-Carbonell 2007; Di Tella et al. 2003; Helliwell and Putnam 2004). Therefore, we use the term "subjective evaluation" to refer all of these general measures. We do not, however, explore the advantages and disadvantages of more hedonistic measures of well-being, such as measures of affect balance or measures that aggregate daily affect (for example, Daily Reconstruction Method [Kahneman et al. 2004]).

We recognize that governments do not rely on income alone as a measure of well-being, and many social indicators are used to judge the effectiveness and the distributional consequences of government policy.

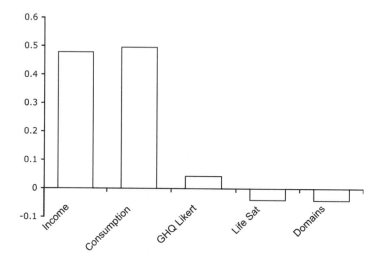

Figure 4. Average standardized scores of well-being for those who commute more than 1 hour per day.

However, willingness to pay (WTP) is widely used as a measure of benefit in cost-benefit analysis, and income is sometimes treated as a complete measure of value. Therefore, it is useful to compare income with life satisfaction, which is increasingly being advocated as an alternative measure of well-being for policy.

We also recognize that a measure of well-being could be used in many policy contexts: in economic evaluations such as cost-benefit or cost-effectiveness studies in (for example) health care, in research on understanding issues such as the causes of well-being throughout the life course, in measuring individual well-being and aggregate well-being for macro policy design, in monitoring distributional and equity concerns and evaluating policy initiatives aimed at distributional issues, and in international comparisons aimed at judging relative country performance and contributing to national-level policy agendas. Precisely what is required of the measure may vary according to context, but the criteria should apply in all circumstances, even if the relative importance of the criteria may vary depending upon the application of the measure.

Notwithstanding some variation according to specific contexts, our general conclusion is that income as a proxy for preference satisfaction performs no better, and sometimes worse, than life satisfaction ratings as a measure of individual well-being for public policy. In Sections 2 and 3, we set out the criteria and assess the accounts according to them before considering some of the implications of our conclusion for research and policy in Section 4.

2. THE CRITERIA

2.1. The Measure Is Conceptually Appropriate

While it may be philosophically interesting to consider the best and most complete account of well-being, policy makers require knowledge only about that part of well-being that is relevant for public policy. This means the account and the measure must include only those things that are relevant to policy—and it must exclude those things that are not relevant. In relation to the former consideration, a distinction can be made between the good life and a life that is good for the individual concerned. The concept of a good life includes values beyond what is good for the individual, such as moral, spiritual, and aesthetic concerns. The concept of well-being most suitable for public policy is that which is good for the individual, that is, prudential value. This is not to say that nonprudential values should not be of concern for government. However, for transparency and clarity, this can be in addition to well-being rather than combined in one well-being measure.

The measure should incorporate all those attributes that are seen to make someone's life better for her; hence, it is an exhaustive measure of prudential value. For example, if the measure excludes something that the individual could have, and society cares about whether she has it for her sake, then the measure may not be sufficiently complete. If an attribute that we care about people having is not picked up by the measure, and this attribute differs between members of the society, then we need to cast doubt either on our intuitions that the attribute is something we should care about or on the measure of well-being.

In relation to what might be excluded from prudential value, some sources of well-being may be illegal or socially illegitimate (Feldman 2002). A contentious issue is whether one individual's well-being is allowed (for policy purposes) to decline when another person's income or consumption rise. Harsanyi (1982, p. 56) proposed that the social welfare function should exclude antisocial preferences, such as "sadism, envy, resentment, and malice." However, one person's consumption may also be viewed as imposing an externality onto other people that they are unable to avoid (Frank 1997; Layard 2006). We may also find inappropriate claims on resources arising from the cultivation of expensive tastes (Cohen 1993; Rawls 1982).

Despite these concerns, we suggest that all sources of well-being should be included at the measurement stage. It is impractical to measure the extent to which an individual's well-being has been derived from illegitimate sources, even assuming those sources could be agreed upon and remain stable. Additional information on the sources of well-being or changes in well-being may still be relevant for the formulation of policy, and methods might be developed to determine these where they are considered particularly important.

Well-being may also arise from areas that society does not perceive to be appropriate areas of concern for government intervention, for example, those relating to religious beliefs. However, attributes of well-being should be excluded from a public policy measure only if they cannot be affected by any government policies (and this is unlikely to be known in advance). While it may be appropriate to exclude some attributes of well-being from being targets of government policy, the consequences of any action designed to improve well-being should be judged by its impact on well-being overall.

Therefore, an ideal measure would include all important consequences to the individual, and whether these should all be considered the remit of policy is then a separate question. Of course, a measure of well-being for public policy needs to be acceptable to policy makers and the public. A measure of prudential value is likely to be have more legitimacy when it is placed alongside (and sometimes traded off for) other objectives (for example, truth, justice, freedoms, knowledge, beauty, and so on), and this is preferable to trying to incorporate these other values within the well-being measure.

2.2. The Measure Is Valid

To be useful for policy, a measure should measure what it purports to. However, it is impossible to fully establish validity in the absence of a gold standard for measuring well-being. Nonetheless, the measure should show how an individual's well-being changes over time and how it compares to that of other individuals. Interpersonal comparison requires that measurement scales referring to different people can be meaningfully compared. Economists have been remarkably reluctant to make interpersonal comparisons (as a good example, see Robbins 1932). However, we cannot escape the fact that most policy decisions involve, either explicitly or implicitly, comparisons of the costs and benefits incurred by different people.

One way of considering whether a measure of well-being is valid is to consider the degree to which the measure is similar to (converges on) other measures to which theoretically it should be similar. If the measure is not correlated with factors that we take to be signs of an individual's well-being—such as health, material resources, facial expressions, her opinions about how her life is going, and opinions of those close to her—then this would be of concern for the measure unless a reasonable explanation could be offered. It should be noted that our intuition on sources of well-being may be incorrect, so correlations of a measure of well-being with an attribute that is commonly thought to be a source of well-being should be treated with caution. A measure has predictive validity if it can correctly predict something that we theoretically think it should be able to predict. For example, low levels of well-being may predict attempts at suicide.

2.3. The Measure Is Empirically Useful

For most policy evaluations, we should like to know something about how much well-being changes as well as whether it goes up or down; that is, the measure should be cardinal. Since Pareto ([1906] 1971), many economists have been reluctant to think in terms of cardinal differences in well-being. However, Ng (1997) argues that people can make statements about how much more or less happy they are in one state over another. Moreover, people do not seem to find it difficult to make decisions between ways of spending their time, money, and energy on things that yield noncomparable benefits: it seems an individual can get by without having a clear idea of exactly how much additional well-being she gets from owning a cat, her relationship with her sister, eating chocolate ice cream, or having a detached garage. Griffin (1986) describes individual judgments of intrinsic reward as "roughly cardinal" and capable of distinguishing big from small differences finely enough to guide individual decisions on what is worth sacrificing or risking now for future gains.

The measure should represent an unbiased assessment of well-being and should not be sensitive to theoretically irrelevant factors. The perfect measure in theory may be unreliable in practice if it is subject to various biases, heuristics, and framing effects. Having said this, policy makers will require a measure that is sensitive to real changes in well-being and is able to distinguish between different levels of well-being. From the policy maker's perspective, being able to show changes that arise as a result of altered circumstances over which the government may have some degree of control is likely to be essential. However, measures should not be so sensitive that they detect differences that are not relevant to the individual or to public policy. A measure's sensitivity needs to be judged by its ability to detect true changes in well-being rather than its variability and divisibility into a large number of different levels.

Finally, any empirically useful measure of well-being for public policy must be practical, that is, easily and cheaply attainable. In order to measure well-being efficiently, there should not be redundancy within the measurement instrument, and additional items should be included only if they provide additional information.

3. DO INCOME AND LIFE SATISFACTION MEET THESE CRITERIA?

This section compares the performance of income as a measure of preference satisfaction and evaluative survey reports against the criteria set out above.

3.1. Is the Measure Conceptually Appropriate?

3.1.1. Preference Satisfaction. The appropriate conception in this context is one that includes only prudential value. Preference satisfaction measures of well-being can incorporate both prudential and nonprudential value. To the extent that income contributes to the satisfaction of nonprudential desires, it will overestimate the prudential part of well-being that we have argued to be relevant to public policy. However, expenditure on nonprudential desires is very small. Even if all charitable donations reflected nonprudential concerns (which they do not of course, as they also result in the purchase of moral satisfaction), they would represent about 2 percent of disposable household income in the United States (Giving USA 2006). Although many desires for nonprudential values may not reveal themselves in financial giving, the levels of expenditure on charity donations suggest that expenditure on nonprudential values does not represent a large part of expenditure.

It is an open question the degree to which people actually think that well-being increases when more of our preferences are satisfied. Even if preference satisfaction is an appropriate account of well-being, the main measurement instrument—income—is also required to be appropriate. Many people would agree that more income is not necessarily always a good thing, but many of us act as if it is. Income certainly does not reflect all that is important to well-being, and, at least in advanced economies, friendship and a good family life are often seen as more important to well-being than is income (Lane 2000). To the extent that the consequences of satisfying our desires show up in our life satisfaction, the effect of income would appear to be small (and sometimes less than the effect of relative income). Many studies have also shown that marriage, health, employment status, and contact with friends and family are robust determinants of happiness (see Dolan, Peasgood, and White [2006] for a review). These factors are independently important to happiness, and desires for them cannot be fully satisfied by increased income.

3.1.2. Subjective Evaluation.   Life satisfaction ratings may correspond to an individual's assessment of her own life or the lives of her family group, those close to her, animal species, or the world more generally, and life satisfaction may arise from sacrifices to her own interests, such as sacrifices for her children. Ng and Ho (2006) argue that life satisfaction has the potential to incorporate beliefs of doing things to benefit others, regardless of whether that benefit has even been realized. Cross-cultural studies have found that less individualistic cultures may incorporate concerns for family and community units in their own life assessments (Diener, Oishi, and Lucas 2003). Some evaluative-style survey questions may have more potential to incorporate nonprudential values than others; for example, questions focusing on living the "best life" possible may lead individuals to think about moral or spiritual values in addition to prudential values.

While personal sacrifice is a theoretical possibility, the addition of nonprudential concerns to an individual's assessment of her life is unlikely to have a substantial effect and hence is arguably of limited concern. In some cases, the incorporation of what may look like nonprudential concerns for justice, and so forth, may actually relate to concerns for own well-being. In other cases, apparent sacrifices for others may enhance well-being because of the impact of behaving ethically and the experience of giving and caring. Whether an individual judges that she is leading a good life and how she would judge her life in terms of how well it is going for her is likely to, in most cases, be extremely similar. Although measures of well-being from an evaluative perspective have the potential to be contaminated by nonprudential values, it is unlikely that they will be contaminated to such an extent that subjective evaluation becomes an inappropriate concept of well-being for public policy (Ng 1997).

However, as Nozick (1974) has famously argued, there may be more to life than experience. While subjective evaluations incorporate more than hedonic affect, they cannot incorporate truth or the degree of authenticity in our experience. If an individual claims to be extremely happy and satisfied with life but is not educated, has no material resources, has low income, and is in very poor health, then we may find it difficult to accept her own assessment of her life as a good proxy for her well-being. This may be because we believe that some objective circumstances really do contribute to well-being and that there must be something wrong with her subjective assessment. Or it may stem from a belief that some objective circumstances are inherently valuable. This would not invalidate subjective evaluation but simply suggests adherence to a substantive good account of well-being.

3.2. Is the Measure Valid?

3.2.1. Preference Satisfaction.
One obstacle to intra- and interpersonal comparisons of preference satisfaction arises where desires are influenced by existing and past circumstances. Since an individual's preferences may be different in different periods of time depending upon recent experience, preference orderings of different situations may change over time. If desires are bought in line with expectations, then in situations of long-standing deprivation, people may be "too subdued or broken to have the courage to desire much" (Sen 1992). As neatly put by Griffin (1986), "Our desires are shaped by our expectations, which are shaped by our circumstances. Any injustice in the last infects the first." As our circumstances change, we are left with no clear vantage point from which to make intertemporal comparisons of our well-being.

Income as a measure of preference satisfaction assumes that only those desires that are met contribute to well-being and that unmet desires will be constant or at least independent of income. However, evidence suggests this is not the case. For example, van Praag (1993) finds that wealthier respondents require greater levels of money to call an income sufficient, and both Easterlin (2000) and Stutzer (2004) find that increases in income lead to greater aspirations. Studies incorporating lagged income have tended to find a negative but weak effect. Di Tella, Haisken-De New, and MacCulloch (2005) analyze German data and find negative coefficients on income in the previous 4 years. Graham and Pettinato (2001) identify a group of "frustrated achievers" who, despite a rapid growth in income, are unhappy because of rising aspirations.

Of course, the key issue for making interpersonal comparisons based on income is being able to accurately adjust income by the marginal utility of income. Unfortunately, the evidence on the elasticity of marginal utility of income is limited and implies a wide range of values. Cowell and Gardiner (1999) review the evidence and find that using risk aversion to measure inequality aversion gives a range of .5–4. Pearce (2003) suggests a range between .5 and 1.2 for the implied value of the elasticity of marginal utility of income from savings behavior. Evans (2005) finds a value of 1.4 from revealed social values from personal tax rates in 20 Organisation for Economic Co-operation and Development (OECD) countries. In the absence of definitive evidence, any rate chosen for use in cost-benefit analysis, including a marginal utility of consumption of 1, will be subject to potential challenge (Evans et al. 2005).

Preference satisfaction as proxied by income converges with some other aspects of well-being, such as health, which lends support to its validity as a measure of well-being. Analysis of OECD countries finds that gross domestic product correlates positively with average years of schooling, life expectancy at birth, healthy life expectancy at birth, mortality risk, and volunteering and negatively with income inequality, relative poverty, child poverty, and child mortality (Boarini, Johansson, and Mira d'Ercole 2006). In terms of predictive validity, income predicts health, life expectancy, and educational attainment—but less so life satisfaction over time.

3.2.2. Subjective Evaluation.

Similar conceptual and measurement problems of intra- and interpersonal comparisons apply to subjective evaluation in that an individual's notion of what makes life go well is likely to be dynamic. What constitutes well-being for an individual will change over time as new opportunities become available (Coyne and Boettke 2006), although there is some evidence to suggest that an individual's satisfaction with life is a relatively stable construct (Eid and Diener 2004). Problems for intertemporal comparisons of well-being arise if individuals (*a*) evaluate their lives as good but would give a different evaluation were they to gain different knowledge or experience and/or (*b*) adapt to their circumstances to the extent that they evaluate their lives as good but would give a different evaluation were they to gain different knowledge or experience. In other words, subjective evaluations may also be related to expectations, and expectations may be related to past circumstances.

In relation to interpersonal comparisons, we may mistrust an individual's assessment of her life in situations where we consider her judgment to be impaired. This may arise if she is incapable of making a reasonable judgment about her life because of mental impairment. We may also consider an individual's judgment to be impaired if it is based on beliefs about herself or the world that are not well informed or are myopic. The evaluative account could be based on "autonomous" and "informed" assessments of her life (Sumner 1996), but neither can be clearly identified. Issues of establishing autonomy are discussed by Haybron (2007), who argues that life satisfaction is not merely a judgment but involves affirming or endorsing one's life, but again, the precise implications for the use of subjective evaluations in policy are far from clear.

A further concern exists relating to whether people alter their true responses in order to give a socially appropriate response. For example, some groups may feel uneasy admitting to feelings of sadness and may distort self-reports to present a favorable outward view. For example, Carstensen and Cone (1983) found a high correlation among the elderly between two frequently used measures of psychological well-being and the Edwards Scale of Social Desirability. While these tendencies may be consistent across one individual in different periods of time, they are problematic if people deliberately alter life satisfaction responses to conform to socially acceptable responses following changes in circumstances. For example, the unemployed or recently widowed may report lower levels of life satisfaction to meet social expectations. However, instead of reflecting response artifact, high correlations between social desirability and well-being measures may reflect content overlap between the scales (Diener 1994).

Some evidence to support interpersonal comparisons can be taken from similarities between personal ratings and informant ratings. For example, Lepper (1998) reports self-other (spouse or close friend or relative) correlations between subjective evaluations of around .5. Additional support for interpersonal comparisons can be gained from the fact that the determinants of life satisfaction identified in cross section (from variation between people) are similar to those identified using within-person analysis in panel data. There is also increasing evidence that brain activity and physiological markers (such as cortisol levels) are strongly associated with subjective evaluations in ways that enable groups with high or low levels of well-being to be identified from these markers.

In terms of convergent validity, life satisfaction ratings converge with other measures, such as others' reports of their life satisfaction, frequency of smiling, and mood ratings (Pavot and Diener 1993; Seidlitz and Diener 1993, Sandvick, Diener, and Seidlitz 1993; Diener and Suh 1997). Interrater reliability of life satisfaction responses has been found to be high, which suggests that individuals are able to recognize and predict the life satisfaction level of others. Associations have been found between positive and negative emotions and startle eye-blink response and facial expressions (Ito and Cacioppo 1999). Blanchflower and Oswald (2007) relate differences in life satisfaction across countries to differences in self-reported high blood pressure.

In relation to predictive validity, life satisfaction measures have also been shown to predict behavior, such as reduced suicide attempts (Koivumaa-Honkanen et al. 2001). Smoking and sleep disturbance were also shown to have a higher prevalence in groups who gave a low evaluation of their life satisfaction and general levels of happiness (Lepper 1998). There is reasonable evidence that happiness is also correlated with morbidity and mortality, at least for some groups (Pressman and Cohen 2005). The health benefits of positive affect have been found in conditions such as strokes (Ostir et al. 2001), the likelihood of catching a cold when exposed to the cold virus and speed of recovery (Cohen et al. 2003), intentional and unintentional fatal injury (Koivumaa-Honkanaen et al. 2002), and future blood pressure (Steptoe and Wardle 2005). There is some evidence that overall happiness and other satisfaction measures are linked to length of life (Deeg and Zooneveld 1989; Danner, Snowdon, and Friesen 2001). Life satisfaction also predicts marital breakup (Gardner and Oswald 2006).

3.3. Is the Measure Empirically Useful?

3.3.1. Preference Satisfaction. Cardinality first requires there to be a single measure of the proxy for preference satisfaction. However, income may vary depending upon whether individual or household income is used, the method by which income is allocated to members of the household, the method by which nominal incomes are translated into real incomes, whether annual or current (for example, the last month) income is used, the extent to which local and national taxation and subsidies are incorporated, and the extent to which income net of saving and dissaving is incorporated (and the method used for assessing changes in wealth and assets, such as changes in the value of housing stock). There is no single income measure and good reasons (for example, from data in the BHPS) to suppose these different measures may show considerable variability. In addition, there are concerns about the reliability of reported income as a measure of actual income (Moore, Stinson, and Welniak 2000), particularly where people such as the self-employed perceive an incentive to misrepresent their income.

Further problems arise if we wish to adjust income to include nonmarket preferences. Methodologies that aim to place a value on the change in well-being following a real or hypothesized change in a nonmarket good are well established (Brent 2006). However, in terms of using these methodologies to give an indication of well-being at the individual level, there is no clear consensus on what to include or how to include it. Despite the potential to adjust individual income to account for the satisfaction of nonmarket preferences, in reality an income measure of well-being is unlikely to incorporate the fulfilment of nonmarket desires. To the extent that the satisfaction of market desires is not perfectly correlated with satisfaction of nonmarket desires, income as a cardinal measure of desire satisfaction will be undermined. Moreover, if nonmarket bads are positively related to income, the relationship between income and preference satisfaction may not even be clearly ordinal. In the BHPS, for example, higher household incomes are significantly negatively correlated with frequency of talking to neighbors (Peasgood 2007).

In addition, and as noted above, it is widely accepted that there are diminishing marginal returns to income, but we could adjust income for this, such that a 1-unit increase on the adjusted income scale represents the same intensity-weighted desire satisfaction for all levels of income, then the adjusted measure of income may be cardinal. However, as noted above, there is considerable disagreement on the elasticity of marginal utility of income. The UK Treasury recommendation of a constant elasticity of 1 implies that the log of income would be approximately cardinal, which suggests that a similar percentage increase in income across the income range leads to a similar enhancement of well-being as desire satisfaction.

At the individual level, and because of a lack of information, an individual's actual (revealed) preferences may contain some mistakes and be contrary to his real interests. Actual preferences may differ from an individual's informed preferences or "the hypothetical preferences he would have if he had all the relevant information and had made full use of this information" (Harsanyi 1996, p. 133) for two main reasons. First, choices may be limited by knowledge, experience, and perceptions, all of which are costly to change. Harsanyi (1996) gives the example of a coffee drinker who has knowledge of the taste of only a selection of possible coffees available.

Second, there is good evidence that people mispredict the effects of their choices on their well-being. We fail to anticipate changes in our preferences caused by ownership, or the "endowment effect" (Kahneman, Knetsch, and Thaler 1991). We make erroneous assumptions about our willpower. The large number of credit card users who incur high interest rates and finance charges has been viewed as implying that many credit card users expect to maintain a zero balance but fail to do so (Ausubel 1991). We overestimate our reactions to a range of events (Wilson and Gilbert 2003) and fail to predict adaptation (Dolan and Kahneman 2008). Moreover, our memories of past events are biased so that we focus on the most intense experiences and ignore duration, and this leads us to make further inaccurate future forecasts (Kahneman, Wakker, and Sarin 1997). Our choices may also diverge from those that maximize well-being because of a desire to rationalize our decisions and have clear reasons for making decisions (referred to as "lay rationalism" by Hsee et al. 2003).

In its favor, income is potentially the most sensitive measure since it is possible to show very small changes, although many studies gather income data in broad ranges. In addition, income data are often routinely gathered and monitored, so it certainly appears to be practical to collect.

3.3.2. Subjective Evaluation.   When respondents are faced with single-item evaluative measures, they may use what would seem a reasonable assumption that the scale is linear, with equal distance between each level. Strictly speaking, we know only that the scale is at least ordinal, and it is possible that reported life satisfaction is a nonlinear function of true life satisfaction, but a number of authors have shown that assuming cardinality or ordinality of the responses to life satisfaction questions is relatively unimportant for the results for the determinants of well-being (Ferrer-i-Carbonell and Fritjers 2004; Frey and Stutzer 2000; Layard, Mayraz, and Nickell 2007).

It is problematic if life satisfaction responses are unduly influenced by what the respondent's attention is drawn to at the time of the assessment. Life satisfaction questions that ask "taking all things together" require a difficult mental task, and respondents are unlikely to retrieve all the information relevant to the true assessment of their lives (Schwarz and Strack 1999). Just as misremembering generates problems for the validity of WTP responses, memory biases may also impact life satisfaction responses. People are seen to construct answers to self-reported measures on the basis of selective use of information stored in memory, which opens them up to the influences of situational factors that affect memory recall processes (Diener 1994).

In relation to framing effects, the impact of question order is of particular concern since it suggests that evaluative questions may be subject to systematic biases. Studies that manipulate item order have generally found small (yet significant) effects of item order (Schimmack and Oishi 2005). Responses can also be influenced by the choice of reference group, which itself can be manipulated. The presence of a handicapped person in the room (Strack, Martin, and Schwarz 1988) enhances judgment, which suggests that comparison standards can easily be changed by making one comparison more accessible.

The degree of sensitivity of life satisfaction questions depends on the scale used. Cummins and Gullone (2000) note that a Likert scale of five to seven response options does not exploit the discriminative capacity of most people, and they argue that an 11-point (0–10) scale is preferable for attaining maximum sensitivity with no loss of reliability. At present, analysis of large data sets has explained only a small proportion of the variation in life satisfaction in terms of an individual's circumstances, indicating either fairly rapid adaptation to new circumstances or that circumstances play only a small part in determining life satisfaction— or that the measures are not sufficiently sensitive to pick up important changes. For example, Argyle (1999) estimates that only 15 percent of the variance in life satisfaction is accounted for by circumstances. Studies of twins led to the conclusion that 55 percent of the variance in negative emotionality and 40 percent of the variance in positive emotionality was accounted for by genetics and that in the long run up to 80 percent of happiness is heritable (Lykken and Tellegen 1996).

However, despite this stability, life satisfaction measures are sufficiently sensitive to show robust change following changes in income, marriage, health, employment status, and frequency of contact with friends and family (Dolan, Peasgood, and White 2006). The single life satisfaction questions have an obvious advantage in terms of time and survey space and have been included in many large surveys and found to have high response rates. However, the limited sensitivity of global life satisfaction responses may require very large samples.

4. DISCUSSION

Different accounts of well-being and different measures in those accounts may lead to different conclusions about who is doing well and who is doing badly and may result in different policy decisions. It is important that any measure for policy purposes satisfy some basic conditions; in this paper, we have suggested three possible criteria. These are that the measure use an appropriate conception of well-being for public policy, be a valid representation of what it purports to measure, and be empirically useful. It is unlikely that any well-being measure will fully meet each criterion, and there may be trade-offs between criteria. Further consideration should be given to these issues in future conceptual and empirical research.

We have considered preference satisfaction (proxied by income) and subjective evaluation (proxied by life satisfaction ratings) against these conditions. Preference satisfaction has a firmer theoretical basis if choices reflect desires and if those desires are informed and considered. This has led many philosophers and some economists to move away from actual preferences and toward idealized preferences. However, it is not at all clear precisely how much information is required for idealized preferences, and the concept itself raises considerable problems for measurement. Income as a proxy for well-being is certainly a long way away from idealized preferences. It may also be some way from representing the full set of preferences, including nonmarket preferences that an individual may hold. Ironically, global assessments of life satisfaction, despite reflecting a subjective-evaluation account of well-being, may actually more closely reflect the satisfaction of idealized preferences than income does.

Without agreement on what constitutes how well an individual's life is going—even from her own perspective—considerations of validity will always be problematic. Empirical evidence is useful, but it cannot really answer the question of validity. Both income and life satisfaction ratings suffer from problems of intra- and interpersonal comparability. There is good evidence that aspirations are not independent of income, and so income can be interpreted only as a measure of the actual number of preferences satisfied rather than the proportion of preferences satisfied. Currently, we know surprisingly little about how people's interpretations of life satisfaction scales change when important things in their life change, for example, having children. Such changed circumstances may alter perceptions of end points: life may be better but reported as the same because our understanding of potential quality of life has been increased, and so on. This is an area where more research is needed.

Although many uncertainties remain, faced with a choice between knowing an individual's income and her self-reported score on a life satisfaction question, the former may well tell us more about her well-being for policy purposes. In terms of empirical usefulness, income and life satisfaction are ordinal rather than cardinal, but ordinal analysis would place a considerable restriction on how well-being measures could be used. Despite appearances, income is unlikely to offer a cardinal measure of well-being. The concept of diminishing marginal utility of income has been around for long time, yet we are no nearer to establishing the extent to which marginal utility diminishes at higher levels of income. It may be more reasonable to treat subjective measures as cardinal (Ferrer-i-Carbonell and Fritjers 2004).

Errors in the reporting and measurement of income can be investigated, since it is an objective and verifiable entity. Of course, the extent to which income is used to meet preferences is more problematic. Some studies have shown that our choices may be subject to faulty reasoning, limited information, and an inability to maximize future outcomes. The extent of and bias in the measurement error this generates is unknown but, given the expanding body of evidence pointing to limitations in choices, is likely to be considerable. In terms of subjective evaluations, there are concerns about the risk of context dependence, and this highlights the need for caution in how we administer surveys.

On the face of it, income is more sensitive than subjective evaluations. However, when we consider sensitivity in terms of important changes in well-being, income loses its comparative advantage. There are still questions about the sensitivity of global life satisfaction ratings because there have been very few studies that evaluate a policy intervention using such ratings. This should be a priority for future research. Income and life satisfaction are both practical to collect, so there is little to choose between them in this regard. However, life satisfaction surveys tend to suffer less from response refusal and missing values.

Overall though, it is clear that both measures of well-being struggle to meet all of the criteria, which may suggest that the measures are not useful—or that the criteria are too strict. However, any measure of well-being that is to be actively used in public policy will probably be treated as if those criteria hold, so we should be clear about exactly what the criteria would be. It is worth emphasizing, of course, that public policy is based on information for groups, and the criteria may be less problematic when applied to groups rather than to individuals. We may lack confidence in preference satisfaction or subjective evaluations providing an indication of well-being for any one individual but still have confidence in the measures for providing information at a group level—so long as measurement error is not related to group-level characteristics.

There are a number of ways in which a more complete set of preferences could be developed for use in policy. It is possible to adjust income by the inclusion of nonmarket production, valuation for safety, environment, public services, and so on. A more radical approach would be to implement policies that bring actual and idealized preferences closer together. For example, more information could be provided about the consequences of important decisions—including not just details about products (as is good practice in WTP studies) but how people feel after purchasing them. It would be interesting to consider whether we would wish to limit the advertising of some products purely on the basis that they do not really contribute to future subjective evaluations. Such changes would not only improve the use of income as a measure of well-being but also increase the extent to which the satisfaction of preferences enhances experienced well-being.

Equally, if subjective evaluations are well informed and well considered, there is less reason to suspect that life satisfaction assessments are not authentic or are myopic. This suggests that judgments are more valid when individuals have good access to information about factors that affect how well their life is going overall, such as knowledge about health, risk of crime, and the risks of poverty in old age. A more developed theoretical model for subjective evaluations that clarifies the links between current well-being, cumulative well-being, and lifetime well-being would also help to reduce the potential ambiguity over the timescale involved when respondents reply to life satisfaction questions and should lead to more focused survey questions.

Measures of subjective evaluation are still being developed, and ongoing improvements in their validity should follow. For example, greater understanding of what peoples' attention is drawn to at the time of questioning will enable researchers to make an explicit and transparent decision about what to draw peoples' attention to during surveys and to gain an understanding of the potential measurement error inherent in subjective measures. In addition, more information could be given about the anchors when asking survey questions. This may go some way to overcoming response shift, although restrictions in opportunities of which an individual is not aware (for example, not ever experiencing being in love but not realizing what she is missing) will remain.

It is important to consider the limitations of using any measure of well-being for public policy. Although income and life satisfaction do not meet the criteria fully, subjective evaluations fare at least as well as preference satisfaction and overall substantially better than income alone as an indirect measure of well-being. Therefore, we suggest that policy making could be more efficient in attempts to enhance well-being if it takes due account of the effect that policies have on people's evaluations of how well their lives are going.

REFERENCES

Argyle, Michael. 1999. Causes and Correlates of Happiness. Pp. 353–373 in *Well-Being: The Foundations of Hedonic Psychology*, edited by Daniel Kahneman, Ed Diener, and Norbert Schwarz. New York: Russell Sage.

Ausubel, Laurence M. 1991. The Failure of Competition in the Credit Card Market. *American Economic Review* 81:50–81.

Blanchflower, David G., and Andrew J. Oswald. 2007. Hypertension and Happiness across Nations. Unpublished manuscript. Dartmouth College, Department of Economics, Hanover, N.H.

Boarini, Romina, Asa Johansson, and Marco Mira d'Ercole. 2006. Alternative Measures of Well-Being. Working Paper No. 476. Organisation for Economic Co-operation and Development, Economics Department, Paris.

Brent, Robert J. 2006. Applied Cost-Benefit Analysis. 2d ed. Cheltenham: Edward Elgar.

Carstensen, Laura L., and John Cone. 1983. Social Desirability and the Measurement of Well-Being in Elderly Persons. *Journal of Gerontology* 38: 713–15.

Cohen, Gerald Allan. 1993. Equality of What? On Welfare, Goods and Capabilities. Pp. 9–29 in *The Quality of Life,* edited by Martha Nussbaum and Amartya Sen. Oxford: Clarendon Press.

Cohen, Sheldon, William J. Doyle, Ronald B. Turner, Cuneyt M. Alper, and David P. Skoner. 2003. Emotional Style and Susceptibility to the Common Cold. *Psychosomatic Medicine* 65:652–57.

Cowell, Frank A., and Karen Gardiner. 1999. *Welfare Weights*. OFT Report No. 282. London: UK Office of Fair Trading.

Coyne, Christopher J., and Peter J. Boettke. 2006. Happiness and Economics Research: Insights from Austrian and Public Choice Economics. Pp. 89–105 in *Happiness and Public Policy: Theory, Case Studies, and Implications,* edited by Yew-Kwang Ng and Lok Sang Ho. New York: Palgrave Macmillan.

Cummins, Robert A., and Eleonora Gullone. 2000. Why We Should Not Use 5-Point Likert Scales: The Case for Subjective Quality of Life Measurement. Pp. 74–93 in *Proceedings of the Second International Conference on Quality of Life in Cities*. Singapore: National University of Singapore.

Danner, Deborah D., David A. Snowdon, and Wallace V. Friesen. 2001. Positive Emotions in Early Life and Longevity: Findings from the Nun Study. *Journal of Personality and Social Psychology* 80:804–13.

Deeg, Dorly J. H., and Robert J. van Zonneveld. 1989. Does Happiness Lengthen Life? The Prediction of Longevity in the Elderly. Chapter 5 in *How Harmfull Is Happiness? Consequences of Enjoying Life or Not*, edited by Ruut Veenhoven. Rotterdam: Universitaire Pers Rotterdam.

Defra (Department for Environment, Food and Rural Affairs). 2005. *Securing the Future—UK Government Sustainable Development Strategy*. London: Defra.

Diener, Ed. 1994. Assessing Subjective Well-Being: Progress and Opportunities. *Social Indicators Research* 31:103–57.

Diener, Ed, Robert A. Emmons, Randy J. Larson, and Sharon Griffin. 1985. The Satisfaction with Life Scale. *Journal of Personality Assessment* 49:71–75.

Diener, Ed, Shigehiro Oishi, and Richard E. Lucas. 2003. Personality, Culture, and Subjective Well-Being: Emotional and Cognitive Evaluations of Life. *Annual Review of Psychology* 54:403–25.

Diener, Ed, and Eunkook Suh. 1997. Measuring Quality of Life: Economic, Social and Subjective Indicators. *Social Indicators Research* 40:189–216.

Di Tella, Rafael, John P. Haisken-De New, and Robert MacCulloch. 2005. Happiness Adaptation to Income and to Status in an Individual Panel. Unpublished manuscript. Harvard Business School and National Bureau of Economic Research, Cambridge, Mass.

Di Tella, Rafael, Robert MacCulloch, and Andrew Oswald. 2003. The Macroeconomics of Happiness. *Review of Economics and Statistics* 85:809–27.

Dolan, Paul, and Daniel Kahneman. 2008. Interpretations of Utility and Their Implications for the Valuation of Health. *Economic Journal* 118:215–34.

Dolan, Paul, Tessa Peasgood, and Mathew White. 2006. Review of Research on the Influences on Personal Well-Being and Application to Policy Making. Defra, London.

Easterlin, Richard. 2000. Income and Happiness: Towards a Unified Theory. *Economic Journal* 111:465–84.

Eid, Michael, and Ed Diener. 2004. Global Judgements of Subjective Well-Being: Situational Variability and Long-Term Stability. *Social Indicators Research* 65:245–77.

Evans, David. 2005. The Elasticity of Marginal Utility of Consumption: Estimates for 20 OECD Countries. *Fiscal Studies* 26:197–224.

Evans, David, Erhun Kula, and Haluk Sezer. 2005. Regional Welfare Weights for the UK: England, Scotland, Wales and Northern Ireland. *Regional Studies* 39:923–37.

Feldman, Fred. 2002. The Good Life: A Defense of Attitudinal Hedonism. *Philosophy and Phenomenological Research* 65:604–28.

Ferrer-i-Carbonell, Ada, and Paul Frijters. 2004. How Important Is Methodology for the Estimates of the Determinants of Happiness? *Economic Journal* 114: 641–59.

Fisher, Irving. 1918. Is "Utility" the Most Suitable Term for the Concept It Is Used to Denote? *American Economic Review* 8:335–37.

Frank, Robert. 1997. Frame of Reference as a Public Good. *Economic Journal* 107:1832–47.

Frey, Bruno, and Alois Stutzer. 2000. Happiness, Economy and Institutions. *Economic Journal* 110:918–38.

Gardner, Jonathan, and Andrew J. Oswald. 2006. Do Divorcing Couples Become Happier by Breaking Up? *Journal of the Royal Statistical Society* 169: 319–336.

Giving USA. 2006. *The Annual Report on Philanthropy for the Year 2005.* Glenview, Ill.: Giving USA Foundation.

Graham, Carol, and Stefano Pettinato. 2001. Happiness, Markets and Democracy: Latin America in Comparative Perspective. *Journal of Happiness Studies* 2:237–68.

Griffin, James. 1986. *Well-Being: Its Meaning, Measurement and Moral Importance.* Oxford: Clarendon Press.

Harsanyi, John C. 1982. Morality and the Theory of Rational Behaviour. Chapter 2 in *Utilitarianism and Beyond,* edited by Amartya Sen and Bernard Williams. Cambridge: Cambridge University Press.

———. 1996. Utilities, Preferences, and Substantive Goods. *Social Choice and Welfare* 14:129–45.

Haybron, Daniel. 2007. Life Satisfaction, Ethical Reflection, and the Science of Happiness. *Journal of Happiness Studies* 8:99–138.

Helliwell, John F. and Robert Putnam. 2004. The Social Context of Well-Being. *Philosophical Translations of the Royal Society of London* 359:1435–46.

Hsee, Christopher K., Jiao Zhang, Frank Yu, and Yiheng Xi. 2003. Lay Rationalism and Inconsistency between Predicted Experience and Decision. *Journal of Behavioral Decision Making* 16:257–72.

Ito, Tiffany A., and John T. Cacioppo. 1999. The Psychophysiology of Utility Appraisals. Pp. 470–88 in *Well-Being and the Foundations of Hedonic Psychology*, edited by Daniel Kahneman, Ed Diener, and Norbert Schwarz. New York: Russell Sage.

Kahneman, Daniel. 2000. Evaluation by Moments: Past and Future. Chapter 38 in *Choices, Values and Frames*, edited by Daniel Kahneman and Amos Tversky. New York: Cambridge University Press and Russell Sage.

Kahneman, Daniel, Jack Knetsch, and Richard Thaler. 1991. The Endowment

Effect, Loss Aversion, and Status Quo Bias. *Journal of Economic Perspectives* 5:193–206.

Kahneman, Daniel, Alan B. Krueger, David A. Schkade, Norbert Schwarz, and Arthur A. Stone. 2004. A Survey Method for Characterizing Daily Life Experience: The Day Reconstruction Method. *Science* 306:1776–80.

Kahneman, Daniel, Peter Wakker, and Rakesh Sarin. 1997. Back to Bentham? Explorations of Experienced Utility. *Quarterly Journal of Economics* 112: 375–405.

Koivumaa-Honkanen, Heli, Risto Honkanen, Markku Koskenvuo, Heimo Viinamäki, and Jaakko Kaprio. 2002. Life Dissatisfaction as a Predictor of Fatal Injury in a 20-Year Follow-Up. *Acta Psychiatrica Scandinavica* 105:444–50.

Koivumaa-Honkanen, Heli, Risto Honkanen, Heimo Viinamäki, Kauko Heikkilä, Jaakko Kaprio, and Markku Koskenvuo. 2001. Life Satisfaction and Suicide: A 20-Year Follow-up Study. *American Journal of Psychiatry* 158: 433–39.

Lane, Robert E. 2000. *Loss of Happiness in Market Economies*. New Haven, Conn., and London: Yale University Press.

Layard, Richard. 2006. Happiness and Public Policy: A Challenge to the Profession. *Economic Journal* 116:C24-C33.

Layard, Richard, Guy Mayraz, and Stephen Nickell. 2007. The Marginal Utility of Income. Unpublished manuscript. London School of Economics, London.

Lepper, Heidi. 1998. Use of Other-Reports to Validate Subjective Well-Being Measures. *Social Indicators Research* 44:367–79.

Lykken, David, and Auke Tellegen. 1996. Happiness Is a Stochastic Phenomenon. *Psychological Science* 7:186–89.

Moore, Jeffrey C., Linda L. Stinson, and Edward J. Welniak Jr. 2000. Income Measurement Error in Surveys: A Review. *Journal of Official Statistics* 16: 331–61.

Nathan, Gad. 1999. *A Review of Sample Attrition and Representativeness in Three Longitudinal Surveys*. National Statistics Monograph Series 13. London: Office for National Statistics.

Ng, Yew-Kwang. 1997. A Case for Happiness, Cardinalism and Interpersonal Comparability. *Economic Journal* 107:1848–58.

Ng, Yew-Kwang, and Lok Sang Ho. 2006. *Happiness and Public Policy, Theory, Case Studies and Implications*. New York: Palgrave, Macmillan.

Nozick, Robert. 1974. *Anarchy, State, and Utopia*. New York: Basic Books.

Osberg, Lars. 1985. The Measurement of Economic Welfare. Pp. 49–87 in *Approaches to Economic Well-Being*, edited by David Laidler. Vol. 26 of the Royal Commission on the Economic Union and Development Prospects for Canada, MacDonald Commission. Toronto: University of Toronto Press.

Ostir, Glenn V., Kyriakos S. Markides, M. Kristen Peek, and James S. Goodwin. 2001. The Association between Emotional Well-Being and the Incidence of Stroke in Older Adults. *Psychosomatic Medicine* 63:210–15.

Pareto, Vilfredo. [1906] 1971. *Manual of Political Economy.* London: Macmillan Press.

Pavot, William, and Ed Diener. 1993. Review of the Satisfaction with Life Scale. *Psychological Assessment* 5:14–172.

Pearce, David. 2003. The Social Cost of Carbon and Its Policy Implications. *Oxford Review of Economic Policy* 19:362–84.

Peasgood, Tessa. 2007. Does Well-Being Depend upon Our Choice of Measurement Instrument? Paper presented at the British Household Panel Survey conference, University of Essex, Colchester, July 5–7.

Pressman, Sarah D., and Sheldon Cohen. 2005. Does Positive Affect Influence Health? *Psychological Bulletin* 131:925–71.

Rawls, John. 1982. Social Unity and Primary Goods. Pp. 159–85 in *Utilitarianism and Beyond*, edited by Amartya Sen and Bernard Williams. Cambridge: Cambridge University Press.

Robbins, Lionel. [1932] 1945. *An Essay on the Nature and Significance of Economic Science.* 2nd ed. London: Macmillan & Co.

Sandvik, Ed., Ed Diener, and Larry Seidlitz. 1993. Subjective Well-Being: The Convergence and Stability of Self-Report and Non-Self-Report Measures. *Journal of Personality* 61:317–42.

Schimmack, Ulrich, and Shigehiro Oishi. 2005. Chronically Accessible versus Temporarily Accessible Sources of Life Satisfaction Judgments. *Journal of Personality and Social Psychology* 89:395–406.

Schwarz, Norbert, and Frank Strack. 1999. Reports of Subjective Well-Being: Judgmental Processes and Their Methodological Implications. Pp. 61-84 in *Well-Being: The Foundations of Hedonic Psychology*, edited by Daniel Kahneman, Ed Diener, and Norbert Schwarz. New York: Russell Sage.

Seidlitz, Larry, and Ed Diener. 1993. Memory for Positive versus Negative Life Events: Theories for the Differences between Happy and Unhappy Persons. *Journal Personality Social Psychology* 64:654–64.

Sen, Amartya. 1992. *Inequality Re-examined.* Oxford: Clarendon Press.

Steptoe, Andrew, and Jane Wardle. 2005. Positive Affect and Biological Function in Everyday Life. *Neurobiology of Aging* 26:S108–S112.

Strack, Fritz, Leonard L. Martin, and Norbert Schwarz. 1988. Priming and Communication: The Social Determinants of Information Use in Judgments of Life-Satisfaction. *European Journal of Social Psychology* 18:429–42.

Stutzer, Alios. 2004. The Role of Income Aspirations in Individual Happiness. *Journal of Economic Behavior and Organization* 54:89–109.

Sumner, L. Wayne. 1996. *Welfare, Happiness and Ethics.* Oxford: Clarendon Press.

United Nations Development Programme. 2006. *Beyond Scarcity: Power, Poverty and the Global Water Crisis.* Human Development Report 2006. New York: United Nations.

Van den Berg, Bernard, and Ada Ferrer-i-Carbonell. 2007. The Well-Being of

Informal Caregivers: A Monetary Valuation of Informal Care. *Health Economics* 16:1227–44.

van Praag, Bernard M. S. 1993. The Relativity of the Welfare Concept. Pp. 362–83 in *Quality of Life*, edited by Amartya Sen and Martha Nussbaum. Oxford: Clarendon Press.

Wilson, Timothy D., and Daniel T. Gilbert. 2003. Affective Forecasting. Pp. 345–411 in volume 35 of *Advances in Experimental Social Psychology*, edited by Mark P. Zanna. New York: Elsevier.

World Values Survey. 2000. World Values Survey Association. Madrid: ASEP/ JDS (aggregate file producer). http://www.worldvaluessurvey.org.

Happiness Inequality in the United States

Betsey Stevenson and Justin Wolfers

ABSTRACT

This paper examines how the level and dispersion of self-reported happiness has evolved over the period 1972–2006. While there has been no increase in aggregate happiness, inequality in happiness has fallen substantially since the 1970s. There have been large changes in the level of happiness across groups: two-thirds of the black-white happiness gap has been eroded, and the gender happiness gap has disappeared entirely. Paralleling changes in the income distribution, differences in happiness by education have widened substantially. We develop an integrated approach to measuring inequality and decomposing changes in the distribution of happiness, finding a pervasive decline in within-group inequality during the 1970s and 1980s that was experienced by even narrowly defined demographic groups. Around one-third of this decline has subsequently been unwound. Juxtaposing these changes with large increases in income inequality suggests an important role for nonpecuniary factors in shaping the well-being distribution.

1. INTRODUCTION

It is now widely understood that average levels of happiness have failed to grow in the United States, despite ongoing economic growth (Easterlin 1995; Blanchflower and Oswald 2004). Yet an average can hide as much as it reveals, and so our task in this paper is to explore the full distribution of happiness through time.

Previous authors have documented the existence of happiness in-

BETSEY STEVENSON is at the Wharton School at the University of Pennsylvania, the Center for Economic Studies and Ifo Institute for Economic Research (CESifo), and the National Bureau of Economic Research (NBER). JUSTIN WOLFERS is at the Wharton School at the University of Pennsylvania, the Centre for Economic Policy Research (CEPR), CESifo, the Institute for the Study of Labor (IZA), and NBER. The authors would like to thank Wharton's Zicklin Center for Business Ethics Research and Zell/Lurie Real Estate Center for generous research support.

[*Journal of Legal Studies*, vol. XXXVII (June 2008)]

equality both within and between demographic groups: the rich are typically happier than the poor; the educated are happier than those with less education; whites are happier than blacks; those who are married are happier than those who are not; and women—at least historically—have been happier than men. These differences are likely interrelated, and in addition, there exists substantial happiness inequality even within narrowly defined demographic groups. We seek to document how each of these factors is changing and how the changing composition of the U.S. population may be contributing to the observed aggregate trends.

The parallel literature on income inequality certainly suggests that this may be a fruitful task, as recent decades have witnessed the partial closure of gender and race gaps, an increase in education and age gaps, and a substantial increase in income inequality within most demographic groups. All told, this literature suggests that the gains from recent economic growth have been quite unevenly distributed. Beyond the pecuniary domain, there have also been important changes in the legal and institutional organization of work, family, leisure, and community life as well as technological changes that may have impacted well-being.

As with previous analyses, we find that, on average, happiness has failed to grow since the 1970s. But beneath this average, we document some important striking differences across groups: two-thirds of the black-white happiness gap has been eroded, and the gender happiness gap has disappeared entirely, with more recent data suggesting that it may even have inverted. Paralleling changes in the income distribution, differences in happiness by education have widened substantially.

Our more striking finding is the substantial decrease in happiness inequality through our sample. We document that the dispersion of happiness fell sharply in the 1970s and 1980s; subsequently, about one-third of this decline has subsequently been unwound. Our decomposition exercise suggests that the real reason for today's lower levels of happiness inequality is not to be found in the relative experiences of particular groups, or the specific experiences of only a few, but rather in a pervasive decline in within-group inequality experienced by even narrowly defined demographic groups.

Beyond these substantive findings, our approach to measuring inequality and our decomposition of changes in the distribution of happiness within and between groups may be of methodological interest, especially for those interested in analysis of ordinal data. Our integrated approach to estimating levels and dispersion of happiness through time and the accounting framework for describing the proximate sources of these changes may also prove to be useful for analyses of other qualitative or attitudinal data.

Before proceeding, it is worth putting our findings into a broader context. In terms of our empirical objectives, our goal is to describe the data rather than to point to causal links. We juxtapose decreasing happiness inequality with rising income inequality not because we believe that this reflects a clear link between the two but rather because, jointly considered, they hint at the intriguing possibility of a decline in inequality in the nonpecuniary domain.

The normative implications of our results are also somewhat limited. For instance, a committed utilitarian cares only about the average level of well-being, and not inequality in well-being. While the usual utilitarian argument for valuing inequality rests on the view that redistribution yields utility gains to the poor that exceed the costs to the rich, this argument—based as it is on diminishing marginal utility—may be more convincing in the pecuniary domain than when evaluating happiness. We should also add that the usual caveats about well-being data apply, and the mapping between true subjective experiences and responses to subjective well-being questions remains quite poorly understood. (Kahneman and Krueger [2006] provide a useful overview of the relevant literature.)

Our findings contribute to the much broader (positive) literature on trends in well-being, and particularly inequality, in the United States. As such, Section 2 provides the broader context, describing trends in economic inequality and in particular its ongoing rise since the 1970s. We also note that there have been a host other social and legal changes that may have had interesting distributional impacts, including changes in the distribution of leisure, regulation impacting families, antidiscrimination legislation, violent crime, and affirmative action.

In Section 3 we highlight the aggregate trends in happiness—both levels and dispersion—and introduce our approach to cardinalizing these descriptive survey responses. Section 4 turns to examining happiness both within and between groups, to assess how the distribution and dispersion of happiness is changing across socioeconomic and demographic lines. We measure changes in a variety of dimensions and assess their joint impact through a decomposition exercise that points to the importance of within-group increases in happiness inequality. Section 5 provides a concluding discussion.

2. BACKGROUND: TRENDS IN INEQUALITY

Income inequality has increased throughout our sample period, which begins in 1972. During the 1970s inequality rose modestly, with the rise stemming largely from changes in residual inequality (Goldin and Katz 2008). The college wage premium fell through the 1970s, which mitigated against larger rises in overall inequality. However, the college wage differential rebounded during the 1980s, and in this decade inequality rose sharply and throughout the distribution. The rise in inequality in the 1990s and early 2000s was concentrated in the top of the income distribution, with the differential between wages at the 90th and 50th percentiles rising through 2005, despite a decrease in 50–10 inequality (Autor, Katz, and Kearney 2008).

Between 1972 and 2006 (our sample period), overall income inequality rose both within and between groups, with an important part of the rise coming from changes in the returns to education, with the education returns both increasing and increasing by a greater amount for higher levels of education (Goldin and Katz 2007). For example, the weekly earnings of full-time, full-year workers with education beyond a college degree rose 34 log points relative to their counterparts with only a high school degree, while the parallel rise for those with only a college degree was 22 log points (Goldin and Katz 2008, p. 139). Over this period wage dispersion also increased within demographic and skill groups (Autor, Katz, and Kearney 2008). In contrast, wage differentials between some groups have narrowed. Specifically, male-female wage inequality narrowed during the 1970s and 1980s and continued to narrow, albeit more slowly, in the 1990s (Blau and Kahn 2006). The black-white wage gap has also narrowed over the past 35 years, with convergence in the 1970s and, after stagnating in the 1980s, further narrowing in the 1990s (Couch and Daly 2003).

Along with this rise in income inequality has come concerns about increasing income volatility and a more general concern about increasing inequality stemming from households bearing more health and retirement risk (Hacker 2006). Income inequality has occurred through both an increase in the dispersion of permanent income and an increase in transitory income volatility (Gottschalk and Moffitt 1994). However, more recent work has argued that increases in income volatility have impacted few families and have not been broadly experienced (Jensen and Shore 2008).

Since households may be able to use insurance, borrowing, or savings, consumption is less variable than income, and it may better reflect material well-being. As such, many studies of economic inequality have turned to measures of consumption inequality, finding evidence of a parallel increase in consumption inequality in the 1980s (Johnson and Shipp 1997; Cutler and Katz 1991; Attanasio, Battistin, and Ichimura 2004). Some authors have argued, however, that consumption inequality was flat or declining in the 1990s and that the overall rise has been small relative to the rise in income inequality (Krueger and Perri 2006). The rise in consumption inequality has occurred both between and within skill groups (Attanasio, Battistin and Ichimura 2004), although this point has been debated in the literature, with Krueger and Perri (2006) suggesting that there was only minimal growth in consumption inequality within skill groups, despite large increases in within-group income inequality. These same authors find that between-group changes in consumption inequality have been similar to the between-group changes in income inequality. Countering this, Johnson and Shipp (1997) argue that most of the rise in consumption inequality has been within groups.

More recently we have learned that leisure—time devoted to neither market nor household work—is another important domain in which inequality has changed over recent decades (Aguiar and Hurst 2007). In particular, the new leisure class is composed of the low skilled who have experienced steady increases in leisure hours over the past 3 decades. While the high skilled experienced an increase in leisure in the 1970s and 1980s, in recent years this increase has been reallocated toward home production. Yet the biggest rises in nonwork, nonhousehold production hours have been focused on the unemployed and disabled low-skilled men, and most of the increase in "leisure" among those with less education is due to changes in employment status. In contrast, among men with more education, the decline in leisure is due to changes within employment status (Aguiar and Hurst 2008).

There have also been important legal changes impacting equality of opportunity. A vast array of legislation and court rulings have coincided with changes in social norms to reduce discrimination and allow individuals to make life choices with fewer restrictions due to characteristics such as race, religion, gender, or sexual preference. Most notably, the 1964 Civil Rights Act outlawed segregation and discrimination against people on the basis of religion, race, national origin, or gender. This legislation has continued to impact hiring and firing decisions, with substantial growth in employment discrimination litigation in the decades since its passage (Donohue and Siegelman 1991). In more recent years, antidiscrimination legislation has expanded to include the disabled with the Americans with Disabilities Act of 1990 and the Family and Medical Leave Act of 1993, which protects individuals against job loss in the case of short-term medical or family issues.

Families have also gained more autonomy over family life with a wave of large-scale deregulation of the family beginning in the 1960s that diminished the role that government plays in family life. A series of state legislative changes and constitutional cases in the 1960s and 1970s increased individual rights surrounding marriage and family, and individuals gained broader access to marriage, divorce, birth control, and abortion.[1] Many of these legal changes occurred simultaneously with social upheaval that resulted in large changes in family life. Divorce rates doubled between the mid-1960s and the mid-1970s, and while they have been falling since the late 1970s, the stock of divorced people has continued to grow (Stevenson and Wolfers 2007a, 2008b). This increase in the number of people who have experienced family disruption has increased the dispersion of family experience. Isen and Stevenson (2008) also document differential changes by education in both family behavior and subjective assessments of marital satisfaction.

Previous studies of subjective well-being have found that both pecuniary and nonpecuniary aspects of life contribute to our reported happiness. The fact that happiness data aggregate across these domains makes them especially interesting. Equally, this also expands the range of possible explanations for the changes in the distribution of happiness we document. In this paper, we refrain from attempting any such explanation, and we now turn to assessing how the average levels of happiness and happiness inequality have changed.

3. AGGREGATE TRENDS IN HAPPINESS

Our analysis is based on responses to the General Social Survey (GSS; Davis, Smith, and Marsden 1972–2006), which asks, "Taken all together, how would you say things are these days—would you say that you are very happy, pretty happy, or not too happy?" This survey was administered to a nationally representative sample of about 1,500 respondents each year from 1972 to 1993 (except 1979, 1981, and 1992) and con-

---

1. See Stevenson and Wolfers (2007a) for further discussion of the legal and social changes impacting families during the 1960s and 1970s.

tinues with around 3,000 respondents every second year from 1994 through to 2004, rising to around 4,500 respondents in 2006 (although only half the respondents were queried about their happiness in 2002 and 2004, followed by two-thirds in 2006). These repeated cross sections are designed to track attitudes and behaviors among the U.S. population and contain a wide range of demographic and attitudinal questions.

Before assessing how answers to these questions have trended over time, it is important to account for any changes in measurement that may affect responses to the happiness question. While these data are relatively consistent, responses to happiness questions are remarkably sensitive to small changes in question order, and hence it is quite important to adjust for changes in survey design. In particular, Smith (1990) notes that reported happiness tends to be higher when preceded by a five-item satisfaction scale (as was the norm except in 1972 and 1985). In addition, among married respondents, reported happiness is higher when preceded by a question about marital happiness (as was the norm, except in 1972). Fortunately, the changes induced by these question order effects can be assessed by way of split-ballot experiments run in subsequent surveys; the Appendix details these adjustments.[2] We show the results of these corrections in Figure 1.

In order to ensure that these time series are nationally representative, all estimates are weighted using WTSALL, and we drop the 1982 and 1987 black oversamples. In order to maintain continuity with earlier survey rounds, we also drop those 2006 interviews that occurred in Spanish and could not have been completed had English been the only option, as Spanish-language surveys were not offered in previous years.[3] Our corrected data series are listed in Table 1.

Having constructed a consistent series, the next challenge is to convert qualitative responses into a meaningful quantitative summary measure. This issue becomes particularly pressing in analyzing the GSS data, as only three response categories are given. The simplest (and most widely used) approach is to equate "not too happy" with a happiness score of 1, "pretty happy" with a score of 2, and "very happy" with a score of

2. While the split-ballot experiments provide a bridge between different versions of the survey, they also mean that it is not possible to simply drop the two outlier years, as results from subsequent surveys also need to be adjusted for the presence of these experimental split ballots.

3. For those interested in replicating our results, the simplest way is to define a weighting variable as follows: gen wt = WTSALL if SAMPLE~=4 & SAMPLE~=5 & SAMPLE~=7 & SPANINT~=2.

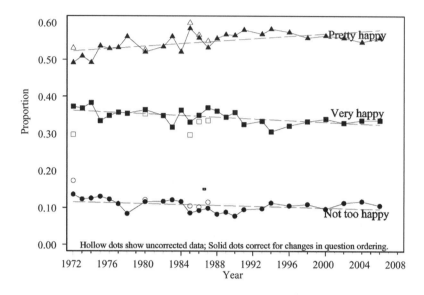

Figure 1. Trends in the distribution of happiness

3. We can then take the mean and variance of these measures each year. The results from this simple approach are presented in Figure 2. Two facts are immediately evident. First, the average level of happiness in the United States is roughly stable, or perhaps slightly declining, a finding that is explored further by Blanchflower and Oswald (2004) and subsequently by Stevenson and Wolfers (2008a). Second, inequality in happiness declined until the mid- or late-1980s, despite the fact that both income and consumption inequality rose through most of this period. Subsequently, happiness inequality rose through the 1990s, although the most recent estimates of inequality still remain below the higher levels seen in the early 1970s.[4] These movements are quite substantial, as we observe an initial decline in the variance of happiness of about 25 percent from the early 1970s to the late-1980s, followed by a rise of about 10 percent by the mid-2000s.

The difficulty with the aggregation shown in Figure 2 is that it arbitrarily assigns qualitative categories scores equal to their rank order, imposing a linear structure in which the difference between being "not

4. The decline in happiness inequality from the 1970s to the early 2000s has also been noted by Brooks (2008).

Table 1. Happiness Trends in the United States

| Year | Survey Responses | | | | Estimated Moments: Happiness ~ N(0, 1) | |
	Not Too Happy (%)	Pretty Happy (%)	Very Happy (%)	Sample Size	Mean	Variance
1972	13.6	49.1	37.3	1,606	.023	1.321
1973	12.3	50.9	36.8	1,500	.027	1.194
1974	12.5	49.2	38.3	1,480	.060	1.279
1975	13.0	53.6	33.4	1,485	−.055	1.106
1976	12.2	52.9	34.8	1,499	−.015	1.112
1977	11.0	53.2	35.7	1,527	.020	1.059
1978	8.4	56.2	35.5	1,517	.048	.871
1980	11.6	52.0	36.4	1,462	.027	1.123
1982	11.7	53.5	34.8	1,505	−.008	1.072
1983	12.1	56.2	31.7	1,573	−.078	.988
1984	11.6	52.1	36.3	1,445	.025	1.123
1985	8.6	58.4	33.1	1,530	−.001	.821
1986	9.2	55.8	35.0	1,449	.026	.912
1987	9.7	53.3	37.0	1,437	.060	1.016
1988	8.2	55.7	36.1	1,466	.061	.880
1989	8.8	56.7	34.5	1,526	.023	.872
1990	7.7	56.5	35.7	1,361	.061	.838
1991	9.5	58.0	32.5	1,504	−.025	.861
1993	9.7	56.9	33.4	1,601	−.011	.900
1994	11.3	58.2	30.5	2,977	−.089	.904
1996	10.5	57.4	32.1	2,885	−.047	.909
1998	10.9	55.9	33.3	2,806	−.030	.967
2000	9.6	56.4	33.9	2,777	.000	.909
2002	11.3	55.8	32.9	1,369	−.043	.979
2004	11.7	54.7	33.6	1,337	−.034	1.029
2006	10.6	55.9	33.5	2,828	−.019	.955

Source. General Social Survey, 1972–2006.

Note. Estimates are based on sample weight WTSALL, omitting black oversamples in 1982 and 1987, as well as those Spanish-language interviews in 2006 that could not have been completed were English required (as in previous years). All data are corrected for question order effects, as described in the Appendix. The mean and variance estimates are based on a generalized ordered probit regression of happiness in which both the level and variance of happiness are a linear function of year fixed effects, as described in equations (6)–(9). These estimates are constructed on the assumption that the latent happiness variable is normally distributed, with mean zero and average variance equal to one. The estimated cut points are $\delta_1 = -1.244$ and $\delta_2 = -.397$.

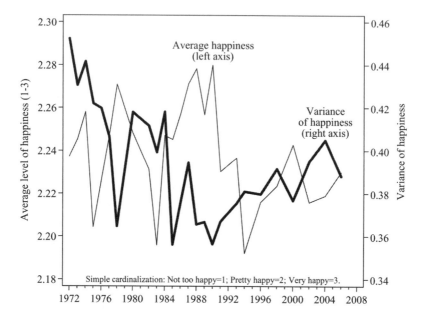

Figure 2. Simple approach to estimating trends in the distribution of happiness

too happy" and "pretty happy" is assumed to be equal to the difference between being "pretty happy" and "very happy." Moreover, it is difficult to know how to interpret comparisons of happiness levels without some sort of normalization. (That is, is by what metric can we interpret the economic significance of the roughly .02 point decline in average happiness levels shown in Figure 2?)

An alternative approach involves using data on the proportions of the population who report themselves as being in each happiness category and imposing a functional form restriction on the distribution of a latent "happiness" index. A common example of this latter approach is the use of ordered probit regressions to estimate trends in well-being, as in Stevenson and Wolfers (2007b, 2008a). In this approach, one assumes that there is a latent variable, happiness, that is normally distributed (and by an innocuous normalization, it is a standard normal). Thus, an ordered probit regression of happiness on year fixed effects recovers the time series of the distribution of happiness. This maximum likelihood procedure simultaneously estimates the cut points above which a person will report being "pretty happy" rather than "not too happy" or "very happy" rather than "pretty happy." In turn, the year fixed effects are interpreted as shifts in the average level of happiness. Unfortunately, the ordered probit (or ordered logit) model is insufficient for our analysis, as we are interested in measuring trends in the dispersion of happiness, whereas these statistical procedures measure shifts in the average level of happiness, while assuming its dispersion is constant.

However, it is fairly straightforward to generalize the ordered probit (or ordered logit) model in order to jointly estimate the time series of both the average level and dispersion of happiness. We can also generalize the specific parameteric assumptions embedded in each particular model. To see this, note that with three response categories, we have essentially two observations each year—the proportion "not too happy" and the proportion "very happy" (the proportion "pretty happy" is the complement and hence perfectly collinear). Thus we can use these two observations to solve for two unknowns and hence recover the parameters of any two-parameter probability density function.[5] Throughout this paper, we will report the mean and variance of happiness implied by these parameters. We do not mean to suggest that the variance is the optimal measure of the dispersion of happiness, but given the restriction to two-parameter distributions, other measures of happiness inequality such as the standard deviation, Gini coefficient, interquartile range, and 90–10 ratio will be a monotonic function of the variance.[6] (For our purposes the variance is particularly convenient, as the decomposition exercise in Section 4 is a relatively straightforward variance decomposition.)

We begin with the usual logic of the standard models for ordered categorical data, assuming that the happiness of an individual, i, from a representative cross section taken in period t, is an unobservable index, y_{it}^*, determined by

$$y_{it}^* = x_{it}\beta_t + \varepsilon_{it}, \tag{1}$$

where x_{it} refers to the individual's observable independent variables and

5. For a related approach, see the appendix to Mankiw, Reis, and Wolfers (2003).

6. Atkinson (1970) describes alternative measures of inequality as applying different weights to various parts of the distribution. In a more applied vein, Kalmijn and Veenhoven (2005) assess different approaches to quantifying inequality of happiness and conclude by endorsing the use of standard deviations.

ε_{it} is the error term. However, we do not observe y_i^* but rather only the ordered categorical variable y_i:

$$y_{it} = \begin{cases} \text{Not too happy} & \text{if } y_{it}^* \leqslant \delta_1 \\ \text{Pretty happy} & \text{if } \delta_1 < y_{it}^* \leqslant \delta_2 \\ \text{Very happy} & \text{if } y_{it}^* > \delta_2, \end{cases} \tag{2}$$

where δ_1 and δ_2 are the unknown cut points that must be estimated.

While the typical ordered probit model further assumes $\varepsilon_{it} \sim N(0, 1)$, at this point we generalize in two directions, allowing for any two-parameter distribution, $F(.)$, and also allowing the variance to vary with observable covariates:

$$\varepsilon_{it} \sim F(0, \ x_{it}\gamma_t). \tag{3}$$

Thus the independent variables, x_{it}, shift both the mean and variance of happiness. We could allow different sets of independent variables, x_{it}^m and x_{it}^v, to shift the mean and the variance, and this amounts to denoting the union of these variables as $x_{it} = x_{it}^m \cup x_{it}^v$ and imposing specific zero restrictions on the β and γ vectors. We will not impose such restrictions, because we want to allow the data to describe which independent variables drive each moment of the distribution.

Because we are interested in using this approach to simply document aggregate time series variation in the mean and variance of happiness, we begin by focusing on the simple case where the only independent variables are a vector of year fixed effects, yielding the time series of both the average level (μ_t) and variance (σ_t^2) of happiness. In this particularly simple case, this model yields simple closed-form expressions, which can be computed without the need for any specialist software. Without assuming any specific functional form, we note

$$\%\text{Not too happy}_t = F_{\mu_t, \sigma_t^2}(\delta_1) \Rightarrow F^{-1}(\%\text{Not too happy}_t) = \frac{\delta_1 - \mu_t}{\sigma_t} \tag{4}$$

and

$$\%\text{Very happy}_t = 1 - F_{\mu_t, \sigma_t^2}(\delta_2) \Rightarrow F^{-1}(1 - \%\text{Very happy}_t) = \frac{\delta_2 - \mu_t}{\sigma_t}, \tag{5}$$

where $F(.)$ is the cumulative distribution function of a distribution characterized by two parameters that map into an average level of happiness in each year μ_t and variance, σ_t^2. The key to identification of this model is that the cut points, δ_1 and δ_2, do not vary through time. That is, we can identify shifts in both the mean and dispersion in happiness if we are willing to assume that the mapping between true feelings of happiness and how respondents choose to answer the survey remains constant through time. (As an aside, while this assumption sounds strong, it is made implicitly in every approach to cardinalizing subjective well-being that we have seen.) Combining equations (4) and (5) yields

$$\mu_t = \frac{\delta_1 F^{-1}(1 - \%\text{Very happy}_t) - \delta_2 F^{-1}(\%\text{Not too happy}_t)}{F^{-1}(1 - \%\text{Very happy}_t) - F^{-1}(\%\text{Not too happy}_t)} \tag{6}$$

and

$$\sigma_t^2 = \left(\frac{\delta_2 - \delta_1}{F^{-1}(1 - \%\text{Very happy}_t) - F^{-1}(\%\text{Not too happy}_t)} \right)^2. \tag{7}$$

The cut points δ_1 and δ_2 define the location and scale over which we are measuring μ_t and σ_t^2, and so we normalize so as to ensure that the average level of happiness across the entire sample is zero and the average variance is one. This normalization implies

$$\delta_1 = \sqrt{\phi} \sum_{t=1}^{\tau} F^{-1}(\%\text{Not too happy}_t) \tag{8}$$

and

$$\delta_2 = \sqrt{\phi} \sum_{t=1}^{\tau} F^{-1}(1 - \%\text{Very happy}), \tag{9}$$

where the constant

$$\phi = \frac{\tau}{\{\sum_{t=1}^{\tau}[F^{-1}(1 - \%\text{VH}) - F^{-1}(\%\text{NTH})]\}^2\{\sum_{t=1}^{\tau}[F^{-1}(1 - \%\text{VH}) - F^{-1}(\%\text{NTH})]^{-2}\}}$$

simplifies the above expressions, the abbreviations %NTH and %VH correspond to the proportions "not too happy" and "very happy," respectively, and τ denotes the number of periods for which we are estimating happiness trends. Our normalization ensures that we recover estimates of μ_t and σ_t that are roughly comparable across assumptions about functional forms and comparable to those from an ordered probit regression (which imposes that this normalization holds for all observations, rather than just hold on average).

Thus, for any specific assumption about the functional form of the underlying latent happiness variable, the simple expressions in equations (6)–(9) can be evaluated using a simple spreadsheet program to compute the time series of both the average level of happiness and its variance.[7] Table 1 provides an example of these calculations for the normal distribution.

We assess the robustness of our estimates of the time series of the distribution of happiness in Figure 3 on the basis of three increasingly fat-tailed assumptions about the distribution of the latent happiness variable: normality, a logistic distribution, and a uniform distribution. The mean and variance estimates are based on equations (6)–(9). While any set of assumptions will seem arbitrary, it is worth noting that the more widely used approach presented in Figure 2 is based on the particularly unappealing assumption that the happiness distribution has three equally spaced mass points corresponding to the three allowable responses.

The key finding is that none of the qualitative (and, indeed, quantitative) implications of our earlier analysis are much changed by alternative approaches to cardinalizing the happiness question, which is quite reassuring. Again, we find only a mild negative trend in average happiness but a clear decline in happiness inequality, with a turning point registered in about the late 1980s and only a gradual increase in the subsequent years. By any measure, happiness inequality in the first third of our sample period is higher than in the final third.

Figure 1 provides some simple intuition for why alternative distributional assumptions yield such similar results: the decline in inequality through to the late 1980s is roughly equally evident whether looking at those who are unusually happy or when looking at those who are unusually unhappy, and as such, placing different weights on the proportion "very happy" relative to the proportion "not too happy" yields similar trends.

Having found that our simple generalization of the ordered probit, ordered logit, and ordered uniform models yields such similar time-series estimates of both the average levels of happiness and its dispersion, the rest of our analysis will focus on the generalized ordered probit model (which assumes normality), although none of our results are materially affected by this focus. An alternative rationale for focusing on the normal distribution is that alternative subjective well-being questions that elicit responses on a 10-point scale tend to yield roughly normally distributed responses (although as Oswald [2008] notes, reported happiness reflects

---

7. This computational simplicity is a useful side effect of the model being just identified. If one were assessing four or more categorical responses, or were to add control variables, then an explicit maximization routine would be required. We explore this further in Section 4.

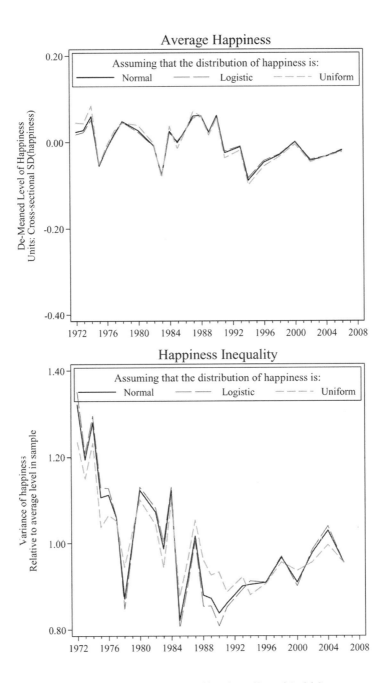

Figure 3. Estimated trends in the distribution of happiness (General Social Survey, 1972–2006).

the conjunction of true happiness and an unknown happiness reporting function).

In order to better assess these changes, we put both mean and dispersion shifts together in Figure 4, showing the combined impact on the distribution of happiness. The estimated distribution of a latent happiness variable, recovered by running a generalized ordered probit regression in which the level and variance of happiness are a linear function of decadal fixed effects, takes account of estimated shocks to both the mean and variance of happiness. (See Table 2 for coefficient estimates underlying the figure.) In order to keep the charts uncluttered, we base these plots on decadal averages of the mean and variance of happiness: the decadal average variance of happiness falls from 1.135 in the 1970s to .979 in the 1980s and to .897 in the 1990s, before rising to .968 in the 2000s; the corresponding numbers for average levels of happiness show much less movement: .015 in the 1970s, .015 in the 1980s, −.023 in the 1990s, and −.024 in the 2000s.[8] This plot shows quite clearly that the magnitude of the changes in dispersion dominates any change in the average level of happiness. For instance, from the 1970s to the 2000s, the happiness level at the 25th (75th) percentile of the happiness distribution rose by .016 points (fell by .094 points), reflecting a .039 point decline in the mean and a .055 point rise (fall) due to increasing happiness inequality. Indeed, Figure 4 shows that while the decline in average levels of happiness made the population in the 2000s less happy on average than in the 1970s, the crossover of the two cumulative distribution functions implies that 32 percent of the population are happier today, and this is due to the offsetting effects of the decline in happiness inequality shrinking the left tail.

Indeed, even as there was not much movement in average levels of happiness in the 1970s and 1980s, there were large increases in happiness at the bottom of the happiness distribution. Figure 5 illustrates, showing annual estimates of the change in well-being since 1972, at various percentiles of the happiness distribution. Percentiles were estimated by running a generalized ordered probit regression in which both the mean and variance of happiness are a linear function of year fixed effects, and we make projections based on the assumed normality of the distribution of happiness. (See Table 1 for coefficient estimates underlying the figure.)

8. The decades we refer to as the 1970s should be understood as the period since the General Social Survey began in 1972; similarly, estimates for the 2000s reflect data from 2000–2006 (the most recent survey), and the 1980s and 1990s refer only to those years in which the General Social Survey was conducted.

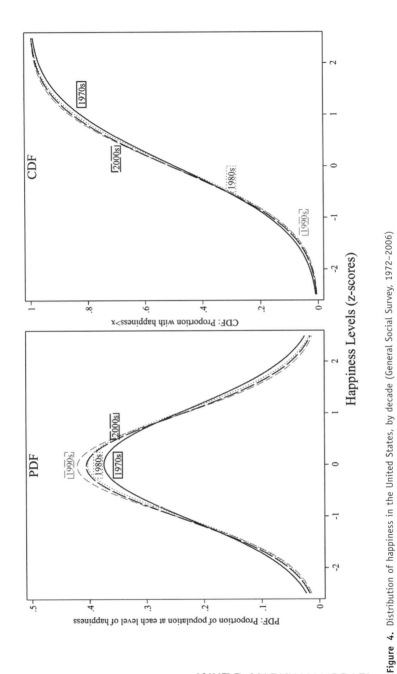

Figure 4. Distribution of happiness in the United States, by decade (General Social Survey, 1972–2006)

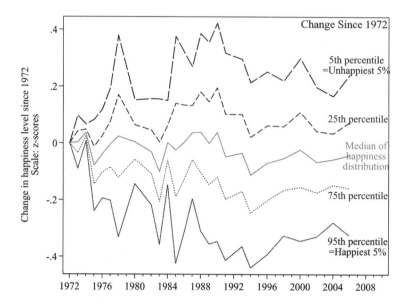

Figure 5. Changes in happiness levels since 1972, by percentile

The (unhappiest) 5th percentile have become .24 points happier since 1972; the 25th percentile have gained around .07 points; the median lost .04 points; the 25th percentile lost .16 points, and the (happiest) 5th percentile lost .33 points. Again, each of these numbers should be considered relative to a cross-sectional standard deviation (normalized to one). In order to compare these magnitudes with their dollar equivalents, note that Stevenson and Wolfers (2008a) estimated that each 10 percent increase in log family income is associated with an increase in happiness of .022 points.[9] Thus, each of these changes in happiness can be converted to a happiness-equivalent percentage change in income, by dividing by .0022 (or multiplying by 45), which suggests that the decline in happiness inequality that we document is very large.

9. The regression reported in figure 8 of Stevenson and Wolfers (2008a) is an ordered probit regression based on these same 1972–2006 GSS data: Happiness = .22ln(Real family income) (standard error = .007), where family income is deflated by the Consumer Price Index Research Series Using Current Methods (CPI-U-RS), and each year's income intervals are converted into point estimates by interval regressions, assuming that income is lognormally distributed. It should be noted that estimates of the happiness-income gradient based on other data sets were often somewhat larger, but most tend to lie in the range of .2–.4.

In the first column of Table 2, we assess these aggregate trends more formally, analyzing the annual time series of happiness inequality (and its mean) derived from our generalization of the ordered probit. (See the Estimated Moments columns of Table 1 for the underlying data.) When we examine decadal averages in happiness inequality, we see that the variance fell by a total of 15 percent from the 1970s to the 2000s, which reflects a decline of 21 percent from the 1970s through the 1990s, about one-third of which reversed in the subsequent decade.

We also assess the magnitude and statistical significance of the overall trend in our annual estimates of inequality. In addition, we allow for a change in the trend; in order to minimize data snooping (and to maximize statistical power), we simply break the sample in half, testing for a break at the (chronological) midpoint of our sample, 1989.[10] In each case, we report Newey-West standard errors, accounting for first-order autocorrelation in happiness inequality. These regressions confirm that the decline in happiness inequality is both economically and statistically significant and that the average decline through the sample period reflects a sharp decline in happiness inequality through the first part of the sample and a subsequent, smaller, rise in the second part, undoing about one-third of the initial decline. We report similar regressions estimates in the bottom half of Table 2, albeit analyzing average levels of happiness rather than its dispersion. These regressions reveal that there is a small, statistically significant overall decline in average happiness. The average level of happiness in the United States is lower in the 1990s and 2000s than it was in the 1970s and 1980s.

Thus far we have shown that in the aggregate, happiness inequality fell sharply during the 1970s and continued to fall in the 1980s, before rising slightly in the 1990s and 2000s. In contrast, average happiness in the population shows little evidence of a trend before the late 1980s, at which point it falls. Yet these broad trends may mask underlying heterogeneity in both the average happiness and the inequality of happiness across socioeconomic and demographic groups. We now turn to digging a bit further into which groups are most affected by these trends.

4. ASSESSING TRENDS WITHIN AND BETWEEN GROUPS

Our approach so far focuses on population aggregates, estimating average happiness and inequality within each year by treating annual ob-

---

10. Given the limited degrees of freedom, we do not test for a discontinuous break in levels in the series, allowing only a change in the trend.

Table 2. Trends in Happiness Inequality and Levels, by Group

	Block 1: Full Sample	Block 2: By Education				Block 3: By Gender		Block 4: By Race		Block 5: By Marital Status		Block 6: By Age		
		College Grad	Some College	High School	<High School	Men	Women	White	Nonwhite	Married	Not married	18–34	35–49	50+
Variance of happiness:[a]														
Decadal averages of Var(happiness):														
1970s	1.135	.921	1.053	1.126	1.316	1.073	1.200	1.049	1.223	1.186	1.045	1.001	1.113	1.270
1980s	.979	.836	.840	.917	1.316	.958	.997	.912	1.055	.990	1.015	.850	.862	1.249
1990s	.897	.884	.827	.849	1.132	.859	.934	.836	.948	.913	.873	.779	.903	1.008
2000s	.968	.956	.912	.955	1.113	.958	.975	.899	1.021	.935	.970	.945	.916	1.021
Full-sample time trend[b]	−.797*	−.036	−.616	−.786+	−.989*	−.644+	−.966**	−.710*	−.991*	−1.038**	−.567*	−.420	−.837	−1.176**
	(.297)	(.390)	(.452)	(.410)	(.358)	(.313)	(.300)	(.265)	(.379)	(.260)	(.257)	(.384)	(.499)	(.195)
Testing for trend break:														
Trend 1972–1989	−2.101**	−1.166	−2.061**	−2.327**	−1.580*	−1.843**	−2.382**	−1.840**	−2.510**	−2.208**	−1.400**	−1.866**	−2.483**	−1.787**
	(.276)	(.724)	(.719)	(.486)	(.587)	(.339)	(.289)	(.244)	(.564)	(.279)	(.368)	(.363)	(.842)	(.492)
Trend 1989–2006	.748**	1.302**	1.097*	1.078*	−.289	.776*	.713**	.628**	.808+	.349	.420	1.295*	1.113*	−.452
	(.202)	(.312)	(.405)	(.399)	(.866)	(.350)	(.232)	(.185)	(.425)	(.264)	(.366)	(.601)	(.462)	(.496)

Variance of average happiness:[c]
Decadal averages of average happiness:

1970s	.015	.104	.052	.046	−.092	−.035	.068	.190	−.287	.254	−.340	−.083	.053	.095
1980s	.015	.171	.023	−.001	−.110	−.011	.038	.181	−.181	.248	−.195	−.059	.006	.115
1990s	−.023	.136	−.030	−.065	−.210	−.022	−.021	.141	−.115	.255	−.249	−.061	−.058	.055
2000s	−.024	.156	−.003	−.124	−.281	−.023	−.025	.149	−.105	.294	−.261	−.069	−.024	.016
Full-sample time trend[d]	−.163*	.055	−.244*	−.570**	−.690**	.056	−.378**	−.187*	.759**	.124	.278	.063	−.350**	−.290*
	(.061)	(.129)	(.109)	(.091)	(.134)	(.083)	(.101)	(.070)	(.193)	(.096)	(.237)	(.100)	(.106)	(.137)
Testing for trend break:														
Trend 1972–89	−.009	.161	−.262	−.279	−.187	.399*	−.420*	−.124	1.386**	−.025	1.352**	.401	−.499*	−.004
	(.164)	(.292)	(.238)	(.281)	(.256)	(.170)	(.193)	(.186)	(.368)	(.230)	(.261)	(.273)	(.232)	(.269)
Trend 1989–2006	−.345*	−.071	−.224	−.915	−1.285**	−.352	−.328	−.263	.016	.301	−.994**	−.338	−.173	−.629**
	(.151)	(.217)	(.155)	(.261)	(.313)	(.192)	(.218)	(.159)	(.281)	(.233)	(.186)	(.209)	(.277)	(.178)

Note. Newey-West standard errors are in parentheses, correcting for first-order autocorrelation. $N = 26$ annual or biennial observations on the means and variance of happiness, estimated using generalized ordered probit from the General Social Survey, 1972–2006. Trend 1972–89 reports β_1. Trend 1989–2006 reports $\beta_1 + \beta_2$. Time trends have been divided by 100 (or, alternatively, the coefficients multiplied by 100).

[a] Relative to sample average.

[b] Variance happiness$_t$ (or mean happiness$_t$) $= \alpha + \beta(\text{Year}_t - 1972)/100$.

[c] Relative to cross-sectional standard deviation of happiness.

[d] Variance happiness$_t$ (or mean happiness$_t$) $= \alpha + \beta_1 I(1972 \leq \text{Year}_t \leq 1989)(\text{Year}_t - 1972)/100 + \beta_2 I(\text{Year}_t \geq 1989)(\text{Year}_t - 1989)/100$.

+ Statistically significant at the 10% level.

* Statistically significant at the 5% level.

** Statistically significant at the 1% level.

servations as distinct cells. We can extend our analysis to consider changes over time within and between categories of demographic groups by estimating separate regressions that consider demographic category × year as the relevant cell. Formally, this simply requires replacing the subscript t in equations (4)−(9) (which denoted separate years as the relevant cells) with the subscript t, d (thus denoting distinct demographic categories in distinct years as the relevant cells). This procedure yields unconditional estimates of differences in happiness levels and inequality both between demographic categories at each point in time and within each demographic category through time. Once we estimate these time series, we report a few summary characteristics in Table 2. For example, by interacting education categories with the year fixed effects, our regression estimates the average level and variance of happiness in each education category through time (and indeed, block 2 of Table 2 describes precisely the evolution of happiness by education and time).

Recall that the first column of Table 2 shows the aggregate trends in happiness and happiness inequality and thus summarizes 26 annual observations. Each subsequent block in Table 2 reports separate regressions that analyze separate demographic category × year cells. Note that levels of happiness and the measure of happiness inequality shown in Table 2 are standardized within each block and hence are comparable across columns within a block, but not comparable between blocks. (Estimates within each block are based on the same cut points, but between blocks these are reestimated and so differ slightly.) We should also be clear in noting that these are raw trends, and so they do not simultaneously account for other factors influencing trends in happiness and happiness inequality.

As such, when interpreting these descriptive analyses—as with all of our demographic breakdowns—it is important to bear in mind that the dramatic changes in the proportions of the population choosing higher education levels or choosing to remain unmarried. If, as seems likely, the marginal member added to (or subtracted from) each group is different from the average, this changing composition will account for some of the time-series variation in the estimated levels and dispersion of happiness within each group. This caveat should also be borne in mind even in Section 4, as it continues to be relevant even despite our best efforts to account for observable differences and compositional change. Nonetheless, this approach does allow us to make some useful within-group time series comparisons, and a few interesting trends emerge.

Focusing on the top half of Table 2, which assesses trends in happiness inequality, the most striking finding is simply that the broad trends seen in the aggregate appear similarly within each of the different demographic groups. Happiness inequality within most groups was highest in the 1970s, fell in the subsequent 2 decades, and rose slightly in the 2000s, although it remains below earlier levels. In contrast, when looking at the average level of happiness in the bottom half of the table, stark differences occur across groups.

To examine patterns in each of the groups more closely, we begin by focusing on the patterns by educational attainment. Recall that returns to education were falling in the 1970s and rose sharply in the 1980s, 1990s, and 2000s. Real wages of men with less than a high school degree and those with only a high school degree stagnated or fell through much of the period, while the real wages of those with a college degree or beyond rose. In contrast, leisure increased among those with less education relative to those with more education. Turning to happiness inequality, block 2 shows that, in the 1970s, average happiness inequality fell with educational attainment. By the 1980s, the differences in happiness inequality between the groups had declined, such that the gap in the dispersion of happiness between those with a college degree and those who had attended, but not completed, college had disappeared. In addition to a decrease in between-group inequality over this period, happiness inequality was much lower for all groups, except among those who had not completed high school. In the 1990s, happiness inequality was little changed among those with some college education, rose for those with a college degree, and fell among those with a high school degree or less. In the most recent period, happiness inequality continued to decline among high school dropouts, despite being higher than in the preceding decade for other groups. By the 2000s, not only was the dispersion of happiness lower within groups compared with the 1970s, but the differences in happiness inequality between groups had been reduced.

In contrast, the bottom half of Table 2 shows that trends in average levels of happiness has varied quite strongly across education groups, with happiness rising among college graduates, falling among those with some college, and falling sharply among those with a high school degree or less. These patterns are what one might expect based on between-group changes in wage inequality (although it is at odds with rising leisure among the less educated).

Turning to examine happiness patterns by gender, we see in the bottom half of the table that women's happiness has fallen, while male happiness followed a statistically insignificant upward trend. This pattern in similar to that seen in Stevenson and Wolfers (2007b), who demonstrate that women's happiness has fallen both absolutely and relative to that of men since the 1970s. Indeed, the gender happiness gap in the 1970s was not only eroded over the subsequent decades, but today, women typically report lower levels of happiness than men. Not surprisingly, happiness inequality for women was also higher than that for men in the 1970s (block 3 in the top half of the table). Yet inequality among both men and women fell in roughly equal measure over the next 2 decades and then rose in the most recent period. These trends have yielded decreased inequality of happiness among both men and women and reduced the difference in the dispersion of happiness between the two groups.

The racial gap in average happiness has also declined since the 1970s, however nonwhites remain substantially less happy—on average—than whites. We find a strikingly large, statistically significant increase in average happiness among nonwhites, while happiness among whites has been declining slightly (in block 4).[11] Examining happiness inequality in the top half of the table shows not only that average levels of happiness were much lower among nonwhites but also that the dispersion of happiness was greater. Happiness inequality fell for both groups through to the 1990s and rose in the 2000s, with inequality lower both within and between racial categories in 2000 than in the beginning of the sample.

Finally, we examine differences in happiness inequality by marital status and by age. One reason for examining differences across marital status is because of the well-known finding that marriage is associated with higher levels of subjective well-being (Blanchflower and Oswald 2004). This pattern is evident in decadal averages of average happiness—in all decades those who are married are happier than those who are not—and there is little trend in their levels of happiness. Moreover, patterns of inequality of happiness are similar for the two groups and match the trends seen for the population as a whole.

Block 6 in Table 2 examines patterns by age, and here some interesting trends emerge. The dispersion of happiness increases with age—a fact

---

11. The GSS race variable allows for a division into white, black and other. Unfortunately there are so few respondents in the "other" category that separating nonwhites into its constituent groups yields particularly imprecise, and thus uninformative, results for these categories. Even so, in further regressions (not shown) breaking out these categories, our estimates for blacks largely track those for obtained for the broader "nonwhite" category.

that is reminiscent of other trends in inequality by age, such as the fact that dispersion in both income and consumption increases with age (Deaton and Paxson 1994). However, the rise in happiness inequality over the life cycle has diminished over the past 35 years and there is less fanning out in the most recent period. The aggregate pattern—of lower levels of happiness inequality in the 1980s and 1990s, rising in the 2000s—is seen for the youngest and oldest age groups, although among prime-age adults happiness inequality is higher in the 1990s than it is in the 1980s. The lower half of the table shows that happiness rises with age, yet the time trend in average happiness has been flat or slightly rising among the young (ages 18–34) and declining among both prime-age and older adults.[12]

The key commonality across all of these results is that happiness inequality has declined within all of these demographic groups. Naturally, these trends may be interrelated, and so we conducted a further analysis based on more narrowly defined demographic groups, breaking the sample up into 24 subsamples reflecting a division into mutually exclusive and collectively exhaustive samples for two genders × three age groups × four education levels. Within 20 of these 24 cases we found a trend decline in happiness inequality, and in no case did with find statistically significant evidence of a trend increase in inequality. We interpret these findings as suggesting a pervasive rise in within-group happiness inequality.

Breaking up the sample into distinct subsamples can go only so far with our limited sample sizes (and this exercise already yielded some fairly small cell sizes). As such, a more formal regression framework is needed if we are also going to account for the influence of further factors. We now turn to developing an appropriate estimation framework in greater detail that will condition on a variety of demographic and socioeconomic variables at once.

A More General Approach

The key to our estimation is simply to generalize the standard ordered probit model so as to allow us to jointly estimate both the mean and variance of happiness as a function of a rich set of covariates.

Given the model defined by equations (1)–(3), when analyzing a data

---

12. Blanchflower and Oswald (2004) report a U shape in life-cycle happiness in which happiness is highest at young and older ages. However, this pattern is what occurs when examining happiness patterns by age conditional on life outcomes such as marriage, income, and employment status. Our results in Table 2 are unconditional.

set with N observations indexed by i, a dependent variable consisting of J ordered response categories, and a covariate vector, x_{it}, the log likelihood function is

$$\ln L = \sum_{i=1}^{N} \sum_{j=1}^{J} I(y_{it} = j) \ln \left[F\left(\frac{\delta_j - x_{it}\beta_t}{\sqrt{x_{it}\gamma_t}}\right) - F\left(\frac{\delta_{j-1} - x_{it}\beta_t}{\sqrt{x_{it}\gamma_t}}\right) \right], \qquad (10)$$

where $F(.)$ is the cumulative distribution function of the error term, and we shall assume that it is normal; we impose no bounds on the latent happiness variable, and hence $\delta_1 = -\infty$ and $\delta_j = \infty$. Two further constraints are required to pin down the location and scale of the estimates, and as before, we impose these constraints so as to ensure that the latent happiness index has a mean of zero and an average variance of one: $\sum_{i=1}^{N} x_{it}\beta_t = 0$ and $\sum_{i=1}^{N} x_{it}\gamma_t = N$. Our interest lies in the β_t vector, which shifts the average level of happiness, and γ_t, which shifts its variance.

Thus, our results in Section 3 can be reframed as solving the maximization problem described by equation (10), where the covariates, x_{it}, were simply a vector of year fixed effects. The advantage of our generalized framework is that we can now estimate different trends by demographic group, conditioning on time-series movements in the level and dispersion of happiness common to other demographic characteristics. By comparison, the approach described in equations (4)–(9) required dividing the sample into mutually exclusive cells—something that is feasible only when assessing a small number of covariates (particularly given the relatively small samples in the GSS). We now turn to expanding the vector of relevant covariates, x_{it}, so that it incorporates not only a vector of year fixed effects but also those year fixed effects interacted with dummy variables for each education, gender, race, marital status, and age group. That is, we estimate

$$\text{Happiness}_{it}^* = \sum_t I(\text{year}_t = t)$$

$$\times \left\{ \left[\sum_e \beta_{e,t} I(\text{educ}_{it} = e) + \sum_s \beta_{s,t} I(\text{sex}_{it} = s) + \sum_r \beta_{r,t} I(\text{race}_{it} = r) \right. \right.$$

$$\left. + \sum_m \beta_{m,t} I(\text{mar}_{it} = m) + \sum_a \beta_{a,t} I(\text{age}_{it} = a) + \sum_r \beta_{r,t} I(\text{region}_{it} = r) \right] \qquad (11)$$

$$+ \left[\sum_e \gamma_{e,t} I(\text{educ}_{it} = e) + \sum_s \gamma_{s,t} I(\text{sex}_{it} = s) + \sum_r \gamma_{r,t} I(\text{race}_{it} = r) \right.$$

$$\left. \left. + \sum_m \gamma_{m,t} I(\text{mar}_{it} = m) + \sum_a \gamma_{a,t} I(\text{age}_{it} = a) + \sum_r \gamma_{r,t} I(\text{region}_{it} = r) \right]^{1/2} \times \varepsilon_{i,t} \right\},$$

where Happiness_{it}^* is the unobserved happiness index, reported according to equation (2), ε_{it} is the error term, the β terms shift the level of hap-

piness differentially for each group in each year, and the γ terms shift
the variance of happiness differentially for each group in each year. Our
omission of income from this equation is purposeful, as we wish to
juxtapose our findings regarding trends in happiness inequality by demographic group, with analogous trends reported in the income inequality literature.

Estimating this full regression yields 26 separate year fixed effects for
both the level and dispersion of happiness for each of 17 different demographic groups (four education groups, two genders, two racial
groups, two marital statuses, three age groups, and four regions), for a
total of $26 \times 2 \times 17 = 884$ coefficient estimates. Thus, instead of showing a regression table, we present these point estimates graphically in
Figure 6 (focusing on average happiness levels for each group) and Figure
7 (focusing on happiness inequality within each group). Instead of showing coefficients relative to an arbitrary omitted group, each panel shows
the predicted levels and dispersion of happiness of someone with the
average sample characteristics, except for the particular characteristic
examined in each panel. Thus, for instance, the top (grey) line in the
first panel of Figure 6 shows the evolution of happiness for someone
with college education but all other (noneducation) covariates set to
their (time-invariant) sample averages (and Figure 7 shows the corresponding variance).

These figures illustrate in more detail the broad trends seen in Table
3. Figure 6 shows that happiness has fanned out by education, with
happiness highest (and rising) for college graduates, but lower and falling
for high school graduates, and declining more steeply for high school
dropouts. Happiness has also become more dispersed by age, albeit only
slightly. Among 35–49 year olds and those over age 50, happiness has
trended downward, while the happiness of 18–34 year olds has trended
upward. As previously seen, happiness has converged along gender and
racial lines. Indeed, the closing of the racial happiness gap is striking
and appears to have nearly been eliminated in recent years, which suggests that the much larger unconditional racial happiness gap seen in
Table 2 may be attributable to the combined impact of racial differences
in educational attainment and widening educational differences in happiness.[13] Happiness differences by marital status narrowed in the 1980s,

13. Again we emphasize that differences by demographic group are merely descriptive
means (or conditional means), and it should not be inferred that these are causal relationships.

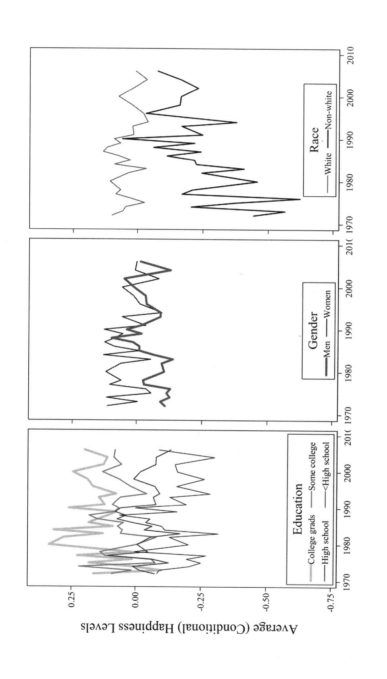

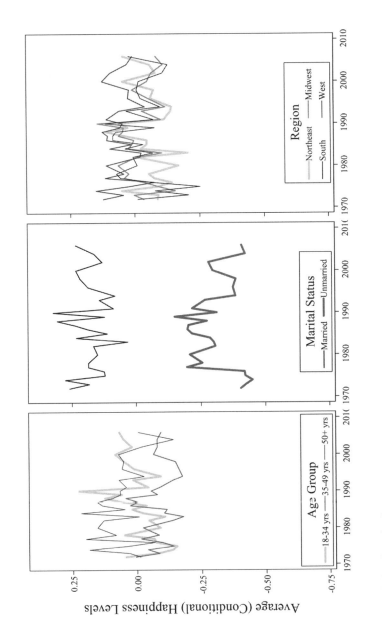

Figure 6. Trends in happiness levels

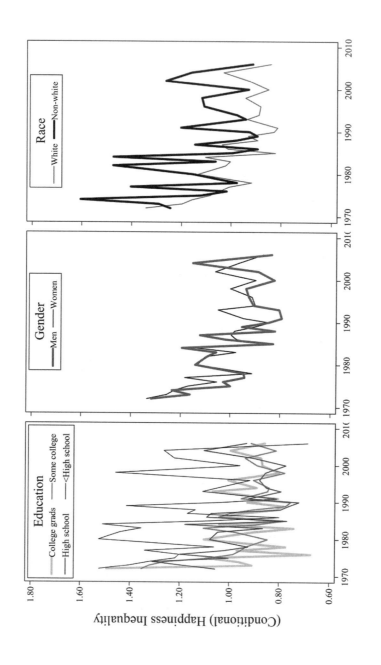

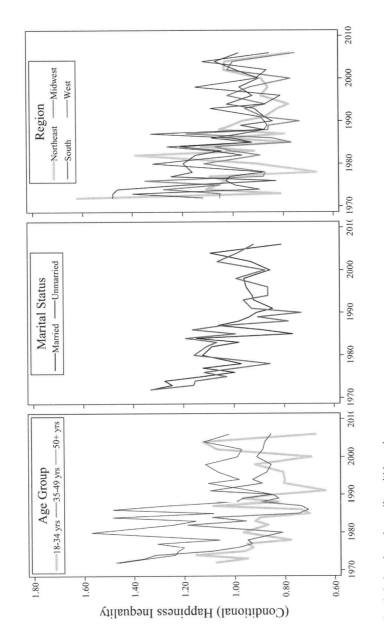

Figure 7. Trends in happiness inequality, within each group

Table 3. Regression Describing the Evolution of Happiness, by Decade

	Block 1: Level of Happiness					Block 2: Variance of Happiness					Block 3: Sample Proportions (%)				
	$\bar{\beta}$	β_{1970s}	β_{1980s}	β_{1990s}	β_{2000s}	$\bar{\gamma}$	γ_{1970s}	γ_{1980s}	γ_{1990s}	γ_{2000s}	$\bar{x}$	x_{1970s}	x_{1980s}	x_{1990s}	x_{2000s}
Constant	.016	.062 (.011)	-.018 (.010)	-.032 (.010)	.084 (.014)	.830	.931 (.011)	.832 (.010)	.730 (.010)	.859 (.014)	100	100	100	100	100
College graduate	.198	.102 (.011)	.194 (.009)	.200 (.008)	.262 (.011)	-.008	-.090 (.011)	-.079 (.009)	.071 (.008)	.005 (.011)	20.5	13.7	17.6	24.6	27.2
Some college	.102	.095 (.010)	.090 (.009)	.075 (.008)	.158 (.010)	-.005	.035 (.010)	-.035 (.009)	-.005 (.008)	.002 (.010)	23.2	16.9	21.1	26.1	30.1
High school graduate	.000	.000 (.010)	.000 (.009)	.000 (.008)	.000 (.010)	.000	.000 (.008)	.000 (.008)	.000 (.009)	.000 (.010)	32.0	33.9	34.3	30.9	27.7
<High school	-.117	-.132 (.008)	-.098 (.008)	-.142 (.009)	-.077 (.012)	.251	.236 (.008)	.334 (.008)	.239 (.009)	.079 (.012)	24.3	35.4	27.0	18.3	15.0
Men	.000	.000 (.007)	.000 (.006)	.000 (.006)	.000 (.008)	.000	.000 (.007)	.000 (.006)	.000 (.006)	.000 (.008)	45.9	47.5	44.8	45.4	46.2
Women	.076	.139 (.007)	.096 (.006)	.038 (.006)	.022 (.008)	.036	.086 (.007)	-.016 (.006)	.054 (.006)	.032 (.008)	54.1	52.5	55.2	54.6	53.8
White	.000	.000 (.010)	.000 (.009)	.000 (.008)	.000 (.010)	.000	.000 (.007)	.000 (.006)	.000 (.006)	.000 (.008)	83.9	87.8	86.4	82.0	78.0
Nonwhite	-.242	-.408 (.010)	-.385 (.009)	-.174 (.008)	-.169 (.010)	.149	.190 (.010)	.123 (.009)	.173 (.008)	.115 (.010)	16.1	12.2	13.6	18.0	22.0
Married	.000	.000 (.007)	.000 (.006)	.000 (.006)	.000 (.008)	.000	.000 (.007)	.000 (.006)	.000 (.006)	.000 (.008)	62.7	72.1	63.9	58.9	55.0
Nonmarried	-.494	-.555 (.007)	-.395 (.006)	-.507 (.006)	-.554 (.008)	-.025	-.141 (.007)	.033 (.006)	-.053 (.006)	.032 (.008)	37.3	27.9	36.1	41.1	45.0
Ages 18–34	.088	.014 (.008)	.058 (.008)	.159 (.008)	.137 (.010)	-.047	-.075 (.008)	-.007 (.008)	-.059 (.008)	-.058 (.010)	35.1	37.0	37.6	33.4	31.1
Ages 35–49	.000	.000 (.008)	.000 (.008)	.000 (.008)	.000 (.010)	.000	.000 (.008)	.000 (.008)	.000 (.008)	.000 (.010)	29.2	25.8	26.9	32.9	31.4

Table (rotated 90° in original). Coefficient estimates, sample proportions, and weighted averages from a generalized ordered probit model. Standard errors in parentheses. For each block the first column is the overall weighted average and the following four columns are the separate decades.

	$\bar{x}\beta_t$					$\bar{x}_t\beta_t$					Sample proportion (%)				
Ages 50+	.147	.138 (.008)	.171 (.008)	.182 (.007)	.072 (.009)	.189	.162 (.008)	.318 (.008)	.126 (.007)	.117 (.009)	35.8	37.2	35.5	33.7	37.5
Northeast	.000	.000	.000	.000	.000	.000	.000	.000	.000	.000	20.8	22.9	21.1	19.7	19.1
Midwest	.026	.030 (.009)	.051 (.009)	.052 (.009)	−.073 (.012)	−.022	.046 (.009)	−.091 (.009)	.046 (.009)	−.110 (.012)	26.1	29.0	27.3	24.3	23.3
South	.103	.129 (.009)	.103 (.008)	.111 (.009)	.060 (.011)	.076	.187 (.009)	.009 (.008)	.091 (.009)	.026 (.011)	34.2	32.2	33.2	35.4	36.2
West	.027	.004 (.011)	.048 (.010)	.061 (.010)	−.034 (.013)	.030	.048 (.011)	.011 (.010)	.077 (.010)	−.031 (.013)	19.0	16.0	18.4	20.5	21.4
Net effect	$\bar{x}_t\beta_t$	.023	.019	−.030	−.015	$\bar{x}_t\beta_t$	1.151	1.101	.910	.933					

Decomposition:

	(β block)					(γ block)				
Baseline	$\overline{x\beta}$	.000	.000	.000	.000	$\overline{x\gamma}$	1.000	1.000	1.000	1.000
Changing coefficients	$\bar{x}(\beta_t - \bar{\beta})$	−.016	.016	−.021	.003	$\bar{x}(\gamma_t - \bar{\gamma})$	.119	.004	−.080	−.077
Changing composition	$(\bar{x}_t - \bar{x})\beta_t$	.038	.003	−.009	−.019	$(\bar{x}_t - \bar{x})\gamma_t$	.032	.006	−.010	.009

Note. Coefficient estimates, sample proportions, and weighted averages are shown from estimating a generalized ordered probit regression in which the unobserved latent happiness index is estimated as Happiness$_{it}^{*} = x_i\beta_t + \varepsilon_{it}$, where $\varepsilon_{it} \sim N(0, x_i\gamma_t)$, where the subscript t refers to separate decades. Cut points are $\delta_1 = -1.29$ and $\delta_2 = .42$. Log likelihood $= -40{,}707.940$. Omitted categories are high school graduates, men, whites, married, ages 35–49, and Northeast. Standard errors are shown in parentheses. $N = 46{,}303$ observations from the General Social Survey, 1972–2006.

but by the end of the sample are similar to what were seen in the 1970s. Happiness trends by region have been roughly common across space.

Figure 7 shows that the decline in happiness inequality since the 1970s has occurred pretty much in parallel across demographic groups. There appears to be a fair bit of noise in these annual estimates, and in no case do the data make a convincing case for sharply different trends in within-group happiness inequality.

We also present a more compact representation of our results in Table 3, where we analyze changes by decade rather than year, so as to reduce the number of coefficient estimates to a manageable size (and reduce statistical noise). This approach has the advantage of allowing distinct patterns by decades to be examined for each group. This analysis contains all of the interactions in Table 2 along with time trends by region but differs from that table in that it shows conditional estimates. The first row of Table 3 reports the decadal trends for our baseline group— 35–49-year-old white, married males with only a high school degree who live in the Northeast. For this group we see that happiness fell in the 1980s and 1990s but rose in the 2000s such that there is little difference in happiness between 1972 and 2006. Among members of this group, inequality in happiness follows the pattern seen in the aggregate population and is lower in the most recent period than in the 1970s. To compare these men with similar men who completed a college degree, we turn to the second row, which reports how the trends differ for college graduates. Adding the second row to the first row provides the trends 35–49-year-old white, married males with a college degree who live in the Northeast. Similarly, adding estimated coefficients for women to those in the top two rows would provide the trends for the equivalent female.

The estimated trends in Table 3 illustrate that some of the unconditional trends in Table 2 reflect the coincidence of trends in other categories. For example, examining those who are not married, we see that, conditional on other trends, happiness inequality was higher in the 1980s than the 1970s, a distinctly different pattern from what we have seen thus far. Yet the broad trends can still be seen—happiness levels are higher among women in the 1970s, with the gender gap narrowing in the ensuing decades. Similarly, happiness levels are lower among nonwhites, yet the gap narrows over the decades. The dispersion in happiness is higher among women and nonwhites in the 1970s, as seen previously.

A Decomposition

The key new finding in this paper is the fact that happiness inequality has declined since the 1970s, even if it has risen somewhat in recent years. In turn, the aggregate trend in happiness inequality shown in Figure 3 reflects the influence of changing average levels of happiness between groups (shown in Figure 6), changing happiness inequality within groups (shown in Figure 7), and changing proportions of the population in each group (Figure 8). In order to assess the combined impact of these separate influences, we now turn to a decomposition exercise, along the lines suggested by Lemieux (2002).

We begin by noting that our full regression, equation (11), expresses the latent happiness index as a function of individual characteristics with time-varying coefficients:

$$\text{Happiness}_{it}^* = x_{it}\beta_t + \sqrt{x_{it}\gamma_t}\varepsilon_{it}, \tag{12}$$

where i denotes the individual observation, t is the time period, $\varepsilon_{it} \sim N(0, 1)$ is the error term, x_{it} is the $(1 \times k)$ vector of binary covariates described more fully in equation (11), where the scalar at the jth position denotes membership in demographic group j, and β_t and γ_t are time-varying $(k \times 1)$ vectors of parameters.

The mean level of happiness in each period can thus be expressed as

$$\mu_t = \bar{x}_t\beta_t, \tag{13}$$

where $\bar{x}_t = \sum_i \omega_{it} x_{it} / \sum_i \omega_{it}$ is a vector in which the scalar at position j represents the proportion of the population in period with t characteristic j and ω_{it} refers to each observation's sampling weight, A simple Oaxaca decomposition allows us to describe changes in the mean as due to changes in the time-varying coefficients versus changes in the composition of the sample:

$$\mu_t = \bar{x}\bar{\beta} + \bar{x}(\beta_t - \bar{\beta}) + (\bar{x}_t - \bar{x})\beta_t, \tag{14}$$

where $\bar{x} = \Sigma_t\Sigma_i\omega_{it}x_{it} / \Sigma_t\Sigma_i\omega_{it}$ is a vector in which the scalar at position j represents the proportion of the whole sample that has characteristic j. The first term in this expression captures the average level of happiness in the sample, which is set to zero by our normalization. The second term captures changes due to time-series movements in the average happiness of various groups, captured by deviations of the betas from their means. Note that the each of the within-group changes shown in Figure

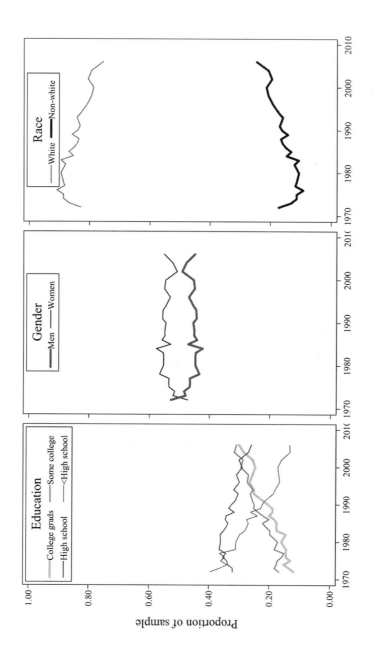

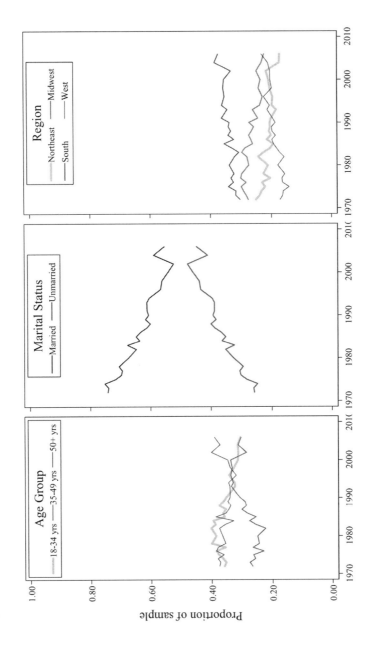

Figure 8. Changes in the proportion of the General Social Survey population with each demographic characteristic

6 are components of this vector, $[\beta_t^1, \ldots, \beta_t^k]$, and we aggregate these time series into a representative fixed-weight index by use of a time-invariant weighting vector $\bar{x}$, which describes the proportions of people in the entire sample with each characteristic. Finally, the impact of changes in the proportion of the sample with each demographic characteristic is captured by the third term.

We show the estimates of these terms estimated using decadal means at the bottom of block 1 in Table 3. The net time series for average happiness is, if anything, somewhat negative over this period. Yet when a fixed-weight happiness is formed, $\bar{x}(\beta_t - \bar{\beta})$, this trend decline disappears. The decadal estimates of the effects of compositional change, $(\bar{x}_t - \bar{x})\beta_t$, illustrate how the population has shifted into demographic categories that have typically been less happy. In particular, the sample proportions (in block 3) show the population is increasingly nonwhite and unmarried—factors associated with lower levels of happiness—while simultaneously becoming older and more educated—factors associated with higher average happiness. On aggregate, these shifts have contributed to reducing the overall happiness in the population.

We can also write the variance of Happiness$_{it}^*$ as the sum of within-group changes in happiness and a component due to changes in happiness levels between groups:

$$V_t = \overbrace{\bar{x}\gamma_t}^{\text{within}} + \overbrace{\beta_t'\Omega_t^x\beta_t}^{\text{between}}, \tag{15}$$

where Ω_t^x is the variance-covariance matrix of x_{it} in period t.[14]

The within-group variance can be further decomposed:

$$\bar{x}\gamma_t = \bar{x}\bar{\gamma} + \bar{x}(\gamma_t - \bar{\gamma}) + (\bar{x}_t - \bar{x})\gamma_t, \tag{16}$$

where the first term captures the average variance of happiness in our sample, which is set to one by our normalization. The second term reflects estimated time-series movements in the variance within each group, aggregated using a fixed-weight index. The third term reflects

---

14. Note that the literature on wage inequality sometimes refers to the first term in equation (15) as residual variance and the second term as explained variance. This terminology reflects the fact that these studies typically begin by running a regression of wages on observable variables (either in a separate regression for each year or, alternatively, in a single regression interacting observable variables with year fixed effects). The second term in equation (15) is explained by these first-stage regressions, while the first term reflects the variance of these residuals. By contrast, we model shifts in the level and dispersion of happiness in a single step: see equation (11).

the changes due to changing composition of the sample into groups prone to greater or lesser degrees of dispersion—a factor emphasized by Lemieux (2006) as an important explanator of rising residual wage in equality.

As with the means, we show the decomposition of the within-group variance using decadal means in block 2 of Table 3. The fixed-weight index of within-group changes in happiness inequality, $\bar{x}(\gamma_t - \bar{\gamma})$, points to a substantial decrease in the within-group variance of happiness through to the 1990s. Turning to the estimated $(\bar{x}_t - \bar{x})\gamma_t$ term, we see a qualitatively similar pattern—albeit with a much smaller quantitative contribution—with the changing composition of the sample contributing to falling dispersion through the 1990s and a rise in dispersion in the 2000s. All told, it appears that compositional change explains very little of the overall rise in residual happiness inequality.

Finally, the between-group variance can be decomposed as follows:

$$\boldsymbol{\beta}_t'\Omega_t^x\boldsymbol{\beta}_t = \bar{\boldsymbol{\beta}}'\Omega^x\bar{\boldsymbol{\beta}} + (\boldsymbol{\beta}_t - \bar{\boldsymbol{\beta}})'\Omega^x(\boldsymbol{\beta}_t - \bar{\boldsymbol{\beta}}) + \boldsymbol{\beta}_t'(\Omega_t^x - \Omega^x)\boldsymbol{\beta}_t, \qquad (17)$$

where Ω^x is the variance-covariance matrix of x_i, estimated using data from all time periods.

We combine these time-series movements in difference in average levels of happiness between groups ($\boldsymbol{\beta}_t$, shown in Figure 6), within-group dispersion in happiness (γ_t, shown in Figure 7), and the proportion of the population with each demographic ($\bar{x}_t$, shown in Figure 8) to yield a useful decomposition of the overall trends in the distribution of happiness, shown in Figure 9.[15] The decompositions come from five models: $\text{Happiness}_{it}^1 = \bar{x}\bar{\boldsymbol{\beta}} + \bar{x}\bar{\gamma}\sqrt{\varepsilon_{it}}$, $\text{Happiness}_{it}^2 = \bar{x}\bar{\boldsymbol{\beta}}_t + \bar{x}\bar{\gamma}\sqrt{\varepsilon_{it}}$, $\text{Happiness}_{it}^3 = \bar{x}_t\bar{\boldsymbol{\beta}}_t + \bar{x}\bar{\gamma}_t\sqrt{\varepsilon_{it}}$, $\text{Happiness}_{it}^4 = \bar{x}_t\bar{\boldsymbol{\beta}}_t + \bar{x}\bar{\gamma}_t\sqrt{\varepsilon_{it}}$, and $\text{Happiness}_{it}^5 = \bar{x}_{it}\bar{\boldsymbol{\beta}}_t + \bar{x}_{it}\bar{\gamma}_t\sqrt{\varepsilon_{it}}$. (See equations (11)–(17) for details on each decomposition.) This figure shows that changes in the variance of happiness are being driven more by changes in within-group variance than by changes in between-group variance. However, there is a slight downward trend in between-group variance that is contributing to the overall decrease in happiness inequality since the 1970s. In sum, the figure illustrates that while the happiness convergence by race and gender played a role in

15. Of course, alternative decompositions exist, and we can vary the order in which compositional versus within-group changes are considered or which period to use as the index base (we choose the sample averages rather than any specific year). Table 3 provides the raw data necessary for these alternative decompositions; our analysis suggests that these alternative approaches do not much change the character of our results.

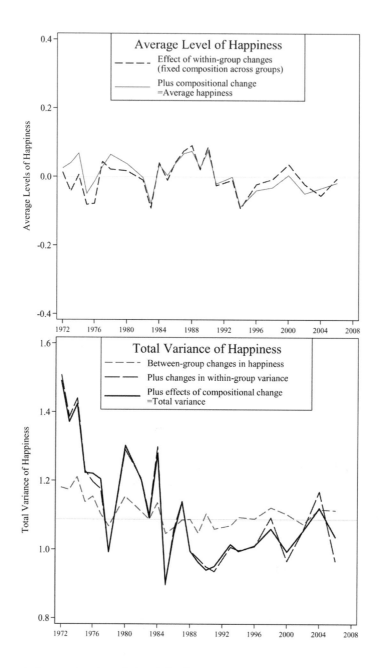

Figure 9. Decomposing the evolution of the distribution of happiness (solid lines show the aggregate observed level of each statistic; dashed lines show results from decompositions that abstract from the role of compositional change).

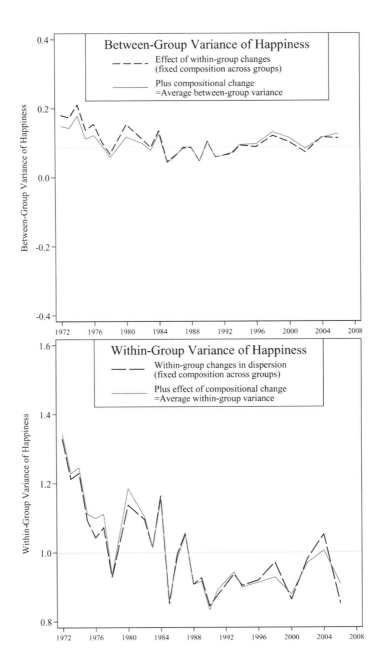

Figure 9. *Continued*

reducing inequality, this role was small compared to the overall decline in the inequality of happiness that is seen within each demographic category.

5. DISCUSSION

While there has been no increase in aggregate happiness over recent decades, there have been large changes in the level of happiness across groups. Much of the racial happiness gap has closed, the gender happiness gap has disappeared and perhaps inverted, and differences in happiness by education have widened substantially. More generally, we document a pervasive decline in happiness since the 1970s, albeit with some reversal over the past decade or so. That these trends differ from trends in both income growth and income inequality suggests that a useful explanation may lie in the nonpecuniary domain. As such, we suspect that our data are best interpreted in the broader context of a host of economic, social, and legal changes impacting equality in the United States over the past 35 years. There is much more work to be done in unraveling just how these forces are affecting the distribution of happiness in the United States.

In addition to the changes in both the level and dispersion of happiness between groups, there have been large demographic shifts that have potentially impacted happiness aggregates. Throughout this paper we have developed an integrated approach to measuring inequality and decomposing changes in the distribution of happiness. We examine how the composition and average happiness have changed both within and between demographic groups, paying particular attention to demographic and socioeconomic factors known to impact happiness such as education, marital status, age, race, and gender. This decomposition points to changes in the dispersion of happiness within groups as the main driver of declining happiness inequality. However, while this is a useful accounting exercise, it still leaves unanswered the question of just what it is that is creating less inequality in the subjectively experienced lives of demographically similar people.

APPENDIX: CORRECTING FOR QUESTION ORDER EFFECTS IN THE GENERAL SOCIAL SURVEY

While the General Social Survey has maintained the same question about happiness since its inception in 1972, responses seem to be quite sensitive to the immediately preceding battery of questions, and this ordering has changed several times. We provide this appendix in the hope that it will help the field settle on a widely accepted and accurate time series.

There are two key changes in question ordering:

1. whether a question probing marital happiness (asked only of married couples) immediately precedes the general happiness question and

2. whether a five-question battery probing domains of satisfaction immediately precedes the happiness question.

The first context occurs every year except in 1972, which is replicated in split-ballot experiments affecting only one-third of the respondents in 1980 and 1987 (those assigned form 3). Smith (1990) notes that these split ballots suggest that levels of happiness among married respondents tend to be higher in these instances in which they are preceeded by a question about marital happiness.

The second change in question ordering affects all respondents in 1972 and 1985, and its impact can be assessed by virtue of the fact that it was replicated for 1986 form 2 respondents and forms 2 and 3 respondents in 1987. Smith (1990) finds that aggregate happiness is higher in the years in which the happiness question is preceded by a five-item satisfaction scale.

Because of the split-ballot experiments run in 1980 and 1987—in which one in three randomly assigned questionnaires dropped the marital satisfaction question—and similar experiments run in 1986 and 1987, in which the satisfaction scale was dropped in one-third and two-thirds of the forms, respectively, we can assess the changes induced by these question order effects. These experiments are particularly useful in that statistically similar populations are assigned different contexts.

Thus, we use these experiments to calculate a set of sampling weights that correct for the undersampling of relatively happy people in 1972, 1980, and 1985–87 as well as the oversampling of happy married people in 1980 (see Table A1).

While our analysis largely follows Smith's suggestions, we differ in two respects. First, we do not simply drop the experimental forms from the sample but include their (appropriately adjusted) responses in computing our time series. And second, we also apply a slightly more sophisticated approach to measuring and correcting for these biases. In particular, given our interest in measuring the full distribution of happiness, it is important that we provide corrections for the share who are very happy, pretty happy, and not too happy.

In order to estimate the extent of these biases, we regress happiness on a dummy variable equal to one for those affected by each sampling change (the first change affected married people in 1972 and married form 3 respondents in 1980 and 1987; the second change affected all 1972 and 1985 respondents as well as the experimental 1986 form 2 respondents and 1987 form 2 and 3 respondents, controlling for year fixed effects, entered separately for both married and unmarried respondents. Our dependent variables are separate dummies

Table A1. Correcting General Social Survey Happiness Data for Question Order Effects

	Raw Data (%)			Corrected (%)			
Year	Not Too Happy	Pretty Happy	Very Happy	Not Too Happy	Pretty Happy	Very Happy	Sample Size
1972	17.2	53.0	29.7	13.6	49.1	37.3	1,606
1973	12.3	50.9	36.8	12.3	50.9	36.8	1,500
1974	12.5	49.2	38.3	12.5	49.2	38.3	1,480
1975	13.0	53.6	33.4	13.0	53.6	33.4	1,485
1976	12.2	52.9	34.8	12.2	52.9	34.8	1,499
1977	11.0	53.2	35.7	11.0	53.2	35.7	1,527
1978	8.4	56.2	35.5	8.4	56.2	35.5	1,517
1980	12.1	52.6	35.3	11.6	52.0	36.4	1,462
1982	11.7	53.5	34.8	11.7	53.5	34.8	1,505
1983	12.1	56.2	31.7	12.1	56.2	31.7	1,573
1984	11.6	52.1	36.3	11.6	52.1	36.3	1,445
1985	10.5	59.9	29.6	8.6	58.4	33.1	1,530
1986	10.2	56.6	33.2	9.2	55.8	35.0	1,449
1987	11.5	55.0	33.5	9.7	53.3	37.0	1,437
1988	8.2	55.7	36.1	8.2	55.7	36.1	1,466
1989	8.8	56.7	34.5	8.8	56.7	34.5	1,526
1990	7.7	56.5	35.7	7.7	56.5	35.7	1,361
1991	9.5	58.0	32.5	9.5	58.0	32.5	1,504
1993	9.7	56.9	33.4	9.7	56.9	33.4	1,601
1994	11.3	58.2	30.5	11.3	58.2	30.5	2,977
1996	10.5	57.4	32.1	10.5	57.4	32.1	2,885
1998	10.9	55.9	33.3	10.9	55.9	33.3	2,806
2000	9.6	56.4	33.9	9.6	56.4	33.9	2,777
2002	11.3	55.8	32.9	11.3	55.8	32.9	1,369
2004	11.7	54.7	33.6	11.7	54.7	33.6	1,337
2006	10.6	55.9	33.5	10.6	55.9	33.5	2,828

Note. Estimates are based on the sample weight WTSALL, omitting black oversamples in 1982 and 1987 and the Spanish-language interviews in 2006 that could not have been completed were English required (as in previous years). The corrected series make adjustments in 1972, 1980, 1985, 1986, and 1987 for question order effects.

corresponding to each of three possible happiness responses. Thus, the ballot experiments identify the effect of changing questionnaire order separate from background trends in happiness by marital status. These estimates suggest that the absence of the question about marital happiness led to a statistically significant decline (of about 5.4 percent) in the proportion of married respondents reporting themselves to be "pretty happy," while the absence of the preceding satisfaction questions led to a statistically significant rise (of about 2.7 percent) in the proportion of respondents claiming they were "not too happy." The aggregate happiness time series is simply the unadjusted annual happiness aggregates less the estimated question order effects (for those subject to the varied question order). The Stata code required to estimate these effects is available on our Web pages.[16]

REFERENCES

Aguiar, Mark, and Erik Hurst. 2007. Measuring Trends in Leisure: The Allocation of Time over Five Decades. *Quarterly Journal of Economics* 122: 969–1006.

———. 2008. The Increase in Leisure Inequality. NBER Working Paper No. 13837. National Bureau of Economic Research, Cambridge, Mass.

Atkinson, Anthony B. 1970. On the Measurement of Inequality. *Journal of Economic Theory* 2:244–63.

Attanasio, Orazio, Erich Battistin, and Hidehiko Ichimura. 2004. What Really Happened to Consumption Inequality in the US. NBER Working Paper No. 10338. National Bureau of Economic Research, Cambridge, Mass.

Autor, David, Lawrence Katz, and Melissa Kearney. 2008. Trends in U.S. Wage Inequality: Revising the Revisionists. *Review of Economics and Statistics* 90: 300–323.

Blanchflower, David, and Andrew Oswald. 2004. Well-Being over Time in Britain and the USA. *Journal of Public Economics* 88:1359–86.

Blau, Francine, and Lawrence Kahn. 2006. The U.S. Gender Pay Gap in the 1990s: Slowing Convergence. *Industrial and Labor Relations Review* 60: 45–66.

Brooks, Arthur C. 2008. *Gross National Happiness: Why Happiness Matters for American—and How We Can Get More of It*. New York: Basic Books.

Couch, Kenneth, and Mary Daly. 2003. The Improving Relative Status of Black Men. *Journal of Income Distribution* 12:56–78.

Cutler, David, and Lawrence Katz. 1991. Macroeconomic Performance and the Disadvantaged. *Brookings Papers on Economic Activity,* pp. 1–74.

Davis, James A., Tom W. Smith, and Peter V. Marsden. 1972–2006. General Social Surveys. National Data Program for the Social Sciences Series No. 18. Chicago: National Opinion Research Center.

Deaton, Angus, and Christina Paxson. 1994. Intertemporal Choice and Inequality. *Journal of Political Economy* 102:437–67.

Donohue, John J., and Peter Siegelman. 1991. The Changing Nature of Employment Discrimination Litigation. *Stanford Law Review* 43:983–1033.

Easterlin, Richard A. 1995. Will Raising the Incomes of All Increase the Happiness of All? *Journal of Economic Behavior and Organization* 27:35–48.

16. See http://bpp.wharton.upenn.edu/betseys or http://www.nber.org/~jwolfers. For those interested in replicating our results, the simplest way is to define a weighting variable as follows: gen wt=WTSSALL if SAMPLE~=4 & SAMPLE~=5 & SAMPLE~=7 & SPANINT~=2.

Goldin, Claudia, and Lawrence Katz. 2007. Long-Run Changes in the Wage Structure: Narrowing, Widening, Polarizing. *Brookings Papers on Economic Activity,* pp. 135–65.

———. 2008. *The Race between Education and Technology.* Cambridge, Mass.: Harvard University Press.

Gottschalk, Peter, and Robert Moffitt. 1994. The Growth of Earnings Instability in the US Labor Market. *Brookings Papers on Economic Activity,* pp. 217–72.

Hacker, Jacob. 2006. *The Great Risk Shift.* New York: Oxford University Press.

Isen, Adam, and Betsey Stevenson. 2008. Women's Education and Family Behavior: Trends in Marriage, Divorce and Fertility. Working paper. University of Pennsylvania, Wharton School, Philadelphia.

Jensen, Shane, and Stephen Shore. 2008. Changes in the Distribution of Income Volatility. Unpublished manuscript. John Hopkins University, Department of Economics, Baltimore.

Johnson, David, and Stephanie Shipp. 1997. Trends in Inequality Using Consumer Expenditures: 1960 to 1993. *Review of Income and Wealth* 43: 133–52.

Kahneman, Daniel, and Alan B. Krueger. 2006. Developments in the Measurement of Subjective Well-Being. *Journal of Economic Perspectives* 20:3–24.

Kalmijn, Wim, and Ruut Veenhoven. 2005. Measuring Inequality of Happiness in Nations. In Search of Proper Statistics. *Journal of Happiness Studies* 6: 421–55.

Krueger, Dirk, and Fanrizio Perri. 2006. Does Income Inequality Lead to Consumption Inequality? Evidence and Theory. *Review of Economic Studies* 73: 163–93.

Lemieux, Thomas. 2002. Decomposing Changes in Wage Distributions: A Unified Approach. *Canadian Journal of Economics* 35:646–88.

———. 2006. Increased Residual Wage Inequality: Composition Effects, Noisy Data, or Rising Demand for Skill. *American Economic Review* 96:461–98.

Mankiw, N. Gregory, Ricardo Reis, and Justin Wolfers. 2003. Disagreement about Inflation Expectations. *NBER Macroeconomics Annual,* pp. 209–48.

Oswald, Andrew J. 2008. On the Curvature of the Reporting Function from Objective Reality to Subjective Feelings. *Economics Letters* 100:369–72.

Smith, Tom W. 1990. Timely Artifacts: A Review of Measurement Variation in the 1972–1989 GSS. GSS Methodological Report. University of Chicago, National Opinion Research Center.

Stevenson, Betsey, and Justin Wolfers. 2007a. Marriage and Divorce: Changes and Their Driving Forces. *Journal of Economic Perspectives* 21:27–52.

———. 2007b. *The Paradox of Declining Female Happiness.* Unpublished manuscript. University of Pennsylvania, Wharton School, Philadelphia.

———. 2008a. Economic Growth and Happiness: Reassessing the Easterlin Paradox. *Brookings Papers on Economic Activity*, spring, pp. 1–87.

———. 2008b. Trends in Marital Stability. Unpublished manuscript. University of Pennsylvania, Wharton School, Philadelphia.

Who Is the Happy Warrior? Philosophy Poses Questions to Psychology

Martha C. Nussbaum

ABSTRACT

Psychology has recently focused attention on subjective states of pleasure, satisfaction, and what is called "happiness." The suggestion has been made in some quarters that a study of these subjective states has important implications for public policy. Sometimes, as in the case of Martin Seligman's "positive psychology" movement, attempts are made to link the empirical findings and the related normative judgments directly to the descriptive and normative insights of ancient Greek ethics and modern virtue ethics. At other times, as with Daniel Kahneman's work, the connection to Aristotle and other ancient Greek thinkers is only indirect, and the connection to British Utilitarianism is paramount; nonetheless, judgments are made that could be illuminated by an examination of the rich philosophical tradition that runs from Aristotle through to John Stuart Mill's criticisms of Bentham.

> Who is the happy Warrior? Who is he
> That every man in arms should wish to be?
> [Wordsworth, "Character of the Happy Warrior," 1807]

> Man does not strive after happiness; only the Englishman does
> that. [Nietzsche, "Maxims and Arrows," 1889]

Psychology has recently focused attention on subjective states of pleasure, satisfaction, and what is called "happiness." The suggestion has been made in some quarters that a study of these subjective states has important implications for public policy. Sometimes, as in the case of

MARTHA NUSSBAUM is the Ernst Freund Distinguished Service Professor of Law and Ethics, Law School, Philosophy Department, and Divinity School, the University of Chicago. I am grateful to Eric Posner for guidance, comments, and suggestions, to all the participants in the happiness conference for their helpful input, and to an anonymous referee for the journal.

[*Journal of Legal Studies*, vol. XXXVII (June 2008)]

Martin Seligman's "positive psychology" movement, attempts are made to link the empirical findings and the related normative judgments directly to the descriptive and normative insights of ancient Greek ethics and modern virtue ethics. At other times, as with Daniel Kahneman's work, the connection to Aristotle and other ancient Greek thinkers is only indirect, and the connection to British Utilitarianism is paramount; nonetheless, judgments are made that could be illuminated by an examination of the rich philosophical tradition that runs from Aristotle through to John Stuart Mill's criticisms of Bentham.

The aim of my paper is to confront this increasingly influential movement within psychology with a range of questions from the side of philosophy. Often these questions have a very long history in the discipline, going back at least to Aristotle; the more thoughtful Utilitarians, above all Mill, also studied them in depth. Some of these questions are conceptual; others are normative. After going through quite a number of them, I will attempt to correct some misunderstandings, within this psychological literature, of my own "objective-list" conception and the role I think it ought to play in public policy. And I will say what I think some appropriate roles for subjective-state analysis in public policy might be.

1. CONCEPTUAL ISSUES

1.1. What Is Pleasure?

Psychologists often talk about pleasure, and also about subjects' hedonic state. Too rarely, however, do they ask some very obvious questions about it that greatly affect any research program involving the concept. Two central questions are, is pleasure a single thing, varying only in intensity or duration, or is it plural, containing qualitative differences? And is it a sensation, or is it something more like a way of attending to the world, or even a way of being active?

Jeremy Bentham famously held that pleasure was a single sensation, varying only along the quantitative dimensions of intensity and duration (see my discussion in Nussbaum 2004b). Modern psychology follows Bentham. Indeed, Kahnemann explicitly traces his own conception of "hedonic flow" to Bentham (see, for example, Kahneman and Krueger 2006, p. 4). And yet, is Bentham correct? Does his account correctly capture the complexity of our experience of pleasures of many sorts? We speak of pleasure as a type of experience, but we also refer to activities as "my pleasures," saying things like, "My greatest pleasures are listening to Mahler and eating steak." We also use verbal locutions, such as "enjoying" and "taking delight in." (The ancient Greeks used such verbal locutions much more frequently than they used the noun.) Such ways of talking raise two questions: Is pleasure a sensation at all, if such very different experiences count as pleasures? And is it single? Could there be any one thing that both eating a steak and listening to Mahler's Tenth, that harrowing confrontation with grief and emptiness, have in common?

These questions were subtly discussed by Plato, Aristotle, and a whole line of subsequent philosophers.[1] Bentham simply ignores them. As Mill writes in his great essay "On Bentham," "Bentham failed in deriving light from other minds." For him, pleasure simply must be a single homogeneous sensation, containing no qualitative differences. The only variations in pleasure are quantitative. Pleasures can vary in intensity, duration, certainty or uncertainty, propinquicy or remoteness, and, finally, in causal properties (tendency to produce more pleasure, and so on). The apparent fact that pleasures differ in quality, that the pleasure of steak eating is quite different from the pleasure of listening to Mahler's Tenth, bothered Bentham not at all; he does not discuss such examples.

Perhaps the reason for this problem is that Bentham's deepest concern is with pain and suffering, and it is somewhat more plausible to think of pain as a unitary sensation varying only in intensity and duration. Even here, however, qualitative differences seem crucial: the pain of a headache is very different from the pain of losing a loved one to death. As Mill says, Bentham's view expresses "the empiricism of one who has had little experience"—either external, he adds, or internal, through the imagination.

Nor was Bentham worried about interpersonal comparisons, a problem on which economists in the Utilitarian tradition have spent great labor, and one that any program to use subjective satisfaction for public policy must face. For Bentham there was no such problem. When we move from one person to many people, we just add a new dimension of quantity. Right action is ultimately defined as that which produces the greatest pleasure for the greatest number. Moreover, Bentham sees no problem in extending the comparison class to the entire world of

---

1. For one good philosophical overview, see Gosling and Taylor (1982); see also the excellent treatment in Taylor (1976). An admirable general philosophical discussion is Gosling (1969).

sentient animals. One of the most attractive aspects of his thought is its great compassion for the suffering of animals, which he took to be unproblematically comparable to human suffering.[2] This attractive aspect, however, is marred by his failure even to consider whether animal pains and pleasures are qualitatively different, in at least some respects, from human pains and pleasures.

What is appealing about Bentham's program is its focus on urgent needs of sentient beings for relief from suffering and its determination to take all suffering of all sentient beings into account. But Bentham cannot be said to have developed anything like a convincing account of pleasure and pain, far less of happiness. Because of his attachment to a strident simplicity, the view remains a sketch crying out for adequate philosophical development.

Modern philosophers starting off from the Greco-Roman tradition have noticed that already in that tradition there is a widespread sense that Bentham's sort of answer will not do. A proto-Benthamite answer is familiar, in views of hedonists such as Eudoxus[3] and the title character in Plato's *Philebus* who represented Eudoxus's position. But there is an equally widespread sense among the Greek thinkers that this view will not do. The young interlocutor Protarchus, in the *Philebus*, is quickly brought by Socrates to reject it: he sees that the sources of pleasure color the pleasure itself, and that the pleasure of philosophizing is just not the same qualitatively as the pleasure of eating and sex. (The name "Philebus" means "lover of young men," and the character is represented as using his unitary view of pleasure to seduce attractive youths.)[4]

Aristotle takes up where the *Philebus* left off. Throughout his work he insists on the tremendous importance of qualitative distinctions among the diverse constituent parts of human life; he later suggests that these distinctions affect the proper analysis of the concept of pleasure. Notoriously, however, he offers two very different conceptions of pleasure, one in book VII and one in book X of the *Nicomachean Ethics*. The first identifies pleasure with unimpeded activity (not so odd if we remember that we speak of "my pleasures" and "enjoyments"). The

2. He denied that animals suffered at the very thought of death, and thus he argued that the painless killing of an animal is sometimes permitted.

3. No writings of Eudoxus survive; we know his views through Aristotle's characterization of them in *Nicomachean Ethics* 1172b9 ff. and by reports of later doxographers; he is usually taken to be the inspiration for the title character in Plato's *Philebus*.

4. In the Greek world, this would not mark him as depraved, only as greedy: he is the Greek equivalent of a womanizer.

second, and probably better, account holds that pleasure is something that comes along with, supervenes on, activity, "like the bloom on the cheek of youth." In other words, it is so closely linked to the relevant activities that it cannot be pursued on its own, any more than bloom can be adequately cultivated by cosmetics. To get that bloom you have to pursue health. Similarly, one gets the pleasure associated with an activity by doing that activity in a certain way, apparently a way that is not impeded or is complete. It would seem that what Aristotle has in mind is that pleasure is a kind of awareness of one's own activity, varying in quality with the activity to which it is so closely linked. In any case, pleasure is not a single thing, varying only in intensity and duration (the Eudoxan position). It contains qualitative differences, related to the differences of the activities to which it attaches.

J. S. Mill follows Aristotle. In a crucial discussion in *Utilitarianism*, he insists that "[n]either pains nor pleasures are homogenous." There are differences "*in kind*, apart from the question of intensity," that are evident to any competent judge. We cannot avoid recognizing qualitative differences, particularly between "higher" and "lower" pleasures. How, then, to judge between them? Like Plato in *Republic* book IX, Mill refers the choice to a competent judge who has experienced both alternatives.

This famous passage shows Mill thinking of pleasures as very like activities (with Aristotle in Book VII) or, with Aristotle in Book X, as experiences so closely linked to activities that they cannot be pursued apart from them. In a later text, he counts music, virtue, and health as major pleasures. Elsewhere he shows that he has not left sensation utterly out of account: he refers to "which of two modes of existence is the most grateful to the feelings." Clearly, however, the unity of the Benthamite calculus has been thrown out, to be replaced by a variegated conception, involving both sensation and activity, and prominently including qualitative distinctions. It is for this reason that philosophers today typically find Mill more subtle and conceptually satisfactory than Bentham.

Modern philosophical discussion of pleasure follows Aristotle and Mill. In one of the best recent accounts, J. C. B. Gosling's (1969) book *Pleasure and Desire*, Gosling investigates three different views of what pleasure is: the sensation view (Bentham/Eudoxus), the activity view (Aristotle's first account), and what he calls the "adverbial" view (pleasure is a particular way of being active, a view closely related to Aristotle's second account). Uneasily, with much uncertainty, he opts, with Aristotle, for the adverbial view.

Now it is obvious that such debates influence the ways in which one would study pleasure empirically. If Aristotle, Mill, and Gosling are correct, it would not make sense to ask people to rank all their pleasures along a single quantitative dimension: this is just bullying people into disregarding features of their own experience that reflection would quickly reveal. People are easily bullied, particularly by prominent psychologists, and so they do answer such questions, rather than respond, "This question is ill-formed." If Mill and Aristotle are right, however, they would quickly agree on reflection that qualitative differences matter.

Moreover, any experiment that simply assumes pleasure to be a hedonic state, something like a sensation, would also be inadequate, say Mill and Aristotle, to the complexity of human experience, since people agree that activity matters: they would not think that the pleasure derived from being plugged into Robert Nozick's "experience machine" was equivalent to a pleasure associated with actually doing the activity oneself (Nozick 1974, pp. 42–45).

1.2. What Is Satisfaction with One's Life as a Whole?

Some of the most influential experiments ask not about pleasure or hedonic flow, but about satisfaction with one's life as a whole. Typical is the question posed by Kahneman, "Taking all things together, how satisfied are you with *your life as a whole* these days? Are you very satisfied, satisfied, not very satisfied, not at all satisfied?" (Kahnemann and Krueger 2006, p. 7 n. 2, emphasis in the original). Notice here the bullying we encountered before: people are simply told that they are to aggregate experiences of many different kinds into a single whole, and the authority of the questioner is put behind that aggregation. There is no opportunity for them to answer something plausible, such as, "Well, my health is good, and my work is going well, but I am very upset about the Iraq war, and one of my friends is very ill." Not only is that opportunity not provided, but, in addition, the prestige of science—indeed of the Nobel Prize itself—is put behind the instruction to reckon all life elements up as a single whole. The fact that people answer such questions hardly shows that this is the way that they experience their lives.

If we bracket that difficulty, however, we arrive at another one. There is a deep ambiguity about the question being asked. The psychologists who pose this question take the question to be a request for a report of a subjective state of satisfaction, which is at least closely akin to the feeling of pleasure. (Kahneman treats this question and the hedonic flow question, on the whole, as different ways of getting at the same thing.)

One might indeed hear the question that way. But one might also hear it in a very different way, as a request for a reflective judgment about one's life, which judgment might or might not be accompanied by feelings of satisfaction, contentment, or pleasure.

Consider J. S. Mill's last words: "You know that I have done my work" (Packe 1954, p. 507). Now I would say that this is in one way an answer to the overall satisfaction question: Mill is reporting, we might say, satisfaction with his life as a whole. He has done what he aimed to do. And yet it seems highly unlikely that Mill, on his deathbed, suffering from physical pain and from the fear of death that he acknowledges not being able to get rid of, is experiencing feelings of satisfaction or pleasure. (Mill once reports that the one great attraction of a belief in a life after death [which he finds himself ultimately unable to accept] is the hope it yields of being reunited "with those dear to him who have ended their earthly life before him"—a loss, he continues, that "is neither to be denied nor extenuated" [Mill 1998, p. 120]. So he would no doubt be struggling, on his deathbed, with the eternal loss of Harriet in addition to his own demise.) While judging that his life is on balance successful, he is almost certainly not experiencing feelings of satisfaction or pleasure.

Since the psychologists who work with this question do not notice this ambiguity, they do nothing to sort things out, so we do not really know which question their subjects are answering. Probably some are answering one question, some the other. What would be needed to progress would be conceptual work to separate the feeling-conception from the judgment-conception, and then a set of questions designed to tease apart those distinct notions.

In my own case, the ambiguity produces something like a contradiction. That is, my own conception of a good life attaches a great deal of value to striving, longing, and working for a difficult goal. So, if I ever notice myself feeling feelings of satisfaction, I blame myself and think that, insofar as I have those feelings, I am like Mill's "pig satisfied" or Aristotle's "dumb grazing animals," and thus, reflectively, I report dissatisfaction with my life as a whole. Nor do I think that I am an unusual case. As I have indicated, Mill's contrast between Socrates and the pig reveals similar values, and anyone whose culture is deeply influenced by romanticism, with its exaltation of longing and yearning (or, indeed, by the more romantic varieties of Christianity, such as Augustine's), would have the same difficulty: insofar as one is feeling satisfied, thus far one's life is not a success. That is what Nietzsche is getting at in my epigraph: having feelings of satisfaction as a goal, he thinks, is a rather base thing, something that he associates with the impoverishment of English culture, as contrasted with German romanticism. Zarathustra, asked whether he is happy, responds, "Do I strive after happiness? I strive after my works."[5] Schiller, Beethoven, and Mahler might have said that they were satisfied with their life as a whole—in the reflective-judgment sense. They probably, however, did not report many feelings of satisfaction, and they would have worried about themselves if they had had such feelings. (Indeed, Mahler's Resurrection Symphony revolves precisely around the contrast between the herdlike feeling of satisfaction and the more exalted judgment that one's whole life is rich and meaningful—because it is governed by an active kind of love. The former is represented by the swoopy, aimless clarinet phrases of the third movement, the latter by the passionate heartbeat that the final movement associates with the wings of the soul.)[6]

1.3. What Is Happiness?

Bentham simply identifies happiness with pleasure. Kahneman on the whole agrees with Bentham. Some psychologists are more subtle. Seligman's conception of authentic happiness, for example, involves both positive emotion and valuable activity (Seligman 2002). But (to return to my question about Socrates and the pig) how are these two constituents related? Are they both necessary for happiness and jointly sufficient? Is one more important than the other? And must the positive emotion be suitably linked to the good activity, a kind of taking delight in one's good activity?

Here is what Aristotle thought: that activity is far and away the main thing, and that pleasure will normally crop up in connection with doing good activities without struggle, the way a virtuous person does them. Pleasure accompanies activity, and completes it, like, he says, the bloom on the cheek of a healthy young person. That example implies, too, that it would be totally mistaken to pry the pleasure apart from the activity and seek it on its own: for it would then not be the bloom on the cheek of a healthy person, it would be the rouge on the cheek of a person who has not bothered to cultivate health. And Aristotle also thought that sometimes the pleasure would not arrive: for example, the courageous person who is about to lose his life in battle is happy, but has no pleasant emotion, because he is losing everything. Wordsworth's very Aristotelian

5. See the excellent treatment of this passage in Birault (1985).
6. See my analysis of the symphony in Nussbaum (2001b).

poem, "Character of the Happy Warrior," tells a similar tale, describing the "happy warrior" as "happy" because he is active in accordance with all the virtues, and yet he has little if any pleasure, and a good deal of pain.[7]

Wordsworth is a useful interlocutor at this point, because we can see that the Aristotelian idea was dominant until Bentham's influence dislodged it, changing the very way that many people, at least, hear the English word "happiness." So powerful was the obscuring power of Bentham's oversimplification that a question that Wordsworth takes to be altogether askable, and which, indeed, he spends 85 lines answering—the question what happiness really is—soon looks to philosophers under Bentham's influence like a question whose answer is so obvious that it cannot be asked in earnest. Thus early twentieth-century philosopher Henry Prichard, albeit a foe of Utilitarianism, was so influenced in his thinking about happiness by Bentham's conception that he simply assumed that any philosopher who talks about happiness must be identifying it with pleasure or satisfaction. When Aristotle asks what happiness is, Prichard argued, he cannot really be asking the question he appears to be asking, since the answer to that question is obvious: happiness is contentment or satisfaction. Instead of asking what happiness consists in, then, he must really be asking about the instrumental means to the production of happiness.[8] Nietzsche, similarly, understands happiness to be (uncontroversially) a state of pleasure and contentment, and expresses his scorn for Englishmen who pursue that goal, rather than richer goals involving suffering for a noble end, continued striving, activities that put contentment at risk, and so forth. Apparently unaware of the richer English tradition about happiness represented in Wordsworth's poem, he simply took English "happiness" to be what Bentham said it was. So, much later, did Finnish sociologist Erik Allardt, when he wrote an attack on the idea that happiness was the end of social planning, entitling his book *Having, Loving, Being*—active things that he took to be more important than satisfaction, which Finns, heir of Nordic romanticism, typically think quite unimportant (Allardt 1975).[9] Like Nietzsche, he understood the "happiness" of the social scientists

7. The complete text of the poem can be found in Appendix A.

8. Prichard (1935), famously discussed and criticized in Austin (1979). My account of Prichard follows Austin's, including his (fair) account of Prichard's implicit premises.

9. A brief summary of some of the argument in English can be found in Allardt (1993). (The original language of the book is Swedish because Allardt is a Swedish-speaking Finn.)

to be a state of pleasure or satisfaction. (He is correct about the social scientists, if not about "happiness.")

Aristotle's richer conception is still present in our lives, and we can see that ideas like Seligman's idea of authentic happiness capture something of its spirit.[10] According to this Aristotelian tradition, what we all can agree about is that happiness (*eudaimonia*) is something like flourishing human living, a kind of living that is active, inclusive of all that has intrinsic value, and complete, meaning lacking in nothing that would make it richer or better. Everything else about happiness is disputed, says Aristotle, but he then goes on to argue for a conception of happiness that identifies it with a specific plurality of valuable activities, including activity in accordance with excellences[11] (valuable traits) of many sorts, including ethical, intellectual, and political excellences, and activities involved in love and friendship. Pleasure, as I have said, is not identical with happiness, but it usually (not always) accompanies the unimpeded performance of the activities that constitute happiness.

Something like this is the idea that Wordsworth is relying on, when he asks, in each of the many areas of life, what the character and demeanor of the "happy Warrior" would be, and answers that question. As J. L. Austin (1979, p. 20) memorably wrote in a devastating critique of Prichard on Aristotle, "I do not think Wordsworth meant . . .: 'This is the warrior who feels pleased.' Indeed, he is 'Doomed to go in company with Pain/And fear and bloodshed, miserable train.'"

As Austin saw, the important thing about the happy warrior is that he has traits that make him capable of performing all of life's many activities in an exemplary way, and he acts in accordance with those traits. He is moderate, kind, courageous, loving, a good friend, concerned for the community, honest,[12] not excessively attached to honor or worldly ambition, a lover of reason, an equal lover of home and family. His life is happy because it is full and rich, even though it sometimes may involve pain and loss.

So would Seligman agree with Aristotle and Wordsworth that the

---

10. For an excellent recent analysis, arguing that the Aristotelian view captures best our intuitive sense of what happiness is, see Nozick (1989, chap. 10).

11. I thus render Greek *aretê*, usually translated "virtue." *Aretê* need not be ethical; indeed it need not even be a trait of a person. It is a trait of anything, whatever that thing is, that makes it good at doing what that sort of thing characteristically does. Thus Plato can speak of the *aretê* of a pruning knife.

12. Here we see the one major departure from Aristotle that apparently seemed to Wordsworth required by British morality. Aristotle does not make much of honesty. In other respects, Wordsworth is remarkably close to Aristotle, whether he knew it or not.

happy warrior is indeed happy? Or does he require pleasant emotion in addition to the good activity? If even Seligman's conception is under-specified, however, Kahneman does not get to the point of noticing a problem at all and simply goes along with Bentham.

(I note that the happy warrior is still happy because he is still able to act well; Aristotle believed, however, that more extreme calamities could "dislodge" one from happiness, by removing one's sphere of ac-tivity. His example is Priam at the end of the Trojan War, who lost his children, his political freedom and power, and his personal freedom.)[13]

When we notice that happiness is complex, we are prepared to face yet a further question in connection with its proper analysis: does hap-piness require self-examination? All the ancient philosophers take issue with some of the popular accounts of *eudaimonia* in their cultural set-ting, by arguing that no life is truly happy unless it is accompanied by reflection. As Socrates says in the *Apology*, "The unexamined life is not worth living for a human being." One sees clearly in Plato's dialogues how controversial this emphasis is. When people are asked to define a virtue (seen as a putative part of happiness), they never include this element of knowledge or reflection—until Socrates patiently shows them that any definition that leaves it out is inadequate. On reflection, how-ever, they always agree with Socrates, and I would say that my contem-porary students do as well when they think about it for a while. Aristotle gives a little more room than Plato does to the nonintellectual elements in virtue, including emotions as at least one part of what each virtue involves. But he, too, sticks to the Socratic commitment, saying that each and every virtue of character requires the intellectual virtue of practical wisdom. Much later, as we saw, J. S. Mill insists that it is better to be Socrates dissatisfied than a pig satisfied.

Wordsworth, as you can see, agrees with the Socratic tradition: the happy warrior's "law is reason." He "depends/Upon that law as on the best of friends," and he strives to become ever "More skilful in self-knowledge."

The commitment to reflection is also a commitment to the ceaseless critical scrutiny of cultural beliefs and cultural authorities. Socrates in-terrogates everyone he meets, and nobody does very well, especially not received cultural authorities. Socrates himself does best only in the sense that he is aware of the incompleteness and fallibility of his knowledge of happiness. Although later Greek philosophers are more willing than

---

13. See my treatment of this passage in Nussbaum (2001a, chap. 10).

Socrates to pronounce on what happiness is, they are no more trustful of their culture, and all are relentless critics of their cultures' dominant understandings of happiness. Aristotle excoriates the undue attention given to the accumulation of wealth, to pleasure, and to manly honor. The Stoics have similar criticisms. And yet, they hold, not implausibly, that if people give it enough thought, they will agree with their proposal, because it honors something that people will understand to be deep in themselves, the source of their human dignity.

The omission of this reflective element in happiness is one of the most disturbing aspects of the conceptual breeziness of contemporary subjective-state psychology, insofar as it is laying the groundwork for normative recommendations. Our democracy has many of the vices Socrates identified in his: haste, macho posturing, an excessive deference to wealth and honor. We badly need the element of reflection, and if prestigious psychologists simply tell us again and again that reflection is not a necessary element of the happy life, we may begin to believe it.

1.4. What Emotions Are Positive?

The part of subjective-state measurement that focuses on moment-to-moment hedonic flow assumes that some emotions are positive and others are negative. Seligman makes a similar assumption and tells us somewhat more about what he is assuming, in keeping with his rather greater interest in philosophical matters. For Seligman, positive emotions, to put it somewhat crudely, are those that feel good. So love would be positive, anger and grief negative, and so forth.

The ancient thinkers adopt a very different account. Again, this issue deeply affects any normative recommendations that may ultimately be based on the conceptual assumptions.

Since the Greeks and Romans (along with the best work on emotions in contemporary cognitive psychology) believe that emotions embody appraisals or evaluations of things in the world, they think it is very important for those appraisals to be correct. Fear, for example, involves (in Aristotle's view) the thought that there are serious damages impending and that one is not entirely in control of warding them off. Anger (again in Aristotle's view) involves the thought that a serious and inappropriate damage has been willfully inflicted on me or someone or something one cares about, and also the thought that it would be good for that damage to be made good somehow.

So we can see that there are a number of things that can go wrong here. One might get the facts wrong, thinking that a danger was present when it was not, or that a wrong had been done when it had not. One might blame the wrong person for the wrong or might wrongly believe that the damage was blameworthy when it was in fact accidental. Finally, one can get the seriousness of the good or bad event wrong: one may get angry over trivia—Aristotle's example is when someone forgets your name, so you see the world has changed little. Or, again Aristotle's example, one might fear a mouse running across the floor.

Because emotions embody appraisals, one can get them to be appropriate only by getting appropriate appraisals. Thus, in the *Rhetoric,* Aristotle gives the aspiring orator recipes for provoking anger in an audience—by convincing them that their enemies have wronged them in some illicit way, for example—and also recipes for taking anger away and calming people down—by convincing them that they had not in fact been wronged in the way they thought, or that the thing was not of much importance.

For all the ancient thinkers, a necessary and sufficient condition of an emotion's being truly positive—in the sense of making a positive contribution toward a flourishing life—is that it be based on true beliefs, both about value and about what events have occurred. This is as true of good-feeling as of bad-feeling emotion. Many instances of good-feeling emotion are actually quite negative, inasmuch as they are based on false beliefs about value. Pleasure is only as good as the thing one takes pleasure in: if one takes pleasure in harming others, that good-feeling emotion is very negative; even if one takes pleasure in shirking one's duty and lazing around, that is also quite negative. If one feels hope, that emotion is good only if it is based on accurate evaluations of the worth of what one hopes for and true beliefs about what is likely.

By the same token, many negative-feeling emotions are appropriate, and even very valuable. Aristotle, like Wordsworth, stresses that the courageous person is not free from fear: indeed, he will appropriately feel more fear and pain at the prospect of losing his life in battle than the mediocre person, because his life, which is at risk, is a valuable life and he knows it. Anger is a sign of what we care intensely about and a spur to justice. Aristotle does not urge people to be angry all the time; indeed, he thinks that the appropriate virtue in this area should be called "mildness of temper," in order to indicate that the good person does not get angry too often. But if someone did not get angry at damages to loved ones or kin, he would be "slavish," in Aristotle's view. Again, compassion is painful, but it is extremely valuable, when based on true beliefs and accurate evaluations of the seriousness of the other person's predicament, because it connects us to the suffering of others and gives us a motive to help them. Grief when a loved one dies is extremely appropriate (although Plato, admiring self-sufficiency, tried to deny this).

The ancient philosophers also stress that happy and sad emotions are conceptually interconnected: to the extent that you value uncertain things that are in the control of chance, you cannot help having both fear and hope about them, since their prospects are in fact uncertain. Where you have love, you will also have anxiety—and, very likely, anger. Where you have gratitude (when someone does something importantly nice for you), there is also conceptual space for anger (if that same person should decide to treat you badly). The Stoics saw clearly that the only way to get rid of negative emotions was not to value the uncertain things of human life at all and to care only for one's own inner states. But Aristotle, and most modern readers of the texts, reject that solution.

Aristotle is correct here. That is, emotions are positive or negative, in the sense relevant to normative thinking, according to the correctness of the appraisals or evaluations they contain. And since human life contains, in fact, many bad accidents and much bad behavior, there is no way a person who values friends, loved ones, work, and political action can avoid having many painful-feeling emotions, such as grief, fear, and anxiety. These emotions are valuable in themselves, as expressions of correct evaluation, and also spurs to good action. Can one imagine a struggle for justice that was not fueled by justified anger? Can one imagine a decent society that is not held together by compassion for suffering? Can one imagine love that does not assume the risk of grief? I believe that C. Daniel Batson's excellent research on compassion (which, I note en passant, has a rare philosophical sophistication and precision) has shown that the painful emotion leads to helping; so it is extremely important not to set out to avoid painful emotional experiences (Batson 1991).

Seligman, in particular, thinks that it is good to promote good-feeling emotions and to minimize bad-feeling emotions, often by thinking hopeful thoughts. But sometimes having a hopeful "take" on the bad thing that has happened seems to trivialize it. The Stoics urged people to respond to the death of a loved one with constructive sentiments, such as "Everyone is mortal, and you will get over this pretty soon." But are they correct? Is this really the way to take the measure of love?[14] It is very interesting to see how Cicero, who in his voluminous correspon-

---

14. See my longer reflections on this question in Nussbaum (1994, chaps. 10 and 12).

dence consoled his friends with positive sentiments like Seligman's, rejects them utterly when his beloved daughter Tullia dies. Among the most moving letters in history are his outpourings of desperate grief to his friend Atticus, to whom he says that he feels that he is in a dark forest, and whose injunctions to put an end to his mourning he angrily rejects, saying that he cannot do it, and moreover, he thinks that he should not, even if he could.[15]

Today, Americans are often are embarrassed by deep grief and tend to give Stoic advice too freely. A colleague in my university lost his son: a young man, troubled, who died either of a drug overdose or by suicide. I wrote him, saying that I thought this was the worst thing that could happen to someone and he had my sympathy. This man, whom I do not know very well, wrote back immediately, thanking me and saying, "I really dislike this American stuff about healing." (He is an American.) I inferred from that response that many other messages he had received had talked about healing, and he had gotten fed up with them. I am with him: it seems a deeply inappropriate way to think of the tragic death of a child.

So I would like to see psychology think more about positive pain, that is, the grief that expresses love, the fear that expresses a true sense of a threat directed at something or someone one loves, the compassion that shares the pain of a suffering person, the anger that says, "This is deeply wrong and I will try to right it."

2. NORMATIVE QUESTIONS

I have suggested, along with Aristotle and Mill, that the Benthamite conception does not adequately capture our concepts of pleasure and happiness, nor does the focus on overall life satisfaction have the conceptual clarity that is imputed to it. However, Benthamism captures something, whether or not that something is coincident with our reflective concepts of pleasure and happiness, so let us now ask whether that something is a good guide to public policy. Should we seek to promote pleasant feelings and to minimize painful feelings? I have already suggested some reasons for doubt in the preceding section, but let us go through the reasons more systematically.

15. See the excellent edition and translation of Cicero's letters by David Shackleton Bailey (1999); the relevant letters are in volume III of *Letters to Atticus*.

2.1. Bad Pleasures, Good Pains

Let us stipulate for the sake of argument that Bentham is correct: pleasure is a single uniform sensation, even if it is produced by activities and objects of many different kinds. Nonetheless, it still seems problematic to conclude, as Bentham quickly does, that pleasure is the single thing that we should be aiming to produce. First of all, even if pleasure were single and homogeneous, a good life for a human being clearly is not single: as Mill and Aristotle argue, it is constituted by activities of many different sorts, which cannot be rendered commensurable on any quantitative scale. Already, then, there is something very important about the good human life that Benthamism does not capture.

But there is an even greater problem: pleasure is simply not normatively reliable, for reasons that we have already anticipated in talking about positive and negative emotions. Some pleasures are bad, namely, those that are closely associated with bad activities. Rich people have pleasure in being ever richer and lording it over others, but this hardly shows that redistributive taxation is incorrect. Racists have pleasure in their racism, sexists in their sexism. In general, bad people have pleasure in their bad behavior. The more philosophical among welfarist economists have been quick to notice this problem. John Harsanyi—after excluding pleasures based upon incorrect and/or incomplete information from the social welfare function—feels the need to exclude, as well, pleasures that he calls "sadistic or malicious," a notion that he unpacks further by emphasizing that a Kantian notion of human equality is tempering his commitment to Utilitarianism. Bad pleasures, for him, will be those that insist on subordinating others and in other ways failing to respect their human dignity and equality (Harsanyi 1982). Analyzing Harsanyi's argument, I have argued that at this point he uses independent moral notions—the notions of dignity and equality—to constrain his welfarism; thus his view cannot be seen as a pure welfarist view (Nussbaum 2001c, chap. 2). It is plausible, as a guide to public policy, precisely because it imports these independent moral notions and refuses to follow Bentham all the way.

We see here another place where Mill wisely departs from Bentham. In his great work *The Subjection of Women* (Mill 1869), he makes it perfectly clear that men take great pleasure in subordinating women, because this helps them to feel superior, to have a pliant servant around the house, and so forth. But then, when reckoning up the gains to society that sex equality would bring with it, Mill does not even pause to con-

sider or reckon up the pain that men will surely be caused by this ab-
rogation of their unearned privileges. He just assumes, anticipating Harsanyi, that these unjust pleasures do not count in the social welfare
function.

Another problem, which we have already encountered in talking
about Wordsworth and about positive and negative emotions, is that
some valuable activities are not accompanied by pleasure. Aristotle's
example is Wordsworthian (perhaps the source for Wordsworth's poem):
the courageous warrior who faces death in battle for the sake of a noble
end. It is absurd to say that this person is pleased at the prospect of
death, says Aristotle. Indeed, the better his life is, the more he thinks
he has to lose, and the more pain he is likely to feel at the prospect of
death. Nonetheless, he is acting in accordance with excellence and is
aware of that, and so he is still happy, in Aristotle's sense. This just goes
to show, says Aristotle, that pleasure does not always go along with the
activities that comprise happiness, only most of the time.

Wordsworth goes yet further: he emphasizes that the experience of
risk and suffering deepens the personality, increasing compassion for
others and making a person "more skilful in self-knowledge." In the
Rhetoric, discussing compassion, Aristotle agrees: he points out that
people who have never faced their own weaknesses, and who think,
optimistically, that they are not very likely to suffer, tend to have little
compassion for the sufferings of others; he calls this a *hubristikê dia-
thesis,* or "overweening disposition" (Aristotle, *Rhetoric,* II.5). Rousseau
develops this insight in *Emile,* talking about the nobles of France, who
fail in sympathy for the poor because they think they are above the
common sufferings of human life (Rousseau 1762). Rousseau's proposed
remedy for this problem is that education should focus on the inculcation
of negative emotion in the form of *pitié,* compassionate pain at the
sufferings of others. He believes that it will not be easy for young Emile
to learn that emotion, because, like all children, he wants to be happy.
But sadness must be dinned into him by repeated teaching about the
common predicaments of human life, the bodily frailty we share with
others, the countless other miseries to which human life is subject. This
lesson is reinforced and deepened by actual suffering: the deaths of animals that the child loves, for example.

Not implausibly, Rousseau connects this teaching with (ultimate) happiness, in the sense of flourishing life: for he thinks that there can be no
happiness in society where there is hierarchy and injustice, and there
can be no justice without a common sentiment of suffering about the

human predicaments. To the extent that privileged groups live a charmed life and insulate themselves from the sufferings of the poor, everyone is missing out on happiness, since they are all living in a bad unjust world. Sponging off the misery of others may feel good, but it is not happiness, for Rousseau or any of the ancient thinkers whom he follows, since they think of happiness, with Aristotle, as living a flourishing life. The teaching of painful compassion is the beginning of social change and of the possibility of real happiness. "Thus from our weakness," he writes, "our fragile happiness is born."

Rousseau's problem would appear to be common in today's United States, where people used to a high standard of living fail to consider and sympathize with the plight of those who do not enjoy such happy lives. Candace Clark's wonderful book *Misery and Company* (Clark 1997), a sociological study of American attitudes to sympathy and compassion, shows that most Americans do not have compassion for the poor, because they believe that the poor brought their misery on themselves. Indeed, they are more sympathetic with people who get stuck in traffic jams!

Another study that should give one pause is the study of adolescent males by Dan Kindlon and Michael Thompson, in their excellent book *Raising Cain* (Kindlon and Thompson 1999). They show that the education of a young male in America is very likely to include the teaching that real men are above suffering. They should never feel, and certainly should never admit to feeling, fear, pain, and weakness. The consequence of this deformed expectation, Kindlon and Thompson argue, is that these boys come to lack an understanding of their own vulnerabilities, needs, and fears, weaknesses that all human beings share. They lack even a language in which to characterize their own inner world, and they are by the same token clumsy interpreters of the emotions and inner lives of others. This emotional illiteracy is closely connected to aggression, as fear is turned outward, with little real understanding of the meaning of aggressive words and acts for the feelings of others. We see too many such males in American public life. We should therefore place greater emphasis on the dangers of the hubristic disposition and, in consequence, on Rousseauian virtues that involve acknowledging one's weakness and vulnerability and reflecting on one's own experiences of loss and suffering.

Strategies are linked to diagnoses. Martin Seligman's diagnosis of Americans is that they are too anxious and unhappy, and so he proposes a public policy focus on happiness in part as a corrective. One might have doubts here. An alternative diagnosis of the American psyche would be that many Americans cannot stand to be unhappy, cannot stand to grieve, cannot stand to look at poverty or the real damages of war. One could argue that this is a larger problem than the problem of excessive unhappiness. Does Seligman's positive psychology risk pushing already hubristic Americans in the direction of even greater hubris?

We all have our own sense of what the deeper problems are. But here I call George Orwell to my aid. In *Nineteen Eighty-Four* he imagines the world of the future as marred by an absence of deep pain and grief, a loss of the sense of tragedy (Nussbaum 2005). "Tragedy, [Winston] perceived, belonged to the ancient time. . . . Such things, he saw, could not happen today. Today there were fear, hatred, and pain, but no dignity of emotion, or deep or complex sorrows." Now it is a long story to show how this absence of deep grief is connected to the politics of the novel. But let me venture to suggest that today's America is all too much like Winston Smith's Oceania in that respect: we do not connect to one another in Rousseau's way, through the sense of tragedy; instead, we connect through the desire for mastery and completeness, which is all too often connected to a narcissistic indifference to the sufferings of others. Pain and loss, acknowledged and thoroughly experienced, rather than pushed away or deflected into aggression, can help us grow "more compassionate, . . . more skilful in self-knowledge," as Wordsworth says.

2.2. Adaptation

One normative worry that has already received a good deal of notice in the literature about subjective states and public policy is the phenomenon of "adaptation": people's preferences adjust to what they know or can expect. Amartya Sen has shown that this happens even at the level of physical health: women who are chronically malnourished and who are taught that they have no right to demand anything following the death of a husband report their heath status as good or fair, despite the evident presence of many diseases. Jon Elster makes the equally important point that people who were not brought up to think of themselves as equal citizens with a full range of citizens' rights will not report dissatisfaction at the absence of equality—until a protest movement galvanizes awareness. Feudalism went on for centuries without such a protest movement, sexism far longer.[16] Empirical work on women shows that they often

16. I discuss Elster's feudalism example with reference to sexism in Nussbaum (2001c, chap. 2), where I also give comprehensive references to Sen's treatment of this question.

report satisfaction at having less education than males, because that is what they are brought up to think is right and proper (Bagchi 1997). So deferring to the subjective experience of pleasure or satisfaction will often bias the social inquiry in the direction of an unjust status quo.

2.3. The Choice of Lives

Seligman's positive psychology and the ancient Greek tradition (along with their heir, J. S. Mill) agree in a limited normative criticism of Benthamism: namely, they agree that a life with feeling alone and no action is impoverished. So they agree that a person who sits around doing nothing, or even just counting blades of grass, or a person plugged in to Robert Nozick's experience machine that generates pleasant experiences, is not living a life of the sort we should try to promote, however pleased that person feels. But there are many further questions once one gets clear about that. First of all, I am not even clear that Seligman has taken a position on Mill's famous claim that it is better to be Socrates dissatisfied than a pig satisfied. He clearly thinks it is better to be Socrates satisfied than a pig satisfied, but Socrates probably had few positive emotions and substantial pain, so what should we say about that comparison and the choices of lives that we might make after thinking about it?

What I am interested in, though, is a slightly different question, absolutely central to the Greeks and Romans, and to their classifications of virtues, and on which they disagree a good deal. There are quite a few types of worthwhile action, and some of them are riskier than others. Should one, then, choose a career that minimizes the risk of reversal and suffering? And should one urge others to choose such lives? If that aim makes sense, they all agree, one will probably choose a contemplative intellectual life. Contemplation is something that one can do under more or less all circumstances: if one is in prison, if one is poor, if one has no friends or family. Other sorts of lives require more specialized external conditions: a life of political action, for example, requires free birth, citizenship, friends, and at least some money. The life of a person who cares for family will be blasted if they all die or if one proves to be childless. So should one rank those lives below the contemplative life?

Now the Greeks exaggerate, here, the nonriskiness of contemplation. Aristotle, taking issue with that familiar picture, noted that it is ridiculous to suppose that someone who is being tortured can go on thinking well, and so the picture of the sage thinking high-minded thoughts while being tortured on the wheel has something unrealistic about it. But still, they have a point, which I shall make with an example.

Eleven years ago I had occasion to spend some time at St. Andrews University in Scotland. I was therefore involved in the commencement and honorary degree ceremonies, and I met the people who were being honored. The two men I shall contrast both had worthwhile lives, worthy of public honor, and they were receiving that honor. But they were very differently placed with respect to positive emotion and happiness. As they stood side by side on the stage, and as, later, I talked with them at various dinners and garden parties, I ruminated on this difference. One of the men was John le Carré, whose real name is David Cornwell. David Cornwell is a very happy man. He was relaxed and genial, gentle, funny. It was clear not only that he felt proud of his achievement but also that he felt in control of his ongoing activity. He loves writing—indeed, he lives in a very remote spot in Cornwall and rarely travels, so that he can write all the time. And nothing, and nobody, disturbs him. He has a lovely wife, also genial and funny, and he clearly enjoys living with her company and that of his books. Of course old age, illness, and death will disrupt that happiness eventually, but in 1996 he was the very image of the contemplative life and its rich human satisfactions, and in 2007, at the age of seventy-six, he seems to be living exactly the same life, productive and calm.

Side by side with him on the podium was John Hume, the Northern Irish politician who won the Nobel Peace Prize with David Trimball in 1998. In 1996, however, there was no peace. Things were going extremely badly, and it was plausible to think that everything Hume had worked for all his life was out the window. He had even been rudely dumped by his own party. John Hume was not a happy man. His face was like a tragic mask. He hardly spoke to a soul. He stood around at the garden parties as if he had no idea where he was. He stood up on the stage to be honored, but no glint of happiness appeared on his face. (And when you think about his life, consider that he might have died the next day, before things began to go better, before the Prize, before his lauded retirement from politics in 2004, at which time he was praised even by Ian Paisley, before this year's astounding reconciliation of Ian Paisley and Gerry Adams, and so forth.)

That is really what the ancient debate is about: Should one pay attention to the risk of ending up in a miserable condition, all one's projects smashed, when one makes one's choice of life? Or should one focus only on the commitments and values one believes important and follow those whatever risks they entail? The ancient thinkers did not believe that it was optional which valuable goals one pursued. So the ones who believe that politics is part of the human good thought that its riskiness was no good argument against it: one has an obligation to pursue it, come what may. It is very moving, again, to read Cicero's letters on that point, for he repeatedly says that in losing Tullia and the Roman republic he has lost the two things that give life meaning, and yet he continues to exhort his son and his friend tirelessly to the political life and to insist that even the philosopher is contemptible if he does not incur risk for the sake of his country.

Benthamism, of course, gives utterly different advice: follow the pleasant and avoid the painful—although, as Mill observes, if one takes seriously the fact that the goal is not just one's own utility, but the greatest pleasure of the greatest number, then one will be bound to notice that in the present defective condition of society, the person who pursues that goal energetically is in for a lot of pain. Mill thinks that in a good society this would not be so, but that, in our present defective one, the good person should make the risky choice. That, however, is Mill, and contemporary Benthamism has no such altruistic thoughts, so far as I can see, and no such critical diagnosis of our present social condition as defective to the extent that individual and universal well-being are badly aligned.

If we now turn to Seligman's somewhat richer normative conception, it would appear that his positive psychology gives the following advice: to the extent that a career offers secure prospects of happiness and still contains some valuable activity, that career is to be preferred to the career that has a large risk of reversal and misery. In other words, do not go into politics, especially in Northern Ireland, and perhaps not in America either! Probably all of us at this conference have given ourselves some such advice, or we would not be in tenured positions in the academy, that safest of careers. But I do not think that this advice is good as a general thing. With Cicero, I think that there are some values that need to be fought for and that each of us ought to do some fighting, and incur some risk, to fight for what is important, even if we are in the protected precincts of the academy. And if the world were such that everyone were as risk averse as most academics by nature are, it would be a horrible place, with much less justice in it, even, than it now has. So some, indeed many, good people must make the riskier choices of lives, or we all will end up with nothing worth living for.

Thus, while I enjoyed the company of David Cornwell more than that of John Hume, and while I found in David Cornwell a kindred contemplative happy spirit, I admired John Hume more and criticized myself for not being more like him. Similarly, when I am in India working with development activists, I often feel awed and humbled by them, because they are out there in the trenches, risking bodily health, contentment, and life itself, while I am sitting in a beautiful building at a new computer, writing. One of India's most admired activists for women's issues, the creative NGO founder Viji Srinivasan, died in her late fifties of respiratory collapse, on a train bound from Delhi to Chennai, because the harsh conditions in which she worked, running a women's organization in rural Bihar, had ruined her health. I have not made such choices: indeed, whenever I travel I ask for time to go to the gym, and I choose a good hotel. My excuse to myself is that I would be very bad at what they do and that what I do is not altogether irrelevant to the pursuit of justice. But it is an uneasy excuse, and I honor them for their choices.

Public policy should make room for, and honor, commitments that are in their very nature fraught with risk, pain, and difficulty, especially commitments to fighting for social justice, as not optional but mandatory parts, in some form, of the good life of any human being. A society that thinks this way will make different policy choices: it will favor, for example, as I do, a program of compulsory national service for all young people, in which they will learn to care for elderly people and do other valuable and unpleasant tasks. Young people in America are encouraged, instead, to follow pleasure and to avoid the risk of unhappiness. To the extent that such recommendations are successful, our country is the poorer.

2.4. Aggregation

Benthamism already aggregates in a questionable way, by funneling all the states associated with diverse activities into a single quantitative calculus. There is, however, another type of aggregation to consider: its aggregation across persons. For the Benthamite, we are to strive to produce the greatest net balance of pleasure over pain for the greatest number. This "sum-ranking," as Amartya Sen and Bernard Williams (1982) aptly call it, seems to treat all people equally: as Bentham says, "each to count for one, and none as more than one." Looked at more closely, however, this approach prevents us from providing a minimum floor of dignity and decent life beneath which no person is to be pushed. The exceeding pleasure of a large number can justify giving a small number a very miserable life. This is yet one more reason to doubt the facile equation of pleasure with happiness. But this criticism of Utilitarianism is so well known and so often discussed that I shall pursue it no further here.

3. PURSUING AN OBJECTIVE LIST: SOME MISUNDERSTANDINGS

In one of the clearest, most rigorous, and most interesting discussions of the subjective-state approach, Paul Dolan and Mathew P. White (2007) contrast it with an objective-list approach, of which I am named as an exemplar. Their article, however, betrays some misunderstandings, and it seems like a good occasion to correct them here.

In *Women and Human Development* (Nussbaum 2001c), *Frontiers of Justice* (Nussbaum 2006), and numerous articles, particularly central being "Capabilities as Fundamental Entitlements" (Nussbaum 2003; see also Nussbaum 2004c), I argue that a good way of thinking about some central political principles that can be the basis for constitutional guarantees is to think of them as a list of capabilities, or opportunities for functioning, which include both the internal education for that functioning and the provision, and protection, of suitable external circumstances for actually choosing the functioning. My list of capabilities is given in Appendix B.

Dolan and White make the objection that this conception is "paternalistic," insofar as it "may be left to policy makers" to decide what well-being is for everyone and then to "impos[e]" it. While this objection might possibly be brought against some versions of the objective-list approach, it surely cannot be brought against mine. Indeed, despite being pleased at being cited in this very good article, I am less than pleased by the fact that the authors appear not to have read chapter 1 of the book they cite (*Women and Human Development*), which is all about the ways in which I would answer the charge of paternalism, or chapter 2 either, in which I fault some objective-list accounts for being insufficiently sensitive to desire and show what role desire plays in my idea of justification. (The book has only four chapters, chapters 3 and 4 being less pertinent to the question they pose.) It is difficult to summarize briefly the results of such lengthy discussions, but let me try.[17]

First of all, the nature of my project must be described: I am not

---

17. All of these points are made in Nussbaum (2001c, 2006, 2003), in more or less identical form, although not in the same order.

trying to provide an account of well-being for all public purposes. I am trying to provide an account of a central group of very fundamental entitlements, those without the securing of which no society can lay claim to basic justice. The account is closely linked to constitution making and to the idea of fundamental constitutional rights (Nussbaum 2007).

Second, the account is explicitly said to be, in John Rawls's sense, a political rather than a comprehensive account (Rawls 1996): it is deliberately narrow and partial, confining itself to a core group of entitlements that can, it is argued, become the object of an overlapping consensus among people who have very different comprehensive views, religious and secular, of the meaning and purpose of human life.

Third, the items on the list, these key political goals, are, crucially, capabilities, not actual functionings. The point here is to leave room for choice. A person who has the right to vote (and really can go out and vote, with no subtle impediments or discrimination) may always choose not to vote; a person who has access to adequate health care can always choose an unhealthy lifestyle. A person who has the freedom of religion may decide to have nothing to do with religion. The only place where my conception is paternalistic, imposing a specific mode of functioning, is when we are speaking of children. Here I would impose compulsory primary and secondary education, and I would also allow the state to intervene in parental health care choices where the health and life of children are at risk. But this is hardly controversial.

It seems obvious that people may endorse a given item as a capability while believing that, for themselves, it would be quite wrong to function in that way. The Amish believe that it is wrong to vote, but they can happily endorse the right to vote as a fundamental entitlement of all citizens in a pluralistic society. A person whose personal choice is to live an extremely unhealthy lifestyle and never go to the doctor can happily endorse a decent national health care program: nobody is forcing her to use it, and she realizes that fellow citizens, whom she respects, do not share her lifestyle preferences. Even the most militantly antireligious people in the United States do not applaud the policies of Marxist nations that suppress religion; they are happy to defend religious liberty.

Fourth, even at the level of specifying the items on the list, the conception leaves much room for the democratic political process to play itself out. A free speech right, for example, is never fully specified in the founding document itself: its contours become clearer over time through a combination of legislative and judicial action. Within limits, different societies may legitimately do this differently, in accordance with their different traditions.

Fifth, the list includes many of the major liberties of choice without which meaningful choice is not possible. If a society does not commit itself to the right of free speech, the right to free association, the freedom of conscience, all in a way that entrenches these entitlements, setting them beyond the vicissitudes of majority vote—as, for example, in a constitution somewhat difficult to amend it is showing, I would argue, deficient concern for human choice and liberty.

Sixth, the list is ultimately justified only through a complex process that involves consulting informed desires of certain types. I shall not elaborate further here, since the entire second chapter of *Women and Human Development* is required to give those conditions.

Seventh, the list is a template for persuasion, not for forcible implementation. If any country is going to put these items into its constitution, it will be only because it has gone through some type of political process internally, for example, a constitutional convention. I am against any sort of forcible intervention in the affairs of another nation, except in the case of genocide.

I am not sure, then, where the objectionable element of paternalism is. If Dolan and White believe that the very fact of having a list of fundamental entitlements specified in a constitution entrenched beyond majority whim is an objectionable form of paternalism, they certainly do not make that argument. Nor do they make any argument trying to show that the capabilities on my list could not become the object of an overlapping consensus, as capabilities, among people who endorse very different comprehensive views of the good life.

I say nothing at all about what account of well-being should be used by administrative agencies when they are not following core constitutional mandates. But the general tenor of my account would be that whatever they do should be respectful to the plurality of comprehensive doctrines that citizens reasonably hold.

4. THE TRUTH IN SUBJECTIVE-STATE ANALYSIS

When, then, is it right to focus on subjective states, in the light of all these normative difficulties? Here we should return to Mill. Mill, out of his long experience of depression, articulates a version of Aristotelianism that is, to my mind, slightly ahead of Wordsworth's. Wordsworth focuses so much on fine activity that he suggests that subjective feelings of plea-sure do not matter at all. In his *Autobiography*, Mill describes himself, during his depression, as still active in accordance with a variety of good purposes. And yet his life felt empty and meaningless. Only the nour-ishment of poetry (prominently including Wordsworth's poetry) lifted him out of his torpor. Shortly after that, he met the love of his life, Harriet Taylor (see my discussion in Nussbaum 2004b). We should pay attention to Mill's experience and realize that it is important to treat depression, whether or not the treatment contributes to enhancing val-uable activities (and usually, of course, it does). Subjective states matter greatly, and sometimes we can produce them through direct interven-tions, even though by and large pleasures are closely associated with activities. Public policy should certainly adopt the treatment of depres-sion as a valuable goal, for example, and it would not do so if it followed purely Wordsworthian lines. (Indeed, my capabilities list makes room for this, making the opportunity for at least some pleasure and the relief of pain a central entitlement.)

Public policy should also focus on the mitigation of the sort of pain that is not an enrichment of the soul or a deepening of self-knowledge, and there is a lot of pain that is not conducive to anything good. If we can totally eliminate hunger and painful childhood diseases, for example, we should do that. We should also strive to eliminate child sexual abuse, domestic violence, and rape, all of which are pains that seem to have no positive educative function. When people have a painful illness that cannot be cured, palliative treatment should be supported by a decent scheme of national medical insurance, and this same decent scheme should adequately cover the treatment of depression and other mental illnesses. The badness of pain should be a central consideration in end-of-life care and in the discussion of physician-assisted suicide.

Beyond this, Dolan and White make sensible recommendations in the area of curtailing environmental pains, such as noise pollution. We can add that nuisance law, as it has evolved, is a sophisticated set of strategies for dealing with the distress that people may cause to others without direct harm, and such laws have a valuable social purpose (Nussbaum 2004a, chap 3). To endorse these proposals we do not need to be Ben-thamites, and we certainly do not need to equate pleasure with happiness.

Indeed, we had better not be Benthamites, or else we are likely to use such insights in ways that dangerously subordinate and oppress. To some people, the distress caused by the presence of a homosexual couple next door is just as acute as the distress caused by the presence of a running sewer next door. The law, however, has learned to distinguish between an actual physical distress directly caused by a bad smell and the type of distress that is mediated by imagining what people are doing behind closed doors. For Bentham, there is no such difference: pleasures and pains vary only in intensity and duration. So, if we are to use the insight that Dolan and White provide us and, centrally, the insight that Mill's *Autobiography* provides us, we had better have more adequate conceptions of pleasure and pain than Bentham did, and we had better have a firm grasp on moral principles (such as the protection of privacy and choice) that are independent of pleasure and pain and whose protection, indeed, has always proved painful to nosy people, which is to say most of the people who are around.

In short: the appeal to subjective well-being, as currently used in the psychological literature, is not utterly useless, but at present it is so riddled with conception confusion and normative naïveté that we had better pause and sort things out before going any further.

APPENDIX A: WORDSWORTH'S POEM

"Character of the Happy Warrior"

Who is the happy Warrior? Who is he
That every man in arms should wish to be?
—It is the generous Spirit, who, when brought
Among the tasks of real life, hath wrought
Upon the plan that pleased his boyish thought:
Whose high endeavours are an inward light
That makes the path before him always bright;
Who, with a natural instinct to discern
What knowledge can perform, is diligent to learn;
Abides by this resolve, and stops not there,
But makes his moral being his prime care;
Who, doomed to go in company with Pain,
And Fear, and Bloodshed, miserable train!
Turns his necessity to glorious gain;
In face of these doth exercise a power
Which is our human nature's highest dower:
Controls them and subdues, transmutes, bereaves
Of their bad influence, and their good receives:
By objects, which might force the soul to abate
Her feeling, rendered more compassionate;
Is placable—because occasions rise

So often that demand such sacrifice;
More skilful in self-knowledge, even more pure,
As tempted more; more able to endure,
As more exposed to suffering and distress;
Thence, also, more alive to tenderness.
—'Tis he whose law is reason; who depends
Upon that law as on the best of friends;
Whence, in a state where men are tempted still
To evil for a guard against worse ill,
And what in quality or act is best
Doth seldom on a right foundation rest,
He labours good on good to fix, and owes
To virtue every triumph that he knows:
—Who, if he rise to station of command,
Rises by open means; and there will stand
On honourable terms, or else retire,
And in himself possess his own desire;
Who comprehends his trust, and to the same
Keeps faithful with a singleness of aim;
And therefore does not stoop, nor lie in wait
For wealth, or honours, or for worldly state;
Whom they must follow; on whose head must fall,
Like showers of manna, if they come at all:
Whose powers shed round him in the common strife,
Or mild concerns of ordinary life,
A constant influence, a peculiar grade;
But who, if he be called upon to face
Some awful moment to which Heaven has joined
Great issues, good or bad for human kind,
Is happy as a Lover; and attired
With sudden brightness, like a Man inspired;
And, through the heat of conflict, keeps the law
In calmness made, and sees what he foresaw;
Or is an unexpected call succeed,
Come when it will, is equal to the need:
—He who though thus endued as with a sense
And faculty for storm and turbulence,
Is yet a Soul whose master-bias leans
To homefelt pleasures and to gentle scenes;
Sweet images! Which, wheresoe'er he be,
Are at his heart; and such fidelity
It is his darling passion to approve;
More brave for this, that he hath much to love;—

'Tis, finally, the Man, who, lifted high,
Conspicuous object in a Nation's eye,
Or left unthought-of in obscurity,—
Who, with a toward or untoward lot,
Prosperous or adverse, to his wish or not—
Plays, in the many games of life, that one
Where what he most doth value must be won:
Whom neither shape nor danger can dismay,
Nor thought of tender happiness betray;
Who, not content that former worth stand fast,
Looks forward, persevering to the last,
From well to better, daily self-surpast:
Who, whether praise of him must walk the earth
For ever, and to noble deeds give birth,
Or he must fall, to sleep without his fame,
And leave a dead unprofitable name—
Finds comfort in himself and in his cause;
And, while the mortal mist is gathering, draws
His breath in confidence of Heaven's applause;
This is the happy Warrior; this is he
That every Man in arms should wish to be.

APPENDIX B: THE CENTRAL HUMAN CAPABILITIES

1. *Life.*   Being able to live to the end of a human life of normal length; not dying prematurely, or before one's life is so reduced as to be not worth living.
2. *Bodily Health.*   Being able to have good health, including reproductive health; to be adequately nourished; to have adequate shelter.
3. *Bodily Integrity.*   Being able to move freely from place to place; to be secure against violent assault, including sexual assault and domestic violence; having opportunities for sexual satisfaction and for choice in matters of reproduction.
4. *Senses, Imagination, and Thought.*   Being able to use the senses, to imagine, think, and reason—and to do these things in a "truly human" way, a way informed and cultivated by an adequate education, including, but by no means limited to, literacy and basic mathematical and scientific training. Being able to use imagination and thought in connection with experiencing and producing works and events of one's own choice, religious, literary, musical, and so forth. Being able to use one's mind in ways protected by guarantees of freedom of expression with respect to both political and artistic speech and freedom of religious exercise. Being able to have pleasurable experiences and to avoid nonbeneficial pain.
5. *Emotions.*   Being able to have attachments to things and people outside ourselves; to love those who love and care for us, to grieve at their absence; in

general, to love, to grieve, to experience longing, gratitude, and justified anger. Not having one's emotional development blighted by fear and anxiety. (Supporting this capability means supporting forms of human association that can be shown to be crucial in their development.)

6. *Practical Reason.*   Being able to form a conception of the good and to engage in critical reflection about the planning of one's life. (This entails protection for the liberty of conscience and religious observance.)

7. *Affiliation.*

   A. Being able to live with and toward others, to recognize and show concern for other human beings, to engage in various forms of social interaction; to be able to imagine the situation of another. (Protecting this capability means protecting institutions that constitute and nourish such forms of affiliation and also protecting the freedom of assembly and political speech.)

   B. Having the social bases of self-respect and nonhumiliation; being able to be treated as a dignified being whose worth is equal to that of others. This entails provisions of nondiscrimination on the basis of race, sex, sexual orientation, ethnicity, caste, religion, national origin.

8. *Other Species.*   Being able to live with concern for and in relation to animals, plants, and the world of nature.

9. *Play.*   Being able to laugh, to play, to enjoy recreational activities.

10. *Control over One's Environment.*

    A. *Political.*   Being able to participate effectively in political choices that govern one's life; having the right of political participation, protections of free speech and association.

    B. *Material.*   Being able to hold property (both land and movable goods), and having property rights on an equal basis with others; having the right to seek employment on an equal basis with others; having the freedom from unwarranted search and seizure. In work, being able to work as a human being, exercising practical reason, and entering into meaningful relationships of mutual recognition with other workers.

REFERENCES

Allardt, Erik. 1975. *Att ha, alska, att vara: Om valfard i Norden* (Having, loving, being: On welfare in the Nordic countries). Borgholm: Argos.

———. 1993. Having, Loving, Being: An Alternative to the Swedish Model of Welfare Research. Pp. 88–94 in *The Quality of Life,* edited by Martha Nussbaum and Amartya Sen. Oxford: Clarendon Press.

Austin, J. L. 1979. *Agathon* and *eudaimonia* in the *Ethics* of Aristotle. Pp. 1–31 in *Philosophical Papers,* edited J. O. Urmson and G. J. Warnock. Oxford and New York: Oxford University Press.

Bagchi, Jasodhara. 1997. *Loved and Unloved: The Girl Child in the Family.* Kolkata: Stree.

Batson, C. Daniel. 1991. *The Altruism Question.* Hillsdale, N.J.: Lawrence Erlbaum.

Birault, Henri. 1985. Beatitude in Nietzsche. Pp. 219–31 in *The New Nietzsche,* edited by David Allison. Cambridge, Mass.: MIT Press.

Clark, Candace. 1997. *Misery and Company.* Chicago: University of Chicago Press.

Dolan, Paul, and Mathew P. White. 2007. How Can Measures of Subjective Well-Being Be Used to Inform Public Policy?" *Perspectives on Psychological Science* 2:71–85.

Gosling, J. C. B. 1969. *Pleasure and Desire.* Oxford: Clarendon Press.

Gosling, J. C. B., and C. C. W. Taylor. 1982. *The Greeks on Pleasure.* Oxford and New York: Clarendon Press.

Harsanyi, John. 1982. Morality and the Theory of Rational Behavior. Chapter 2 in *Utilitarianism and Beyond,* edited by Amartya Sen and Bernard Williams. Cambridge: Cambridge University Press.

Kahneman, Daniel, and Alan B. Krueger. 2006. Developments in the Measurement of Subjective Well-Being. *Journal of Economic Perspectives* 20:3–24.

Kindlon, Dan, and Michael Thompson. 1999. *Raising Cain: Protecting the Emotional Life of Boys.* New York: Ballantine Books.

Mill. John Stuart. 1869. *The Subjection of Women.* New York: D. Appleton Co.

———. 1998. The Utility of Religion. Pp. 69–122 in *Mill: Three Essays on Religion.* Amherst, N.Y.: Prometheus Books.

Nozick, Robert. 1974. *Anarchy, State, and Utopia.* New York: Basic Books.

———. 1989. *The Examined Life.* New York: Simon & Schuster.

Nussbaum, Martha. 1994. *The Therapy of Desire: Theory and Practice in Hellenistic Ethics.* Princeton, N.J.: Princeton University Press.

———. 2001a. *The Fragility of Goodness: Luck and Ethics in Greek Tragedy and Philosophy.* Updated ed. Cambridge: Cambridge University Press.

———. 2001b. *Upheavals of Thought: The Intelligence of Emotions.* New York: Cambridge University Press.

———. 2001c. *Women and Human Development.* New York: Cambridge University Press.

———. 2003. Capabilities as Fundamental Entitlements. *Feminist Economics* 9: 33–59.

———. 2004a. *Hiding from Humanity: Digust, Shame, and the Law.* Princeton, N.J.: Princeton University Press.

———. 2004b. Mill between Bentham and Aristotle. *Daedalus* 133(2):60–68.

———. 2004c. On Hearing Women's Voices: A Reply to Susan Okin. *Philosophy and Public Affairs* 32:193–205.

———. 2005. The Death of Pity: Orwell and American Political Life. Pp. 279–99 in *On "Nineteen Eighty-Four": Orwell and Our Future,* edited by Abbot

Gleason, Jack Goldsmith, and Martha C. Nussbaum. Princeton, N.J.: Princeton University Press.

⸺. 2006. *Frontiers of Justice: Disability, Natoinality, Species Membership*. Cambridge, Mass.: Harvard University Press.

⸺. 2007. Constitutions and Capabilities: "Perception" against Lofty Formalism. Supreme Court Foreword 2006. *Harvard Law Review* 121:4–97.

Packe, Michael St. John. 1954. *The Life of John Stuart Mill*. New York: Macmillan.

Prichard, H. A. 1935. The Meaning of *agathon* in the *Ethics* of Aristotle. *Philosophy* 10:27–39.

Rawls, John. 1996. *Political Liberalism*. Expanded paper ed. New York: Columbia University Press.

Rousseau, Jean-Jacques. 1762. *Emile, ou de l'éducation*. Book IV. Paris.

Seligman, Martin. 2002. *Authentic Happiness: Using the New Positive Psychology to Realize Your Potential for Lasting Fulfillment*. New York: Free Press.

Sen, Amartya, and Bernard Williams. 1982. Introduction to *Utilitarianism and Beyond*, edited by Amartya Sen and Bernard Williams. Cambridge: Cambridge University Press.

Shackleton Bailey, David, ed. and trans. 1999. *Cicero: Letters to Atticus, III, 166–281*. Loeb Classical Library 97. Cambridge, Mass.: Harvard University Press.

Taylor, C. C. W. 1976. *Plato: Protagoras*. Oxford: Clarendon Press.

Two Recommendations on the Pursuit of Happiness

Christopher K. Hsee, Fei Xu, and Ningyu Tang

ABSTRACT

While any improvement in wealth and consumption will likely increase happiness, the increased happiness may or may not last long. In this article we offer two recommendations to make the increased happiness sustainable. The first one—to invest resources to promote adaptation-resistant rather than adaptation-prone consumption—seeks to make the increased happiness sustainable within a generation. The second recommendation—to invest resources to promote inherently evaluable rather than inherently inevaluable consumption—seeks to make the increased happiness sustainable across generations.

Most of us now possess more wealth and enjoy better consumption goods than our parents' and grandparents' generations. Are we happier? Research suggests that in developed countries wealth has increased multiple times since the Second World War, but reported happiness and life satisfaction have virtually stagnated (Blanchflower and Oswald 2004b; Easterlin 1974, 1995). A question weighs on the minds of researchers, policy makers, and the general public alike: how can happiness increase as wealth accumulates and consumption improves? In recent decades, psychologists, economists, and other behavioral scientists have all tried to address this question (for example, Clark, Frijters, and Shields 2007;

CHRISTOPHER K. HSEE is the Theodore O. Yntema Professor of Behavioral Science and Marketing at the University of Chicago Booth School of Business. FEI XU is Professor and NINGYU TANG is Associate Professor at the Antai College of Economics and Managment, Shanghai Jiaotong University. The authors thank Reid Hastie, Eric Posner, Alois Stutzer, and Yang Yang for comments on drafts of this article. They also thank the Templeton Foundation, National Natural Science Foundation of China (grant 70832004), and their respective universities for research support.

[*Journal of Legal Studies*, vol. XXXVII (June 2008)]

Diener and Oishi 2000; Diener and Biswas-Diener 2002; Diener et al. 1999; Easterlin 1995; Frey and Stutzer 2004, 2002; Kahneman 1994; Kahneman, Diener, and Schwarz 1999; Kahneman, Wakker, and Sarin 1997; Layard 2005; Oswald 1997; Parducci 1995; Seligman 2002; Tian and Yang 2007; Veenhoven 1991).

This article examines how to increase the average happiness level within a generation and across generations. One way is to further increase the wealth of the society (for example, gross domestic product per capita) and thus its corresponding consumption levels. Many economists endorse this approach. Another approach is to optimize the way in which wealth is consumed without increasing the amount of aggregate wealth per se. These two approaches are complementary. In this article, we focus on the latter approach and refer to the scientific study of this approach as "hedonomics," to distinguish it from economics (Hsee, Hastie, and Chen 2008).

Within the hedonomic approach, we offer two specific recommendations to increase the average level of happiness in a society. The first recommendation is based on the observation that some experiences are prone to hedonic adaptation and other experiences are relatively resistant to hedonic adaptation, which suggests an emphasis on pursuing adaptation-resistant rather than adaptation-prone positive experiences and avoiding adaptation-resistant rather than adaptation-prone negative experiences. The second recommendation rests on the observation that the influence of wealth on happiness can be either relative or absolute, which suggests a focus on producing goods that are inherently easy to evaluate and have an absolute effect on happiness, rather than goods that are inherently difficult to evaluate and have only a relative effect on happiness. These recommendations have different implications. The first is to produce prolonged happiness within a generation; the second is to increase happiness across generations.

Certain caveats are in order. First, we do not assume that the pursuit of the average happiness of a society is the only goal policy makers should pursue; we simply assume that it should be an important consideration. Although many scholars have realized the importance of happiness (for example, Cabanac and Bonniot-Cabanac 2007; Diener et al. 2000; Kahneman et al. 2004; Layard 2005) and may have even over-emphasized its importance (for discussions, see, for example, Frey and Stutzer 2007; Loewenstein 2008), policy makers are far from using happiness principles to guide their decisions, and articles such as this may help them move toward that direction.

Second, the shades of meaning expressed by the word "happiness" operate at different levels. The kind of happiness derived from reading Tolstoy's *War and Peace* or from volunteering at a homeless shelter differs from the kind of happiness enjoyed while watching a situation comedy or riding a Ferris wheel. Some people might prefer using the terms "meaningful," "rewarding," or "satisfying" to words such as "happy" or "pleasant" when describing the first type of experience. While the distinction of these different levels of happiness is important, the current article is concerned only with hedonic (positive versus negative) aspects of experiences.

Finally, the recommendations we offer in this article are not intended to comprise an exhaustive list of methods to increase happiness. Numerous other ways exist, such as promoting positive personalities and traits (for example, Lyubomirsky 2007; Seligman 2002). Our approaches are not concerned with individual personality or idiosyncratic beliefs but rely on how wealth is used and perceived. In the rest of this article, we review the relevant literature and elaborate on each recommendation in turn. In the general discussion section, we explore the relationship between the two recommendations.

1. PROMOTING ADAPTATION-RESISTANT CONSUMPTION

Any improvement in a consumption variable, be it an increase in the size of a home or an increase in the speed of a computer, can at least temporarily raise one's happiness. The problem is that the increased happiness may not last long. One of the obstacles to creating lasting happiness is hedonic adaptation. Hedonic adaptation is the tendency to feel less hedonically sensitive to an ongoing stimulus with the passage of time (see, for example, Diener, Lucas, and Scollon 2006; Frederick and Loewenstein 1999; Helson 1964). For example, a person who upgrades his laminate countertop to granite may feel happy at first, but as time goes by he adapts to the granite countertop and no longer feels particularly happy while in his kitchen. Hedonic adaptation applies to a wide range of experiences, including both positive events such as marriage (Lucas and Clark 2006) or winning a lottery (Brickman, Coates, and Janoff-Bulman 1978) and negative events such as the loss of a family member (Oswald and Powdthavee 2008) or becoming disabled (Brickman, Coates, and Janoff-Bulman 1978; Ubel, Loewenstein, and Jepson 2005).

Given that humans are so remarkably adaptable, the question arises, do we adapt to everything? To answer this, imagine three isolated societies: the baseline society, the short-commute society, and the large-home society. In the baseline society, the average living space is 400 square feet per person and the average commute time between home and work is 60 minutes per day. The large-home society is the same as the baseline society except that the government subsidizes more spacious buildings so that the average living space is now 500 square feet per person while the commute time remains 60 minutes. The short-commute society is the same as the baseline society except that instead of subsidizing better housing, the government uses the same amount of resource to subsidize faster transportation systems so that the average commute is now 30 minutes per day while the average living space remains 400 square feet per person.

Relative to the baseline society, will members in the large-home society or in the short-commute society be happier? We predict that in the short run people in the large-home society may be happier but in the long run people in the short-commute society will be happier. When people move from a small home to a large home they will initially feel happy, but before long they will adapt and become hedonically insensitive to the new home size. When people's commuting decreases, they will also initially feel happy, but they will not easily adapt or become insensitive to this improvement.

Consistent with our data, Stutzer and Frey (2004) found that people who commuted long hours on average had higher income but that this higher income did not compensate for the long commute in terms of their happiness. Frey and Stutzer's analysis suggests that people do not adapt to commuting but seem to adapt to a higher labor income.

Generally speaking, events that are stable and certain are easy to adapt to, and events that are variable or uncertain are difficult to adapt to (Kurtz, Wilson, and Gilbert 2007; Frederick and Loewenstein 1999; Kahneman and Thaler 1991). Thus, unstable or uncertain good events will create longer lasting happiness than their stable and certain equivalents, and unstable or uncertain bad events will create longer lasting misery than their stable and certain equivalents. Consistent with these views, Kurtz et al. (2007) found that a gift from a mysterious source (uncertain condition) created longer lasting happiness than an equivalent gift from a certain condition. In the negative domain, Smith et al. (2008) found that colostomy patients with hope of recovery (uncertain outcome) adapted more slowly to their misery than colostomy patients without hope of recovery (see also Van Boven and Gilovich [2003] for a related point regarding experiences versus material possessions and Scitovsky [1978] for a discussion regarding pleasure versus comfort).

The size of a home is rather stable and certain. In contrast, the thrill or misery of a rush-hour commute remains uncertain. The commuter has to cope with new situations every day—catching trains, traffic delays, and so on. Moreover, long commutes incur high opportunity costs and leave commuters with less time to sleep, less time to spend with family members, and less time and energy to engage in intimate relationships. Since sleep, social interaction, and intimate relationships are inherently evaluable types of experiences and are essential to one's happiness (Kahneman et al. 2004; Blanchflower and Oswald 2004a, 2004b), we predict that people in the short-commute society will be happier.

The trade-off between home size and commute time is just one example of a trade-off between adaptation-prone versus adaptation-resistant events. We face similar choices all the time: whether to use our money to buy a better car or to take a vacation, whether to use our money to remodel our kitchen or to dine out with friends, or, more broadly, to pursue what Scitovsky (1978) distinguished as comfort or pleasure activities. There are at least two reasons why individuals and marketers often fail to make hedonomically optimal decisions involving such trade-offs. First, they fail to anticipate the power of hedonic adaptation (Wilson and Gilbert 2005). Second, even if they could accurately predict hedonic adaptation, a consumer's decisions are often driven by anticipated immediate pleasure, while a marketer's decisions are often driven by anticipated immediate profits. An improvement in an adaptation-prone condition (for example, larger living space) may generate more short-term, immediate happiness than an equally costly or effortful improvement in an adaptation-resistant event (for example, shorter commute time), even though in the long run the reverse is true. Therefore, consumers and marketers tend to favor the short-lived but adaptation-prone improvement.

This fact provides policy makers with the opportunity to play a constructive role and fund research that better identifies which improvements are adaptation prone and which are adaptation resistant. With this information, government funds could be allocated to support adaptation-resistant improvements rather than adaptation-prone improvements and government policies adopted to encourage businesses to do likewise.

2. PROMOTING INHERENTLY EVALUABLE CONSUMPTION

One of the most fundamental questions for students of happiness is whether happiness is relative or absolute. By saying that happiness is absolute, we mean that happiness depends on the absolute amount of wealth and the absolute consumption level, regardless of whether it also depends on relative wealth and consumption levels. By saying that happiness is relative, we mean that happiness depends only on relative wealth and consumption levels, that is, the difference between one's wealth and consumption levels and one's knowledge (perception) about the wealth and consumption levels of other people (Festinger 1954). While standard economic theory assumes the importance of absolute values, many psychologists and a growing number of economists believe that happiness is relative (for example, Clark, Frijters, and Shields 2007; Easterlin 1995; Luttmer, 2005; McBride 2001; Parducci 1995).

Yet this begs the question, is happiness always relative? More than a mere intellectual curiosity, this question carries important social implications. Understanding whether relative or absolute wealth and consumption levels determine happiness helps predict what happens when wealth and consumption levels rise from one generation to the next. If happiness depends on absolute wealth and consumption levels, then raising wealth and consumption levels across generations is likely to increase happiness. If happiness depends only on relative wealth and consumption levels, then raising wealth and consumption levels across generations is just a zero-sum game and is unlikely to affect happiness.

Existing findings are mixed. Some suggest that raising wealth cannot increase happiness, as consistent with the relative view. For example, although real (inflation-adjusted) income in developed countries has increased multiple times in the last half-century, reported life satisfaction has remained virtually the same (see, for example, Easterlin 1974, 1995). Other data suggest that raising wealth can increase happiness, as consistent with the absolute view. For example, reported life satisfaction is on average higher in wealthy nations than in poor nations (for example, Diener et al. 1993; Kahneman 2008; Leigh and Wolfers 2006; Stevenson and Wolfers 2008), and increases in reported happiness are associated with increases in gross domestic product per capita (for example, Di Tella, MacCulloch, and Oswald 2003).

We assert that happiness is neither always relative nor always absolute but instead depends on the nature of the consumption experience. To illustrate, imagine three isolated societies: the baseline society, the better jewelry society, and the better heater society. In the baseline society, members on average have only inexpensive jewelry and ineffective heating systems. The better jewelry society is identical to the baseline society in all aspects except that members on average possess better jewelry, for example, larger diamonds. The better heater society is also identical to the baseline society except that members on average possess better heating systems and enjoy warmer temperatures in the winter. Within each society, some members possess better jewelry than others, and some members possess better heating systems than others.

In which society are members the happiest on average and in which society are members the least happy on average? According to the relativist view, happiness is derived only from comparison. Because the three societies are isolated, then on average members in the three societies will be equally happy (or unhappy), and within each society those who possess better jewelry or better heating systems are happier than those who possess inferior jewelry or inferior heating systems. According to the absolute view, happiness depends on absolute consumption levels, so members in the better jewelry society and members in the better temperature society will be happier on average than members in the baseline society.

We propose that members in the better jewelry society will not be happier than members in the baseline society, yet members in the better heating society will be. Hsee et al. (forthcoming) distinguish between two types of consumption variables: type A (inherently evaluable) and type B (inherently inevaluable). A variable is type A if human beings (and maybe even primates) have an innate, shared, and stable scale to assess its desirability. Examples include ambient temperature, amount of sleep, orgasm, availability of social companions (or loneliness), stress, fatigue, and so on. Conversely, a variable is type B if human beings have no innate scale to gauge its desirability and must evaluate it on the basis of external reference information, for example, comparison with what other people possess. Examples include the size of a diamond, the brand of a purse, the horsepower of a car, the price of a stock, and so on.

We wish to make several clarifications. First, type A and type B variables are not two discrete states but form two ends of a continuum, with the great majority of consumption variables falling in between. Furthermore, certain consumption variables are inherently inevaluable in some range and inevaluable in other ranges. For example, the difference between a 10-inch television screen and a 20-inch television is likely inherently evaluable, because an increase from 10 to 20 inches would reduce the viewer's eye strain; however, the difference between a 60-inch screen and a 90-inch screen is less likely to be inherently evaluable. The same can be said of the size of a home. Second, type A variables may differ from type B variables in that they are more associated with basic survival needs (Veenhoven 1991), and they are better suited for private consumption (Frank 2000; Solnick and Hemenway 2005). Finally, experiences with both type A and type B variables are subject to the influence of external reference information, including social comparison. The key difference between the two types of experiences is not whether they can be affected by external reference points but whether they have an inherent and stable reference scale. Type A experiences may be thought to resemble a foam ball, while type B experiences resemble a Play-Doh ball. Bouncing either one will distort its shape, but the foam ball will return to its original or "inherent" form, whereas the Play-Doh ball will flatten because has no inherent shape but instead retains changes in response to environmental forces.

Whether happiness during the consumption of a good is absolute or relative depends on whether the relevant variable of the good is type A or type B (Hsee et al. forthcoming). If it is type A, happiness is absolute; if it is type B, happiness is relative. This proposition has been supported by both lab and field data (Hsee et al. forthcoming). In a large-scale telephone interview study conducted during the winter, randomly selected respondents from China's 31 officially designated large cities were asked about their happiness with their room temperature and with their jewelry possessions. The results support our inherent-evaluability thesis: within each city, people who owned more expensive jewelry reported greater happiness about their jewelry than people who owned less expensive jewelry, and people who enjoyed warmer room temperatures reported greater happiness about their room temperatures than people in colder rooms. Between cities, however, residents of cities with more expensive jewelry were not any happier on average about their jewelry than residents of cities with less expensive jewelry, yet respondents in cities with warmer room temperatures were still happier on average about their room temperatures than those in cities with colder room temperatures. Assuming that respondents compare themselves to people within a city than between cities, we consider these results evidence for our proposition that room temperature (a type A variable) has an absolute effect on happiness while jewelry value (a type B variable) has only a relative effect on happiness.

Our analysis has implications for how to increase happiness across generations. A generation is a social milieu, like a society. Just as people in the better jewelry society are not happier on average than people in the baseline society but people in the warmer temperature society are happier, our future generation will not be happier than us if increased wealth is spent on improving type B consumption but will be happier than us if it is spent on improving type A consumption. (The reader may dispute the cross-generation analogy, because in the society example, the societies are isolated, but people in a new generation may compare themselves with an old generation. Indeed, they may, but people in the old generation may also have compared themselves with an even older generation. To the extent that a new generation is always better off than an old generation by roughly the same rate, this cross-generational comparison will yield a constant effect on each generation and will not make one generation happier than another.)

Thus, to make future generations happier, we recommend investing resources in improving type A variables—letting every family enjoy heating in the winter and air conditioning in the summer; developing effective drugs for people with sleeping disorders, depression, or migraine headaches; building better sanitary systems so that fewer people will suffer from insect bites and diseases; providing services and organizing events so that people could more easily socialize with each other; and so on. Compared with previous generations, we already have more comfortable room temperatures, more effective medicines, better sanitary systems, better communication systems, and so on. Yet there is significant room for improvement, especially in developing countries.

Our analysis seems at odds with the Easterlin paradox—the finding that happiness has not increased in the last few decades in developed countries while wealth has (for example, Blanchflower and Oswald 2004a, 2004b; Easterlin 1995). As wealth increases, type A consumption should also improve. Then why does life satisfaction refuse to follow suit? There are several possible reasons. First, when reporting life satisfaction, respondents may attend more to money and goods than to the hedonomic quality of their consumption experiences. Second, happiness with money and consumption is only one component of life satisfaction; other determinants of life satisfaction may have worsened across generations and neutralized any improvements in inherently evaluable consumptions. Third, improvements in developed countries in recent decades may have focused on type B variables, and according to our theory, improvements in type B variables across generations do not increase happiness. This speculation is corroborated by findings that in less developed nations life satisfaction does increase as wealth increases (for example, Clark, Frijters, and Shields 2007) and that life satisfaction in less developed countries is lower on average than life satisfaction in developed countries (for example, Diener et al. 1993; Kahneman 2008; Leigh and Wolfers 2006). To the extent that inherently evaluable variables relate more to basic biological needs than to higher order needs, developing nations have more room to improve inherently evaluable goods than do developed nations.

Even in developed countries, there are still deficiencies in domains we believe are type A. For example, not all Americans have adequate heating in the winter, and many suffer from insomnia, depression, and social isolation. The free-market system does not always encourage manufacturers to produce type A goods rather than type B goods. It may be more profitable to manufacture imitation diamonds than more cost-effective medicines and more profitable to design fashionable winter coats than warmer winter coats. This is where policy makers can play a constructive role by investing government resources to develop type A goods or services or introducing regulatory policies to provide incentives to businesses to do so.

To achieve this, policy makers first need to know which variables are type A and which are type B. Theoretically, type A versus type B is defined by the extent to which one has an inherent evaluation scale for that variable. Operationally, one can identify whether a variable is type A or type B by drawing on people's intuition. While lay intuition may not always be correct, it should not be systematically wrong either. Alternatively, one may adopt a more scientific method to empirically identify a variable as type A or type B. Suppose that x_1 and x_2 are two levels of variable X. Recruit three groups of respondents (or primates?) who have not socially learned about which level of X is desirable or undesirable. Let everyone in group 1 experience x_1, everyone in group 2 experience x_2, and some in group 3 experience x_1 and some in group 3 experience x_2, and then assess everyone's happiness. The three groups should be isolated, but members in each group should know what level of X other members get. Define $D_{between} = e_{group1}(x_1) - e_{group2}(x_2)$ and $D_{within} = e_{group3}(x_1) - e_{group3}(x_2)$, where $e_{group1}(x_1)$ is the mean happiness level of group 1, $e_{group2}(x_2)$ is the mean happiness level of group 2, and $e_{group3}(x_1)$ and $e_{group3}(x_2)$ are the mean happiness levels of those in group 3 who receive x_1 and x_2, respectively. Notice that $D_{between}$ reflects X's absolute effect and D_{within} reflects X's absolute effect or its relative effect or both. Assume that $D_{within} > 0$. Then whether X is type A or type B can be identified as follows. If $D_{between}$ is close in magnitude to D_{within}, then X is type A. If $D_{between}$ is small relative to D_{within} or is zero, then X is type B.

One could apply this method to a wide range of variables and then classify them as type A or type B or somewhere in between, hence forming a type A/B menu. We believe that such a menu would be highly valuable to policy makers. If they intend to make future generations happier, policy makers could use this menu to decide where to invest their resources.

3. GENERAL DISCUSSION

To increase the average happiness of members in a society, policy makers could adopt an economic approach to stimulate the economy and increase individual wealth and consumption, which will likely increase happiness. But the increased happiness may not continue. To ensure sustainable happiness, policy makers need to know how to allocate resources, a question that hedonomics seeks to address. In this article we have made two hedonomic recommendations: (1) invest resources to improve adaptation-resistant consumption and (2) invest resources to improve type A (inherently evaluable) consumption.

These two recommendations are theoretically distinctive and are intended to serve different purposes. Improving adaptation-resistant consumption can produce long-lasting happiness within the life span of a generation. Improving inherently evaluable consumption can increase happiness from one generation to the next.

Figures 1–4 describe how our theory predicts the change in happiness as the consumption variable improves over time. Across the four graphs, the consumption variable is either adaptation prone or adaptation resistant and either inherently evaluable or inherently inevaluable. In each figure, the x-axis is time. The solid curve is the consumption variable, and each step-up indicates an improvement in the consumption variable. Each dashed curve represents the happiness of one generation with that variable. In our illustrations, there are two consecutive generations.

In all the four cases (Figures 1–4), an improvement in the objective consumption variable leads to an improvement in happiness within a given generation. However, how long the increased happiness lasts within the generation depends on whether the consumption variable is adaptation resistant or prone. In the adaptation-resistant case, the im-

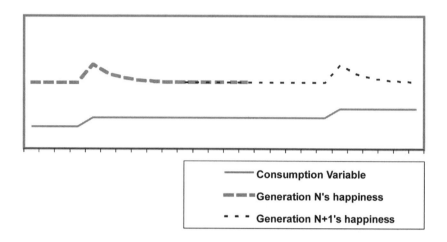

Figure 1. Happiness with an adaptation-prone, inherently inevaluable consumption variable

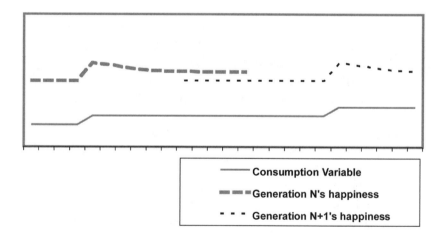

Figure 2. Happiness with an adaptation-resistant, inherently inevaluable consumption variable.

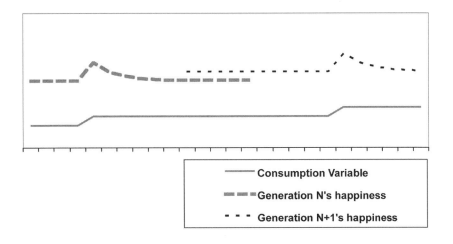

Figure 3. Happiness with an adaptation-prone, inherently evaluable consumption variable

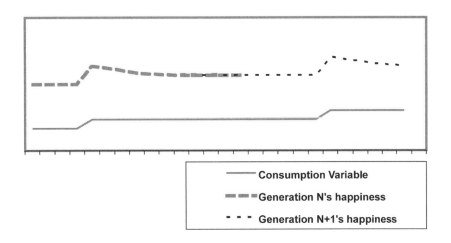

Figure 4. Happiness with an adaptation-resistant, inherently evaluable consumption variable

proved happiness tapers off very slowly. In the adaptation-prone case, it retreats rapidly. However, an improvement in an adaptation-resistant variable does not necessarily lead to an improvement in happiness across generations. Whether the new generation is happier than the old generation depends on whether the consumption variable is inherently evaluable or inevaluable. In the inherently evaluable case, the new generation is happier; in the inherently inevaluable case, it is not. In sum, hedonic adaptation and inherent evaluability lead to different consequences. How adaptation prone a consumption variable is determines how fast happiness within a generation tapers off after an improvement in the variable. How inherently evaluable a consumption variable is determines how much happiness increases from one generation to the next when there is an improvement in the variable between the two generations.

The messages from this analysis can be summarized as follows:

1. Any improvement in a consumption variable can make the affected people happier, at least for a short while.
2. To make the increased happiness sustainable across time within a generation, the improvement has to be adaptation resistant.
3. To make a new generation happier than an old one, the improvement has to be inherently evaluable.

Despite the theoretical separation between hedonic adaptation and inherent evaluability, we suspect that these two constructs are related. Specifically, adaptation-resistant variables are usually those that are inherently evaluable, and vice versa. For example, compared with the size of a diamond, ambient temperature is both more inherently evaluable and more resistant to adaptation. Although the twentieth time taking a bath in 20°C water will be less irritating than the first bath in 20°C water, it will still be less pleasant than the twentieth time taking a bath in 40°C water. This speculation is corroborated by results from the field study on jewelry and room temperature previously cited. Recall that variation in room temperature revealed both a within-city effect and a between-city effect, whereas difference in jewelry value revealed only a within-city effect. Presumably room temperature was something the respondents normally experience and had adapted to. The fact that it still exerted a significant between-city effect suggests that adaptation to temperature is slow or incomplete. It awaits future research to further identify the relationships between hedonic adaptation and inherent evaluability.

To conclude, we recommend prioritizing the improvement of inherently evaluable and adaptation-resistant consumptions. Such improvements not only will produce long-lasting happiness within a generation but also will make the next generation happier.

REFERENCES

Blanchflower, David G., and Andrew J. Oswald. 2004a. Money, Sex and Happiness: An Empirical Study. *Scandinavian Journal of Economics* 106: 393–415.

———. 2004b. Well-Being over Time in Britain and the USA. *Journal of Public Economics* 88:1359–86.

Brickman, Philip, Dan Coates, and Ronnie Janoff-Bulman. 1978. Lottery Winners and Accident Victims: Is Happiness Relative? *Journal of Personality and Social Psychology* 36:917–27.

Cabanac, Michel, and Marie-Claude Bonniot-Cabanac. 2007. Decision Making: Rational or Hedonic? *Behavioral and Brain Functions* 3:1–45.

Clark, Andrew E., Paul Frijters, and Mike Shields. 2007. Relative Income, Happiness and Utility: An Explanation for the Easterlin Paradox and Other Puzzles. *Journal of Economic Literature* 46:95–144.

Diener, Ed, and Robert Biswas-Diener. 2002. Will Money Increase Subjective Well-Being? *Social Indicators Research* 57:119–69.

Diener, Ed, Richard E. Lucas, and Christie N. Scollon. 2006. Beyond the Hedonic Treadmill: Revising the Adaptation Theory of Well-Being. *American Psychologist* 61:305–14.

Diener, Ed, and Shigehiro Oishi. 2000. Money and Happiness: Income and Subjective Well-Being across Nations. Pp. 185–218 in *Culture and Subjective Well-Being*, edited by Diener Ed and Eunkook M. Suh. Cambridge, Mass.: MIT Press.

Diener, Ed, Ed Sandvik, Larry Seidlitz, and Marissa Diener. 1993. The Relationship between Income and Subjective Well-Being: Relative or Absolute? *Social Indicators Research* 28:195–223.

Diener, Ed, Eunkook M. Suh, Richard E. Lucas, and Heidi L. Smith. 1999. Subjective Well-Being: Three Decades of Progress. *Psychological Bulletin* 125: 276–302.

Di Tella, Rafael, Robert J. MacCulloch, and Andrew Oswald. 2003. Macroeconomics of Happiness. *Review of Economics and Statistics* 85:809–27.

Easterlin, R. A. 1974. Does Economic Growth Improve the Human Lot? Some Empirical Evidence. Pp. 89–125 in *Nations and Households in Economic Growth: Essays in Honour of Moses Abramovitz*, edited by Paul A. David and Melvin W. Reder. New York: Academic Press.

————. 1995. Will Raising the Incomes of All Increase the Happiness of All? *Journal of Economic Behavior and Organization* 27:35–47.

Festinger, Leon. 1954. A Theory of Social Comparison Processes. *Human Relations* 7:17–140.

Frank, Robert H. 2000. *Luxury Fever: Money and Happiness in an Era of Excess.* Princeton, N.J.: Princeton University Press.

Frederick, Shane, and George Loewenstein. 1999. Hedonic Adaptation. Pp. 302–29 in *Well-Being: The Foundations of Hedonic Psychology*, edited by Daniel Kahneman, Ed Diener, and Norbert Schwarz. New York: Russell Sage Foundation.

Frey, Bruno S., and Alois Stutzer. 2002. *Happiness and Economics: How the Economy and Institutions Affect Human Well-Being*: Princeton, N.J.: Princeton University Press.

————. 2004. Economic Consequences of Mispredicting Utility. IEW Working Paper No. 218. University of Zurich, Institute for Empirical Research in Economics, Zurich.

Helson, Harry. 1964. Current Trends and Issues in Adaptation-Level Theory. *American Psychologist* 19:26–38.

Hsee, Christopher K., Reid Hastie, and Jingqiu Chen. 2008. Hedonomics: Bridging Decision Research with Happiness Research *Perspectives on Psychological Science* 3:224–43.

Hsee, Christopher K., Yang Yang, Naihe Li, and Luxi Shen. Forthcoming. Wealth, Warmth and Well-Being: Whether Happiness Is Relative or Absolute Depends on Whether It Is about Money, Acquisition or Consumption. *Journal of Marketing Research.*

Kahneman, Daniel. 1994. New Challenges to the Rationality Assumption. *Journal of Institutional and Theoretical Economics* 150:18–36.

————. 2008. The Sad Tale of the Aspiration Treadmill—the Edge Annual Question. http://www.edge.org/q2008/q08_17.html#kahneman.

Kahneman, Daniel, Ed Diener, and Norbert Schwarz, eds. 1999. *Well-Being: The Foundations of Hedonic Psychology.* New York: Russell Sage Foundation.

Kahneman, Daniel, Alan B. Krueger, David A. Schkade, Norbert Schwarz, and Arthur A. Stone. 2004. A Survey Method for Characterizing Daily Life Experience: The Day Reconstruction Method. *Science* 306:1776–80.

Kahneman, Daniel, and Richard H. Thaler. 1991. Economic Analysis and the Psychology of Utility: Applications to Compensation Policy. *American Economic Review* 81:341–46.

Kahneman, Daniel, Peter. P. Wakker, and Rakesh Sarin. 1997. Back to Bentham? Explorations of Experienced Utility. *Quarterly Journal of Economics* 112: 375–405.

Kurtz, Jaime L., Timothy D. Wilson, and Daniel T. Gilbert. 2007. Quantity versus Uncertainty: When Winning One Prize Is Better Than Winning Two. *Journal of Experimental Social Psychology* 43:979–85.

Layard, Richard. 2005. *Happiness: Lessons from a New Science*. New York: Penguin.

Leigh, Andrew, and Justin Wolfers. 2006. Happiness and the Human Development Index: Australia Is Not a Paradox. *Australian Economic Review* 39: 176–84.

Loewenstein, George F. 2008. That Which Makes Life Worthwhile. Commentary on National Time Accounting: The Currency of Life, by Alan B. Krueger, Daniel Kahneman, David Schkade, Norbert Schwarz and Arthur A. Stone. Working paper. Carnegie-Mellon University, Department of Social and Decision Sciences, Pittsburgh.

Lucas, Richard E., and Andrew E. Clark. 2006. Do People Really Adapt to Marriage? *Journal of Happiness Studies* 7:405–26.

Luttmer, Erzo F. P. 2005. Neighbors as Negatives: Relative Earnings and Well-Being. *Quarterly Journal of Economics* 120:963–1002.

Lyubomirsky, Sonia. 2007. *The How of Happiness: A Scientific Approach to Getting the Life You Want*. New York: Penguin Press.

McBride, Michael. 2001. Relative-Income Effects on Subjective Well-Being in the Cross-Section. *Journal of Economic Behavior and Organization* 45: 251–78.

Oswald, Andrew J. 1997. Happiness and Economic Performance. *Economic Journal* 107:1815–31.

Oswald, Andrew J., and Nattavudh Powdthavee. 2008. Death, Happiness, and the Calculation of Compensatory Damages. *Journal of Legal Studies* 37: S217–S251.

Parducci, Allen. 1995. *Happiness, Pleasure, and Judgment: The Contextual Theory and Its Applications*. Mahwah, N.J.: Lawrence Erlbaum Associates.

Scitovsky, Tibor. 1976. *The Joyless Economy: An Inquiry into Human Satisfaction and Consumer Dissatisfaction*. New York: Oxford University Press.

Seligman, Martin. 2002. *Authentic Happiness: Using the New Positive Psychology to Realize Your Potential for Lasting Fulfillment*: New York: Free Press.

Smith, Dylan M., George Loewenstein, Aleksandra Jankovich, and Peter Ubel. 2008. The Dark Side of Hope: Lack of Adaptation to Temporary versus Permanent Colostomy. Working paper. Carnegie-Mellon University, Department of Social and Decision Sciences, Pittsburgh.

Solnick, Sara J., and David Hemenway. 2005. Are Positional Concerns Stronger in Some Domains Than in Others? *American Economic Review* 95:147–51.

Stevenson, Betsey, and Justin Wolfers. 2008. Economic Growth and Subjective Well-Being: Reassessing the Easterlin Paradox. Working paper. University of Pennsylvania, Wharton School, Philadelphia.

Stutzer, Alois, and Bruno S. Frey. 2004. Stress That Doesn't Pay: The Commuting Paradox. Working Paper No. 151. University of Zurich, Institute for Empirical Research in Economics, Zurich.

Tian, Guoqiang, and Liyan Yang. 2007. A Formal Economic Theory for Happiness Studies: A Solution to the Happiness-Income Puzzle. Texas A&M University, Department of Economics, College Station.

Ubel, Peter A., George Loewenstein, and Christopher Jepson. 2005. Disability and Sunshine: Can Hedonic Predictions Be Improved by Drawing Attention to Focusing Illusions or Emotional Adaptation? *Journal of Experimental Psychology: Applied* 11:111–23.

van Boven, Leaf Van, and Thomas Gilovich. 2003. To Do or to Have? That Is the Question. *Journal of Personality and Social Psychology* 85:1193–1202.

Veenhoven, Ruut. 1991. Is Happiness Relative? *Social Indicators Research* 24: 1–34.

Wilson, Timothy D., and Gilbert, Daniel T. 2005. Affective Forecasting: Knowing What to Want. *Current Directions in Psychological Science* 14:131–34.

Hive Psychology, Happiness, and Public Policy

Jonathan Haidt, J. Patrick Seder, and Selin Kesebir

ABSTRACT

We consider three hypotheses about relatedness and well-being including the hive hypothesis, which says people need to lose themselves occasionally by becoming part of an emergent social organism in order to reach the highest levels of human flourishing. We discuss recent evolutionary thinking about multilevel selection, which offers a distal reason why the hive hypothesis might be true. We next consider psychological phenomena such as the joy of synchronized movement and the ecstatic joy of self-loss, which might be proximal mechanisms underlying the extraordinary pleasures people get from hive-type activities. We suggest that if the hive hypothesis turns out to be true, it has implications for public policy. We suggest that the hive hypothesis points to new ways to increase social capital and encourages a new focus on happy groups as being more than collections of happy individuals.

Question: What is the difference between society and the sun? Answer: If you really want to, you can stare directly at the sun. But to see society, you must use special glasses. Social scientists generally use one of two kinds: glasses that reveal atoms (individuals) and glasses that reveal networks (groups of connected individuals). Psychologists and some economists seem to prefer looking at individuals. We model people as agents who have beliefs and desires and who act to maximize the satisfaction of their desires given their beliefs. We revel in demonstrations that people sometimes do not maximize, and we advance our sciences by bringing in unconscious desires, discounting curves, and errors in the reasoning processes by which people make inferences from their beliefs.

When we put on the atomizing glasses, a research agenda and a humanitarian project appear before us: we must fully understand the

JONATHAN HAIDT is Associate Professor and J. PATRICK SEDER and SELIN KESEBIR are graduate students in the Department of Psychology, University of Virginia.

[*Journal of Legal Studies*, vol. XXXVII (June 2008)]

workings of the human mind in order to engineer environments (through legislation, education, and other policy levers) that will maximize the happiness of individuals and that will protect people from the occasional traps of a free society in which people sometimes choose badly. We ask questions such as, How should we compensate people to maximize their satisfaction after a loss, knowing as we do that people adapt quickly to most losses? And how can we encourage people to make choices that will benefit themselves most in the long run, knowing as we do that people tend to overweigh present utility and to take no action when faced with too many choices or a lack of social consensus?

Many sociologists, anthropologists and economists, however, prefer the "network" glasses, which help them see groups as organic entities. Groups are composed of individuals, but you cannot study those individuals in isolation. You look at the emergent properties of the group; you identify the links between individuals; you show how a culture is rooted in events of the past and how it is shaped by its economic, environmental, and intergroup context. When looking through these glasses, the complexity of society and the interdependence of its parts are so apparent that many viewers develop contempt for the reductionism often practiced by psychologists. When looking through these glasses, social engineering often seems foolish. Societies are chaotic systems. Parameters can be changed, but efforts to intervene directly, particularly by changing individuals through therapy or education, seem naïve.

Of course, both pairs of glasses are essential for the social sciences, and many of the best practitioners use both. However, empirical research on happiness and well-being to date has been conducted overwhelmingly by psychologists, now joined by some economists, who rely upon the atomizing glasses. In this paper we will put on the group-vision glasses and try to report on a few phenomena that might be relevant to discussions of law, public policy, and happiness. In particular, we will make the case that human beings evolved by a process of multilevel selection, including group-level selection, and that it is useful to see people as being (in a metaphorical sense) hive creatures like bees. Human lives do not make sense without some discussion of human hives. If we want to increase human happiness, we must go beyond simple conceptions of sociality (in which people need and are affected by relationships) and examine humanity's communal, tribal, and religious needs as well.

1. THREE HYPOTHESES ABOUT RELATEDNESS

You do not need special glasses to know that relatedness is important for well-being. Many surveys confirm that social support, in the form of friendships and marriage, is one of the biggest environmental contributors to well-being (Myers 2000). We shall call this claim the dyadic hypothesis, which states that people need relationships to flourish. The hypothesis is about dyads: one individual tied to another. It does not claim that people need groups to flourish, only that they need friends, lovers, and other individuals who are responsive to their needs. We consider this to be among the best-supported hypotheses in the scientific study of well-being, and we will say no more about it (see Baumeister and Leary [1995] for a review).

A stronger and more controversial hypothesis is the moral community hypothesis, which states that people need to be bound into a community that shares norms and values in order to flourish. This hypothesis was stated forcefully by Emile Durkheim, whose pioneering study of suicide concluded that the suicide rate in European countries "varies inversely with the degree of integration of the social groups of which the individual forms a part" (Durkheim [1897] 1951, p. 208). Factors that increased social integration (having a large family, being Catholic or Jewish rather than Protestant, being in a nation at war) decreased suicide rates; factors that increased self-sufficiency (for example, wealth and education) were associated with higher rates of suicide. Durkheim believed that marriage protects against suicide not because of the dyadic conjugal bond but because it creates a domestic society.

Durkheim gave us the concept of anomie, or normlessness, the condition of a society in which there is no clear and agreed-upon set of rules for behavior, and people are freed—or forced—to follow their own desires. Complete freedom to pursue one's preferences may seem self-evidently good to many economists, but for Durkheim it is a recipe for misery and social decay. Durkheim thought that when people are left to their own devices, they can never satisfy their limitless acquisitiveness. Only by being a member of a group that imposes limits and sets standards for good behavior can people achieve their desires and find satisfaction.

Durkheim's early findings about suicide rates appear to hold true today (Eckersley and Dear 2002), and a modern Durkheimian can easily explain why well-being has remained flat and depression rates have risen as Western nations have doubled or tripled their wealth per capita in recent decades (Diener and Seligman 2004; Twenge 2000). The moral community hypothesis also helps explain why regular participation in religious worship is a strong predictor of well-being and of charitable giving (Brooks 2006; Diener and Clifton 2002; Diener et al. 1999; Myers 2000). Religion (in general) makes people depend less upon themselves and more upon God and each other. It makes them less atomic and more networked or hivish. We believe that the moral community hypothesis is probably true, although it requires more caveats than does the dyadic hypothesis. For example: when groups become too binding, suicide rates go up, driven in part by the shame of those who do not live up to the group's standards. (Durkheim called this kind of suicide "altruistic suicide.") Furthermore, there are probably individual differences in personality, which Durkheim did not consider, that moderate the benefits people derive from being bound tightly into a group. People who score high on the trait of openness to experience, for example, are likely to chafe more at restraint and to enjoy the anomie, variety, and creativity of life in big cities (McCrae 1996).

An even stronger relatedness hypothesis is the hive hypothesis, which says that the self can be an obstacle to happiness, so people need to lose their selves occasionally by becoming part of an emergent social organism in order to reach the highest levels of human flourishing. This hypothesis is essentially the moral community hypothesis with the additional claim that the most effective moral communities (from a well-being perspective) are those that offer occasional experiences in which self-consciousness is greatly reduced and one feels merged with or part of something greater than the self. We acknowledge that this hypothesis is speculative. There is research on the "curse of the self" (Leary 2004), but we know of no research that directly compares groups that vary on the degree of self-loss they afford. We are inspired, however, by two recent books that review the historical and anthropological evidence on dance, drill, and the joys of synchronized movement and conclude that the loss of self in group ritual is generally beneficial (Ehrenreich 2006; McNeill 1995). In the rest of this paper we will suggest that the hive hypothesis is plausible enough to merit serious scientific scrutiny. We further suggest that if it is true, it has important implications for legal and policy interventions aimed at increasing happiness.

2. MULTILEVEL SELECTION AND HAPPINESS

Economists care about preference satisfaction, but where do these preferences come from? Evolutionary psychology offers what is arguably the most comprehensive explanation: we want things that helped our ancestors succeed at leaving surviving offspring in the environments in which the human mind was shaped by natural selection (Barkow, Cosmides, and Tooby 1992). Our love of sweet and fatty foods, even when we know that we now eat too much of them; the desire for prestige and our concern for the opinions of others, even when we wish not to care; the desperate passion to protect our own children and the rapidly declining concern we show for more distantly related children—all of these human preferences flow readily from an analysis of the preferences that led early hunter-gatherers to succeed as individuals. David Buss (2000) has even offered a catalog of evolutionarily informed methods for increasing human happiness in the modern environments we now inhabit. But nearly all analyses of happiness from evolutionary psychology, such as those from economics, focus on individuals and their preferences. Might there be group-level preferences too? Might individuals be happiest when their groups are doing things that led, over eons of evolution, to group success?

Evolution works at multiple levels simultaneously. Genes jockey with other genes during meiosis to get on to the very few trains (eggs and sperm) that will make it into the next generation. Individuals compete with other individuals for the resources and mates that will enable them to leave more and better-provisioned offspring. And groups compete with other groups for land, hunting rights, or larger shares of the pie generated by cooperation in large-scale societies. Darwin ([1871] 1998, p. 166) believed that morality evolved in part by natural selection working at the group level: "A tribe including many members who, from possessing in a high degree the spirit of patriotism, fidelity, obedience, courage, and sympathy, were always ready to aid one another, and to sacrifice themselves for the common good would be victorious over most other tribes; and this would be natural selection."

For the next hundred years, many writers on evolution followed Darwin's lead and assumed that cooperative traits in humans and other animals evolved for the good of the group, or even the good of the species. But in 1966 George Williams demolished such arguments by analyzing many cases of adaptations that had been claimed to be adaptations at the group level, such as restraints on fertility and consumption when food supplies are limited. He argued that in all cases these behaviors can be better explained by the natural selection of alternative alleles (gene variants) as individuals competed with other individuals. Donning the atomizing glasses, he concluded that a fleet herd of deer is really just a herd of fleet deer; nothing is gained by talking about groups because the fitness of a group is just the "summation of the adaptations of its members" (Williams 1966, p. 17). The free-rider problem appeared to be insoluble: any gene that created self-sacrificing altruists would be replaced in the population by genes that created individuals who benefited from the acts of altruists without incurring costs themselves. In 1976 Richard Dawkins's book *The Selfish Gene* brought Williams's ideas to the masses, including the masses of young researchers being trained in biology and the human sciences, and group selection was declared not only dead but an outright heresy for the next generation (Dawkins 1976).

But Williams looked in the wrong places. He examined behaviors in dozens of species that are not adept at solving the free-rider problem. Solutions to free riding are indeed rare in nature, but when they happen, the results can be profound. In fact, they are called "major evolutionary transitions" (Maynard Smith and Szathmary 1997), and there is good reason to believe that one or more such transitions occurred for humans, who are very good at solving free-rider problems.

Several such transitions are now widely accepted: replicating molecules joined together to form chromosomes, prokaryotes merged together to form eukaryotic cells, single-cell eukaryotes stayed together after division to form multicellular organisms, and some multicellular organisms stayed together after birth to form hives, colonies, and societies (Maynard Smith and Szathmary 1997). In each of these cases, cooperation by entities at one level led to enormous gains for the emergent group, largely through division of labor. These gains are so vast that the superorganisms produced by group-level selection tend to spread rapidly, transforming ecosystems by taking the richest environmental niches and relegating closely related species to the margins (as the close relatives of bees, ants, and humans can attest). Group-level analyses are no longer heretical; in a sense, all life forms are now understood to be groups, or even groups of groups (for state-of-the-art reviews, see Wilson, Van Vugt, and O'Gorman 2008; Wilson and Wilson 2007).[1]

---

1. Some biologists claim that group selection is still controversial (for example, Dawkins 2006), but these authors are for the most part still relying on Williams's analysis from

To identify a major transition, one must find the mechanisms that suppressed free riding at the lower level and allowed individual units to cohere into a superorganism. For bees and ants, the mechanisms involve the suppression of breeding by individuals and the concentration of breeding in a queen. For humans, those mechanisms are generally thought to involve cultural and biological adaptations such as religion and religiously inclined minds (Wilson 2002) or practices of shaming, gossip, and other low-cost control techniques that coevolved with minds prone to shame and reputational concerns (Richerson and Boyd 2005). Both McNeill (1995) and Ehrenreich (2006) suggest that one cooperation-enhancing biological mechanism that has been exploited by most cultures, often as part of religious practice, is synchronous movement.

An important fact about major transitions is that they are never complete. The advantages of free riding by lower-level units are always present (for example, intragenomic conflict, worker bees that lay their own eggs, and warriors who hold back and let others take the risks), and so groups at each level (genomes, individuals, hives) exist in a continual state of tension and can survive only as long as they have mechanisms that continually suppress selfishness by lower-level units. In this paper we follow those who suggest that social and religious practices that increase "hiving" are such mechanisms (Wilson 2002). We suggest that putting on the group-vision glasses can help social scientists to see the interlocking biological, psychological, and cultural innovations that enable large human groups to stay together and act in a coordinated fashion.

In the next section we discuss a few of these interlocking innovations, particularly rhythm, synchronous movement, and festivals. Consistent with the hive hypothesis, we suggest that some of the most intense and long-lasting forms of happiness come about when people do the sorts of things and experience the sorts of feelings that helped their ancestors' groups be successful.

3. MOVEMENT AND JOY

One of the first things you see through the group-vision glasses is the extraordinary measures many groups take to create and maintain their cohesiveness. Ecstatic group rituals, for example, were a regular and

---

1966 and have not addressed newer theories in which cultural and genetic traits coevolve. See Borello (2005) for a review of the history of the debate.

nearly universal practice among tribal societies at the time of European contact (Ehrenreich 2006). These celebrations were usually held to mark life transitions (that is, births, deaths, weddings, successes) or historical or astronomical events that were practically or symbolically relevant to the group. They typically involved feasts, special costumes, masks, drumming, chanting, and dancing to the point of exhaustion. A common feature of these rituals was that some or all members of the group transcended ordinary consciousness, often achieving a trance state. A related goal was for all members of the group to merge with the group. "As the dancer loses himself in the dance," wrote the anthropologist Radcliffe-Brown ([1922] 1964, pp. 251–52), "he reaches a state of elation in which he feels himself filled with an energy beyond his ordinary state . . . at the same time finding himself in complete and ecstatic harmony with all of the fellow members of his community."

Durkheim ([1915] 1965) coined the term "collective effervescence" to describe ecstatic group rituals and their effects. He considered the intense passion and joy generated by these periodic events to be essential to the long-term maintenance of a cohesive group. The anthropologist Victor Turner ([1969] 1995) proposed the Latin word *communitas* to describe the inspiration and revitalization experienced by those who participate in ecstatic group rituals. Turner believed that all societies went through an eternal oscillation between structure, in which the hierarchical relationships among roles and positions is affirmed, and *communitas*, in which structure is temporarily abolished and the relationships among people are affirmed.

Durkheim and Turner can help us understand many of the most joyful human celebrations. Whether we look at initiation rites in New Guinea, carnivals in medieval Europe, or Halloween in San Francisco, we find many common elements, including costuming, dancing, the mocking of authority, and the gleeful switching of roles (for example, dressing as though one were of another sex, caste, or class). Boundaries are dissolved, equality rules, and people celebrate with those of all ranks and social positions. Turner believed that these temporally limited periods of antistructure are not just safety valves for the oppressed to vent resentment; rather, they bond and humanize all members of the group, making the structures they later return to more humane and stable. Turner thought there was a necessary dialectic between structure and *communitas*: "[T]he immediacy of communitas gives way to the mediacy of structure, while . . . men are released from structure into communitas only to return to structure revitalized by their experiences of communitas. What is certain is that no society can function adequately without this dialectic" (p. 129). It should be noted, however, that because *communitas* is both subversive and regenerative, people in positions of power sometimes feel threatened by it and resist it. Turner saw the hippie movement of his own time, and the violent reaction against it, in this light.

Although a variety of "techniques of ecstasy" (Eliade 1964) appear across cultures, McNeill (1995) and Ehrenreich (2006) maintain that rhythmic drumming and moving together in time are the most widespread and perhaps powerful methods used in pursuit of *communitas*. Both authors speculate that these cultural innovations played a role in human evolution. These techniques have been around long enough (millennia, and perhaps tens of millennia), and they have such powerful effects on individuals, that it would be hard to imagine that there were no adaptive consequences, no reduction in the Darwinian success of individuals who were unwilling or unable to participate. The human love of rhythm, dance, parades, cheerleading, yoga classes, and other kinds of moving together in time may be like our love of sweets, prestige, and our own children: they are pleasures for us now (in part) because ancient people who had a heritable tendency to enjoy synchronized movement were more likely to participate in such activities, reap the benefits of closer social ties, and leave more surviving offspring than those who did not.

The recent discovery of mirror neurons, which are much more extensive in human brains than in those of other primates, may be relevant here. Mirror neurons are an unusual class of neurons that fire either when a person performs an action or when the person simply sees another person performing the action (Iacoboni et al. 1999). In other words, when the person next to us moves in a particular way, motor systems in our brains begin reacting as though we were moving that way, making it easier for us to match the motor patterns of others. The phrase "monkey see, monkey do" is a mischaracterization of monkeys, who do not imitate, but it is apt for humans (Tomasello, Kruger, and Rater 1993). The great expansion of mirror neurons in human brains probably predates cultural practices of synchronization, so this expansion may be seen as a preadaptation (Mayr 1960)—a feature that arose under one selection pressure (such as improved learning through imitation) but was then available as a substrate for newer traits (such as group synchronous movement) that were shaped by other selection pressures.

If synchronous collective activities provide such potent and pleasurable ways to foster group connections and commitments, and if such activities were practiced in nearly every culture, why do we make so little use of them in the modern West? Ehrenreich (2006) shows that early European explorers generally reacted with disgust to the wild abandon of ecstatic group rituals, which they often misperceived as sexual or orgiastic in nature. These rituals were seen to be pointless, animalistic, and antithetical to the Western ideal of autonomous, rational selves that had emerged in Europe during the early modern period. McNeill (1995) and Ehrenreich (2006) also review research showing that early and medieval Christian worship included collective dancing within churches, but such dancing and other forms of exuberance were gradually pushed out of churches and into public squares beginning in the thirteenth century as the church became more hierarchical and dogmatic. These celebrations mutated into profane festivals and carnivals. As cities and festivals grew in subsequent centuries, public festivities became more characterized by drunkenness and criminal activity, making it ever easier for church and secular authorities to justify limiting them or shutting them down. The Reformation (especially Calvinism, which outlawed dancing and many other sources of pleasure) and the industrial revolution both encouraged virtues and social structures that were antithetical to such ecstatic practices and collective, egalitarian celebrations.

In spite of attempts to suppress them, vestiges of these ancient practices remain. Carnival celebrations in Catholic countries are direct descendants of these practices. Some African-American forms of worship may be direct descendants too, a kind of pipeline bringing ancient African practices into modern Christianity, particularly charismatic forms such as Pentecostalism (Ehrenreich 2006). Other practices are new inventions, suggesting that people, even Westerners, will find ways to satisfy their need for *communitas*. Ehrenreich argues that audiences at musical and sporting events are now more physically active and synchronized than they were 50 years ago when police enforced "no dancing" rules at concert halls. The scene inside and outside of many sport and musical events now often has a variety of carnivalesque elements, including face painting and body decoration. And "ravers" in the 1990s created their own version of ecstatic communal ritual when they found a drug (not coincidentally nicknamed Ecstasy) that increases feelings of love, even toward strangers, and combined it with new forms of music that were beat heavy and repetitive, to which they danced to exhaustion. "There is no question," writes sociologist Tim Olavson, "that they

[Durkheim and Turner] would not be surprised to witness the rave phenomenon were they alive today; nor would they wonder, as so many politicians, anxious parents, and even social scientists currently do, why the rave experience so strongly attracts contemporary youth" (Olavson 2004, p. 96). The motivation to seek periodic experiences of intense joy and connection through synchronous movement with others may be a fundamental human need that modern Western societies fail to acknowledge and satisfy.

4. HIVES AND EMERGENT ORGANISMS

The idea of society as an organism is a recurring theme in the history of social thought. Herbert Spencer ([1896] 1975) popularized the term "super-organism" to refer to human societies. Drawing a direct analogy between societies and biological organisms, he wrote about the sustaining, distributing, and regulating systems of a society. Like Spencer, many of the early psychologists, including Wundt (1911), Le Bon ([1896] 1920), McDougall (1920), and Freud (1922), thought of groups as something more than just collections of individuals. With regard to the emergence of group behavior Le Bon ([1896] 1920, p. 30) wrote, "The psychological crowd is a provisional being formed of heterogeneous elements, which for a moment are combined, exactly as the cells which constitute a living body form by their reunion a new being which displays characteristics very different from those possessed by each of the cells singly."

These early psychologists were interested in the psychology of people in groups, which they envisioned as something emergent, something that came into being only when individuals were in the right spatial and psychological configuration. Yet group psychology did not fare well in the coming decades, partly because of overstatements by some proponents that bordered on the metaphysical. Floyd Allport (1924, p. 4) wrote, "There is no psychology of groups which is not essentially and entirely a psychology of individuals. Social psychology must not be placed in contradistinction to the psychology of the individual; it is a part of the psychology of the individual, whose behavior it studies in relation to that sector of his environment comprised by his fellows."

Much like the idea of group selection, the idea of a group mind was declared scientifically dead and placed off-limits. The scientific study of groups (without group minds) continued in psychology, but it never achieved the importance that the early psychologists had envisioned (see Forsyth and Burnette [2005] for a review).

This rejection of the group-vision glasses marked the beginning of the nearly exclusive focus on the individual that was to be the hallmark of social psychology for the rest of the twentieth century. Don Campbell (1994, p. 23) wrote, "Methodological individualism dominates our neighboring fields of economics, much of sociology, and all of psychology's excursions into organizational theory. This is the dogma that all human social group processes are to be explained by laws of individual behavior." This unfortunate turn in the history of psychology leaves us now ill equipped to understand and respond to many mass phenomena.

The commitment to individualism may be one reason why the joy and happiness that flows from merging with a group is rarely mentioned in psychology. As Ehrenreich (2006) points out, if homosexual love is "the love that dare not speak its name," group love is the love that has no name at all, except for obscure terms such as *communitas*. Yet many of us have felt it at some point in our lives, perhaps while playing a team sport, singing in a choir, marching and chanting at a protest rally, or working closely with friends to achieve a noble goal. We lose ourselves, forget our petty concerns, and feel suffused with energy and purpose. Such memories often stand out as peak moments of happiness when people reflect on their lives, so even if such experiences are rare, these peaks may be important for the study of well-being (Kahneman 1999).

A further reason to study such experiences is that if they really do increase group cohesiveness, then they may increase well-being indirectly as well as directly. For example, strong social ties and mutual trust within a community, referred to as "social capital" (Coleman 1988), has many salutary societal effects. Social capital contributes to economic growth, positive health outcomes, greater subjective well-being, and lower crime and mortality rates (Folland 2007; Helliwell 2003; Putnam 2000). Similarly, people often derive satisfaction from their collective identities. Researchers have consistently found that being part of a group with which one strongly identifies is associated with greater well-being. A positive relationship has been found between group identification and indicators of mental well-being for people who are deaf (Bat-Chava 1994), people who attend group therapy (Marmarosh and Corazzini 1997), religious people (Diener and Clifton 2002), members of ethnic minorities (Branscombe, Schmitt, and Harvey 1999; Goodstein and Ponterotto 1997; Munford 1994), and members of stigmatized groups

(Crocker and Major 1989). Participation on sports teams as a leisure activity and identification with a sports team have also been found to predict well-being (Wann 2006). These findings strongly suggest that people derive satisfaction from the sense of being a part of something larger than themselves. As for whether these groups are more effective at increasing well-being when they are as cohesive as hives, we cannot yet say. But there are good reasons to think that the periodic loss of self, in the company of others with whom one shares an identity, would have many beneficial effects.

5. THE BENEFITS OF TRANSCENDING THE SELF

Ehrenreich (2006) traces the Western loss of openness to collective joy to the profound changes in selfhood that began to occur in early modern Europe. It was during this period that people came to believe "that the essence of the Western mind, and particularly the Western male, upper-class mind, was its ability to resist the contagious rhythm of the drums; to wall itself up in a fortress of ego and rationality against the seductive wildness of the world" (p. 9) (on the related contrast between independent and interdependent construals of the self, which is the foundation of modern cultural psychology, see Markus and Kitayama 1991). This adaptation was highly functional in the new capitalist economy, but it came with certain costs. One of the largest may have been an increased tendency for people to experience depression and anxiety. Clinical depression is not a modern invention; clear cases can be found in letters, poems, and other texts from the ancient world. But the prevalence of depression may have increased in Europe in the sixteenth and seventeenth centuries; many commentators from that era, but not earlier ones, described epidemics of "melancholy" sweeping the continent (Ehrenreich 2006, chap. 7). Now that we have better records, we can say with more confidence that rates of depression in Western nations rose during the twentieth century (Diener and Seligman 2004; Twenge 2000), even as those nations grew vastly richer. Wealth is weakly correlated with happiness (Diener and Biswas-Diener 2002), but isolation and separation, which are characteristic of modern ways of living, are strongly correlated with depression (on the dyadic relatedness hypothesis, see Baumeister and Leary 1995).

The social psychologist Mark Leary supports Ehrenreich's analysis in his book *The Curse of the Self* (Leary 2004). Leary maintains that our goal-focused, judgmental, worry-prone, internally chattering self is a modern creation that often sabotages our well-being and renders us blind to our greater potentials. Indeed, he proposes that one of the most important things we can do to improve our well-being is to learn techniques for quieting the self. "Had the human self been installed with a mute button or off switch," Leary (2004, p. 46) writes, "the self would not be the curse to happiness that it often is."

People attempt to switch off the self in a variety of ways, which may be placed on a continuum from short-term distractions to those that produce sustained and sometimes life-changing effects. On the short-term end of the spectrum we find some techniques that are generally beneficial, such as transportation into narrative worlds via television, books, movies, or video games (see, for example, Green, Brock, and Kaufman 2004). But we also find activities that entice people into making myopic trade-offs: a brief period of escape from the self is paid for, with interest, later on. For example, millions of people abuse alcohol, drugs, and food (for example, binge eating) as methods of escape from the self (Baumeister 1991). The guilt and anxiety they feel afterward only increases their motivation to escape the self again, often through the same means.

At the other end of the continuum are behaviors and experiences that can potentially bring about sustained transcendence or modification of the self. Included here are skills of mental and bodily control such as meditation and yoga. Also included here are the fruits of some educational practices, such as some Christian educational methods in which children and young adults are taught to be more like Jesus and less like their materialistic, self-absorbed, secular peers. As explained in the opening line of the Christian bestseller *The Purpose Driven Life*, "It's not all about you" (Warren 2002). Given that highly religious people are happier than secular people (Myers 2000), it is worth asking if the benefits of religion derive not just from participation in religious communities but from the successful alteration of the self.

And finally, many people experience a "quantum change" (Miller and C'de Baca 2001) after a "peak experience" (Maslow [1964] 1964) or a moment of intense awe (Keltner and Haidt 2003). Whether induced by rhythmic movement, hallucinogenic drugs, or in many cases by no known trigger, many people have experienced a profound psychological state involving a loss of concern about the self, transcendence of dichotomies, and overwhelming positivity including feelings that the world is good and desirable. These experiences have much in common with the religious conversion experiences described by William James ([1902] 1961) in *The Varieties of Religious Experience*. James reviewed hundreds of first-hand accounts from Christian and Islamic sources and identified what he called the "state of assurance," characterized by overwhelmingly positive feelings including "the loss of all the worry, the sense that all is ultimately well with one, the peace, the harmony, the willingness to be, even though the outer conditions should remain the same" (p. 248). Such turning points, epiphanies, and conversions are often reported to enrich lives for many years afterward. The long duration of the benefits of these experiences, in comparison to the rapid adaptation that people usually make to pleasures and successes (Frederick and Loewenstein 1999), should make such phenomena of great interest to social scientists interested in well-being.

6. POLICY IMPLICATIONS

We have argued (along with all other evolutionists) that human minds were shaped by natural selection to enjoy doing things that increased our ancestors' Darwinian fitness. We have further argued (along with some but not all other evolutionists) that natural selection works at multiple levels, including the group level, and that it shaped human minds to enjoy doing things that increased the success of our ancestors' groups. Selfishness, greed, and competition within groups can never be eliminated, but groups vary in the degree to which they succeed in suppressing selfishness and creating esprit de corps. Under some circumstances, human groups can be quite successful in suppressing selfishness and eliciting a willingness to sacrifice, and even to die, for the good of the group.

If group selection played a role in shaping our minds and pleasures, then it can be expected to have led to a shift in the nature of cooperation and conflict. As with bees and ants, group selection reduces conflict within groups, but it generally increases conflict across groups. And as technological innovations enabled human groups to better kill their opponents and oppress their own ranks, the dark side of this trade-off has gotten ever darker. Hive psychology can be dangerous. The images of Fascist spectacles at Nuremberg and Rome, with acres of uniformed men moving in lockstep, still haunt us. Many social scientists now have a visceral disgust at any hivelike social formation and will likely recoil from our suggestion that anything good can come from exploring these ancient capacities of the human mind.

We see two crucial distinctions, however, between traditional hiving and fascism. First, we must distinguish between small and large hives. If hiving comes naturally to us, then it is hiving or bonding with dozens or hundreds of other people, not with tens of thousands. The cost/benefit ratio of having many small hives within one's nation is probably very positive, leading to increased trust, cooperation, love, and interdependence at a local level.[2] When nations or ethnic groups become hives, however, the calculus is radically different, and the potential for violence, internal repression, and even genocide becomes so great that no set of benefits could outweigh the risks. If fostering thousands of local hives was a likely precursor to national hivishness, then we would not advocate playing with fire. We suspect, however, that just the opposite may be true. An anomic nation in which individuals are hungry for connection and meaning may be ripe for takeover by a nationalistic demagogue, whereas a nation composed of strong communities with high levels of social capital in which people are tightly bound into many crosscutting groups may be less likely to succumb to such seduction.

A second distinction that must be drawn is between festivals and spectacles. Fascist rallies and parades were designed to awe passive onlookers and reinforce hierarchy and subservience. They fostered unity around the godlike figure of the leader. They had little in common with the techniques of ecstasy used by most traditional societies to bond members as equals, and they certainly did not dissolve structure in *communitas,* as Turner had described. It may be that massive social superorganisms forged through spectacle to serve the will of a leader are always dangerous, whereas smaller social organisms that emerge spontaneously from the actions of people who want to love and trust each other are generally safe.

We note a third distinction: a hive is not the same as a mob. Groups that form spontaneously in response to a perceived moral outrage are often dangerous, as individuals become more willing to commit violent actions that they would be unlikely to commit on their own. The psy-

---

2. We acknowledge that some small hivish groups, particularly those composed of adolescent males, can be quite destructive, particularly if they compete for territory as happens with urban street gangs. But when groups are more mixed by age and sex, and when people participate in multiple crosscutting nonnested groups so that they have multiple identities, the dangers of small hives may be minimal compared to their benefits. See Berreby (2005) for an exploration of these trade-offs.

chology of a mob seems to draw on well-studied mechanisms of deindividuation that release people from the moral constraints of ordinary life and make violent and selfish behavior more likely (Diener 1979). Hives of the sort we have been discussing clearly involve a kind of deindividuation as well, but when deindividuation is in the service of communion and celebration, rather than collective social action, the predominant emotion seems to be love, not anger.

We therefore take the view that hivishness is a basic aspect of human nature that can be used for good or for evil. When hives are small, egalitarian, and communally oriented, they are likely to be harmless to others and beneficial to the participants. When hives are large, hierarchical, and united by the goal of taking what the members believe to be morally corrective action, they are likely to pose a grave danger to others. What, then, are the implications of hive psychology for public policy? We offer three.

6.1. Encourage Local Festivals and Dances

If the hive hypothesis is true, then an increase in the availability of music, dance, and street festivals should increase happiness and trust while decreasing alienation and crime. A less obvious prediction is that synchronized or line dancing should be more beneficial than freestyle dances in which each person moves as she pleases.

Any legal or policy changes would have to meet the definition of "libertarian paternalism" (Thaler and Sunstein 2003). Options can be made available and defaults can be set, but people must be able to opt out easily from new policies. A high rate of opting out should be taken as a rejection of a policy. But with that said, it may be possible for urban planners, local governments, and even schools to make it easier for beneficial festivities to arise. Through tax policies and zoning regulations, localities can increase the number of venues for live music and can take other steps to help local musicians. By building an outdoor amphitheater and putting on a free weekly concert featuring the most popular local bands, a town can encourage its citizens to dance together (as happens on Friday evenings in our town of Charlottesville, Virginia). By making it easy for local groups to close off city streets, towns can increase the frequency of residential block parties featuring music and dancing.

Thinking small and trying to catalyze the efforts of local entrepreneurs might pay off handsomely in terms of social capital and well-being. Thinking big and exerting central control may backfire. For example, large citywide and city-sponsored events may easily spiral out of control, leading to violence and increasing distrust. Large civic projects such as museums, opera houses, and monuments may encourage spectacle rather than festival: participants are passive, save for a bit of clapping and walking, and they attend to the object or performer; they do not come away feeling closer to each other.

Synchronous movement may also be effective in corporations and other business settings. In some Japanese companies (and even some small rural towns) there are morning or midday exercises in which all members participate. Members of Japanese police and fire departments similarly exercise, moving together in sync every morning. Organizational researchers have argued that the main function of these exercises is team building and evoking a group orientation (Tayeb 2005). To our knowledge no causal relations between synchronous movement and employee morale has yet been proved, but we predict that experimental studies would show such an effect, particularly if the activities are led by employees and if managers participate in them as equals.

6.2. Think about Happy Groups, Not Just Happy Individuals

Sometimes aiming directly at a goal can cause you to miss it. Some have argued that direct attempts to increase one's own happiness fall into this category (Schooler, Ariely, and Loewenstein 2003). An instructive example can be found in a surprising place: poultry science. Muir (1996) showed that to maximize egg production in a large multihen cage, it was not a good idea to selectively breed the hens that lay the most eggs. Those egg champions were also the most aggressive birds, so when a number of such chickens shared a cage, they spent their time fighting. Cagewide fertility dropped substantially. The better way of maximizing individual productivity, it turned out, was to selectively breed the cages that collectively produced the most eggs. This is in fact a form of artificial group selection. Predictably, it leads to the spread of genes that suppress aggression and competition within groups.

Recent wisdom from organizational science suggests that the same processes may apply to human groups. Robert Sutton (2007) argues that the best organizations are those that strictly enforce the "no asshole rule," which says that if star performers make others feel belittled and demoralized, they should either change their ways or be fired. As with those cages of chickens, rewarding individual performance at the expense of a civilized work environment can be counterproductive. More generally, given the complex interdependencies that characterize each human group, a focus on individual-level variables may lead to unexpected and unwelcome consequences at the group level. Starting at the group level instead may be the wiser strategy.

This strategy may be particularly useful for increasing well-being. Many of the goods that are known to contribute to well-being, such as wealth and high status, are positional goods: relative position matters more than absolute levels, so competitors are trapped in a zero-sum game (Frank 1999). Increasing the average per capita income in a nation over time seems to have no effect on the subjective well-being of its citizens (Diener and Seligman 2004). But participation in hives is not like this. One person's ability to enjoy the ecstatic loss of self is, if anything, increased by the success of those around her. And the trust and cooperation engendered by such practices is a public good. As Robert Putnam (2007) points out, he and his wife get to enjoy the fruits of living in a town with high social capital even though they never participate in the social clubs and civic events that build that capital.

6.3. Reexamine Diversity

There are good moral reasons for celebrating diversity in order to encourage inclusiveness. But there are good empirical reasons for warning that emphasizing differences, rather than commonalities, can be harmful (Haidt, Rosenberg, and Hom 2003). Social psychological research on minimal groups shows that people can easily be divided and turned against each other when socially meaningless differences (such as being an overestimator versus underestimator of the number of dots on a page) are made salient (Tajfel et al. 1971). When socially meaningful differences such as race, religion, and language are emphasized, division and distrust seem inevitable. A recent study by Putnam (2007) confirms that residential diversity does indeed decrease trust and social ties (or bridging capital) among members of different groups. Surprisingly, however, Putnam found that diversity reduced social capital within groups (or bonding capital) as well. Putnam (2007, p. 149) summarizes his findings as follows: "Diversity seems to trigger not in-group/out-group division, but anomie or social isolation. In colloquial language, people living in ethnically diverse settings appear to 'hunker down'—that is, to pull in like a turtle." Turtling is the exact opposite of hiving. We therefore believe that the unquestioning celebration of diversity should give way to more careful scrutiny and to a full cost-benefit analysis. It may be that diverse democracies such as the United States can best accommodate immigration and racial diversity by emphasizing similarities and shared citizenship, as Putnam (2007) suggests. We add a more speculative suggestion:

the turtling effects of diversity may be muted if people from diverse backgrounds can take advantage of the ancient and universal bonding mechanisms we have discussed in this paper.

7. CONCLUSION

When bank robber Willie Sutton was asked why he robbed banks, he is reputed to have replied, "Because that's where the money is." Social scientists seem to have taken Sutton's (mythical) comment a bit too literally. When studying happiness and well-being, we value money as much as Sutton did. We invest a great deal of effort in quantifying relationships between well-being and gains or losses of money. But if we were to step back and identify the sources of people's greatest joys, we would rebalance our research portfolios. We would invest much more in the study of collective pleasures, group love, and experiences of ecstatic self-loss, because that's where the joy is.

REFERENCES

Allport, Floyd. 1924. *Social Psychology*. Boston: Houghton Mifflin.

Barkow, Jerome H., Leda Cosmides, and John Tooby, eds. 1992. *The Adapted Mind: Evolutionary Psychology and the Generation of Culture*. New York: Oxford.

Bat-Chava, Yael. 1994. Group Identification and Self-Esteem of Deaf Adults. *Personality and Social Psychology Bulletin* 20:494–502.

Baumeister, Roy F. 1991. *Escaping the Self*. New York: Basic Books.

Baumeister, Roy F., and Mark R. Leary. 1995. The Need to Belong: Desire for Interpersonal Attachments as a Fundamental Human Motivation. *Psychological Bulletin* 117:497–529.

Berreby, David. 2005. *Us and Them: Understanding Your Tribal Mind*. New York: Little, Brown.

Borello, Mark E. 2005. The Rise, Fall and Resurrection of Group Selection. *Endeavor* 29:43–47.

Branscombe, Nyla R., Michael T. Schmitt, and Richard D. Harvey. 1999. Perceiving Pervasive Discrimination among African-Americans: Implications for Group Identification and Well-Being. *Journal of Personality and Social Psychology* 77:135–49.

Brooks, Arthur C. 2006. *Who Really Cares: The Surprising Truth about Compassionate Conservatism*. New York: Basic Books.

Buss, David M. 2000. The Evolution of Happiness. *American Psychologist* 55: 15–23.

Campbell, Donald T. 1994. How Individual and Face-to-Face Group Selection Undermine Firm Selection in Organizational Evolution. Pp. 23–38 in *Evolutionary Dynamics of Organizations,* edited by Joel A. C. Baum and Jitendra V. Singh. New York: Oxford.

Coleman, James S. 1988. Social Capital in the Creation of Human Capital. *American Journal of Sociology* 94:S95–S120.

Crocker, Jennifer, and Brenda Major. 1989. Social Stigma and Self-Esteem: The Self-Protective Properties of Stigma. *Psychological Review* 26:608–30.

Darwin, Charles. [1871] 1998. *The Descent of Man and Selection in Relation to Sex.* Amherst, N.Y.: Prometheus Books.

Dawkins, Richard. 1976. *The Selfish Gene.* London: Oxford University Press.

———. 2006. *The Good Delusion.* Boston: Houghton Mifflin.

Diener, Ed. 1979. Deindividuation, Self-Awareness, and Disinhibition. *Journal of Personality and Social Psychology* 37:1160–71.

Diener, Ed, and Robert Biswas-Diener. 2002. Will Money Increase Subjective Well-Being? A Literature Review and Guide to Needed Research. *Social Indicators Research* 57:119–69.

Diener, Ed, and Donald Clifton. 2002. Life Satisfaction and Religiosity in Broad Probability Samples. *Psychological Inquiry* 13:206–9.

Diener, Ed, and Martin E. P. Seligman. 2004. Beyond Money: Toward an Economy of Well-Being. *Psychological Science in the Public Interest* 5:1–31.

Diener, Ed, Eunkook M. Suh, Richard E. Lucas, and Heidi L. Smith. 1999. Subjective Well-Being: Three Decades of Progress. *Psychological Bulletin* 125: 276–302.

Durkheim, Emile. [1897] 1951. *Suicide.* Translated by John A. Spalding and George Simpson. New York: Free Press.

———. [1915] 1965. *The Elementary Forms of the Religious Life.* Translated by Joseph W. Swain. New York: Free Press.

Eckersley, Richard, and Keith Dear. 2002. Cultural Correlates of Youth Suicide. *Social Science and Medicine* 55:1891–1904.

Ehrenreich, Barbara. 2006. *Dancing in the Streets.* New York: Metropolitan.

Eliade, Mircea. 1964. *Shamanism: Archaic Techniques of Ecstasy.* Translated by W. R. Trask. New York: Pantheon Books.

Folland, Sherman. 2007. Does "Community Social Capital" Contribute to Population Health? *Social Science and Medicine* 64:2342–54.

Forsyth, Donelson R., and Jeni Burnette. 2005. The History of Group Research. Pp. 3–18 in *The Handbook of Group Research and Practice,* edited by Susan Wheelan. Thousand Oaks, Calif.: Sage.

Frank, Robert H. 1999. *Luxury Fever: Why Money Fails to Satisfy in an Era of Excess.* New York: Free Press.

Frederick, Shane, and George Loewenstein. 1999. Hedonic Adaptation. Pp.

302–29 in *Well-Being: The Foundations of Hedonic Psychology*, edited by Daniel Kahneman, Ed Diener. and Norbert Schwarz. New York: Russell Sage Foundation.

Freud, Sigmund. 1922. *Group Psychology and the Analysis of the Ego*. London and Vienna: International Psychoanalytical Press.

Goodstein, Renée, and Joseph G. Ponterotto. 1997. Racial and Ethnic Identity: Their Relationship and Their Contribution to Self-Esteem. *Journal of Black Psychology* 23:275–92.

Green, Melanie C., Timothy C. Brock, and Geoff F. Kaufman. 2004. Understanding Media Enjoyment: The Role of Transportation into Narrative Worlds. *Communication Theory* 14:311–27.

Haidt, Jonathan, Evan Rosenberg, and Holly Hom. 2003. Differentiating Diversities: Moral Diversity Is Not Like Other Kinds. *Journal of Applied Social Psychology* 33:1–36.

Helliwell, John F. 2003. How's Life? Combining Individual and National Variables to Explain Subjective Well-Being. *Economic Modelling* 20:331–60.

Iacoboni, Marco, Roger P. Woods, Marcel Brass, Harold Bekkering, John C. Mazziotta, and Giacomo Rizzolatti. 1999. Cortical Mechanisms of Imitation. *Science* 286:2526–28.

James, William. [1902] 1961. *The Varieties of Religious Experience*. New York: Macmillan.

Kahneman, Daniel. 1999. Objective Happiness. Pp. 3–25 in *Well-Being: The Foundations of Hedonic Psychology*, edited by Daniel Kahneman, Ed Diener, and Norbert Schwarz. New York: Russell Sage Foundation.

Keltner, Dacher, and Jonathan Haidt. 2003. Approaching Awe: A Moral, Spiritual, and Aesthetic Emotion. *Cognition and Emotion* 17:297–314.

Leary, Mark R. 2004. *The Curse of the Self*. New York: Oxford University Press.

Le Bon, Gustave. [1896] 1920. *The Crowd: A Study of the Popular Mind*. London: Benn.

Markus, Hazel R., and Shinobu Kitayama. 1991. Culture and the Self: Implications for Cognition, Emotion, and Motivation. *Psychological Review* 98: 224–53.

Marmarosh, Cheri L., and John G. Corazzini. 1997. Putting the Group in Your Pocket: Using Collective Identity to Enhance Personal and Collective Self-Esteem. *Group Dynamics: Theory, Research, and Practice* 1:65–74.

Maslow, Abraham H. [1964] 1994. *Religions, Values, and Peak Experiences*. New York: Penguin.

Maynard Smith, John, and Eors Szathmary. 1997. *The Major Transitions in Evolution*. Oxford: Oxford University Press.

Mayr, Ernst. 1960. The Emergence of Evolutionary Novelties. Pp. 349–80 in *The Evolution of Life*. Vol. 1 of *Evolution after Darwin*, edited by Sol Tax. Chicago: University of Chicago Press.

McCrae, Robert R. 1996. Social Consequences of Experiential Openness. *Psychological Bulletin* 120:323–37.

McDougall, William. 1920. *Group Mind: A Sketch of the Principles of Collective Psychology, with Some Attempt to Apply Them to the Interpretation of National Life and Character.* New York: G. P. Putnam's Sons.

McNeill, William H. 1995. *Keeping Together in Time: Dance and Drill in Human History.* Cambridge, Mass.: Harvard University Press.

Miller, William R., and Janet C'de Baca. 2001. *Quantum Change.* New York: Guilford.

Muir, William M. 1996. Group Selection for Adaptation to Multiple-Hen Cages: Selection Program and Direct Responses. *Poultry Science* 75:447–58.

Munford, Maria B. 1994. Relationship of Gender, Self-Esteem, Social Class, and Racial Identity to Depression in Blacks. *Journal of Black Psychology* 20: 157–74.

Myers, David G. 2000. The Funds, Friends, and Faith of Happy People. *American Psychologist* 55:56–67.

Olavson, Tim. 2004. "Connectedness" and the Rave Experience: Rave as New Religious Movement? Pp. 85–106 in *Rave Culture and Religion*, edited by Graham St. John. New York: Routledge.

Putnam, Robert D. 2000. *Bowling Alone: The Collapse and Revival of American Community.* New York: Simon & Schuster.

———. 2007. E Pluribus Unum: Diversity and Community in the Twenty-First Century. *Scandinavian Political Studies* 30:137–74.

Radcliffe-Brown, Alfred R. [1922] 1964. *The Andaman Islanders.* Glencoe, Ill.: Free Press.

Richerson, Peter J., and Robert Boyd. 2005. *Not by Genes Alone: How Culture Transformed Human Evolution.* Chicago: University of Chicago Press.

Schooler, Jonathan W., Dan Ariely, and George Loewenstein. 2003. The Pursuit and Monitoring of Happiness Can Be Self-Defeating. Pp. 41–70 in *Psychology and Economics*, edited by Juan Carrillo and Isabelle Brocas. Oxford: Oxford University Press.

Spencer, Herbert. [1896] 1975. *Principles of Sociology.* Westport, Conn.: Greenwood Press.

Sutton, Robert I. 2007. *The No Asshole Rule: Building a Civilized Workplace and Surviving One That Isn't.* New York: Warner Business Books.

Tajfel, Henri, Michael G. Billig, Robert P. Bundy, and Claude Flament. 1971. Social Categorization and Intergroup Behaviour. *European Journal of Social Psychology* 1:149–77.

Tayeb, Monir H. 2005. *International Human Resource Management: A Multinational Company Perspective.* Oxford: Oxford University Press.

Thaler, Richard H., and Cass R. Sunstein. 2003. Libertarian Paternalism. *American Economic Review* 93:175–79.

Tomasello, Michael, Ann C. Kruger, and Hilary H. Rater. 1993. Cultural Learning. *Behavioral and Brain Sciences* 16:495–511.

Turner, Victor. [1969] 1995. *The Ritual Process: Structure and Anti-Structure.* New York: Aldine De Gruyter.

Twenge, Jean M. 2000. The Age of Anxiety? The Birth Cohort Change in Anxiety and Neuroticism, 1952–1993. *Journal of Personality and Social Psychology* 79:1007–21.

Wann, Daniel L. 2006. Understanding the Positive Social Psychological Benefits of Sport Team Identification: The Team Identification–Social Psychological Health Model. *Group Dynamics: Theory, Research and Practice* 10:272–96.

Warren, Rick. 2002. *The Purpose Driven Life: What on Earth Am I Here For?* Grand Rapids, Mich.: Zondervan.

Williams, George C. 1966. *Adaptation and Natural Selection: A Critique of Some Current Evolutionary Thought.* Princeton, N.J.: Princeton University Press.

Wilson, David S. 2002. *Darwin's Cathedral: Evolution, Religion, and the Nature of Society.* Chicago: University of Chicago Press.

Wilson, David S., Mark Van Vugt, and Rick O'Gorman. 2008. Multilevel Selection Theory and Major Evolutionary Transitions: Implications for Psychological Science. *Current Directions in Psychological Science* 17:6–9.

Wilson, David S., and Edward O. Wilson. 2007. Rethinking the Theoretical Foundation of Sociobiology. *Quarterly Review of Biology* 82:327–48.

Wundt, Wilhelm. 1911. *Völkerpsychologie—Sprache, Mythus und Sitte Erster Band: Die Sprache.* Leipzig: Verlag von Wilhelm Engelmann.

Illusory Losses

Cass R. Sunstein

ABSTRACT

Recent empirical work demonstrates that healthy people make large mistakes when evaluating the welfare of those suffering from apparently serious health problems. Significant adverse conditions often inflict little or no hedonic damage—sometimes because people adapt to them, and sometimes because those who suffer many losses do not, after a time, focus on them. These findings have important implications for the legal system, especially for awards for pain, suffering, and hedonic losses, where juries are likely to overestimate the effect of injuries on happiness. There are two important qualifications. First, some injuries, such as chronic pain, do inflict significant hedonic losses because people cannot adapt and inevitably focus on them. Second, people may suffer capability loss without suffering hedonic loss, and that loss should be compensable. The legal system might be improved by civil damages guidelines to correct hedonic judgment errors by juries. Broader implications include the appropriate priorities for governments attempting to improve the welfare of their citizens.

> Nothing in life matters quite as much as you think it does while you are thinking about it. [Kahneman and Thaler 2006, p. 229]

1. SIX CLAIMS

In this essay I attempt to defend six principal claims:

1. In advance, people greatly exaggerate the hedonic effects of many adverse events, largely because they do not anticipate their remarkable

CASS SUNSTEIN is the Karl N. Llewellyn Distinguished Service Professor, Law School and Department of Political Science, University of Chicago. I am grateful to Bruce Ackerman, John Donahue, Elizabeth Emens, Robert Hahn, Peter Huang, Christine Jolls, Tracey Meares, Eric Posner, Margo Schlanger, Adrian Vermeule, and an anonymous referee for valuable comments on a previous draft, and to Madeline Fleisher, Bryan Mulder, and Matthew Robson for superb research assistance. Thanks too to participants in superb

[*Journal of Legal Studies*, vol. XXXVII (June 2008)]

capacity to adapt to changes. This capacity stems in part from a distinctive feature of human attention: those who suffer many losses do not focus, constantly or much, on those losses. It follows that many losses are illusory or at least exaggerated, in the sense that they inflict far less hedonic damage than people anticipate.

2. Both juries and judges are likely to make hedonic judgment errors, in a way that produces inflated damage awards. One reason for these errors is that in evaluating losses, observers suffer from adaptation neglect; another reason is that the legal system asks juries and judges to focus on, and thus to attend to, losses to which plaintiffs might well devote little attention in their ordinary lives. In short, the legal system almost certainly produces focusing illusions in tort cases.

3. It is important for the legal system to distinguish between harms that impose enduring losses, such as chronic pain and mental illness, and harms that do not, such as losses of fingers and toes. The distinction between enduring and illusory losses—for which ringing in the ears and loss of toes are illustrative cases—has many implications for economic and regulatory policy.

4. Without acknowledging that it is doing so, the legal system appears to be awarding capability damages under the name of hedonic damages. Juries award damages for the loss of capabilities, even in contexts in which people are not suffering a loss in the enjoyment of their lives. It is not clear whether jurors are explicitly aware of the importance of capabilities or whether they are instead making hedonic judgment errors.

5. It would be desirable to reform the legal system with the aid of a civil damages schedule, designed to accomplish three distinctive tasks: translating hedonic losses into monetary terms, correcting hedonic judgment errors, and assessing capability damages where appropriate.

6. An understanding of hedonic judgment errors raises the serious possibility that many policies, both fiscal and regulatory, are ill directed. Government might be expending resources in the false hope that the expenditures will improve well-being. There are complex questions, however, about the relationships among hedonic effects, capabilities, meaning, and the ingredients of good lives. A sensible society is not

workshops at Harvard Law School and at Yale Law School and a conference on the legal implications of recent happiness research, held at the University of Chicago Law School in June 2007; George Loewenstein and Peter Ubel provided especially helpful comments.

concerned only about "happiness" or even subjective well-being, although both of these certainly matter.

Now for the details.

2. DOLLARS AND WELFARE

The legal system must often assign monetary values to actual or apparent welfare losses. When those losses are purely monetary, the assignment need not be difficult. If a defendant has deprived a plaintiff of $10,000, the legal system will require the defendant to pay $10,000 to the plaintiff. But the legal system has a great deal of difficulty in turning some welfare losses into monetary equivalents.

2.1. Doctrine

Suppose that Jones has lost the use of two toes, or that Smith has become blind, or that Wilson has been paralyzed from the waist down, or that Holmes has developed a high degree of posttrauma anxiety, or that Johnson has been subject to racial harassment, or that Benson has suffered a loss of cognitive capacity, or that Dickerson has become impotent. The legal system allows people to recover for pain and suffering. The adverse effects captured in the idea of pain and suffering are undoubtedly real, and the legal system should attempt to deter them and to provide compensation. Indeed, hedonic losses are often the most serious injuries that people face—far more serious than strictly economic losses. But the resulting damage awards are notoriously variable (Leebron 1989), and it is not clear that they are in any sense rational or coherent (Viscusi 1988; Bovbjerg, Sloan, and Blumstein 1989; Rodgers 1993). An initial problem, which I will explore below, is that of the extreme difficulty of translating pain and suffering into monetary equivalents.

In many states, people are also permitted to recover hedonic damages, designed to capture people's loss of enjoyment of their lives. The line between pain and suffering on the one hand and hedonic damages on the other can be obscure; events that impose suffering also impose hedonic losses. The basic distinction is that hedonic damages cover not affirmative distress or suffering but forgone gains, as when people are unable to engage in valued activities, such as athletics (see *Day v. Ouachita Parish School Bd.*, 823 So. 2d 1039, 1044 [La. Ct. App. 2002]; *Allen v. Wal-Mart Stores, Inc.*, 241 F.3d 1293, 1297 [10th Cir. 2001]). Hedonic damages might be sought, for example, for the loss of a dog (see, for example, *Campell v. Animal Quarantine Station*, 63 Haw. 557, 632 P.2d 1066 [Haw. 1981]; *Knowles Animal Hosp. v. Wills*, 360 So. 2d 37 [Fla. Dist. Ct. App. 1978]), for the inability to engage in sexual relations (see *Varnell v. Louisiana Tech University*, 709 So. 2d 890, 896 [La. Ct. App. 1998]), for the loss of a limb (see *Pierce v. N.Y. Cent. R.R. Co.*, 409 F.2d 1392 [Mich. 1969]; *Matos v. Clarendon Nat. Ins. Co.*, 808 So. 2d 841, 849 [La. Ct. App. 2002]), for the loss of use of an elbow (see *Kirk v. Wash. State Univ.*, 746 P. 2d 285, 292 [Wash. 1987]), for depression and self-consciousness as a result of amputation of an arm (see *Coleman v. Deno*, 832 So. 2d 1016 [La. Ct. App. 2002]), for reduced cognitive capacity or mental retardation (see *Nemmers v. United States*, 681 F. Supp. 567 [C.D. Ill. 1988]), or for becoming bedridden and thus requiring constant care (see Berla, Brookshire, and Smith 1990). Here too, it is extremely difficult to translate the relevant interest into monetary equivalents.

Even before the translation occurs, juries and judges investigating hedonic damages and pain and suffering are asked, in a sense, to serve as "hedometers," assessing the adverse welfare effects associated with one or another loss. For purposes of analysis, I shall henceforth refer to both pain and suffering and hedonic damages as "hedonic losses," while recognizing that the principles behind them are distinct. The idea of hedonic losses is meant to capture the utility or (subjective) welfare losses produced by some adverse event. I use the term "hedonic" to underline the connection with the emerging literature attempting to measure hedonic effects; the word "utility," understood in the standard way, would work equally well.

Of course it is reasonable to ask about the theory on which the relevant judgments of judges and juries are supposed to be based. As the law now stands, the working theory is one of appropriate compensation or "making whole"—with the understanding that the compensatory award is supposed to restore plaintiffs to the hedonic state, or the level of welfare, that they would have occupied if the injury had not occurred (for discussion, see McCaffery, Kahneman, and Spitzer 1995). Under appropriate assumptions, the award of compensation, properly calculated, will also create the right deterrent signal, and hence accurate awards will promote social welfare as well. If those who are harmed seek and receive compensation, compensatory and deterrent goals should generally march hand in hand. As we shall see, however, the two goals often diverge—as when a monetary award for serious pain, or chronic headaches, does little or nothing to make the plaintiff "whole" but does deter the kinds of acts that create serious pain or chronic headaches. In such cases, an award that is hard to defend in compensatory terms might nonetheless be justified as a means of promoting optimal deterrence.

2.2. Measurement

How can judges and juries possibly serve as hedometers, lacking as they do direct access to people's experience? On a standard economic approach, the legal system should start with willingness to pay (WTP) (see, for example, Viscusi 1998). As we shall see, WTP might well reflect a hedonic forecasting error, in a way that complicates standard arguments for cost-benefit analysis as well as legal awards. But even if a forecasting error is not involved, there is no obvious way to ascertain the relevant amounts. Courts might ask, "How much would people pay to reduce a risk of some injury?" Suppose that Jones faces a 1/200,000 risk of losing his dog, of becoming impotent, or of being paralyzed from the waist down. How much would Jones pay to eliminate that risk? A method of this kind is used in the context of mortality risks, where the value of a statistical life (VSL) is ascertained by asking about monetary valuation as measured by reference to WTP (Viscusi 1994). Either revealed preference or contingent valuation studies might be used for this purpose.

But this approach is barred in tort cases (Viscusi 1988), which ask not about valuation of risks but instead about injuries after they occur. Technically, of course, the answer to the two questions might well turn out to be identical. If Jones would be willing to pay $10 to eliminate a 1/200,000 chance of losing his dog, the loss of his dog would seem to be worth $2 million. But this statement of equivalence raises many questions, at least if it is meant to capture actual behavior. Risk aversion, risk seeking, and various cognition distortions might ensure that people would pay far less, or far more, than $10 to avoid a risk of 1/200,000, even if the ultimate loss would be worth $2 million. In any case it is far from clear that most people would produce a monetary figure for a 1/200,000 risk of some injury, such as the loss of an arm, equal to 1/200,000 the amount that they would produce for a certainty of the same injury.

To assess hedonic damages, courts might be inclined to ask, "How much would people have to be paid to incur the relevant loss?" The question might be how much people would demand to give up three fingers, or two toes, or sexual capacities, or the use of an arm. This question is often described as involving "willingness to accept," or WTA (see Korobkin 2003). But the legal system bans courts from asking the

WTA question, whether it is phrased in terms of WTA to face risks or WTA to face actual losses (see McCafferey, Kahneman, and Spitzer 1995). There are two possible reasons, involving loss aversion and humiliation. Both of these may mean that people's WTA would be excessive if measured against the loss.

It is well established that people are highly averse to losses, in the sense that they will demand more to give up a good than they would be willing to pay to obtain that good in the first instance (see Thaler 1991). By itself, this point does not establish that WTA is the wrong measure; perhaps people's WTA more accurately captures the welfare loss than WTP (for a good discussion, see Korobkin 2003). But evidence suggests that loss aversion may well reflect a hedonic forecasting error: people greatly exaggerate the actual hedonic harms associated with a loss from the status quo (see Kermer et al. 2006). If the baseline is actual experience, then loss aversion is a mistake, because people are predicting a level of hedonic loss that they will not actually experience. And if this is so, then the WTA question is the wrong one; people's answers will not map onto the actual harm once the loss comes to fruition. In principle, the actual harm should provide the standard. I shall emphasize this point throughout, because it raises the possibility that in many domains, people's judgments about hedonic effects will be wrong.

In addition, it would seem to be humiliating for people to acknowledge that for a certain amount, they would be willing to allow someone to take two of their toes (see Korobkin 2003). Because they seek to avoid the humiliation, their answer to the question might greatly overstate the hedonic loss. Suppose that people were asked, "How much would you have to be paid to accept some physical injury?" Their response, including the humiliation involved in offering any answer at all, might be far higher than their hedonic loss. An obvious problem is the signaling effect of any affirmative answer. Those who say that they are willing to trade their toes for money might be offering a damaging signal about their concern for their own integrity, bodily and otherwise. Hence people's unwillingness to accept a monetary amount in return for some loss may not reflect the hedonic effect of the loss; the number may be inflated because of the signaling effect of acceptance.

Perhaps the right question is instead, "How much would people, having experienced the loss, need to be paid to feel adequately compensated for that loss?" This question, one involving "making whole" as distinct from "selling price," seems to capture the judgments actually made relevant by the legal system (see McCafferey, Kahneman, and

Spitzer 1995). It also has the advantage of focusing directly on people's experience—a strong point in favor of WTA over WTP. But the "making whole" question raises its own puzzles. How much money would be necessary to make a person as well off as he would be if he had not been injured at all? Suppose that someone has lost a spouse or a child, or that he now faces chronic (and severe) headaches, or that his face has been permanently disfigured. What amount of money would restore the plaintiff to her preinjury state? Perhaps a certain answer makes sense if it would enable the person to obtain medication to cure the headaches or an operation to correct the disfigurement. But if these are not feasible, what amount of money would restore the status quo? A standard answer refers to the amount that would make the injured person indifferent as between the injury and the injury with the compensation. But in cases of chronic and severe pain, or permanent disfigurement, we could easily imagine cases in which no amount would suffice.

Or suppose that someone has lost two toes or been paralyzed from the waist down. When asked how much would make them whole, it is possible that people would sincerely say that they would have to be paid (say) $100,000 for the loss of two toes, or $5,000,000 to be compensated for paralysis. But perhaps those very people do not suffer such a large hedonic loss from the relevant conditions. Perhaps they are not greatly suffering, or not suffering at all, but would nonetheless claim (sincerely) that very high amounts are necessary to compensate them (see Smith et al. 2006). I will explore this puzzle in some detail below, because it raises serious doubts about the standard economic analysis in many domains of law and policy.

Both WTP and WTA measures therefore face serious problems. Those problems might be overcome if the legal system had direct access to people's welfare. Armed with an actual hedometer, legal institutions might be able to make accurate measurements of the harmful effects of various losses. Those involved in law might be able to know, for example, whether or not the loss of two toes, or a pet, or serious disfigurement imposes a great deal of hedonic loss (see, for example, *Washington v. Aetna*, 886 So. 2d 572 [La. 2004]). The results of an accurate hedonic assessment would represent substantial progress, and a great deal of effort has been devoted toward making such progress (see, for example, Layard 2005; Kahneman et al. 2004; Ubel and Loewenstein 2008). Let us now see how the resulting findings might bear on law.

3. ADVERSE CONDITIONS AND HEDONICS

3.1. Resilience and Measurement

A major finding is that human beings are unexpectedly resilient. As a result, many apparently significant injuries do not inflict substantial long-term hedonic harms (Kahneman, Diener, and Schwarz 1999; Gilbert 2006). Perhaps above all, it is important to distinguish between those adverse conditions that impose large and persistent losses and those adverse conditions that, because of human resilience, impose only transitional, short-term, or modest losses.

For purposes of law and policy, a key point here is that people are often unable, in advance, to anticipate the hedonic effects of adverse events, and their inability on this count produces hedonic forecasting errors (see, for example, Gilbert et al. 1998). A central problem here is adaptation neglect: people neglect the extent to which they will be able to adapt to adverse changes and conditions. Adaptation is generally not a product of self-conscious efforts to minimize the effects of such changes; we are speaking of a general feature of human beings, not of successful efforts to embrace some form of Stoicism (Nussbaum 1996). Recall that, for the moment, my concern is genuinely hedonic losses. As we shall see, it is possible that people will not suffer such losses, strictly speaking, but will nonetheless suffer losses of an important kind.

It is reasonable to ask how hedonic effects are being measured. Most of the relevant work involves questions about global happiness or life satisfaction. People are asked, on a scale of (say) 0–8, about how happy they are, or how satisfied they are, with their lives. Skeptics might ask, "Do answers to such questions tell us anything at all?" This is a legitimate question, but people's answers do turn out to be associated with independent tests of hedonic state, including frequent smiling, smiling with the eyes, quality of sleep, happiness ratings by friends, self-reported health, frequent expressions of positive emotions, and being sociable and outgoing (Kahneman and Kruger 2006). To date, no empirical work falsifies or even seriously undermines the suggestion that reports of global happiness are in fact reflective of actual happiness, understood as subjective mental states.

Skeptics might persist at this point, suggesting that what matters is not global life satisfaction but some aggregation of life moments. And, in fact, efforts have been made to assess people's subjective well-being in this way (see Kahneman et al. 2004). We should not be surprised to find that in some domains, answers to global questions will be different from aggregations of moments. Asked about how their life is going, divorced or unmarried people might give relatively less positive answers, focusing as they might on the fact that they are unmarried; but perhaps unmarried people experience more, and not less, in the way of moment-by-moment happiness. I will return to this possibility below.

It would also be sensible for skeptics to worry that whatever the measure, people who suffer from adverse conditions might be engaging in scale recalibration to reflect those conditions. Perhaps colostomy patients rank themselves high, on a bounded scale, on the ground that they are relatively happy, considering their condition; but perhaps they would rank themselves much lower if they were comparing themselves to healthy people. If so, the surprisingly high rankings of those with adverse conditions suggest not high levels of subjective well-being but a sense that things are going well enough, all things considered. This conjecture is apparently wrong. A number of efforts have been made to test for scale recalibration, and thus far the verdict is clear: there is no evidence of recalibration, and considerable evidence to the contrary (Ubel and Loewenstein 2008). I shall be speaking here mainly of findings about global life satisfaction, because these are the most numerous, but on occasion I will refer to moment by moment measures as well.

3.2. Adaptation Neglect and Hedonic Forecasting Errors

Let us begin with the limited hedonic effects of many positive changes. Lottery winners are not happier, a year later, than other people are (Frey and Stutzer 2002, pp. 410–11). Marriage is often thought to be associated with increases in happiness, but after a few years, married people are not happier than they were before (compare Clark et al. [2003] with Easterlin [2003]). Apparently marriage produces a significant hedonic boost, but the boost is short-lived, and people return fairly quickly to their premarriage state. Increases in salary have a similar feature; a 20 percent increase is highly welcome, but after a short period, people do not show a significant long-term change in self-reported happiness or life satisfaction.

With respect to many negative changes, including those that concern the legal system, the hedonic effects are often surprisingly small. It is remarkable but true that paraplegics are only modestly less happy than other people (Kahneman and Krueger 2006).[1] Young people who have

---

1. An interesting question, not explored in the hedonic literature, is the extent to which discrimination and stigma might contribute to the (admittedly modest) decrease in happiness or perhaps in more significant decreases in moment-by-moment happiness.

lost a limb as a result of cancer show no less happiness than similarly situated young people who have not had cancer (Ubel and Loewenstein 2008). Moderately disabled people recover to their predisability level after 2 years (Oswald and Nattavudh 2005). Kidney dialysis patients do not show lower levels of happiness than ordinary people (see Oswald and Nattavudh 2005). Colostomy patients report levels of happiness that are about the same as people who have not had colostomies (see Smith et al. 2006). Intriguingly, those with colostomies greatly exaggerate their actual level of happiness before they had colostomies—while those with reversed colostomies report that before the reversal, they were far less happy than they were in fact (see Ubel and Loewenstein 2008). I will return to these findings below.

From this evidence, it is fair to conclude that healthy people systematically overestimate the adverse effects of many physical problems. Those who face such problems experience unexpectedly little in the way of hedonic loss (Ubel and Loewenstein 2008). As I have noted, it is possible to question the relevant findings; social scientists do not yet have hedometers. But from the existing work, the basic conclusions follow whether we rely on global measures of happiness or life satisfaction or on moment-by-moment measures of mood and happiness, which might seem to be even more reliable (see Ubel and Loewenstein 2008).

In a less dramatic vein, assistant professors greatly overstate the effect of an adverse tenure decision on their subjective happiness (Gilbert and Wilson 2000). They expect that this decision will affect their happiness for many years and, in part for that reason, greatly want to be tenured. But after a few years have passed, those who were denied tenure show no less happiness than those who were tenured. Many voters believe that the outcome of an election will greatly affect their happiness a month after the election is held. But in that month, supporters of losing and winning candidates are as happy as they were before the election (Gilbert and Wilson 2000). People have been found to overestimate the welfare effects of personal insults, the outcomes of sports events, and romantic breakups; in all of these circumstances, the adverse effects, while real and for a time severe, are surprisingly small and short-term (Gilbert and Wilson 2000).

3.3. Enduring versus Illusory Losses (or Loud Unpleasant Noises versus Fewer Toes)

To say this is not to deny that some advantageous events and conditions create large and enduring gains and that some adverse events and con-

ditions impose serious and persistent losses. Various drugs, such as Pro-
zac, apparently create long-term boosts in subjective well-being. It is
easy to imagine changes in the allocation of time—from, say, commuting
and work to socializing, vacations, and leisure—that would produce
enduring benefits (see Frank 2000). Hence it is quite false to say that
people's resilience and their capacity for adaptation ensure that social
changes and interventions are powerless to affect happiness or life satisfaction. The task is to ensure that any changes counteract persistent
rather than illusory losses or that they produce gains to which people
will not quickly adapt.

On the negative side, consider the instructive and in a sense defining
example of loud, unpleasant noise, which people much dislike and which
they do not dislike less as time passes (Frederick and Loewenstein 1999).
With respect to highway noise, people show approximately the same
level of irritation over a period of more than a year—and as time passes,
they become more pessimistic, not less so, about their ability to adjust
to the noise (Weinstein 1982). The physiological effects of noise do not
diminish in children over a significant period of time (Frederick and
Loewenstein 1999). A study of college students finds greater levels of
annoyance at dormitory noise at the end of the year than at the beginning
(Frederick and Loewenstein 1999). Unpleasant noise reduces people's
enjoyment of their lives, and it continues to reduce their enjoyment for
significant periods of time. We should conclude that tortious behavior
that causes (for example) loud ringing in the ears will impose very serious
and quite long-term hedonic losses.

Many adverse conditions belong in the same category as noise. Just
as people overestimate the hedonic harm of many physical losses, such
as kidney dialysis and colostomies, so too people underestimate the hedonic effect of adverse effects, such as depression and chronic pain (see
Ubel, Loewenstein, and Jepson 2003). Leading sources of low levels of
happiness include mental illness (such as anxiety and depression) subjectively reported bad health (above all, pain imposes severe and continuing hedonic losses), unemployment (Frederick and Loewenstein
1999), and separation from a spouse (Layard 2005, p. 64). The process
of divorce is bad, but not as bad as separation; notably, people adjust
fairly quickly and return to their predivorce state (Clark et al. 2003).

More speculatively, we might suggest that some medical conditions
produce significant and enduring losses to the extent that people do not
stabilize but instead must anticipate medical results and consider, with
some frequency, whether they are getting better or worse. Certain can-

cers, in which significant periods of time are spent expecting and receiving results, might well fall in the same category as noise. Similarly, the process of adaptation might be slowed, and focusing might be increased, if people are worrying about whether an adverse condition can be improved or reversed. Also speculatively, we might suggest that some conditions impose significant and enduring losses to the extent that they produce discrimination and stigma of the kind to which people do not easily adapt and on which they tend to focus. Serious facial disfigurement, for example, might produce enduring hedonic losses because of the social consequences of having a disfigured face.

It is therefore important to distinguish among four phenomena: (1) gains that are significant and enduring, such as those produced by relief of chronic pain, (2) gains that are largely illusory, such as those produced by increases in salary, (3) losses that are significant and enduring, such as those produced by pain, depression, and anxiety, and (4) losses that turn out to be low or even illusory (at least in the long term), such as those produced by loss of limbs or by colostomies. For purposes of the legal questions on which I am focusing here, the latter two phenomena are the most important.

3.4. Failures of Affective Forecasting

From these findings, we can draw two general conclusions. The first is that many apparently serious losses inflict relatively little in the way of long-term hedonic harm. The second is that people do not anticipate this fact; they expect far more harm than they actually experience. A key reason is that people neglect the power of psychological mechanisms that immunize them from the kinds of hedonic losses that they expect to face in the event that things go wrong. It is important to try to understand the sources of the resulting errors.

In many cases, people are subject to immune neglect; they do not see the power of their internal psychological immune system, which greatly diminishes the welfare effects of apparently significant changes. A related problem is that people demonstrate a kind of impact bias (see Gilbert et al. 1998), in the form of a tendency to exaggerate the effect of future events on their own emotional states. The exaggerations are sometimes described as a consequence of duration bias (Gilbert et al. 1998), understood as a tendency to overestimate of the length of time during which undesirable effects will have an emotional impact.

The implication for the legal system is clear. If ordinary people make mistakes in forecasting the effects of adverse events in their own lives, there is every reason to think that juries (and judges) will make similar mistakes in assessing the effects of those events on plaintiffs, especially but not only when they are projecting future losses. Hedonic judgment errors are likely to affect those involved in the legal system as well as ordinary people in ordinary life. As we shall see, the same point applies to policymakers, including regulators.

3.5. Adaptation, Attention, and Focusing Illusions

Why, exactly, do adverse events often have relatively little effect on people's subjective well-being? The general phenomenon is adaptation. The most obvious mechanism involves diminished sensitivity to a change over time; what once seemed a large hedonic boost or a serious hedonic loss often becomes part of life's furniture. People do not anticipate this fact—hence adaptation neglect. A second mechanism, which might be defined as a distinct phenomenon, involves attention. When apparent losses inflict surprisingly little hedonic harm, it is often because people do not much focus on those losses after a period of transition (see Kahneman et al. 2007). There is some evidence that adaptation is the dominant explanation for people's erroneous hedonic forecasts with respect to health conditions. In particular, drawing people's attention to the possibility of adaptation reduces hedonic errors, whereas efforts to reduce focusing illusions had no such effect (Ubel, Loewenstein, and Jepson 2005).

A great deal of work explores the possibility of adaptive preferences, which arise as people adapt their preferences to the existing circumstances (see, for example, Elster 1983). Consider the tale of the fox and the sour grapes. Knowing that they are unavailable, the fox does not want the grapes; his preference is a product of their unavailability, to which he has adapted (Elster 1983). The point might be counted as a challenge to utilitarianism or to any account that emphasizes subjective mental states: If people do not want opportunities or goods that are unavailable, is it so clear that the unavailability of those opportunities or goods can be defended by reference to people's wants? Whether or not this question can be answered, it is clear that when people's preferences have adapted to a social situation, their hedonic state will be much better than outsiders will anticipate.

For an apparent real-world example, consider a study of self-reported health in India, a year after the Great Bengal Famine of 1943 (see Nussbaum 1999, p. 139). Only 2.5 percent of widows said that they were "ill," and none said that they were in "indifferent" health. By contrast,

45.6 of widowers said that they were either ill or in indifferent health. The irony was that the widows were in significantly worse health than the widowers (Nussbaum 1999). Evidently the widows adapted to their situation and generally believed that their health was good. In law, economics, political science, and philosophy, analysis of adaptive preferences has proved especially illuminating (Elster 1983), but we continue to lack an adequate understanding of the mechanisms of adaptation. Several different factors seem to be at work.

The term "hedonic adaptation" refers to the adjustment over time in the intensity of people's emotional reactions to adverse events, in a way that ensures unexpectedly limited losses in terms of subjective happiness (see Frederick and Loewenstein 1999, p. 303). As I have noted, people's affective responses to a bad event or condition typically abate as time passes (see Ubel, Loewenstein, and Jepson 2003). Those who have been denied tenure, or lost the use of a limb, or have had a colonoscopy, will react intensely at first, but after a year, their affective response will be much smaller. When moderately disabled people show little or no hedonic loss, adaptation, thus understood, is the key reason.

A distinctive mechanism, which can also be taken as a separate explanation for the general phenomenon of adaptation, involves the operation of human attention (see Kahneman and Sugden 2005). When people lose the use of an arm, they do not think, most of the time, about the fact that one of their arms does not work. Instead they focus on the central features of their hours and their days—their jobs, their meals, their relationships, the book they are reading or the television show they are watching. To the extent that significant losses do not produce hedonic damages, it is frequently because people's attention is not directed, most of the time, to those losses. Kahneman and Thaler (2006, p. 229) describe the problem in a wonderful maxim, my epigraph here: "Nothing in life matters quite as much as you think it does while you are thinking about it."

A failure to focus on what has been lost helps to explain the absence of substantial hedonic effects from apparently large losses. Focusing illusions help in turn to account for people's surprise at the absence of such effects. People are surprised because they focus specifically on the loss, indeed they are often asked specifically to do so, and thus conclude that it has large hedonic effects, neglecting to see that those who have experienced the loss do not, most of the time, focus on it. For hedonic forecasting, the general point is that when asked to focus on a particular aspect of life or a particular ingredient in welfare, observers are likely to make serious blunders, simply because in life, people do not usually focus on any particular aspect or any particular ingredient. As we shall soon see, many of the puzzles in the social science literature on subjective well-being are best explained in this light.

Consider a simple demonstration of a focusing illusion. Many people appear to believe that they are less happy than they would be if they lived in California (see Schkade and Kahneman 1998). This belief is held by both people who live in California and people who do not live in California. But in fact, those who live in California are not happier than those who live elsewhere. Focusing on California weather in particular, Californians and Ohioans believe that they would be happier in California even though weather is not, in fact, an important determinant of most people's happiness. Failures in affective forecasting are often a product of a focusing illusion: people focus on a particular loss without seeing that after the loss has occurred, they are not likely to focus (much) on that loss.[2] When primed to think about weather, or any other factor that is a small ingredient in the subjective well-being of most people (such as, for example, the ability to perform well in sports), focusing illusions lead people to give excessive attention to that factor.

Contingent-valuation studies run into an exceedingly serious problem for this reason (see Bateman and Willis 1999). In such studies, people are specifically asked to value some good, event, or state of affairs (including modest improvements in climate). If the focusing illusion is at work, the resulting numbers will be unrealistically high. We could easily imagine such a study with respect to the loss of two toes, an arm, or a leg. If nothing in life matters quite as much as people think it does when they are thinking about it, then contingent-valuation studies are likely to inflate the importance of certain goods, because they are explicitly designed to make people think about (the relevant) "it." It should be easy to see that a similar problem might infect judges and juries, which are, by hypothesis, being focused on a particular loss.

These points, and an understanding of attention in particular, help to explain why some conditions do in fact produce serious or enduring losses. Noise is the exemplar here; loud and unpleasant noises create such losses because it is hard not to focus on them. In the same vein, conditions that impose enduring losses command attention; people necessarily focus on them. It is hard, for example, not to attend to chronic

2. Note, however, the failure to replicate the finding of a focusing illusion in Ubel, Loewenstein, and Jepson (2005).

pain. By definition, depression and anxiety cannot be put to one side. To the extent that social situations draw constant attention to a condition, people will attend to that condition. When people are separated from their spouses, they are focused, much of the time, on that fact. A few years afterward, divorce becomes a background fact, not a source of constant attention. Parents whose children are suffering or needing constant attention will experience serious hedonic losses; it is hard not to attend to the needs or distress of one's children, and such distress can serve, for parents, as exceedingly loud noise (with remarkable amplifiers).

Other puzzles in the hedonic literature can be similarly understood. Marriage produces a short-term burst in life satisfaction, because those who are recently married are thinking, much of the time, about their recent marriage. But after a few years, marriage becomes part of life's furniture, and it ceases to create the hedonic boost—even if the union is entirely happy.

We are now in a position to understand one of the most counterintuitive findings in the hedonic literature. The life satisfaction of many disabled people is not greatly lower than that of able-bodied people, and for some kinds of disabilities, life satisfaction is essentially the same. At the same time, many disabled people believe that they were happier before they were disabled, and there is clear evidence that they would pay a great deal to return to their predisability state (see Samaha 2007). If the analysis here is correct, disabled people are themselves subject, or made subject, to a focusing illusion when they are asked how their lives were (would be) different when they were (if they were) not disabled, or how much they would pay not to be disabled in terms of money or remaining years of life.[3] I am not sure that this claim is correct; we do not have sufficient evidence to know for sure. But if the claim seems preposterous, consider the following question: "Would you be happier if the weather in your city—say, Chicago, Boston, New York, or Philadelphia—were automatically converted to the weather of Los Angeles or San Francisco?" You might well say yes. But you would be wrong.

3. It is possible, however, that disabled people are showing an implicit appreciation of the importance of capabilities, an issue that I take up below.

4. LEGAL IMPLICATIONS

4.1. Juries, Adaptation, and Attention

For the legal system, there is a concrete implication. Juries and others are likely to make hedonic judgment errors, often exaggerating the hedonic effects of losses.[4] The first problem is that juries and judges will almost certainly suffer from adaptation neglect. The second problem is that when asked to award damages for a certain loss, the attention of the jury (and the judge) is specifically fixed on the loss in question. It is as if juries were asked, "Would you be happier in California?" Deliberately focused on a particular injury, juries are unlikely to see that most of the time, the plaintiff may not be much focused on the particular injury. The very circumstances of trial invite adaptation neglect and create the focusing illusion.[5] In the legal system, juries and judges are asked specifically to think about the importance of the things that they are intensely thinking about.

Suppose, for example, that a plaintiff has lost two fingers or an arm, and the jury is asked to monetize the loss, including the pain and suffering associated with it. Because of the power of the psychological immune system, it is not implausible to think that the loss is short-term and very small. After a period of adjustment and (admittedly nontrivial) transition costs, those who lose two fingers, or even an arm, may be only modestly worse off, in hedonic terms, than those who have suffered no such loss. In fact they might not be worse off at all; recall that there is no discernible hedonic difference between ordinary people and those who have lost a limb as a result of cancer (see Ubel and Loewenstein 2008).

Juries and judges are unlikely to understand this point. In all probability, they too will show adaptation neglect and suffer from a focusing illusion, akin to those asked whether they would be happier if they lived in California. It is sensible to think that in the award of damages, the legal system is likely to be showing a systematic bias as a result. And, in fact, it is not difficult to find cases in which such a bias is exhibited,

---

4. An illuminating discussion, overlapping with the treatment here and focused on hedonic damages in particular, is Bagenstos and Schlanger (2007).

5. Admittedly, this is true for plaintiffs as well as for juries. Those who bring suit will likely focus on their injury—likely more so than those who do not bring suit. On purely hedonic grounds, it might well make sense to discourage (some) plaintiffs from bringing suit, because litigation will prevent hedonic adaptation. To the extent that the suit focuses the plaintiff on the relevant condition, the problem I am describing—exaggerated damage awards—is reduced.

with substantial damage awards for adverse events that are unlikely to have inflicted serious hedonic losses (see, for example, *Dauria v. City of New York*, 577 N.Y.S. 2d 64 [App. Div. 1991]; *Coleman v. Deno*, 832 So. 2d 1016 [La. Ct. App. 2002]; *Squibb v. Century Group*, 824 So. 2d 861 [La. Ct. App. 2002]; *Thornton v. Amtrak*, 802 So. 2d 816 [La. Ct. App. 2001]; *Keefe v. E & D Specialty Stands, Inc.*, 708 N.Y.S. 214 [N.Y. App. Div. 2000]). Consider, for example, a $1 million award for the loss of feeling and strength in a hand (see *Keefe v. E & D Specialty Stands, Inc.*, 708 N.Y.S. 2d 214) or an award of $1.5 million for the amputation of a finger (*Thornton v. Amtrak*, 802 So. 2d 816).

We might reach a similar conclusion for hedonic damages. If someone has lost a dog, he is likely to suffer, and the legal system should award compensation. But the suffering will not usually last a long time.[6] Or suppose that someone has lost mobility, so that she can no longer ski or play tennis. If the question is how much that person has lost in terms of enjoyment of life, understood in hedonic terms, the answer is, very plausibly, little or nothing.

It is both true and important that even if long-term harms are not likely, the short-term harms might be severe. People might experience a degree of distress, fear, mourning, and grief for which a significant degree of compensation is justified. Large monetary awards might well be given for short periods of intense suffering or sense of loss. The only point is that juries are likely to exaggerate the long-term effects and to that extent to award excessive damage awards. If short-term harms are severe, they should be recognized and compensated as such.

The existence of hedonic forecasting errors also suggests the possibility that juries are awarding insufficiently large sums in cases in which the hedonic loss is likely to be high. Recall that for some losses, people underestimate that loss. Suppose, for example, that a plaintiff is suffering chronic back pain. The pain may be relatively low level, but it might be persistent. It is not difficult to find cases in which juries award low damage awards in such instances (see, for example, *Levy v. Bayou Indus. Maint. Serv.*, 855 So. 2d 968, 980 [La. Ct. App. 2003], awarding $50,000 for postconcussion syndrome, including vertigo and migraine headaches). Consider, for example, a $4,000 award for an accident producing headaches three to four times per week and persistent pain in the hands, knees, and shoulders (*Hatcher v. Ramada Plaza Hotel & Conf. Ctr.*,

---

6. I put to one side the question whether the dog's loss should be treated as a loss for the dog, not for human beings; I would answer that question affirmatively.

2003 Conn. Super. LEXIS 255 [Conn. Super. Ct. 2003]), a $25,000 award to 19-year-old woman whose accident causes a painful hip deformity, headaches, ringing in the ears, permanent arthritis in the hip, and backaches (*Frankel v. Todd*, 260 F. Supp. 772 [E.D. Pa. 1966]), an award of $47,000 for an accident causing herniation in the lower back, accompanied by permanent radiating pain and restriction (*Ledesma v. Long Island R.R.*, 1997 WL 33346870 [E.D.N.Y. 1997]), or an award of $30,000 for permanent pain in the neck and knee from a herniated cervical disc and torn meniscus (*Russo v. Jordan*, 2001 N.Y. Slip Op. 20062U, 9 [N.Y. Misc. 2001]). In all these cases, the award seems far too low, because the relevant injury is likely to be enduring.

In the abstract, low-level back pain, headaches, ringing in the ears, and pain in the neck and knee may not seem especially serious; these are familiar phenomena, unlike loss of a limb. It is easy to imagine a jury judgment that while headaches are unpleasant, they are part of daily life, and that the loss of a limb is devastating. But to the extent that headaches, ringing in the ears, and similar conditions are severe, they are likely to operate in the same way as noise: as problems that do not improve much over time. People might well undervalue such injuries with the thought that such conditions arc ordinary parts of human experience—unlike, say, the loss of toes. But those who face chronic pain, severe headaches, or loud ringing in the ears suffer massive hedonic losses, and jurors are unlikely to appreciate that fact.

It is possible of course that some juries and judges might distrust claims of back pain and to be discounting the award because of the risk of faking. But even if those involved in the legal system do believe the claims, they will probably underestimate the adverse effects of certain losses over time. Imagine, for example, what it means to be subject to loud ringing in the ears or to persistent headaches. The same points apply to cases in which tortious behavior produces depression or anxiety. In such cases, the hedonic injury is very serious, and significant damage awards are justified (see, for example, *Hall v. Brookshire Bros., Ltd.*, 831 So. 2d 1010 [La. Ct. App. 2002]; *Levy v. Bayou Indus. Maint. Servs.*, 855 So. 2d at 980). Juries and judges might well fail to see this point.

4.2. Capability Damages

If the discussion thus far is correct, awards for pain and suffering, and for hedonic damages, are often inflated from the hedonic point of view. But does this mean that they are inflated from the correct point of view?

The very ideas of "pain and suffering" and "hedonic damages" suggest attention to subjective mental states; the law's official theory speaks in explicitly hedonic terms. But it is reasonable to think that subjective mental states are not all that matter and that the legal system is attentive to that fact. If an injury causes a significant diminution of cognitive functions, without adversely affecting moods, something has been lost. Let us now shift gears, moving from a purely Benthamite perspective, focused only on subjective mental states, to an Aristotelian one, focused on what people are able to do and to be.

Loss of Capabilities. Suppose that Jones loses the use of a leg; suppose too that the loss does not affect Jones's self-reported happiness. After a difficult but short period of adjustment, Jones is as happy as he was before the loss. Suppose too that the effort to measure Jones's moment-by-moment happiness finds that he is no less happy than he was before (see Kahneman et al. 2004). In other words, Jones has experienced no hedonic loss. Should the legal system therefore disregard Jones's injury?

What Jones has lost is a capability (compare Sen 1985; Nussbaum 2001; Sen 1999).[7] He cannot walk on his leg; he certainly is unable to run. He is unable to engage in many activities that he used to be able to take for granted. Jones may not be in pain and he may not be suffering. Jones may not be suffering hedonic damage in the sense that no hedometer can show that Jones enjoys his life less than he did before. Might the legal system nonetheless award damages? If the answer is yes, it is not justified by a hedonic loss. Instead the loss involves a capability. That loss may be real and significant, even if hedonic measures are unable to capture it. Consider, as apparently supporting evidence, the fact that most people would be willing to pay significant amounts to avoid a loss of a capability, even if they could be persuaded that the loss would inflict no hedonic harm.[8]

7. I am not using the idea of capabilities in the same sense as Sen and Nussbaum, but my use belongs in the same general family, focusing as it does on the capacity to function rather than subjective mental states.

8. It is important to see, of course, that whether someone has lost a capability depends on how social institutions react to the relevant losses. If someone has lost the use of a foot, perhaps he is able to use a prosthetic foot, and perhaps the prosthetic foot can function quite well. The same might be true for legs. And even if people are using wheelchairs, the capability loss produced by wheelchair use is a product of how social institutions accommodate people in wheelchairs. One way to understand the Americans with Disabilities Act is to see it as an effort to reduce the risk that impairments will turn into capability losses.

The claim on behalf of capability losses is a normative one, based on the objective harm faced by those who lose physical or cognitive abilities. If people have had colostomies or if they are on dialysis machines, they have suffered a significant loss whatever their hedonic state. Consider here two remarkable findings. As we have seen, people with colostomies do not show less happiness than people without colostomies; but at the same time, they say that they would give up to 15 percent of their lives to be able to live without a colostomy (see Loewenstein and Ubel 2006). Similarly, dialysis patients show little adverse hedonic effect, but many of them say that they would willingly yield over half their remaining years in order to have normal kidney function (see Loewenstein and Ubel 2006)! It is possible that these answers indicate a hedonic loss that is not adequately captured by efforts to measure subjective well-being. But they also seem to suggest a concern for capabilities, not merely for hedonic states.

Hedonic Judgment Errors or Recognition of Capabilities? In invoking this evidence, I do not mean to suggest that people's statements on such points should be taken as authoritative.[9] Begin with the case of healthy people. If such people are horrified at the prospect of having a colostomy, and if they cannot bear the thought of being on a dialysis machine, they might well believe, quite falsely, that the relevant change would make life barely livable; so the evidence suggests (see, for example, Ubel et al. 2001). Hedonic judgment errors of this kind might well be impervious to debiasing (for evidence that some debiasing strategies help and that others do not, see Ubel, Loewenstein, and Jepson 2005). It is imaginable, for example, that people would be willing to demand a great deal to lose a leg, even if they could be given a fully adequate prosthetic (perhaps better than the original) and even if they could be given reliable evidence that they would suffer no hedonic loss after a (brief) period of transition. People's conclusions about what they would pay to avoid or to eliminate a loss might well reflect a hedonic judgment error or a heuristic that is productive of blunders, and if so, those conclusions should not be taken as a basis for policy. If a hedonic judgment error is at work, people are not, in fact, showing an appreciation of capability losses.

The judgments of those who have actually suffered such losses would seem to be entitled to more weight. Because colostomy or dialysis pa-

---

Nonetheless, it remains true that many injuries produce significant and long-term losses of that kind even if no long-term hedonic harm is experienced.

9. This seems to me the tendency in Loewenstein and Ubel (2006).

tients would give up significant amounts of their lives to be well, we do appear to have reason to think that they are (recognizing that they are) suffering a real loss whatever their hedonic states. Compare a person who has lost cognitive capacities; such a person may believe that he has suffered a real loss even if his hedonic state is good. But it is possible that colostomy or dialysis patients too are vulnerable to focusing illusions, no less than those in Chicago or Cleveland who might be willing to give up a great deal to have the weather enjoyed by people in Los Angeles. Recall that colostomy patients report wildly and inaccurately high levels of happiness before they had colostomies and that people whose colostomies have been reversed say that they were far less happy than they were in fact (see Smith et al. 2006).

In short, I am not claiming that when people say that they want to avoid conditions that do not impose hedonic losses, they are actually motivated by a recognition of capability losses; a hedonic judgment error may well be responsible.[10] My only claim is that when people have lost a capability, they have lost something significant from the normative point of view, even if they have suffered no hedonic loss.

Law and Well-Being. For those who believe that the legal system should accept this view, two difficult questions remain. First, what kinds of capability losses are legally cognizable? Second, how can capabilities be translated into monetary equivalents? At first glance, a notion of normal human functioning would seem to provide the baseline from which to measure capability loss (for discussion, see Satz 2006). It would follow that if someone has lost the use of a leg or an arm, or of cognitive or sexual abilities, a capability loss is involved. I will return below to the question of monetization.

Recognition of the importance of capabilities has broader importance for thinking about well-being, whether it is measured in terms of self-reports involving global life satisfaction (see Frank 2000) or in terms of moment-by-moment measures, designed to capture daily experience (see Kahneman et al. 2004). Those who are able to run, or to have sexual experiences, are better off than those who lack these capabilities, even if the difference cannot be picked up in hedonic terms. Those who are poorly educated have less in the way of capability than those who are well educated, even if hedonic measures cannot identify a difference between the two groups. It is possible that people with less education

10. Compare Loewenstein and Ubel (2006), which appears to honor people's judgments even though they might well be based on cognitive errors.

do not show more negative affect or less positive affect, during their days, than people with a great deal of education (compare Kahneman et al. 2004), but education as such contributes to a richer life. Even if well-educated people do not seem happier according to a hedometer, their enjoyments are more numerous and qualitatively distinct; for good Millian reasons, taken up below, education is valuable whatever its effects on utility, narrowly conceived.

An emphasis on subjective measures is important, because subjective experience matters a great deal. But purely hedonic accounts, focused solely on people's moods, miss aspects of well-being to which sensible societies and legal systems are attuned. It is easy to imagine a group of people who score well on some hedonic measure—perhaps they are all generally at 6, on a scale of 0–8, in terms of positive affect during their days—whose lives are not very good, even in terms of their own considered judgments. As we will see, capabilities are not the only supplement to hedonic measures, but for purposes of what concerns the legal system, they are the most important such supplement.

In a variety of cases, supposedly hedonic damages are probably best justified as capability damages. For example, courts have awarded hedonic damages for loss of the ability to engage in sports (see *Day v. Ouachita Parish School Bd.*, 823 So. 2d at 1044; *Allen v. Wal-Mart Stores, Inc.*, 241 F. 3d at 1297). Hedonic damages have been awarded for the loss of the senses of taste and smell (see *Daugherty v. Erie R.R. Co.*, 169 A. 2d 549 [Pa. Sup. Ct. 1961]). Courts have also awarded significant hedonic damages for the loss of a limb, in a way that may reflect, or be defensible in terms of, a capability loss rather than a hedonic forecasting error (see *Pierce v. N.Y. Cent. R.R. Co.*, 409 F.2d 1392; *Matos v. Clarendon Nat. Ins. Co.*, 808 So. 2d 841). Hedonic damages have been awarded where the tort victim could no longer engage in sexual activities as a result of the injury (see *Varnell v. Louisiana Tech University*, 709 So. 2d at 896). Or consider a case in which the injury rendered the plaintiff mentally retarded; the court awarded hedonic damages for the plaintiff's loss of ability to, among other things, go on a first date, parent children, read, and debate the politics of the day (see *Nemmers v. United States*, 681 F. Supp. 567). It is possible that the court believed that the plaintiff was less happy in some subjective sense. If so, the court might well have been wrong. But the plaintiff lost a capability, indeed a set of capabilities, and might be taken to have deserved damages for that reason.

Consider the possibility that many people who have suffered significant neurological damage are not less happy than they were before; there is no reason to believe that people with Down's Syndrome are unhappy, and they may in fact be unusually happy. Does it follow that damage awards should be low, or zero, for tortious behavior that has produced certain neurological damage or Down's Syndrome in infants? If loss of capabilities matters, significant damage awards would be justified even without an effect on subjective well-being.

Normative Issues. The idea of capability damages will be puzzling to those with strongly Benthamite inclinations, who think that such well-being is all that matters. And it is true that the term "hedonic damages" has an unmistakably Benthamite ring; if it is using a nonhedonic measure, the legal system is relying on a theory of harm that is not captured by the law's own rubric. My principal suggestion is that many cases that award such damages are best justified on the ground that they reflect an implicit commitment to the importance of capabilities (compare the overlapping conclusions in Bagenstos and Schlanger [forthcoming]). People receive monetary compensation not because they enjoy their lives less but because they have lost a capability. A key question, which a reading of the cases cannot answer, is whether the decisions are animated by some kind of hedonic judgment error or instead an intuitive but sensible judgment about capabilities.

The normative issues are complex, and I can offer only a few brief remarks here. Suppose that Jones has been severely injured and suffers a serious loss in cognitive capacities. Suppose too that the pain and suffering have been modest and that there is little or no loss in subjective well-being. Should Jones receive capability damages? Under the official theory of hedonic damages, the question is whether Jones has suffered a diminution in his enjoyment of life. If that idea is understood in purely hedonic terms, there is a real doubt whether damages should be available; perhaps the relevant hedometers are unable to pick up any loss. But it is plausible to think that Jones has lost some enjoyment of life whatever the (relevant) hedometers say. Jones is now unable to have certain kinds of enjoyments that are available only to those who operate at particular cognitive level. The loss of (the capacity for) those enjoyments ought to matter.

For some of the cases, John Stuart Mill's distinction between higher and lower pleasures is clearly relevant (see Mill 1863). Thus Mill writes, "[I]t is an unquestionable fact that those who are equally acquainted with, and equally capable of appreciating and enjoying, both, do give a most marked preference to the manner of existence which employs their higher faculties. . . . [No] intelligent human being would consent to be a fool, no instructed person would be an ignoramus, no person of feeling and conscience would be selfish and base, even though they should be persuaded that the fool, the dunce, or the rascal is better satisfied with his lot than they are with theirs" (Mill 1863, chap. 2). When hedonic damages are awarded for the loss of cognitive capacities, judges and juries might well be responding to a logic of this kind. Whether or not they are responding to that logic, significant damage awards are justified for such losses.

If it is correct to emphasize the importance of capabilities, the general argument applies to a wide range of losses, including those that do not involve higher-level cognitive functions. If Jones is unable to engage in sexual relationships or to participate in certain athletic activities, it is plausible to say that his enjoyment of life has been impaired, once the right content has been given to that concept. It is true, however, that use of the idea of capability makes less sense for those losses that are essentially hedonic. If a person was once able to play tennis, but no longer can, is there a genuine loss if no hedometer can identify it? The answer to that question may be "no" even if we are confident that those with serious cognitive impairments, however happy, have lost some of the enjoyment of life. Perhaps the answer is "yes," because the person has lost an option, and because the option has value. I will return to this issue shortly.

Of course it is true that the category of capability loss does not require plaintiffs to be compensated for any inability to engage in some task. If someone is no longer able to do calligraphy, or to reach the top shelf on her tiptoes, or to hit certain high notes when singing in the shower, compensation may not be justified. (The analysis might be different if the plaintiff is calligrapher or an opera singer.) The task is to identify those losses that are sufficiently basic or foundational to justify a monetary award. Development of a full theory would be a large task, but at a glance at the cases suggest that whatever the content of the theory, losses of a leg, of sexual capacities, of mobility, and of cognitive function are strong candidates for inclusion. Compare in this regard the Americans with Disabilities Act, which labels people "disabled" if they have an impairment that significantly limits "major life activities"; the inquiry into "major life activities" might similarly be understood in terms of capability losses.

4.3. Translating (Hedonic and Capability) Losses into Money

Suppose that Jones has suffered a loss of a leg and that the loss produces a stated hedonic injury. We might agree that the loss is less serious than the loss of both legs but more serious than the loss of three toes. What is the monetary value of the loss? Perhaps the same method can be used to answer that question regardless of whether we are investigating hedonic losses or capability losses.

Willingness to Pay? If we were speaking in economic terms, we might ask how much Jones would be willing to pay to eliminate a 1/100,000 risk of losing the loss of a leg. As we have seen, this is a standard approach in the valuation of mortality and morbidity risks. Suppose that the focus is on Jones's hedonic loss. If so, the discussion thus far should be enough to show that Jones's willingness to pay may reflect a hedonic forecasting error. Perhaps Jones would be willing to pay $50 to avoid that risk, which implies a loss of $5 million, even though the hedonic loss from a lost leg would not be terribly serious. Recall that loss aversion itself appears to be a hedonic forecasting error (see Kermer et al. 2006).

Alternatively, suppose that the focus is on Jones's capability loss. Perhaps Jones is concerned that the loss of a leg is a loss of a capability. He might want to pay a certain amount to preserve the option value of having his leg, or he might want to pay that amount of preserve the capability as such. In principle, his willingness to pay might be a good measure of the relevant value. But it is hard to imagine that faced with small probabilities of such losses, people can generate figures that reliably capture the capability values of significant harms, especially in view of the difficulty of measuring the actual effects of such losses before they have occurred.

If the goal of compensation is to restore people to the status quo, then people's willingness to pay, before the fact, is an unreliable measure. The gold standard consists of people's actual experience, and as we have seen, willingness to pay is likely to reflect a hedonic judgment error. In fact, it may be a mistake to rely on people's judgment about necessary compensation even after they are injured. Of course their judgment is least reliable in the period immediately following the injury. At that point, their focus on the injury and its removal may reflect a focusing illusion, no less than when people are asked about the weather. And long after the injury has occurred, a focusing illusion might also distort their judgments, whether we are speaking in hedonic terms or in terms of capabilities. Recall that colostomy and dialysis patients would pay a great deal (in terms of remaining years of life!) to be well, even though available measures suggest that they are no less happy than they were before.

An argument in favor of willingness to pay might take the following form. The legal system attempts to produce the right deterrent signals. Suppose that people believe, before the fact, that the loss of a limb is terrible and would be willing to pay a great deal to reduce the risk of that loss. Suppose that the legal system awards them a relatively low amount, capturing the actual (as opposed to the wrongly anticipated) loss. Knowing about the prospect of a low award and anticipating the risk of loss, other people, facing that risk, will take extensive precautions against that risk. If so, the willingness-to-pay figure might be used even if it is based on an error, because use of that figure is necessary to avoid those precautions. The argument cannot be ruled out of bounds, but it probably relies on heroic assumptions about the sensitivity of ordinary people to likely awards from the legal system. Accurate awards—sometimes lower and sometimes higher than what people would be willing to pay to avoid—will have behavioral effects at the margin, but it is doubtful that those effects would be large.

Scaling without a Modulus.   Loosened from willingness to pay, however, jurors are likely to produce highly unpredictable results. Indeed, the problem of translating hedonic or capability harms into monetary equivalents is a large source of inequality and variability in the legal system. Studies of pain-and-suffering awards show a great deal of noise, in the form of variations unexplained by differences in the cases (see Leebron 1989). The same is true of awards for sexual harassment (Sharkey 2006). Experimental work suggests that some of the unpredictability comes from the fact that when translating injuries into dollars, jurors are being asked to scale without a modulus—that is, to assign monetary values along an unbounded numerical scale without being given a modulus, or standard, by which to establish a meaning for the various points on the scale (see Sunstein, Kahneman, and Schkade 1998; Kahneman, Schkade, and Sunstein 1998).

Imagine, for example, that people are asked to offer a numerical equivalent for the brightness of a light, or the loudness of a noise, on a bounded scale of 0 to infinity. There is every reason to believe that their judgments would have a high degree of unpredictability—not because of disagreement on anything substantial, but because of the nature of the scale. This problem certainly infects awards for pain and suffering: what is the monetary equivalent of 3 months with migraine headaches, or 6 months of rehabilitation of a broken leg, or back pain for the next 20 years? The same is true for hedonic damages, for jurors are not given a modulus by which to decide on the economic value of some loss of the enjoyment of life. What is the monetary equivalent of the loss of a dog, a limb, cognitive functioning, or sexual capacities? Now suppose that we are not speaking in hedonic terms at all, and the question is the monetary value of a loss of a capability. What is the dollar value of such a loss?

The translation of hedonic or capability losses into monetary equivalents raises daunting problems. But at the very least, it would be valuable to be able to know what is lost in welfare terms, before any attempt is made at translation. My minimal suggestion here has been that judges and juries are likely to make serious blunders in answering the welfare question.

4.4. Toward Civil Damages Guidelines

We can now identify two serious problems in the current situation. First (and this is the more established problem), juries and judges are likely to have difficulty in generating monetary figures to reflect pain, suffering, and loss of enjoyment of life. Because it is difficult to scale without a modulus, and because anchors will have a significant effect, unjustified inequality and excessive and insufficient awards are inevitable. Second (and this is the problem uncovered by the happiness literature), juries and judges are likely to make hedonic judgment errors. My emphasis has been on the second problem, but if we take the two together, we will be inclined to consider large-scale reforms. Proceeding from scratch, no sensible person could possibly want to produce damage awards by asking ordinary people, with little guidance, to assign monetary amounts to losses with which they are unlikely to have had much experience.

The most obvious response would be a set of civil damages guidelines, charged with the task of rationalizing the current situation. The guidelines would place heavy reliance on existing knowledge about hedonic harms, so as to avoid the risk of high awards for illusory losses and low awards for such harms as chronic pain, migraines, anxiety, and depression. To the extent that the short-term hedonic losses are present even when long-term adaptation occurs, the guidelines would take that point into account. To the extent that discrimination and stigma play a role in producing hedonic or other harm, the guidelines would consider that point as well (see Bagenstos and Schlanger forthcoming). A significant part of the harm of certain injuries consists of the resulting social stigma, on which it might be difficult not to focus and from which both economic and noneconomic injuries may follow. Those injuries deserve to count (Bagenstos and Schlanger forthcoming). Moreover, a large advantage of the guidelines is that they would make it less necessary, and perhaps even unnecessary, for disabled plantiffs to "perform" their disability or their suffering in court, in a way that could be embarrassing and even humiliating.

The guidelines would also attempt to make sensible translations into monetary equivalents, perhaps by drawing workers' compensation awards, which reflect a similar attempt at rationalization. Willingness-to-pay figures would provide at least a start here; perhaps the best approach would begin with WTP for hedonic and capability losses and make suitable adjustments when WTP depends on a demonstrable error. Finally, the guidelines would make judgments about capability damages, clearly distinguishing them from hedonic harms.

The development of such guidelines would have a significant technocratic dimension. The goal would not be to build on ordinary intuitions, which are unreliable. It would instead be to incorporate what has been learned about the actual effects of various losses. To the extent that the legal system is concerned with the consequences for subjective well-being, the distinction between persistent and illusory losses would play a key role. In addition, a great deal of attention would have to be paid to ranking capability losses and turning them into monetary equivalents. That task would have a technocratic feature, but it would be inescapably normative. Which capabilities are foundational? How does the loss of an arm compare with the loss of sexual function? For capability losses, reflective judgments, made perhaps by representative and diverse panels, would be most valuable.

If civil damages guidelines were in place, the role of judges and juries would be limited and analogous to that of judges under the Federal Sentencing Guidelines. Attention would continue to be paid to particular circumstances: the loss of a hand is worse for a concert pianist than for a professor of comparative literature. In the criminal context, of course, the Federal Sentencing Guidelines have been subject to vigorous objections; they seem to reflect errors and biases of various sorts, and rule-based systems may not, in the abstract, be better than standard-based alternatives. We cannot entirely exclude the possibility that civil damages guidelines would be even worse than the status quo. But the current system of awards deserves some kind of award for combining unjustified inequality with cognitive errors. There is every reason to try to do better.

4.5. Broader Lessons

These remarks bear on much larger questions. In this section, I offer some notes on the relationship between happiness on the one hand and willingness to pay and income growth on the other.

Willingness to Pay and Happiness. As I have suggested, many economists and economically oriented lawyers work with the WTP criterion. If people are willing to pay $50 to eliminate a 1/100,000 risk of losing a foot, there is a good argument that government should start with that number in deciding on appropriate policies. Suppose, however, that people's WTP is a product of a systematic bias, perhaps in the form of a focusing illusion. If so, the connection between WTP and welfare effects will be weakened and possibly very weak (Sunstein 2007). People may be purchasing goods from which they receive little hedonic benefit, and they may be failing to purchase goods from which they receive significant hedonic benefits. (To be sure, people are willing to pay for nonhedonic reasons, as for example when they give to those in need; but often, at least, the motivation is hedonic.) And if this is so, there are serious problems with reliance on WTP, because it operates as a crude proxy for welfare effects, understood in hedonic terms. In short, hedonic forecasting errors raise serious problems for standard ways of conducting cost-benefit analysis.

We can see the point most clearly in connection with contingent-valuation studies. Suppose that people are asked, "How much would you be willing to pay to ensure that climate in your city does not increase by a certain amount by a certain date or to avoid a 1/100,000 chance of losing a finger?" The problem is that such questions specifically focus people on a certain loss and for that reason create a grave risk of a focusing illusion (see Kahneman and Sugden 2005). To the extent that contingent-valuation studies elicit WTP, there is a serious problem.

Perhaps markets will reduce the problem, because the budget constraint, and the full menu of possible expenditures, looms much larger in the market domain than in the circumstances of surveys. Perhaps in their daily lives, people will not suffer serious focusing illusions when deciding how much to pay to reduce risks, because they are alert, at the relevant times, to the opportunity costs of the expenditures. When people have experience and obtain prompt feedback, they are far less likely to err (Thaler and Sunstein 2008). Nonetheless, sellers of products would very much like to generate focusing illusions in order to ensure that people will buy their products. And it is entirely possible that even in the market domain, WTP reflects a systematic distortion with respect to losses that seem to be significant (but are not) and with respect to losses that seem to be relatively trivial (but are large). A great deal of work remains to be done on this problem, which seems to unsettle many of the standard claims and views in economic analysis of policy and law (for preliminary thoughts, see Sunstein 2007).

Income Growth, Happiness, and Capability. One of the most striking findings in modern social science is that increases in economic growth are not correlated with increases in measures of happiness or reported life satisfaction (see, for example, Layard 2005; Kahneman and Krueger 2006). The United States, France, and Japan all experienced dramatic increases in real income in the twentieth century but showed no increase in subjective well-being (Diener and Suh 2002). An especially striking finding involves China (see Kahneman and Krueger 2006). Between 1994 and 2005, China experienced explosive growth in average real income—250 percent in fact. In that same period, life satisfaction has actually declined, with a reduction in reported satisfaction from 80 percent to 70 percent and an increase in reported dissatisfaction from 21 percent to 35 percent (Kahneman and Krueger 2006).

For purposes of self-reported happiness according to global measures, what appears to matter is relative economic position, not absolute economic position (see Frank 2000). People's self-reported happiness, by global measures, is greatly affected by their position in the economic hierarchy rather than by their absolute wealth. Apparently those who are in a high position, in a relevant hierarchy, impose positional externalities on others, causing hedonic damage (Frank 2000). By contrast, significant shifts in absolute economic position produce little or no hedonic change. From existing evidence, it is odd but not implausible to say that if the gross domestic product (GDP) of America or France doubled in some period of years, we would not pick up any increase in people's life satisfaction. (Return to the case of China.) This conclusion seems counterintuitive but on reflection may not be: Do we really believe that people now living are much happier than people who lived (say) 5 decades earlier and that those who lived 5 decades earlier were happier than those who preceded them? Even when GDP grows every decade, does subjective well-being grow correspondingly? Recall the importance of attention to people's well-being. Those who have relatively less money, and inferior goods and services, are likely to focus on that fact. But if everyone has more money, and better goods and services, people are less likely to attend to the improvement. The problem, for those who believe that subjective well-being is our lodestar, is that existing evidence suggests that economic growth is not a good way to increase national well-being.

I have noted that some people believe that what matters is not global measures of happiness but measures of moment-by-moment happiness. Perhaps global measures are a crude way of capturing what really matters, which is happiness as it is actually experienced (see Kahneman et al. 2004). But even if this is so, absolute income is a poor measure of moment-by-moment happiness; across a certain threshold, there is no evidence that wealth is correlated with positive affect or with an absence of negative affect (see Kahneman et al. 2004, 2007). Even relative economic position, though correlated with global measures, is not correlated with measures of moment-by-moment happiness (Kahneman et al. 2004)—findings that again suggest the importance of attention. We might therefore conclude that whether global or moment-by-moment measures are the appropriate guide, economic growth does not much matter to people's welfare.

But there is an important qualification. From the discussion thus far, it should be clear that self-reported happiness is not the only thing that is important, even if welfare, properly understood, is our lodestar. Happiness may not increase with growth in GDP, but one result of GDP growth may well be increases in longevity, health, and opportunity.[11] From the standpoint of increasing human welfare, it is good to enable people to live 80 healthy years than 40 less healthy years, even if their level of daily happiness does not increase. If increases in GDP are correlated with longer and healthier lives, and with better opportunities and greater education, such increases appear to promote welfare even if subjective happiness stays constant. Recall here the view that capabilities have independent importance. To the extent that increases in GDP increase literacy, promote health, and ensure greater opportunity, they are valuable whatever happens to subjective happiness.

This point receives indirect support from some intriguing differences

11. For discussion, see Sen (1985). Sen argues that the concern should be capabilities, not economic growth, but it is nonetheless true that growth is (imperfectly) correlated with improvements in capabilities.

between measures of global life satisfaction and measures of moment-by-moment happiness. For example, global life satisfaction is positively affected by whether one is married, has children, or is wealthy—but moment-by-moment happiness is not. (In fact, divorced women report both lower life satisfaction and higher moment-by-moment happiness than married women; see Kahneman et al. 2004.) It is tempting to think that the moment-by-moment measures are more accurate, because they are more reliable than global measures, which seem to be a stab in the dark. Consider the fact that experimenters can easily prime those who answer general questions about happiness or life satisfaction, for example, by asking them first how many dates they have had in the past month (see Kahneman and Krueger 2006). Such questions significantly affect reported life satisfaction. Perhaps those who are not specifically primed engage in a kind of self-priming, asking certain questions (am I married, do I have children, or am I wealthy?) in a way that produces inaccurate measures of how happy they are in fact. On this view, moment-by-moment measures are far better; if people are saddened by asking questions about their global life satisfaction, their sadness should matter only to the extent that it shows up in their actual experience.

On a different view, however, global measures produce not inaccurate proxies but more reflective judgments, in which people assess how well their lives are actually going. It is easy to imagine somewhat negative answers to that question despite high levels of moment-by-moment happiness, produced by hedonically good lives in which people see friends a great deal, have long vacations, and greatly enjoy their days. Such people might nonetheless conclude that their lives are not particularly satisfying, perhaps because they lack depth or meaning. Similarly, it is easy to imagine highly positive reactions to global life satisfaction questions despite not-high levels of moment-by-moment happiness. The high levels of life satisfaction and the not-high levels of moment-by-moment happiness might be produced by lives in which people work hard, serve others, and have a great deal of stress.

I am not insisting that, in fact, most people are giving reflective answers to questions about global life satisfaction, offering a mixture of judgments about their moods, their capabilities, and their assignments of meaning. What is clear is that even if social gains along various dimensions do not register on either global or moment-by-moment measures, they should nonetheless count as gains; consider a population that is better educated, significantly healthier, and given more options about what to do with their lives. If economic growth produces those gains, it is valuable even if it does not have significant hedonic effects.

But if the goal really is welfare, we might pursue the relevant ends directly and focus on economic growth only to the extent that it is responsible or a good proxy for the relevant improvements. If the evidence on subjective happiness is taken seriously, the consequences for law and policy would appear to be significant, because economic growth would be demoted to a secondary matter, to be promoted only to the extent that it helps achieve primary goals, which might in any case be pursued directly (see Kahneman and Krueger 2006, pp. 18–21).

A Note on Meaning.   I have mentioned the idea of meaning, and that idea deserves independent analysis. If someone loses cognitive capacities, the loss is not only one of a capability; his life also becomes less meaningful. And if someone is usually in a good mood, perhaps because life is constantly fun, he might nonetheless think, on reflection, that his activities are superficial or even silly and that something is missed by moment-by-moment measures of his moods. A global life satisfaction question might, in principle, pick up this concern, but perhaps people take that question in hedonic terms. And even if an absence of meaning is not reflected in people's answers to survey questions or to subjectively felt experience, it nonetheless matters; much fiction, most prominently Aldous Huxley's *Brave New World*, explores that point. Perhaps some damage awards can be justified as reflecting meaning loss (though here again monetization is extremely difficult).

Whether or not this is so, we can now see an additional difficulty with purely hedonic measures. Those who are always in happy moods may nonetheless be missing an important ingredient of well-being. Happiness, understood in hedonic terms, does matter a great deal, but well-being includes heterogeneous and plural goods.

5. CONCLUSION

In many contexts, the legal system requires people to make difficult hedonic judgments. If people make serious hedonic judgment errors in their own lives, it is highly likely that juries and judges will make equivalent errors. In particular, there is a serious risk that adjudicative institutions will significantly overestimate the hedonic losses associated with certain injuries. The exaggerations stem in part from a failure to appreciate people's powers of adaptation (adaptation neglect); they also stem from the kind of focusing illusion that people demonstrate when thinking about the effects of weather. Often apparently significant losses turn out to be illusory, at least if they are understood in hedonic terms.

There are two particular implications. The first is that those involved in awarding damages must clearly distinguish between those injuries that involve persistent harm and those injuries that do not. Some injuries fall within the same category as unpleasant noises, to which people do not adapt and on which people cannot help but focus; other injuries, such as the loss of toes, inflict little hedonic harm. The second implication is that capability damages deserve independent analysis. Even if little or no hedonic loss is suffered, it is reasonable to conclude that people deserve to be compensated in the event of a loss or serious injury to capabilities.

I have suggested that the legal system now suffers from serious problems in making hedonic judgments and in translating hedonic and capability losses into monetary equivalents. The natural response is a set of civil damages guidelines, incorporating sensible assessments of monetization, the best available information about hedonic effects, and reflective judgments about capability losses.

It should be clear that these points have implications for how policymakers might think about a range of questions outside of the domain of adjudication. These include the limits of the willingness-to-pay criterion, the value of national income growth, and appropriate priority setting for governments concerned to improve social well-being. The minimal conclusion is that if hedonic states matter, governments should give far higher priority than they now do to the relief of mental illness and chronic pain.[12] More generally, it would not be surprising if governments make significant hedonic judgment errors in fiscal and regulatory policy. If so, efforts to correct the resulting errors would produce major welfare gains.

REFERENCES

Bagenstos, Samuel, and Margo Schlanger. 2007. Hedonic Damages, Hedonic Adaptation, and Disability. *Vanderbilt Law Review* 60:745–87.
Bateman, Ian J., and Kenneth G. Willis. 1999. *Valuing Environmental Preferences*. New York: Oxford University Press.

12. To the extent that certain conditions are accompanied by stigma, and to the extent that stigma imposes continuing hedonic harm, the analysis should be similar.

Berla, Edward P., Michael L. Brookshire, and Stun V. Smith. 1990. Hedonic Damages and Personal Injury: A Conceptual Approach. *Journal of Forensic Economics* 3:1–8.

Bovbjerg, Randall R., Frank A. Sloan, and James F. Blumstein. 1989. Valuing Life and Limb in Tort: Scheduling Pain and Suffering. *Northwestern University Law Review* 83:908–76.

Clark, Andrew E., Ed Diener, Yannis Georgellis, and Richard E. Lucas. 2003. Lags and Leads in Life Satisfaction: A Test of the Baseline Hypothesis. Working Paper No. 2003–14. CNRS and DELTA-Federation Jourdan, Paris.

Diener, Edward, and E. Suh. 2002. National Differences in Subjective Well-Being. Pp. 438–41 in *Well-Being: The Foundations of Hedonic Psychology*, edited by Daniel Kahneman, Ed Diener, and Norbert Schwarz. New York: Russell Sage Foundation.

Easterlin, Richard. 2003. *Building a Better Theory of Well-Being*. Discussion Paper No. 742. IZA, Bonn.

Elster, John. 1983. *Sour Grapes: Studies in the Subversion of Rationality*. New York: Cambridge University Press.

Frank, Robert. 2000. *Luxury Fever: Money and Happiness in an Era of Excess*. Princeton, N.J.: Princeton University Press.

Frederick, Shane, and George Loewenstein. 1999. Hedonic Adaptation. Pp. 303–11 in *Well-Being: The Foundations of Hedonic Psychology*, edited by Daniel Kahneman, Ed Diener, and Norbert Schwarz. New York: Russell Sage Foundation.

Frey, Bruno S., and Alois Stutzer. 2002. *Happiness and Economics: How the Economy and Institutions Affect Human Well-Being*. Princeton, N.J.: Princeton University Press.

Gilbert, Daniel. 2006. *Stumbling on Happiness*. New York: Alfred A. Knopf.

Gilbert, Daniel, Elizabeth C. Pinel, Timothy D. Wilson, Stephen J. Blumberg, and Thalia P. Wheatley. 1998. Immune Neglect: A Source of Durability Bias in Affective Forecasting. *Journal of Personality and Social Psychology* 75: 617–38.

Gilbert, Daniel, and Timothy Wilson. 2000. Miswanting: Some Problems in the Forecasting of Future Affective States. Pp. 178–97 in *Feeling and Thinking: The Role of Affect in Social Cognition*, edited by Joseph Forgas. New York: Cambridge University Press.

Kahneman, Daniel, Ed Diener, and Norbert Schwarz, eds. 1999. *Well-Being: The Foundations of Hedonic Psychology*. New York: Russell Sage Foundation.

Kahneman, Daniel, and Alan Krueger, 2006. Developments in the Measurement of Subjective Well-Being. *Journal of Economic Perspectives* 20:3–24.

Kahneman, Daniel, Alan Krueger, David Schkade, Amy Kirlla, and Claude Fischler. 2007. The Structure of Well-Being in Two Cities. Unpublished manuscript. Princeton University, Woodrow Wilson School of Public and International Affairs, Princeton, N.J.

Kahneman, Daniel, Alan B. Krueger, David A. Schkade, Norbert Schwarz, and Arthur A. Stone. 2004. A Survey Method for Characterizing Daily Life Experience: The Day Reconstruction Method. *Science* 3:1776–80.

Kahneman, Daniel, David Schkade, and Cass Sunstein. 1998. Shared Outrage and Erratic Awards: The Psychology of Punitive Damages. *Journal of Risk and Uncertainty* 16:49–86.

Kahneman, Daniel, and Robert Sugden. 2005. Experienced Utility as a Standard of Policy Evaluation. *Environmental and Resource Economics* 32:161–81.

Kahneman, Daniel, and Richard Thaler. 2006. Anomalies: Utility Maximization and Expected Utility. *Journal of Economic Perspectives* 20:221–34.

Kermer, Deborah A., Erin Driver-Linn, Timothy D. Wilson, and Daniel T. Gilbert. 2006. Loss Aversion Is an Affective Forecasting Error. *Psychological Science* 17:649–53.

Korobkin, Russell. 2003. The Endowment Effect and Legal Analysis. *Northwestern University Law Review* 97:1227–94.

Layard, Richard. 2005. *Happiness: Lessons From a New Science*. New York: Penguin Press.

Leebron, David. 1989. Final Moments: Damages for Pain and Suffering Prior to Death. *New York University Law Review* 64:256–363.

Loewenstein, George, and Peter Ubel. 2006. Hedonic Adaptation and the Role of Decision and Experience Utility in Public Policy. Paper presented at the conference Happiness and Public Economics, London, September.

McCaffery, Edward J., Daniel J. Kahneman, and Matthew L. Spitzer. 1995. Framing the Jury: Cognitive Perspectives in Pain and Suffering Awards. *Virginia Law Review* 81:1341–1420.

Mill, John Stuart. 1863. *Utilitarianism*. London: Parker, Son, & Bourn.

Nussbaum, Martha. 1996. *The Therapy of Desire: Theory and Practice in Hellenistic Ethics*. New York: Cambridge University Press.

———. 1999. *Women and Human Development: The Capabilities Approach*. New York: Cambridge University Press.

———. 2001. *Women and Human Development*. New York: Cambridge University Press.

Oswald, Andrew, and Powdthavee Nattavudh. 2005. *Does Happiness Adapt? A Longitudinal Study of Disability with Implications for Economists and Judges*. Unpublished manuscript. University of Warwick, Department of Economics, Warwick.

Rodgers, Gregory. 1993. Estimating Jury Compensation for Pain and Suffering in Product Liability Cases Involving Nonfatal Personal Injury. *Journal of Forensic Economics* 6:251–62.

Samaha, Adam. 2007. What Is The Social Model Good For? Unpublished manuscript. University of Chicago Law School, Chicago.

Satz, Ani B. 2006. A Jurisprudence of Dysfunction: On the Role of "Normal

Species Functioning" in Disability Analysis. *Yale Journal of Health Policy, Law and Ethics* 6:221–67.

Schkade, David, and Daniel Kahneman. 1998. *Does Living in California Make People Happy? Psychological Science* 9:340–46.

Sen, Amartya. 1985. *Commodities and Capabilities*. New York: Elsevier Science.

———. 1999. *Development as Freedom*. New York: Knopf.

Sharkey, Catherine M. 2006. Dissecting Damages: An Empirical Exploration of Sexual Harassment Awards. *Journal of Empirical Legal Studies* 3:1–45.

Smith, Dylan M., Ryan L. Sheriff, Laura Damschroder, George Loewenstein, and Peter A. Ubel. 2006. Misremembering Colostomies: Former Patients Give Lower Utility Ratings Than Do Current Patients. *Health Psychology* 25: 688–95.

Sunstein, Cass R. 2007. Willingness to Pay vs. Welfare. *Harvard Law and Policy Review* 1:303–30.

Sunstein, Cass R., Daniel Kahneman, and David Schkade. 1998. Assessing Punitive Damages (with Notes on Cognition and Valuation in Law). *Yale Law Journal* 107:2071–2154.

Thaler, Richard. 1991. *Quasi Rational Economics*. New York: Russell Sage Foundation.

Thaler, Richard A., and Cass R. Sunstein. 2008. *Nudge: Improving Decisions through the Science of Choice*. New Haven, Conn.: Yale University Press.

Ubel, Peter A., and George Loewenstein. 2008. Pain and Suffering Awards: They Shouldn't Be (Just) about Pain and Suffering. *Journal of Legal Studies* 37: S195–S216.

Ubel, Peter A., George Loewenstein, John Hershey, Jonathan Baron, Tara Mohr, David A. Asch, and Christopher Jepson. 2001. Do Nonpatients Underestimate the Quality of Life Associated with Chronic Health Conditions Because of a Focusing Illusion? *Medical Decision Making* 21:190–99.

Ubel, Peter A., George Loewenstein, and Christopher Jepson. 2003. Whose Quality of Life? A Commentary Exploring Discrepancies between Health State Evaluations of Patients and the General Public. *Quality of Life Research* 12: 599–607.

———. 2005. Disability and Sunshine: Can Hedonic Predictions Be Improved by Drawing Attention to Focusing Illusions or Emotional Adaptation? *Journal of Experimental Psychology Applied* 11:111–23.

Viscusi, W. Kip. 1988. Pain and Suffering in Product Liability Cases: Systematic Compensation or Capricious Awards? *International Review of Law and Economics* 8:203–20.

———. 1994. *Fatal Tradeoffs*. New York: Oxford University Press.

———. 1998. *Rational Risk Policy*. New York: Oxford University Press.

Weinstein, Neil D. 1982. Community Noise Problems: Evidence against Adaptation. *Journal of Environmental Psychology* 2:87–97.

Pain and Suffering Awards: They Shouldn't Be (Just) about Pain and Suffering

Peter A. Ubel and George Loewenstein

ABSTRACT

In this paper, we challenge the conventional view that pain-and-suffering awards should be interpreted literally as a compensation for feelings of pain and suffering. People adapt to conditions as serious as paraplegia and blindness, returning rapidly to near-normal levels of happiness, which means that pain-and-suffering awards based literally on pain and suffering would be small. We argue that compensation for these types of conditions should be larger than would be dictated by pain and suffering alone because people legitimately care about more than just the pain and suffering that results from an injury; they also care about a variety of other factors, such as their capabilities to perform various functions, that often do not affect happiness. We propose the outlines of a method for determining noneconomic damages that divides the problem into three judgments, each to be made by the constituency most competent to make it.

1. INTRODUCTION

The question of how, or even whether, to value damages associated with pain and suffering is of critical importance for legal practice and theory. Empirical studies have found that noneconomic damages account for a large fraction of personal injury tort suits (Viscusi 1988), and the difficulty of placing a monetary value on such damages is often held responsible for arbitrary, capricious awards (Abel 2006). Geistfeld (1995), for example, estimates that the severity of a victim's injury accounts for

PETER UBEL is the George Dock Collegiate Professor of Internal Medicine at the University of Michigan. GEORGE LOEWENSTEIN is the Herbert A. Simon Professor of Economics and Psychology at Carnegie Mellon University. We thank Cynthia Estlund, Sam Gross, an anonymous reviewer, and participants at the conference for helpful comments and suggestions.

[*Journal of Legal Studies*, vol. XXXVII (June 2008)]
© 2008 by The University of Chicago. All rights reserved. 0047-2530/2008/370S2-0008$10.00

only 40 percent of the variation in pain-and-suffering awards, with the remainder potentially attributable to ostensibly unjustifiable factors such as race, gender, and the perceived attractiveness of the victim.

While experts disagree about what actually influences juries in making these awards, they largely agree about what ought to influence juries— they should base pain-and-suffering awards on how much misery a victim will experience due to an injury. In other words, pain and suffering, as applied to legal awards, should be interpreted literally—in hedonic terms. Thus, Geistfeld (1995, p. 781) defines pain and suffering as "a category of damages including not only physical *pain*, but also a wide range of intangible injuries such as fright, nervousness, grief, anxiety, and indignity." All of these intangible injuries, it can be seen, are varieties of feeling states as opposed to objective outcomes. Schwartz and Silverman (2004, p. 1045) cite the judgment of an appellate court in California to the effect that "[t]he standard pain-and-suffering instruction . . . describes a unitary concept of recovery not only for physical pain but for fright, nervousness, grief, anxiety, worry, mortification, shock, humiliation, indignity, embarrassment, apprehension, terror or ordeal." In this list, only the last element allows for any interpretation other than as a hedonically charged feeling state. All the other papers that we were able to locate imply a similarly hedonic perspective.

In this paper we question whether pain and suffering should, in fact, be interpreted in literal, hedonic terms. Drawing on our own and others' research on the measurement and valuation of health states, we argue that while pain and suffering do warrant inclusion as an element of awards, hedonic interpretations of the concept have illogical and normatively unacceptable implications for award amounts.

Several scholars have dwelled on the nub of the problem with the hedonic interpretation of pain and suffering—the phenomenon of adaptation. As we document in some detail, most people adapt substantially to diverse conditions as serious as paraplegia, kidney failure, and blindness, returning to close to baseline levels of happiness after a brief period of adjustment. In Section 2, we review research showing that such adaptation is real and not an artifact of measurement problems; people with these conditions really do experience high levels of happiness. However, as we document in Sections 3 and 4, three groups of people—those who do not have such conditions, those who do have the conditions, and even those who used to have the conditions but recovered from them—display great consistency in the desire to not have the conditions.

We believe that the reason for the discrepancy between hedonic measures and stated preferences (as well as preferences revealed by protective and remediative measures) is that people care about many things that are not purely hedonic, such as meaning, capabilities, and range of feeling and experience. If this is the case, it would be seriously misguided to ignore the expressed distaste of all three groups for the health conditions in question and to base valuations of noneconomic damages on a notion of well-being that is far narrower than that adopted by individuals themselves.

In Section 5, we propose the outlines of a method for determining noneconomic damages that, we believe, avoids many of the egregious problems of the current system.[1] Our method minimizes problems created by hedonic adaptation and is designed to circumvent the challenges that juries would face in balancing hedonic and nonhedonic losses when determining awards. It also minimizes several other major problems that plague pain-and-suffering awards, including horizontal and vertical inequities in compensation, discrepancies between awards based on willingness to pay versus willingness to accept, and arbitrariness that arises from the fact that juries evaluate a given injury in isolation—that is, without considering the range of possible injuries—a task that people are not well suited to accomplish. The proposed procedure divides the valuation problem into three judgments, each to be made by the constituency that is most competent or otherwise best equipped to make it.

Before plunging in, we should note that we lack legal training and that, therefore, there is a high likelihood that we will overlook important legal issues. Our expertise is in the psychology of judgment, decision making, adaptation, and valuation of health states. In this paper, we bring some of the insights from this research to bear on the problem of valuing pain and suffering.

---

1. Our emphasis in this paper is on awards for pain and suffering. We recognize that there are other categories of noneconomic damages, such as awards for hedonic damages. For example, Bagenstos and Schlanger (2006) distinguish pain-and-suffering damages, which compensate people for physical discomfort and negative emotions, from hedonic damages, which compensate people for limitations on their ability "to participate in and derive pleasure from the normal activities of daily life" (p. 3). Similarly, Price (1993) provides evidence that courts consider hedonic damages to refer either to a loss of enjoyment of life or to loss of life's pleasures. By these definitions, a person who is permanently comatose, or even someone who has died, has suffered hedonic damages and deserves compensation even though neither would be in a position to experience pain or suffering. Although our paper focuses on how to value pain-and-suffering awards, many of our arguments also apply to hedonic damages. In both cases, we think the emphasis of the awards should be broadened to move beyond purely hedonic assessments.

2. HEDONIC ADAPTATION

2.1. Hedonic Adaptation Defined

Hedonic adaptation refers to any action, process, or mechanism that reduces the affective consequences—emotional effects—of an otherwise stable circumstance (Frederick and Loewenstein 1999). In the context of tort claims, hedonic adaptation occurs whenever a person's postinjury health status remains stable but his emotional response to the injury fades.

Hedonic adaptation can be aided by other forms of adaptation. For example, people can physically adapt to disabilities. Early in their disability, people may have a hard time performing certain activities of daily living. But over time, through physical therapy and the use of assistive devices, their ability to perform such activities tends to increase.

Hedonic adaptation can also be aided by changes in people's social or work environments. A person whose employer is willing and able to accommodate his injury may be able to regain satisfaction from work, or even achieve new, higher, levels. Even if a person's injury precludes him from performing his previous job, he may find a new line of employment and thereby regain some of his previous well-being.

Hedonic adaptation is rarely complete, but in a wide range of circumstances, it is surprisingly strong. For instance, one study found that people with quadriplegia reported a frequency of negative affect similar to that of control respondents (Wortman and Silver 1987). Another study observed almost no difference in quality of life or psychiatric symptomatology in young patients who had lost limbs to cancer compared with those who had not (Tyc 1992).

In one of our own studies (Riis et al. 2005), we surveyed 50 dialysis patients and 50 healthy control subjects, matched by age, race, education, and gender, and asked each group to provide global estimates of the moods they experienced in a typical week: how much time they spent in a very unpleasant mood (-2), unpleasant mood (-1), neutral mood (0), pleasant mood ($+1$), and very pleasant mood ($+2$). We also asked them to estimate the moods they thought they would experience if their health changed, with healthy controls imagining that they developed kidney failure and dialysis patients imagining that they had never had kidney failure.

As shown in Table 1, and consistent with adaptation, both healthy controls and patients reported that their mood in a typical week was

Table 1. Mood Estimates (-2 to $+2$)

	Current	Predicted If in the Other State of Health
Healthy control subjects	.61	$-.17$
Dialysis patients	.78	1.10

positive for the majority of their waking hours, and indeed there was no statistically significant difference in the moods of those two groups.

Hedonic adaptation is not universal, across either people or conditions (Lucas et al. 2004; Oswald and Blanchflower 2004; Lucas 2005). Some conditions appear to defy adaptation more than others, and some circumstances impede adaptation (Ubel 2006). For example, paradoxically, and perhaps surprisingly, the prospect of hope for relief of a condition can impede adaptation to it.[2] Inevitably, also, there are individual differences both in general propensity to adapt and in ability to adapt to specific conditions (Smith et al. 2005).

2.2. Is Hedonic Adaptation Real?

Given the subjectivity of well-being measures, it is reasonable to ask whether hedonic adaptation is real. Supporting such reservations, researchers have documented a number of biases that affect subjective reports of well-being. For example, people's self-reports of how happy they are "in general these days" are powerfully influenced by how happy they are at the moment when they respond, including fluctuations that depend on random factors such as whether the sun is shining when they are asked (Schwarz and Strack 1999). People also tend to naturally "norm" their responses relative to points of reference, such as the people with whom they spend time. A patient who spends time with other patients, therefore, is likely to report higher levels of welfare than one who spends time with healthy people. Nevertheless, a series of studies

2. See Frederick and Loewenstein (1999) for limited evidence on this point. More definitively, in Smith et al. (2008), we asked patients who had just received colostomies to rate their own happiness and life satisfaction and then provide updates about their state of mind at regular intervals thereafter. The main focus of the study was a comparison of the trajectory of happiness and life satisfaction of patients whose colostomies were irreversible with those whose colostomies were potentially reversible at some point in the future. Consistent with prior research, patients with irreversible colostomies displayed indications of adaptation almost immediately after they underwent the procedure. Those with reversible colostomies displayed chronically low levels of happiness and life satisfaction, with little improvement over time.

we have conducted have convinced us that hedonic adaptation is real and not an artifact of measurement problems.

One possible problem with the measures of happiness that have informed studies of adaptation is that when asked vague global questions about happiness, people with health problems may be motivated to minimize their severity and thus may provide overly rosy reports of their own well-being. To test if that was the case, in our dialysis study (Riis et al. 2005), in addition to asking patients and healthy control subjects for global evaluations of well-being, we also elicited self-reports of moment-to-moment happiness from both groups using an ecological momentary assessment method for an interval of 1 week. We sent both groups home with Palm Pilots that were programmed to beep at random points during the day and ask subjects about their mood. We assumed that they would be less likely to provide overly rosy reports of their well-being when asked to report "the mood you were experiencing when this Palm Pilot beeped" than when asked more vague and global questions about mood. The data from the Palm Pilots showed that the moods of patients and controls were strikingly similar, with both groups reporting significantly more positive than negative affect, and with neither group reporting significantly better moods than the other. This finding provides strong evidence that patients with kidney failure really do emotionally adapt to their illness.

Another vulnerability of measures of happiness based on subjective ratings is the problem of scale recalibration: when people's circumstances change, their interpretations of these subjective scales might systematically change in response. For example, following the onset of an illness or disability, a person may spend more time with other people who are sick or disabled, and when asked to report his happiness on a 0–100 scale, he may automatically compare his own happiness to that of other sick people.[3] Alternatively, people who have experienced ex-

---

3. In fact, we found evidence of scale recalibration in an experiment we conducted among participants in the Health and Retirement Study, a large, nationally representative sample of people 50 years and older in the United States (Ubel et al. 2005). In a random subset of 1,031 participants, we asked people to report their overall health on a 0–100 scale. Across participants, we randomly varied the definition of 100 on the scale to represent "perfect health," "perfect health for someone your age," or "perfect health for a 20-year-old." Participants' responses supported the existence of scale recalibration. People with the scale labeled "perfect health" or "perfect health for someone your age" gave similar ratings (73.1 and 72.9, respectively, not significant), whereas people with the scale labeled "perfect health for a 20 year-old" gave lower ratings (with a mean of 65.0, $p < .001$) than the other groups.

treme misery during the initial phase of adjustment to an illness or disability may anchor the bottom of the scale on the low point of their experience, which would tend to raise subsequent reports of well-being. Having had paraplegia for some period of time, a person might rate himself at 80 on the scale only because he realizes how much he has improved from his despair immediately following the onset of the condition.

Mixed evidence that scale recalibration could be a problem was obtained in a telephone interview study of 256 Parkinson's patients (Smith et al. 2006a). In the lead-in to the interview, half the respondents were informed that researchers were "calling people with Parkinson's disease to find out about their life satisfaction and well-being." The other half were informed that researchers were "calling people in the northeastern United States to find out about their life satisfaction and well-being." This design allowed them to test whether patients, when told that the interview was part of a study of Parkinson's disease, automatically norm their responses relative to other Parkinson's patients. Consistent with such norming, respondents reported greater health satisfaction when the survey was introduced as a survey of Parkinson's patients rather than the general population. However, this recalibration did not generalize to ratings of general life satisfaction; respondents reported similarly high levels of life satisfaction under both conditions. Thus, patients' high levels of life satisfaction cannot be attributed to conversational context.

Two other studies further explored the impact of the measurement scale on self-reports of happiness. In Baron et al. (2003), we assessed people's quality-of-life ratings for a series of common health conditions. Across ratings, we varied whether or not the response modes were ambiguous. We speculated that if scale recalibration accounted for the high ratings given by patients, then patients should provide lower ratings relative to healthy persons if they responded on a more ambiguous scale. No such effect occurred.

In Lacey et al. (forthcoming), we asked 407 patients with diabetes and a comparison group of 418 people without diabetes to rate a series of health conditions (such as emphysema and quadriplegia) and conditions unrelated to health (such as an unpleasant boss and a chronically difficult commute to work) on a 0–100 quality-of-life rating scale. Upon completing this task, we asked them to rate what their quality of life would be if they had diabetes requiring daily insulin injections. One goal of the study was to see if patients with diabetes would use the scale differently than healthy persons. If patients with diabetes view their lives more positively than they otherwise would because they use the scale differently, then they should rate not only the disease scenario but also emphysema, unemployment, and an unpleasant boss more highly than healthy people would. As predicted, diabetes patients gave higher quality-of-life ratings for the disease scenario than did healthy people ($p <$ .01). However, we found no evidence for scale recalibration, because both groups of subjects evaluated items other than diabetes nearly identically.

In summary, the best evidence to date suggests that hedonic adaptation is substantial following a wide range of life circumstances. Therefore, people with a wide range of tort-related injuries are likely to adapt to their injuries and experience long-lasting happiness despite living with a chronic injury.

3. PREFERENCES VERSUS HAPPINESS

Given the apparent reality of hedonic adaptation, it can be seen that valuations that interpret pain and suffering in a literal, hedonic fashion would assign little negative value to a wide range of conditions beyond that associated with a typically brief (albeit sometimes severe) period prior to adaptation. Yet there is ample evidence that people have a strong preference to be in a healthy state, even after they have adapted hedonically to a health condition.

Evidence of a distaste for illness and chronic disability comes from myriad studies that assess the preference for health states using decision-based (as opposed to happiness-based) measures. One such measure, the time trade-off (TTO) method, asks subjects to imagine that they have a health condition and will live with it to a specific age, typically 70. They are then asked how much of their remaining lifespan they would give up to live instead in a healthy state, with a greater willingness to give up life-years indicating a lower evaluation of the health condition (Torrance 1976). The TTO measure is commonly used by medical researchers to determine the disutility created by specific health conditions as part of assessing the cost-effectiveness of interventions designed to prevent or alleviate the conditions (Gold et al. 1996). If people do rapidly adapt emotionally to a given health condition, then one might anticipate that people with the health condition would not be willing to give up much of their remaining lifespan to rid themselves of it.

However, patients' responses to TTO surveys belie this view. For example, dialysis patients state that they would give up almost half their remaining years to once again live with normal kidney function (Torrance 1976). Similarly, Smith et al. (2006b) measured the well-being of people with colostomies against those without and failed to find any significant difference in self-reported mood. Yet people with colostomies report, on average, that they would give up almost 15 percent of their remaining lifespan to regain normal bowel function.

It could be objected that the patients who make these decisions have a strong preference for avoiding these health states because they do not appreciate how much they have adapted to their circumstances. Indeed, there is a large literature, including the dialysis study discussed earlier, supporting the idea that people mispredict how happy they would be if they face adversity (Wilson and Gilbert 2003).

Such mispredictions are not limited to healthy persons but can also be seen in patients, who have experienced both health and sickness. In a number of studies, we not only asked healthy people how happy they would be if they were sick but also asked people with illness or disabilities to estimate how happy they would be if they were healthy. Invariably, we found that patients believe they would be substantially happier if they were healthy—indeed, they typically predict an increase in happiness equal to the decrease in happiness predicted by healthy people if they were sick (see Riis et al. 2005; Smith et al. 2006b). Table 1 presents healthy subjects' predictions of how happy they would be if they were on dialysis and dialysis patients' predictions of how happy they would be if they were healthy. Not only did healthy people believe that they would be more miserable if they were on dialysis, but patients on dialysis also estimated that they would be substantially happier if they were not on dialysis. Thus, both groups agreed that they would be substantially happier if healthy than on dialysis, although no such pattern was observed in their self-reported levels of happiness.

In a longitudinal study (Smith et al., forthcoming), we surveyed patients while they were waiting for kidney transplants and asked them about their quality of life and their level of function across various life domains. We also asked them to predict how their quality of life would change in the year following a successful transplant. Then we resurveyed them 1, 6, and 12 months after their transplant. Table 2 summarizes some of our results.

Prior to transplant, patients reported a mean quality of life of 65 (on a 0–100 scale) and predicted that this would rise to 91 in the year following their transplant. One year after transplant, their quality of life

Table 2. Quality-of-Life Reports and Beliefs (0–100)

Time of Survey	Quality-of-Life Report	1-Year Prediction	Recall of Pretransplant
Pretransplant	65	91	. . .
Posttransplant:			
1 month	78	. . .	57
6 months	80	. . .	55
12 months	83	. . .	48

had risen to 83 but significantly less than predicted ($p < .01$). More important for our current discussion, however, their memory of their pretransplant quality of life had changed. They now believed that their pretransplant quality of life had been lower than it really was. As the table shows, while their own quality of life was increasing through the year, their memory of pretransplant life was changing so that it seemed worse with each passing month.[4]

The similarity of the error made by healthy persons (predicting the happiness of patients) and patients (predicting the happiness of healthy people) probably has a common cause: both groups are likely relying on similar, incorrect, intuitive theories about the impact of disability on happiness. These errors raise the possibility that when patients say they would give up a significant amount of their lifespan or pay a large amount of money to rid themselves of a health condition, they are merely demonstrating their ignorance about hedonic adaptation.

But we think patients deserve more credit than this. While the counterfactuals of patients may result from the same mistakes that healthy persons make, it is difficult to dismiss their responses as purely mistakes.

---

4. We found similar evidence of recall bias among patients who had received colostomies at the University of Michigan over the last 5 years. In a cross-sectional survey (Smith et al. 2006b), we asked 194 colostomy patients about their current mood and past mood. One hundred of these patients had had their colostomies reversed in the intervening years, an intervention that was not an option for the remaining 94 patients. Yet, despite ridding themselves of a colostomy, these patients were no happier than the group who still had a colostomy, reporting similar levels of quality of life, positive affect, and negative affect. In other words, having a colostomy appeared to have a negligible effect on happiness. Yet when we asked people to reflect on how happy they had been in the past, the groups diverged. Patients with colostomies remembered being significantly happier in the past, while those without colostomies remembered being less happy ($p < .01$ for interaction). We believe that the most likely explanation for this divergence is that patients' memories were driven by recall bias. Colostomy patients thought back to their happiness before colostomy and believed that they must have been significantly happier then, while those without a colostomy believed the opposite.

Their belief that they would be happier if they were healthy can be interpreted in a different fashion—as providing a strong indication that they would like to be healthy, whatever the validity of their prediction.[5]

We believe that the main reason that healthy people and sick people want to be healthy is only weakly related to a mistaken belief that disabilities produce unhappiness. Indeed, after conducting numerous studies of the hedonics of health conditions and convincing ourselves that people with serious conditions really are happy, both of us remain steadfast, and we suspect largely unchanged by the research, in our powerful desire to remain healthy.

If the sole goal of pain-and-suffering awards is to compensate people for the emotional consequences of their injuries, then we might favor a system of awards based on the types of measures of experience utility—moment-to-moment mood—that we have collected in our own research. However, we have fundamental doubts about whether the goal of such awards is simply to compensate for noneconomic damages. We believe that the main reason that most people state a willingness to sacrifice valued resources for health is not that they underestimate adaptation but that happiness is not the only thing that matters in life. Hence, there are noneconomic damages that warrant compensation even when people fully adapt, emotionally, to a sickness or injury.

4. WHAT HEDONIC MEASURES MISS

Imagine, for a moment, that you have experienced kidney failure, are receiving dialysis three times a week, and have substantially—even completely—adapted emotionally to the situation. In other words, you are as happy now as you were before experiencing kidney failure. Let us also assume, for the purposes of our argument, that you are able to maintain your normal full-time job or have found alternative employment that is not only gratifying but that gives you the same financial rewards as your previous employment. Is there any way in which you are suffering now that deserves compensation, despite the economic and emotional neutrality of your current circumstances? We contend that there are many things that matter to people in their lives independent of how those circumstances influence their long-term emotions.

---

5. Indeed, the first author has spoken to kidney transplantation patients who say that only after being relieved of kidney failure did they realize how unhappy they used to be when they had to receive dialysis three times a week.

4.1. Capabilities

Disability, by definition, involves the loss of some ability, some kind of normal physical functioning. It could be, and in fact has been, argued that such abilities, or capabilities, are important for welfare even if they have little or no impact on hedonics. This is the central insight of the capabilities approach to welfare proposed by Amartya Sen (1985, 1992) and elaborated on by Martha Nussbaum (2000). It was originally designed to deal with problems of social injustice, and specifically the idea that people may be content with poor social and physical conditions or injustice because they have adapted to them or have never experienced anything else. As Nussbaum (2000, p. 114) expresses it, aspirations for a better life can be squelched by "habit, fear, low expectations, and unjust background conditions that deform people's choices and even their wishes for their own lives." Sen and Nussbaum delineate a series of central human capabilities, such as health, freedom from assault, political voice, property rights, equal employment, and access to education, as well as others that involve self-actualization, such as expression of emotion, affiliation with others, and recreation, that they view as universal desiderata. Some of these capabilities, such as health and recreation, are very likely to be undermined by disability and hence, it could be argued, warrant compensation even if an individual is unaffected hedonically because of adaptation or for other reasons.

4.2. Emotional and Experiential Variety

Consider a person who suffers brain damage from an industrial accident and is turned into a happy simpleton because of the injury. It is possible for this person to be emotionally happier than he was prior to the injury, his neuroses dampened by brain damage, his balance of positive and negative affect now much better than before. Would this victim have no grounds for a pain-and-suffering award? John Stuart Mill ([1863] 1973) addressed this question when he stated that it would be better to be a human dissatisfied than a pig satisfied. Clearly, many philosophers (Griffin 1989), as well as both authors of this paper, believe that there are dimensions of richness of experience and complexity and sophistication of thought that have value over and above simple happiness. To the extent that disability limits such experience, according to this perspective, it detracts from welfare, even if it does not detract from happiness.

4.3. Altruistic and Moral Motives

Yet a third category of desired things that may be imperfectly, or even negatively, related to happiness are those that one does out of duty or a sense of morality. People take care of children and aging parents, even when those duties seem onerous and detract from happiness. Thus, for example, becoming a burden on one's children or parents, instead of a caretaker of them, should therefore be counted as a loss, even if it is not accompanied by acute mental suffering.

4.4. The Myth of "Making Whole"

A final nail in what we would like to think is the coffin of a hedonic interpretation of pain-and-suffering awards is the observation that such awards cannot possibly compensate for the conditions for which they are intended to compensate. This stands in sharp contrast to common ways of viewing pain-and-suffering awards.

The idea of giving a victim—someone who has become blinded or paraplegic or severely brain damaged—an amount of money that would make them whole almost certainly is not possible. For a start, in many cases, as we have discussed at length, people emotionally adapt to injuries, so there is nothing that needs to be made whole, in an emotional sense. In these cases, the goal of a pain-and-suffering award cannot be to restore people to their previous emotional state, since they have largely returned to that emotional state without such compensation. In cases in which people do not recover emotionally from serious injuries, on the other hand, there is no evidence that we are aware of that giving them monetary compensation will restore them to their previous emotional state, so it is often impossible, in any case, to make people "whole." Physical injuries and monetary awards seem like examples of things that legal scholars have referred to as being incommensurable (Sunstein 1994).

5. HOW TO VALUE PAIN AND SUFFERING: A TRIPARTITE PROPOSAL

What does it mean to compensate someone for pain and suffering resulting from an injury to which they have emotionally adapted? We contend that the compensation should include hedonic losses associated with the injury—any loss of pleasure or increase in pain and misery—but should also incorporate other factors. Thus, a person who suffers a brain injury, and has become a happy simpleton, has experienced an important loss that deserves compensation, even thought his moment-to-moment mood may be better than ever.

Pain-and-suffering awards, we believe, should be based on a mixture of factors. In part, they should capture the value that society puts on the noneconomic elements of an injury, to deter people from injuring others. If no value is placed on pain and suffering, then potential causers of damage will not sufficiently internalize the risks they impose on society (Arlen 1990, 1993). Damages for pain and suffering are also, in part, intended to provide some relief from actual hedonic pain and suffering, even if they do not restore individuals to their former level of happiness. How, then, is it possible to place a value on pain and suffering once one recognizes that compensating pain and suffering in a literal hedonic sense is impossible and in any case normatively indefensible? We believe that the key is to abandon the illusion that damage awards should compensate for hedonic losses. Instead, we believe, damages should be calibrated to an evaluation of the overall losses imposed by the injury, including but not limited to hedonic effects. We propose a specific proposal for how to assess such damages, breaking the problem into three decisions, each to be made by the people who are the most competent to make it.

The first part of the decision would involve convening a representative panel of citizens to categorize and rank a list of injuries from worst to least bad. The second would involve legislation to determine a maximum value for noneconomic damages and an appropriate value for each rank or category of injury. The third, which would be the task of juries, would be to position the particular damages of a specific plaintiff within the list of injuries ranked by the panel of citizens. We have no idea if such a solution would be politically feasible or legally permissible, but we suspect that it could attain more normatively justifiable awards and diminish problems of vertical and horizontal inequity.

5.1. Ranking and Categorizing Representative Injuries

The first part of our proposed solution involves recruiting a random panel of citizens to develop a thorough, albeit incomplete, list of injuries categorized into groups, with the groups ranked on the basis of the appropriate level of compensation for those particular injuries. Loss of a pinkie toe, for example, might be in one of the most mild categories of injury, because such an injury has almost no long-term emotional consequences and has negligible effects on physical, social, and job functioning. A below-the-knee leg amputation without significant chronic pain would be ranked as a more severe injury, and an amputation accompanied by serious pain would be ranked as being even more severe. Decisions about an injury's proper category would take into account not only the emotional consequences of the injury but also the person's ability to function across important life domains—social functioning, work functioning, sexual functioning, sleep, and the like.

Panelists would hear testimony from experts who would inform them about the likely material consequences of an injury (for example, whether it would be possible for an individual with the injury to drive a car and what type of job, if any, he or she might be capable of holding). In addition, experts would be permitted to testify about evidence concerning the degree to which people do or do not adapt hedonically to the particular condition.[6] We are unsure of if such testimony would have much impact on rankings, but this is the main point at which it would enter into the valuation of damages.

Such an approach to ranking would have a number of benefits. First, the panelists would be ranking injuries in a comparative fashion. Considerable research, including research specifically related to legal damages, suggests that comparative judgments are superior to one-at-a-time judgments (Hsee, Blount, and Bazerman 1999; Sunstein et al. 2002; Ariely et al. 2003). Second, the panel would have both the time and the expert input needed to make informed judgments. Yet, unlike experts, as a representative sample of the population, such a panel would be largely immune to the specific interests that can cloud experts' judgment and make it impossible for such experts to reach a consensus.

Of course, there are many details that would need to be worked out about how best to create such a grouping of citizens, who should be involved in making the list, and so on. But such a task is possible. For example, in the early 1990s the state of Oregon created a list of health conditions to help it allocate its Medicaid funds more efficiently. The goal was to determine which health conditions benefit most from treatment and are most important to treat and which, therefore, would receive

---

6. Such inputs could be implemented, of course, only if there are substantial data documenting the impact of common injuries on broad measures of well-being. But these data are rapidly accumulating and could readily be made available for the injuries being ranked. This approach could help to eliminate the influence of mispredictions and misrememberings on awards. It would likely lead to smaller awards for many physical disabilities to which most people emotionally adapt, while potentially leading to larger awards for conditions causing physical pain, which typically have a larger effect on subjective well-being than mere loss of physical function. The general public typically overestimates how much physical disabilities affect well-being but underestimates how much pain influences subjective well-being (Damschroder et al. 2005).

funding priority, eliminating funding for less important and less valuable treatments and thereby saving enough money to expand Medicaid coverage to a wider group of people (Ubel 2000). In developing this list, Oregon convened a series of community meetings to see what people valued most in health-care interventions. The Oregon Health Commission organized a number of committees to develop different parts of the list. They put out a preliminary list and received feedback and made many changes to the list over several iterations before arriving upon one that was acceptable to a majority of people. That list has been in existence now for well more than a decade and has continued to play an important role in Oregon's Medicaid system. In addition, our proposal has other legal precedents, such as workers' compensation claims, which are frequently based on preexisting lists of work-related injuries. For example, the *Iowa Worker's Compensation Manual* (Iowa Workforce Development 2007) stipulates benefits for loss of a thumb that are twice as great as for loss of a second finger, and 12/7th as great as for loss of a first finger, but just shy of a quarter as great for loss of an arm.[7]

5.2. Determining Money Amounts

Given the logical and practical impossibility of determining an amount of money that would make a plaintiff "whole," we believe that the task of determining the general value of monetary awards is, or should be, a political one and not subject to the idiosyncrasies of individual juries and judges. The real issue, as highlighted by Jennifer Arlen (1985) in a paper on damages for accidental death, is to determine levels of compensation that make the correct trade-off between compensating those who are harmed and limiting the liability of those who harm others. That is, individuals not only are directly affected by receiving damages for pain and suffering; they also have to pay such damages, either directly or indirectly, when the firms they are employed by, own, and buy goods from pay such damages or when the government they finance through taxes pays damages.

One possible mechanism for determining damages in a specific case would be for federal or state legislators to determine a maximum value for an award of pain and suffering. Determination of such a maximum could, and probably should, be informed by the list produced in the process outlined in Section 5.1. That is, legislators would be in a better

7. The values represent the number of weeks of benefits payable for 100 percent loss, or loss of use, of the body member.

position to specify a maximum if they had full knowledge of not only to what type of injury this maximum would apply but also the range and variety of lesser possible injuries.

Although this might seem like a difficult task for a legislature to tackle, in fact, several state legislatures have already dealt with a very closely related problem—the problem of assigning a damage cap for certain types of damages. There is some evidence that existing damage caps sometimes distort awards, in some cases constraining awards that, according to empirical analyses, should have been larger (Viscusi and Born 2005) and in other cases actually increasing small awards by creating a kind of anchor or focal point for awards (Pogarsky and Babcock 2001). The ranking procedure we have outlined would help to avoid both of these problems.

Once a monetary cap has been established, the award could be determined by using the cardinal score, as described above. As an alternative, for example, panelists participating in stage 1 could be given information on the maximum award and then set a range of awards for each category of injury. If they settled, say, on 10 categories of injury, the top category may qualify for between 80 and 100 percent of the maximum award. The next category may qualify for between 70 and 90 percent of the maximum. This would allow for overlap between categories and for a range of awards based on the particulars of the individual victim. Exactly how monetary awards would be assigned to categories would need to be resolved. The main point of the proposed method, however, is to separate the two tasks—ranking injuries on the basis of hedonic and nonhedonic factors and determining appropriate monetary awards—and to separate both of these from the task given to juries.

5.3. The Task of Juries

As we have already pointed out, jurists are likely to mispredict the hedonic consequences of many injuries, overestimating the long-term impact of physical disabilities while underestimating the impact of factors such as chronic pain. For this reason, juries should not be asked to make such determinations. In addition, there are several other tasks at which juries have been shown to fail. As documented in the empirical literature on damages, the existing jury system produces a great degree of horizontal inequity; similar plaintiffs often end up with vastly different awards. Such inequities occur, in part, because the current system requires juries to make decisions that they are ill-equipped to make—most notably to convert pain and suffering into inherently incommensurable monetary terms (Sunstein 1994). Juries are prone to affective forecasting errors, anchoring effects, and random sources of variability from jury to jury, which leaves the level of any given award unacceptably arbitrary.

But beyond the legal mandate for use of juries and the psychological and cultural investment in the jury process, the jury system has an important strength that the proposed framework seeks to exploit. Each injury is, in fact, unique and fits in with the victim's preinjury life in a unique fashion; the jury system creates the opportunity to individualize awards to take account of each victim's unique circumstances.

While people perform poorly in making certain types of judgments and decisions, such as translating between incommensurable scales, they are extremely good at other types of tasks. Specifically, people are very good at ranking things, comparing things, and categorizing them. The task that we propose to give to juries draws on exactly these capabilities. We propose to give juries the task of determining which group of injuries ranked by the panel of citizens proposed in Section 5.1 most closely resembles that of the victim at hand. In addition, juries could help determine if the victim has extenuating circumstances that should drive the award to either the lower or upper end of acceptable compensation for that group of injuries. For example, a victim may have a spinal cord injury at the level of C-7. A jury's job will be to determine if the evidence of this injury is compelling and if there is culpability and then to judge into which group of injuries this injury best fits. If this injury is common enough, it might actually already be on the list, which would simplify the judgment. If it is not on the list, then the jury will need to determine how the injury at hand compares in severity to the ordered grouping of injury categories. Finally, the jury would be asked to determine if this particular victim is suffering more or less than the average person with such an injury.

Our proposal does not do away with jury trials but instead enables juries to involve themselves in the kind of judgments they are best suited to make. We cannot predict how our proposal would influence the relative size of awards for various injuries, although we anticipate that some purely physical injuries—the kind that do not cause much pain or loss of function—will receive relatively smaller awards. The loss of a finger, for example, may end up lower on the severity list than less visible injuries that have more emotional or functional impact. It seems unlikely, however, that the majority of awards would be unchanged under the new system. It would be quite a coincidence if a careful assessment of the functional impact of common injuries did not cause significant departures from the amounts awarded by the current system, which gives such large play to affective forecasting errors. And even if this unlikely scenario came to pass, at least we would have more confidence in our system than we currently do.

6. CONCLUSION

In this paper we have argued that pain-and-suffering awards cannot, and should not, be measures of either subjective pain and suffering or what it would take to alleviate pain and suffering. Instead, awards should be based on a determination of the impact of the injury on both hedonic and nonhedonic aspects of experience—on how an injury influences not only people's long-term moods and feelings but also their ability to function in important life domains.

We have also argued that individual juries are not equipped to determine the emotional impact of specific injuries and, therefore, that a separate deliberative body should review a list of the most common injuries and rank them on the basis of their impact. By removing juries from having to perform this difficult task, we can focus them, instead, on doing the tasks they are best equipped to accomplish. By relieving juries of this task, we not only avoid problems created by hedonic adaptation but also alleviate other problems that have plagued the jury system.

The current system for determining the value of pain-and-suffering awards evolved during a time when experts were largely ignorant about hedonic adaptation or insights from decision research that can help identify what kind of decisions juries are equipped, and not equipped, to make. The determination of pain-and-suffering awards should be revised to take account of recent advances in understanding human judgment and decision making.

REFERENCES

Abel, Richard. 2006. General Damages Are Incoherent, Incalculable, Incommensurable, and Inegalitarian (but Otherwise a Great Idea). *DePaul Law Review* 55:253–329.

Ariely, Dan, George Loewenstein, and Drazen Prelec. 2003. Coherent Arbitrariness: Stable Demand Curves without Stable Preferences. *Quarterly Journal of Economics* 118:73–106.

Arlen, Jennifer H. 1985. An Economic Analysis of Tort Damages for Wrongful Death. *New York University Law Review* 60:1113–36.

———. 1990. Reconsidering Efficient Tort Rules for Personal Injury: The Case of Single Activity Accidents. *William and Mary Law Review* 32:41–103.

———. 1993. Compensation Systems and Efficient Deterrence. *Maryland Law Review* 52:1093–1136.

Bagenstos, Samuel R., and Margo Schlanger. 2006. Hedonic Damages, Hedonic Adaptation, and Disability. Public Law and Legal Theory Research Paper No. 06–09–01. Washington University School of Law, St. Louis.

Baron, Jonathan, David A. Asch, Angela Fagerlin, Christopher Jepson, George Loewenstein, Jason Riis, Margaret G. Stineman, and Peter A. Ubel. 2003. Effect of Assessment Method on the Discrepancy between Judgments of Health Disorders People Have and Do Not Have: A Web Study. *Medical Decision Making* 23:422–34.

Damschroder, Laura J., Brian J. Zikmund-Fisher, and Peter A. Ubel. 2005. The Impact of Considering Adaptation in Health State Valuation. *Social Science and Medicine* 61:267–77.

Frederick, Shane, and George Loewenstein. 1999. Hedonic Adaptation. Chapter 16 in *Foundations of Hedonic Psychology: Scientific Perspectives on Enjoyment and Suffering*, edited by Daniel Kahneman, Ed Diener, and Norbert Schwarz. New York: Russell Sage Foundation.

Geistfeld, Mark. 1995. Placing a Price on Pain and Suffering: A Method for Helping Juries Determine Tort Damages for Nonmonetary Injuries. *California Law Review* 83:773–852.

Gold, Marthe R., Joanna E. Siegel, Louise B. Russell, and Milton C. Weinstein, eds. 1996. *Cost-Effectiveness in Health and Medicine*. New York: Oxford University Press.

Griffin, James. 1989. *Well Being: Its Meaning, Measurement, and Moral Importance*. Oxford: Clarendon Press.

Hsee, Christopher K., Sally Blount, and Max Bazerman. 1999. Preference Reversals between Joint and Separate Evaluations of Options: A Review and Theoretical Analysis. *Psychological Bulletin* 125:576–90.

Iowa Workforce Develpment. 2007. Division of Workers' Compensation. *Iowa Workers' Compensation Manual*. Des Moines: Division of Workers' Compensation. http://www.iowaworkforce.org/wc/2007ratebook.pdf.

Lacey, Heather P., Angela Fagerlin, George Loewenstein, Dylan M. Smith, Jason Riis, and Peter A. Ubel. Forthcoming. Unbelievably Happy? Exploring Whether Scale Recalibration Accounts for the Happiness Gap. *Health Psychology*.

Lucas, Richard E. 2005. Time Does Not Heal All Wounds: A Longitudinal Study of Reaction and Adaptation to Divorce. *Psychological Science* 16:946–50.

Lucas, Richard E., Andrew E. Clark, Yannis Georgellis, and Ed Diener. 2004. Unemployment Alters the Set Point for Life Satisfaction. *Psychological Science* 15:8–13.

Mill, John Stuart. [1863] 1973. Utilitarianism. Pp. 399–472 in *The Utilitarians*. Garden City, N.Y.: Anchor Press/Doubleday.

Nusbaum, Martha. 2000. *Sex and Social Justice*. New York: Oxford University Press.

Oswald, Andrew J. and David G. Blanchflower. 2004. Money, Sex, and Happiness: An Empirical Study. *Scandinavian Journal of Economics* 106: 393–416.

Pogarsky, Greg, and Linda Babcock. 2001. Damage Caps, Motivated Anchoring, and Bargaining Impasse. *Journal of Legal Studies* 30:143–59.

Price, Douglas L. 1993. Hedonic Damages: To Value a Life or Not to Value a Life? *West Virginia Law Review* 95:1055–90.

Riis, Jason, George Loewenstein, Jonathan Baron, Christopher Jepson, Angela Fagerlin, and Peter A. Ubel. 2005. Ignorance of Hedonic Adaptation to Hemodialysis: A Study Using Ecological Momentary Assessment. *Journal of Experimental Psychology: General* 134:3–9.

Schwartz, Victor E., and Cary Silverman. 2004. Hedonic Damages: The Rapidly Bubbling Cauldron. *Brooklyn Law Review* 69:1037–71.

Schwarz, Norbert, and Fritz Strack. 1999. Reports of Subjective Well-Being: Judgmental Processes and Their Methodological Implications. Pp. 61–84 in *Well-Being: The Foundations of Hedonic Psychology*, edited by Daniel Kahneman, Ed Diener and Norbert Schwarz. New York: Russell Sage Foundation.

Sen, Amartya. 1985. *Commodities and Capabilities*. Amsterdam: North-Holland.

———. 1992. *Rationality and Freedom*. Cambridge, Mass.: Harvard University Press.

Smith, Dylan M., Kenneth M. Langa, Mohammed U. Kabeto, and Peter A. Ubel. 2005. Health, Wealth, and Happiness: Financial Resources Buffer Subjective Well-Being after the Onset of a Disability. *Psychological Science* 16:663–66.

Smith, Dylan M., George Loewenstein, Aleksandra Jankovich, Christopher Jepson, H. Feldman, and Peter A. Ubel. Forthcoming. Mispredicting and Misremembering: Patients Overestimate Improvements in Quality of Life after Renal Transplant. *Health Psychology*.

Smith, Dylan M., George Loewenstein, Aleksandra Jankovich, and Peter A. Ubel. 2008. The Dark Side of Hope: Lack of Adaptation to Temporary versus Permanent Colostomy. Working paper. University of Michigan, Ann Arbor.

Smith, Dylan M., Norbert Schwarz, Todd Roberts, and Peter Ubel. 2006a. Why Are You Calling Me? How Study Introductions Change Response Patterns. *Quality of Life Research* 15:621–30.

Smith, Dylan M., Ryan L. Sherriff, Laura Damschroder, George Loewenstein, and Peter A. Ubel. 2006b. Misremembering Colostomies? Former Patients

Give Lower Utility Ratings than Do Current Patients. *Health Psychology* 25: 688–95.

Sunstein, Cass R. 1994. Incommensurability and Valuation in Law. *Michigan Law Review* 92:779–861.

Sunstein, Cass R., Daniel Kahneman, David Schkade, and Ilana Ritov. 2002. Predictably Incoherent Judgments. *Stanford Law Review* 54:1153–1216.

Torrance, George W. 1976. Social Preferences for Health States: An Empirical Evaluation of Three Measurement Techniques. *Socioeconomic Planning Science* 10:129–36.

Tyc, Vida L. 1992. Psychosocial Adaptation of Children and Adolescents with Limb Deficiencies: A Review. *Clinical Psychology Review* 12:275–91.

Ubel, Peter A. 2000. *Pricing Life: Why It's Time for Health Care Rationing.* Cambridge, Mass.: MIT Press.

———. 2006. *You're Stronger than You Think: Tapping the Secrets of Emotionally Resilient People.* New York: McGraw-Hill.

Ubel, Peter A., Aleksandra Jankovic, Dylan Smith, Kenneth M. Langa, and Angela Fagerlin. 2005. What Is Perfect Health to an 85-Year-Old? Evidence for Scale Recalibration in Subjective Health Ratings. *Medical Care* 43:1054–57.

Viscusi, W. Kip. 1988. Pain and Suffering in Product Liability Cases: Systematic Compensation or Capricious Awards? *International Review of Law and Economics* 8:203–20.

Viscusi, W. Kip, and Patricia H. Born. 2005. Damages Caps, Insurability, and the Performance of Medical Malpractice Insurance. *Journal of Risk and Insurance* 72:23–43.

Wilson, Timothy D., and Daniel T. Gilbert. 2003. Affective Forecasting. Pp. 345–411 in vol. 35 of *Advances in Experimental Social Psychology*, edited by Mark P. Zanna. San Diego, Calif.: Academic Press.

Wortman, Camille B., and Roxane C. Silver. 1987. Coping with Irrevocable Loss. Pp. 189–235 in *Cataclysms, Crises, and Catastrophies: Psychology in Action.* Master Lecture Series 6. Washington, D.C.: American Psychological Association.

Death, Happiness, and the Calculation of Compensatory Damages

Andrew J. Oswald and Nattavudh Powdthavee

ABSTRACT

This paper presents a study of the mental distress caused by bereavement. The greatest emotional losses are from the death of a spouse, the second greatest from the death of a child, and the third from the death of a parent. The paper explores how happiness regression equations might be used in tort cases to calculate compensatory damages for emotional harm and pain and suffering. We examine alternative well-being variables, discuss adaptation, consider the possibility that bereavement affects someone's marginal utility of income, and suggest a procedure for correcting for the endogeneity of income. Although the paper's contribution is methodological and further research is needed, some illustrative compensation amounts are discussed.

1. INTRODUCTION

This paper presents a study of the impact upon a person's happiness of the death of a loved one—especially a child, a spouse, or a parent. It uses longitudinal data on randomly sampled individuals. Although our results may be applicable in other ways in social science, we have in

ANDREW J. OSWALD is Professor of Economics at the University of Warwick. NATTAVUDH POWDTHAVEE is Lecturer in Economics at the University of York. This paper has benefited from the comments of participants in a June 2007 University of Chicago Law School workshop and in seminars at University of Birmingham, the Institute of Education London, London School of Economics, University of Nottingham, University of Sheffield, Uppsala University, and University of Warwick. For particularly helpful suggestions, we thank Matthew Adler, Valentina Corradi, Dan Gilbert, Amanda Goodall, Carol Graham, Jon Haidt, Dan Hamermesh, Peter Hammond, Peter Huang, Emily Jackson, Emanuel Kohlscheen, Nicola Lacey, George Loewenstein, Alan Neal, Dennis Novy, Eric Posner, Mark Stewart, Cass Sunstein, Ken Wallis, a referee, and an anonymous court judge. We thank Alex Dobson for research assistance. The Economic and Social Research Council (ESRC) provided sup-

[*Journal of Legal Studies,* vol. XXXVII (June 2008)]

mind, for concreteness, one particular application. Thinking of a court setting the size of damages for emotional loss, we try to suggest ways to assign a financial value to the unhappiness caused by another's death.[1]

Our methods do not draw upon answers to complex questions about how intensely the person values (or valued) that loved one. Although it may go without saying, we wish to emphasize from the start that this kind of inquiry is a difficult and morally sensitive one[2] and that—perhaps hidden to lay readers by the later algebra and econometrics—the results rely on a simple form of averaging across different people. Whatever its methodological contribution, this paper is some way from the last word on the topic.

A tort occurs where there is a breach of a duty fixed by civil law. If a tort is committed, the law allows a victim to claim compensation. The underlying principle is one of *restitutio in integrum*. The claimant should be restored, by the payment of compensatory damages, to his or her original position.

Many of the valuable things in life—love, friendship, health—come without price tags attached. If their financial value is to be judged, therefore, some method has to be found for assigning pecuniary amounts in situations that do not appear to have any intrinsically financial aspect. In most countries, it is judges who set damages, and they do so by using rules of thumb with conceptual foundations that are ad hoc (see, for example, Elliott and Quinn 2005, pp. 345–47). From an economist's perspective, the law literature here can be difficult to understand. Elliott and Quinn (2005, p. 340), for example, make the (to an economist confusing) statement, "[I]t is not . . . easy to calculate the value of a lost limb, or permanent loss of general good health, and even if it were, money can never really compensate for such losses." Moreover, financial settlements can in practice be so small that their intellectual basis is

---

port through a research professorship to the first author. The British Household Panel Survey data were made available through the U.K. Data Archive. The data were originally collected by the ESRC Research Centre on Micro-social Change at the University of Essex, now incorporated within the Institute for Social and Economic Research. Neither the original collectors of the data nor the archive bears any responsibility for the analyses or interpretations presented here.

1. Terminology varies across countries. We do not focus upon the distinction between the terms "hedonic damages" and "pain-and-suffering awards." For simplicity we treat these as similar; the paper is about the general problem, namely, how to set a level of financial compensation for emotional loss. In the United States, only a small number of states officially recognize the concept of hedonic damages.

2. Tetlock (2003) discusses conditions under which human beings are willing to countenance taboo trade-offs.

perplexing. In *West and Son Ltd. v. Shephard* ([1964] App. Cas. 326) in the United Kingdom, the claimant was a married woman who was 41 years old when severely injured. She was left paralyzed in all limbs and unable to speak. A lump-sum award of £17,500 for loss of amenity (over and above a settlement for harm to her earnings) was upheld by the House of Lords.[3] In today's terms, that is about 5 percent of the lifetime income for a successful professional white-collar worker. It seems implausible that many people would contentedly accept complete paralysis in return for a tiny sum of money.

Damages for the death of loved ones are generically low in some nations. In the United Kingdom, the Fatal Accidents Act 1976 (c. 30) provides a lump sum currently set at £10,000 (approximately U.S.$20,000) in damages for bereavement. This one-off payment "is designed to provide some compensation for the nonpecuniary losses associated with bereavement. It is only available to the husband or wife of the deceased, or, if the deceased was unmarried and a minor, to the parents. It does not give children a claim for the death of a parent" (Elliott and Quinn 2005, p. 350).

A U.K. judge and law professor sent us the following view:[4]

The area you are concerned with is hugely problematic for English lawyers—the US approach has been much more forceful on this kind of front.

Expressions such as "diminution of quality of life" for a tort victim have been found for some time, but the notion of "loss of pleasure" of life is not the normal way in which lawyers in the English courts tend to talk about such heads of loss.

Nevertheless, we do struggle with similar issues—particularly in jurisdictions such as that in which I sit (sex, race, disability, etc. discrimination claims) when it comes to awarding sums under the head of "injury to feelings". The appellate level courts have been consistent in stressing that this is "not a scientific exercise", and have tended to indicated broad "bands" within which awards should normally be made. Awards of a trivial or "tokenistic" nature are strongly discouraged—and the usual framework would consist of three bands (injury to be taken seriously, but not having that great an impact; mid-range injury to feelings, which would be the case where the particular impact on the individual is shown to have

---

3. All pound values in the paper are real and expressed in 1996 values. Currently, £1 equals approximately U.S.$2.

4. Anonymous, private communication, May 2, 2007.

been quite dramatic; and the top end, which is reserved for "outrageous" cases and is only rarely available to the judge).

So what should courts do? Here we explore the empirical foundations of losses from bereavement and, using happiness regression equations (that is, regression equations in which a measure of happiness is the dependent variable), suggest methods for valuation.[5] The analysis could be viewed as an empirical analogue of Posner's (2001) call for a better understanding of the emotions and legal practice (earlier writing includes Kahan and Nussbaum [1996]).[6] Posner and Sunstein (2005) discuss related ideas: they point out that in the United States there are logical inconsistencies in how lives are valued in regulatory policy compared to in tort law. They note that the conventional wisdom in the U.S. legal profession is that damages for wrongful death can be arbitrary, and they argue that in some cases courts appear to misunderstand the nature of hedonic loss.

This paper's aim is to sketch an alternative to willingness-to-pay (WTP) methods in the setting of emotional damages. This is not because we think WTP necessarily lacks validity, although we do believe that answering questions, even probabilistically worded, such as "What number of dollars would compensate you for the death of your daughter?" is likely to be hard for everyone and morally offensive to many. Our purpose is to see what numbers come out of an alternative method. In actual courtroom settings, it seems possible that a complementary mixture of methods might one day be used.

Later we use regression equations in which a measure of subjective well-being is the dependent variable. Intuitively, our method can trace out a form of indifference curve between income and any kind of life event (such as bereavement). This is achieved, put loosely, by measuring how many happiness points are gained on average by a higher income of X thousand dollars and how many happiness points are lost by the death of a loved one and then calculating the ratio of the two. Doing so provides a statistical measure of the marginal rate of substitution

5. There is a large medical and psychiatric literature on the impact of bereavement on people. We shall not attempt to summarize that research field, but a readable introduction can be found in Middleton et al. (1997), and an important paper is Lehman et al. (1993).

6. Peter Hammond pointed out to us that our approach is reminiscent of Robert Nozick's idea that interpersonal comparisons can be used to equate a criminal's incremental disutility brought about by his or her punishment with the victim's disutility due to the crime.

between the pleasure of money and the pain from the death of a loved one.

For pedagogical simplicity, we often treat the data on well-being as though they were cardinal. This is formally unattractive and can be altered without affecting the paper's main points, but it has the advantage that it allows regression equation coefficients to be read off in a way that is easily interpreted. Moreover, there has been much recent econometric work, at the borders between psychology, epidemiology, and economics, on happiness and well-being, where it has been found that the precise kinds of econometric estimators do not affect the key findings. Here we follow methods explained in sources such as Argyle (2001), Clark and Oswald (2002), Diener et al. (1999), Di Tella, McCulloch, and Oswald (2001, 2003), Frey and Stutzer (2002), Oswald (1997), van Praag and Ferrer-i-Carbonell (2004), and van Praag and Baarsma (2005). Redoing our later equations using ordered logit estimators, for example, leaves the substance unchanged.

A central issue in the paper is how much, if any, extra happiness is produced by a greater level of income. There has been a long debate on this topic. It is still not settled. Currently the consensus position is that there is probably a statistically significant but small positive effect. In other words, money buys some extra happiness, but not a large amount. Methodological approaches vary: Kahneman et al. (2006) and Gardner and Oswald (2007) provide recent evidence from different ends of the spectrum. Clark, Frijters, and Shields (2006) survey the literature. Later in the paper we attempt to contribute to ideas on how to instrument an income variable.

What should we believe about the extent of hedonic adaptation, that is, the idea that human beings habituate to tragedy? Bagenstos and Schlanger (2007) make an argument that the existence of such adaptation largely nullifies the case for compensatory damages. The concept of adaptation has a long history, valuably summarized in Frederick and Loewenstein (1999) and Fujita and Diener (2005) and discussed conceptually in Menzel et al. (2002), Rayo and Becker (2007), Ubel, Loewenstein, and Jepson (2005), and Dolan and Kahneman (2008). There is good evidence for habituation in utility levels, for example, Lucas et al. (2003). In its most extreme form this is known as set point theory: whatever life throws at them, people return to an original well-being point.[7] Brickman, Coates, and Janoff-Bulman (1978) is sometimes in-

---

7. Set point theory is not usually expressed formally but might be thought about in

terpreted as support for complete adaptation, although Easterlin et al. (2006) and our own longitudinal work (Oswald and Powdthavee 2008) shed doubt on the claim that severely disabled people return fully to their original level of well-being.

The paper does not say a great deal about differences ex ante and ex post. Our methods seem to apply even in a world where people are poor at affective forecasting (Gilbert et al. 1998; Hsee and Hastie 2006). Nor do we draw upon other nonsubjective measures of well-being and distress such as suicide rates (for example, as Stevenson and Wolfers [2006] do); there may be some, presumably small, bias in our results if suicide rates are immediately higher among bereaved relatives. Although our methods could also be applied to the field of employment law— Huang and Moss (2006) contains an interesting discussion of related issues—that avenue is not be pursued here.

2. CONCEPTS

The idea of compensatory damages for emotional harm seems a natural one. Assume that a person's utility (or "happiness") is negatively affected by the death of a loved one. A person's utility is an increasing function of his or her earned income, y, plus any nonlabor income, i. There is some choice behavior, a, that is taken optimally by the individual. Costs of action are a function $c = c(a)$.

Write the direct utility function and maximization problem, assuming a separable form, as

$$\text{Maximize } u = u(a, y + i) - c(a) - D$$

and the indirect utility function then as

$$v = v(y + i) - D = \max u,$$

where the action, a, is set optimally at the argmax a^* of u and D stands for the emotional cost of a death.

---

the following way. Assume that, where t is continuous time, utility u is described by a differential equation $du/dt = a\, dx/dt + b - cu$, in which x is some variable that influences well-being and a, b, and c are nonnegative parameters. This equation has the solution $u(t) = ax(t) - \int_0^t cu(\tau)d\tau + K$, where K is a constant determined partly by the size of the b parameter. The integral term means that the longer utility has been above its set point, the lower must current utility be. In the short term, a positive shock to x raises u. Then utility erodes back to the long-run steady state, which is determined solely by parameters b and c. In steady-state equilibrium, x does not affect long-run utility, $u^* = b/c$. There is complete adaptation.

In a tort case, in which some party has been negligent, there may exist a sum of money, *s*, that satisfies for the victim the *restitutio in integrum* requirement that

$$v(y + i + s) - D = v(y + i),$$

or, in words, utility after the death and the compensation equals utility without the death occurring. Given monotonicity and concavity of the utility function, the appropriate value of *s* is an increasing, convex function of *D*.

The financial sum *s* can be thought of as redressing the disutility consequences of *D*, namely, as the correct amount of emotional damages in a tort case in which the aim is to return the bereaved to the original utility level. In the harsh language of microeconomic theory, a person receiving *s* is indifferent between whether their loved one lived or died. This has, even to us, an inhuman sound to it;[9] perhaps future work will get to the bottom of why, but this paper does not. The remainder of the paper is concerned with methods that attempt to assess the appropriate value of *s*.

3. EMPIRICS

Empirically, a key difficulty is deciding the extent of the emotional hurt caused to a person by the death of a loved one. Ideally, a statistical inquiry has to have a number of features:

1. Individuals in a sample must be followed over a reasonably long period, so that information on them is available before and after bereavement;
2. The bad life event must be exogenous.
3. There needs to be a control group of individuals unaffected by the event.
4. The sample should be reasonably representative of the adult population.
5. A set of control variables, including income, should be available in the data set, so that confounding influences can be differenced out.

---

8. Cooter (2003) refers to our problem as the search for a "repugnant formula" and argues that in some legal settings there are things—such as dollars and the life of a child— that are incommensurable: "[T]he loss of a child is an extreme example of incompensable losses" (p. 1098).

To our knowledge, no econometric study of this type on the emotional losses of the deaths of loved ones has been published (some, including Clark et al. [2004] and Riis et al. [2005], and the seminal panel data paper on unemployment by Winkelmann and Winkelmann [1998] look at other life events, including the death of a spouse,[9] and do satisfy a number of these requirements). Powdthavee (2005, 2007, 2008) studies crime, joblessness, and friendships. Ferrer-i-Carbonell and van Praag (2002) and Groot, van den Brink, and Plug (2004) explore the negative effect on well-being of various diseases. Oswald and Powdthavee (2008) examine happiness levels after disability.

The data source used in the paper is the British Household Panel Survey (BHPS). This is a nationally representative sample of households that contains over 10,000 adult individuals and was conducted between September and Christmas of each year from 1991 (see Taylor et al. 2002). Respondents are interviewed in successive waves; households who move to a new residence are interviewed at their new location; if an individual splits off from the original household, the adult members of his or her new household are also interviewed. Children are interviewed once they reach age 11 (although we later drop the children from our sample). Since its inception, BHPS has remained representative of Britain's population.

This paper draws on individual-level data from eight of the years: waves 2–5, wave 9, wave 11, and wave 14, which were collected between 1992 and 2005.[10] In these survey waves, which are the ones that provide detailed information on bereavement, the BHPS asks randomly selected adult individuals the same question about important events that happened to them or their family members in the last year.

3.1. Survey Question

> Would you please tell me anything that has happened to you (or your family) which has stood out as important? This might be things you've done, or things that have been of interest or concern; just whatever comes to mind as important to you. Also state whether the event happened to you, one of your family member, or someone else from outside the household.

9. We use the terms "spouse" and "partner" largely interchangeably. The latter includes those who are unmarried but cohabit.

10. The wave 2 data were collected between late 1991 and early 1992. The wave 3 data were collected between late 1993 and early 1994, and so on.

This is asked as an open-ended question, so the answers could be anything from ill health to getting a job promotion. Around 6 percent of the sample answered "death" as one of the major events that took place in the previous year. Respondents were also asked to state whose death it was. The answers to this question ranged from "child" to "friend." These are the data used in the paper.

As far as we are aware, the only other paper on well-being to use these responses from BHPS—that is, the open-ended questions—is innovative work by Ballas and Dorling (2007). Their methods and main purpose are different from ours, and the two projects began independently. Nevertheless, although they are not concerned with the calculation of emotional damages, Ballas and Dorling (2007) note some negative effects from the death variables (dummy variables for different kinds of deaths that indicate whether a respondent has lost a child/partner/parent) (using a form of mental well-being equation, namely, one based on a subquestion from the 12 on the GHQ list of questions), and their first draft slightly predates our own. More broadly, it is known in the literature on happiness that spousal bereavement has large negative consequences (see, for instance, Diener et al. 1999; Easterlin 2003; Blanchflower and Oswald 2004). To the best of our knowledge, the published happiness literature using regression equations has not examined the influence of the death of a child and other bereavements of this kind. There is, however, a relevant psychiatric literature, such as Li et al. (2005). There is also some evidence that marital well-being declines after the death of a child in the family (Broman, Riba, and Trahan 1996).

The analysis uses two measures of mental well-being. One is a psychological distress score (from 0 to 12). The other is a life satisfaction score (from 1 to 7).

The BHPS contains a mental health measure, a GHQ score. This has been used internationally by medical researchers and other investigators as an indicator of psychological strain or stress. Recent applications of GHQ scores include Cardozo et al. (2000), Clark and Oswald (1994, 2002), Martikainen et al. (2003), Pevalin and Ermisch (2004), Robinson, McBeth, and MacFarlane (2004), and Shields and Wheatley Price (2005).

A GHQ score is one of the most commonly adopted questionnaire-based methods of assessing psychological distress. It amalgamates answers to the following list of 12 questions:

Have you recently

1. been able to concentrate on whatever you are doing?

2. lost much sleep over worry?
3. felt that you are playing a useful part in things?
4. felt capable of making decisions about things?
5. felt constantly under strain?
6. felt you could not overcome your difficulties?
7. been able to enjoy your normal day-to-day activities?
8. been able to face up to your problems?
9. been feeling unhappy and depressed?
10. been losing confidence in yourself?
11. been thinking of yourself as a worthless person?
12. been feeling reasonably happy all things considered?

Responses are made on a four-point scale of frequency of feeling in relation to a person's usual state: they are "not at all," "no more than usual," "rather more than usual," and "much more than usual."

As a measure of mental strain, the paper takes a simple summation. It is coded here so that people answer with respect to their usual state; the responses with the two lower well-being values score 1, and those with the two higher well-being value score 0. This is the BHPS variable HLGHQ2: it converts valid answers to questions wGHQA to wGHQL to a single scale by recoding 1 and 2 values on individual variables to 0, and 3 and 4 values to 1, giving a scale running from 0 (the least distressed) to 12 (the most distressed). Medical opinion is that normal individuals score around 1 or 2 on the GHQ measure. Numbers near 12 are rare and correspond to clinical depression. For reasons not fully understood, GHQ scores are trending slightly up through time in Britain (Oswald and Powdthavee 2007), and we adjust for that in the later analysis.

In some cases the paper uses as an alternative a life satisfaction question. This form has been widely used in the happiness literature. The wording in the BHPS survey is, "All things considered, how satisfied or dissatisfied are you with your life overall using a 1–7 scale?"

3.2. Results

The data set provides information on more than 2,000 bereavements. Table 1 summarizes the occurrence of the deaths in the data.

As might be anticipated, the death of a loved one has psychological consequences. Figure 1 charts, on a GHQ scale of 0 to 12, the levels of respondents' mental distress 12 months before and after the death of a

Table 1. Data on Deaths of Loved Ones in the British Household Panel
Survey, 1992–2005

Death	GHQ-12 Analysis		Life Satisfaction Analysis	
	N	% of Sample	N	% of Sample
Child	120	.14	49	.17
Partner	278	.32	89	.31
Father	521	.60	148	.52
Mother	700	.81	300	1.06
Sibling	430	.50	161	.57
Friend	455	.53	139	.49
N	86,623		28,418	

Note. The values are taken from people answering "death" to the GHQ
question about important life events. The question was asked only intermittently. The GHQ mental distress questions were asked every year of the
sample. The life satisfaction question was first introduced in wave 6 of the
British Household Panel Survey. It was then dropped for wave 11 but rein-
troduced again for wave 12. This limits what can be done in any consecutive-
year analysis. Means and standard deviations in the later analysis are as
follows: mean of life satisfaction = 5.23 (SD = 1.31 [overall], .78 [within];
mean of GHQ-12 psychological distress = 1.90(SD = 2.94 [overall], 2.11
[within]).

child, a partner, or a parent.[11] Higher GHQ-12 values signify worse
psychological well-being. The figure uses a subsample of individuals on
whom we have strictly consecutive yearly observations. The data are
from the years 1992–95 because, for this survey question, these are the
only consecutive years available. As would be expected, child deaths are
relatively unusual ($N = 37$). Fifty-nine respondents experienced the
death of a partner ($N = 59$), and 386 experienced the death of a parent.
The three increases in mental distress are significantly different from
zero at the 1 percent level. For death of a child, $t = -2.905$ ($p > .000$);
for the death of a partner, $t = -6.773$ ($p > .000$); and for the death of
a parent, $t = -2.9730$ ($p > .000$). The figure depicts raw means; they
are not regression corrected.

Bereavement is painful. Figure 1 shows that psychological distress
(that is, GHQ-12) is initially around 1.3 among those who will lose a
child and slightly below 3 among those who go on to lose a partner in
the next year. Mental distress then rises abruptly to 3.5 in the year that
the person reports having had a child die and to 6.3 if the person lost

11. For simplicity, we only used wave 2 to wave 5 (and so ignore the discontinued
waves, that is, waves 9, 11, and 14) in our longitudinal plots of psychological distress for
those who lost someone to death.

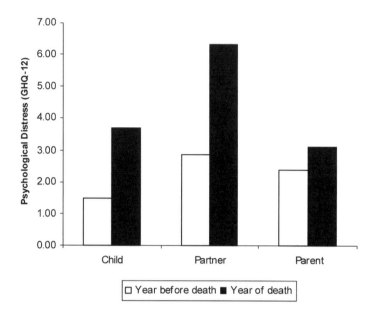

Figure 1. Respondents' levels of psychological distress before and after the death of a child, partner, or parent.

a spouse. A smaller increase is discernible among those who had a parent die. Ideally, we would exploit data on the circumstances of the bereavement, including to what extent it was a premature death, but that information is not available in the BHPS data set.

To allow the extent of any hedonic adaptation to be explored, Figures 2 and 3 extend the graphs for a further year and broaden the categories of bereavement. The data are from the years 1992–95, and t is the year of the death. There are very small numbers of multiple deaths in the sample (.08 percent). Figure 2 shows the distress of respondents who lost a child ($N = 27$) or a partner ($N = 59$). Figure 3 plots the mean psychological distress scores of those in the sample who lost a mother ($N = 120$), father ($N = 119$), a sibling ($N = 80$), or a friend ($N = 114$). As can be seen, there is evidence of an increase in the mean levels of psychological distress after all types of death. For example, the mean level of individual GHQ mental strain is 2.5 in the year before losing a father. In the actual year of a father's death, a person's psychological distress increases to approximately 3.2. One year later, however, psychological distress has fallen again to around 2.5. Similar patterns of

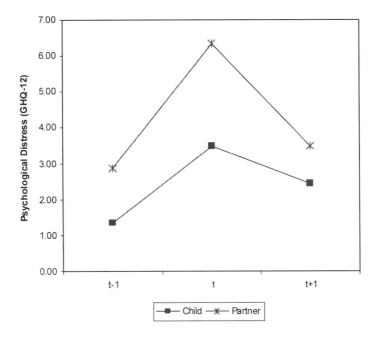

Figure 2. Adaptation after deaths of partner or child; *t* is the year of the death

apparent hedonic adaptation are seen for other types of death. For spousal bereavement, these graphs reinforce the earlier results of Clark et al. (2004), Easterlin (2003), and Gardner and Oswald (2006). Other types of death have not, to our knowledge, been systematically studied (though, as explained, Ballas and Dorling [2007] is in part a counterexample).

We now turn to regression equations. Table 2 presents cross-sectional life satisfaction equations. We treat bereavement as exogenous (partly because it seems reasonable to do so, and partly because it is difficult to know how to instrument for others' deaths). Assuming cardinality in the seven-point-scale life satisfaction scores (1 = very dissatisfied, . . . , 7 = very satisfied), column 1 includes deaths as the only independent variables in the least squares regression. The econometric analysis is restricted to those of working age (ages 16–65). This is to reduce the risk of, say, anticipated natural death of children and parents.

The coefficient on death of father is −.249 in column 1 of Table 2, which implies that the bereavement loss is approximately a quarter of

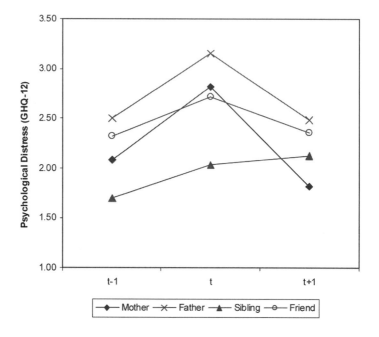

Figure 3. Adaptation after deaths of mother, father, sibling, or friend; *t* is the year of the death.

a life satisfaction point. Its robust standard error is .106, so the null of zero can be rejected at the 5 percent level. The coefficients on death of mother and spousal partner are −.268 and −.894, respectively. Both coefficients are statistically well determined at the 5 percent level. On the other hand, the coefficients on death of a child, sibling, and friend are not statistically significantly different from zero. It should be noted, nevertheless, that the coefficient on child death in is large in an absolute sense. Later in the paper, we show that this effect becomes statistically significant in larger samples.

Column 2 of Table 2 increases the number of independent variables. The *R*-squared values remain modest, at less than 10 percent of the variance explained, which suggests that much remains to be discovered, perhaps about the role of (here unobservable) personalities. Income is deflated by the consumer price index. Compared to column 1, the coefficients on variables for the death of a mother and death of a father variables decline a little in size, while there is a slightly bigger decline in the coefficient size for the death of a partner.

In column 2, the coefficient on real household income is .105, with a statistically well-determined effect (its standard error is .015). This makes it possible to work out how much income would be required to offset the distress from an event such as bereavement. To compensate for the loss of a mother, the necessary sum here is £20,000 per annum. Per annum compensation for the loss of a partner is £64,000 and is £41,000 for the loss of a child.

A difficulty here is that income may be endogenous. In column 3, we instrument income by income measured at $t - 1$. The instrumental variables (IV) coefficient on income is .163 and is statistically significant at the 1 percent level. Here, to compensate for the loss of a mother is £10,000 per annum. To compensate for the loss of a partner is £36,000 per annum, and to compensate for the loss of a child is £34,000 per annum. These numbers are smaller than before because the estimated marginal effect of income has increased. However, lagged income is arguably not ideal as an instrumental variable, and later in the paper we consider alternatives.

Column 4 includes a measure of average income over time, which represents a more permanent measure of household income. The coefficient on average income over time is .202, with a standard error of .023. Using this coefficient, we need approximately £10,000 per annum to compensate for the loss of a mother, £32,000 per annum to compensate for the loss of a partner, and £21,000 per annum for the loss of a child.

Life satisfaction data are collected in the BHPS in wave 7 and intermittently afterward. On this measure of well-being, does bereavement have a long-lasting effect? Table 3 estimates life satisfaction equations as a function of events that occurred long before the survey. In particular, the logic of Table 3 is to see if, controlling for deaths in the immediate period, there is any scarring effect on those who experienced death prior to wave 7. Such scarring mostly seems to disappear (although some small negative effects, insignificantly different from zero, can be seen). There are two exceptions: long-dead friends carry a long-term happiness penalty, and a long-dead child carries a small long-term happiness gain. We do not feel qualified to speculate on psychological explanations for these patterns.

Using data on psychological distress measured by a GHQ score, Table 4 explores the consequences of the death of loved ones on a different measure of well-being. Estimation of GHQ equations goes back to the ordered estimators of Clark and Oswald (1994), and our equation form

Table 2. Life Satisfaction Regression Equations with Death Variables

	OLS (1)		OLS (2)		IV (3)		OLS (4)	
Death of father	−.249*	(.106)	−.157	(.105)	−.182	(.127)	−.170	(.105)
Death of mother	−.268**	(.080)	−.214**	(.078)	−.163+	(.084)	−.213**	(.078)
Death of partner	−.894**	(.242)	−.670**	(.250)	−.590*	(.275)	−.661**	(.251)
Death of sibling	.014	(.168)	−.051	(.167)	.117	(.166)	−.047	(.167)
Death of child	−.395	(.245)	−.430+	(.242)	−.556+	(.287)	−.430+	(.240)
Death of friend	.096	(.119)	.090	(.116)	.131	(.130)	.110	(.115)
Personal and household characteristics:								
Male			−.046*	(.019)	−.046*	(.021)	−.051**	(.019)
Age			−.066**	(.006)	−.073**	(.007)	−.070**	(.006)
$Age^2/100$			.075**	(.007)	.083**	(.008)	.079**	(.007)
Real household income per capita (£10,000s)			.105**	(.015)	.163**	(.033)	.004	(.015)
Mean income over time							.202**	(.023)
Living as couple			−.152**	(.028)	−.163**	(.031)	−.151**	(.028)
Widowed			−.497**	(.077)	−.426**	(.082)	−.474**	(.077)
Divorced			−.664**	(.047)	−.593**	(.050)	−.642**	(.047)
Separated			−.814**	(.070)	−.787**	(.082)	−.789**	(.071)
Single			−.454**	(.033)	−.437**	(.036)	−.452**	(.033)
Unemployed			−.447**	(.054)	−.410**	(.065)	−.424**	(.054)
Retired			.030	(.047)	.023	(.052)	.023	(.047)

	(1)	(2)	(3)	(4)
Family care		−.123** (.039)	−.104* (.043)	−.107** (.039)
Student		.084* (.042)	.114* (.053)	.074+ (.042)
A-level education		.077** (.028)	.067* (.031)	.071* (.028)
University education		.091** (.028)	.072* (.032)	.069* (.028)
Household size		.013 (.011)	.013 (.012)	.021* (.011)
Number of children:				
Ages 0–2		.030 (.031)	.063+ (.035)	.019 (.031)
Ages 3–4		.031 (.031)	.071* (.035)	.025 (.031)
Ages 5–11		−.033+ (.017)	−.004 (.020)	−.025 (.017)
Ages 12–15		−.049* (.022)	−.052* (.025)	−.037+ (.022)
Ages 16–18		−.047 (.038)	−.068 (.046)	−.046 (.038)
Home ownership		.183** (.026)	.167** (.028)	.171** (.026)
Constant	5.164** (.010)	6.475** (.125)	6.528** (.146)	6.418** (.126)
R^2	.002	.059	.052	.063
N	23,417	22,927	18,113	22,927

Note. The data are from British Household Panel Survey waves 9, 11, and 14. The seven-point-scale life satisfaction question was asked first in wave 7 (that is, in 1997), with 1 = very dissatisfied with life and 7 = very satisfied with life. The instrument for income is lagged income. Standard errors are in parentheses. A dummy variable such as "Death of father" means that the interviewee's father died during the 12 month-period prior to interview. The income variable is real income deflated by the consumer price index. Year dummies are included for all regressions. OLS = ordinary least squares; IV = instrumental variables.

$^+ p < .1.$
$^* p < .05.$
$^{**} p < .01.$

Table 3. Life Satisfaction Ordinary Least Squares Regression Equations with Death and Deaths before Wave 7 of the British Household Panel Survey

	Coefficient	SE
Death of father	−.175[+]	.105
Death of mother	−.209**	.078
Death of partner	−.660**	.251
Death of sibling	−.051	.167
Death of child	−.432[+]	.240
Death of friend	.106	.115
Previously had death of child	.385*	.167
Previously had death of partner	−.181	.241
Previously had death of father	−.013	.069
Previously had death of mother	.056	.075
Previously had death of friend	−.293**	.094
Previously had death of sibling	.063	.134
Real household income per capita (£10,000s)	.004	.015
Mean income over time	.202**	.023
Constant	6.411**	.126
R^2	.0636	
N	22,927	

Note. The data are taken from British Household Panel Survey waves 9, 11, and 14. The "previously had death" variables refer to events up to 12 years earlier. Other personal and household characteristics and year dummies are included in the regression.

[+] $p < .1$.

* $p < .05$.

** $p < .01$.

is similar in structure, but they did not have controls for deaths of different loved ones. The dependent variable here is GHQ-12 measured cardinally (where 12 is the worst possible psychological well-being).

Table 4 has a larger sample than the previous regression tables. In column 1 of Table 4, only death variables are included. Now all of the death dummies enter the distress equation with positive and statistically significant coefficients. The largest effect comes from the death of partner. Next is the effect of a child's death. The smallest effect on psychological distress comes from death of sibling.

Column 2 shows results from a full specification. Most coefficients on death are relatively little changed. Ordinary least squares estimates imply the following: per annum compensation is £78,000 for the death of a father, £61,000 for the death of a mother, £206,000 for the death of a partner, £32,000 for the death of a sibling, £137,000 for the death of a child, and £51,000 for the death of a friend.

Column 3 estimates an individual random effects (RE) model of psychological distress that includes death variables as the independent variables. Per annum compensation is £101,000 for the death of a father, £87,000 for the death of a mother, £286,000 for the death of a partner, £39,000 for the death of a sibling, £221,000 for the death of a child, and £55,000 for the death of a friend. Column 4 of Table 4 presents IV RE estimates, using income at $t - 1$ to instrument for current real income. Now per annum compensation is £55,000 for the death of a father, £59,000 for the death of a mother, £172,000 for the death of a partner, £20,000 for the death of a sibling, £141,000 for the death of a child, and £38,000 for the death of a friend. Column 5 includes mean income over time (that is, permanent income) in an RE regression. Per annum compensation is £40,000 for the death of a father, £35,000 for the death of a mother, £115,000 for the death of a partner, £16,000 for the death of a sibling, £89,000 for the death of a child, and £22,000 for the death of a friend.

Column 6 of Table 4 reports fixed effects (FE) estimates. These can allow for genetic and unchanging personality variables. Most of the coefficients on the death variables remain similar in size. For example, the coefficient on death of a mother is .861 in RE and .877 in FE; the coefficient on death of a partner is 2.834 in RE and 2.752 in FE. However, the coefficient on income is not very precisely determined.

Some readers of earlier drafts of this paper—we thank especially George Loewenstein—were concerned about the possibility that bereavement and income might not appear in a separable way in a well-being equation. This is an important issue. If the marginal utility of income is affected by experiencing the loss of a loved one, the calculations above are incorrect (or at least incomplete). We spent some time examining different functional forms. However, we could not find strong evidence for the idea that bereaved people have a different marginal utility of income. Table A1 sets out one illustrative test that shows it is not possible to reject the null hypothesis that all interaction terms have coefficients of zero. Could this merely be for the reason that such tests lack power because of relatively small sample sizes for bereavements? Our experiments suggested not. For instance, when we estimated equations for the subsample of people who had suffered bereavement, the point estimate of their marginal utility of income was similar to that for the much larger subsample of people who did not experience bereavement. Thus, it does not appear that there are problems caused by a low-power test. Instead, the data suggest that it is reasonable simplification to assume that well-being can be written as an additively separable linear equation.

Table 4. Psychological Distress Regression Equations with Death Variables

	OLS (1)	OLS (2)	RE (3)	IV RE (4)	RE (5)	FE (6)
Death of father	1.259** (.164)	1.172** (.162)	.998** (.117)	.940** (.130)	.998** (.117)	.877** (.127)
Death of mother	1.001** (.139)	.928** (.137)	.858** (.105)	1.008** (.116)	.861** (.105)	.877** (.115)
Death of partner	3.498** (.406)	3.115** (.409)	2.835** (.273)	2.936** (.317)	2.834** (.273)	2.752** (.306)
Death of sibling	.562** (.209)	.486* (.207)	.386* (.183)	.336+ (.199)	.385* (.183)	.279 (.204)
Death of child	2.074** (.552)	2.074** (.547)	2.193** (.330)	2.413** (.372)	2.201** (.330)	2.422** (.358)
Death of friend	.802** (.196)	.776** (.194)	.544** (.146)	.646** (.161)	.537** (.146)	.422** (.157)
Personal and household characteristics:						
Male		−.497** (.034)	−.508** (.033)	−.522** (.036)	−.501** (.033)	
Age		.078** (.009)	.070** (.008)	.074** (.009)	.076** (.008)	
Age²/100		−.091** (.012)	−.084** (.010)	−.089** (.011)	−.090** (.010)	−.063** (.015)
Real household income per capita (£10,000s)		−.151** (.022)	−.099** (.017)	−.171** (.035)	−.020 (.020)	−.012 (.021)
Mean income over time					−.247** (.032)	
Living as couple		.162** (.049)	.104* (.043)	.077 (.048)	.106* (.043)	−.039 (.062)
Widowed		.590** (.133)	.701** (.102)	.609** (.112)	.680** (.102)	.754** (.168)
Divorced		.673** (.086)	.514** (.061)	.427** (.065)	.494** (.061)	−.014 (.093)
Separated		1.372** (.125)	1.326** (.084)	1.346** (.094)	1.302** (.084)	1.097** (.107)
Single		.204** (.055)	.182** (.047)	.160** (.052)	.190** (.047)	.114 (.080)

	(1)	(2)	(3)	(4)	(5)	(6)
Unemployed		.884** (.070)	.855** (.052)	.835** (.059)	.828** (.052)	.768** (.064)
Retired		−.039 (.071)	−.080 (.060)	−.107 (.065)	−.077 (.060)	−.111 (.075)
Family care		.278** (.061)	.243** (.046)	.232** (.051)	.222** (.047)	.161** (.059)
Student		.216** (.057)	.130* (.058)	−.007 (.073)	.134* (.058)	−.043 (.080)
A-level education		−.212** (.047)	−.201** (.040)	−.169** (.045)	−.183** (.040)	.083 (.110)
University education		−.151** (.048)	−.197** (.042)	−.176** (.047)	−.155** (.042)	.027 (.103)
Household size		−.049** (.016)	−.024$^+$ (.014)	−.029$^+$ (.016)	−.031* (.014)	.014 (.019)
Number of children:						
Ages 0–2		.054 (.044)	.054 (.040)	.044 (.045)	.055 (.040)	.065 (.048)
Ages 3–4		−.036 (.044)	−.035 (.040)	−.061 (.044)	−.040 (.040)	−.058 (.047)
Ages 5–11		−.036 (.028)	−.078** (.023)	−.093** (.026)	−.088** (.023)	−.128** (.030)
Ages 12–15		.076* (.034)	.046$^+$ (.028)	.060$^+$ (.031)	.040 (.028)	.010 (.034)
Ages 16–18		−.058 (.059)	−.040 (.053)	−.022 (.061)	−.044 (.053)	−.019 (.062)
Home ownership		−.261** (.044)	−.214** (.037)	−.220** (.041)	−.205** (.037)	−.085 (.053)
Constant	1.895** (.017)	.874** (.199)	1.056** (.180)	1.076** (.204)	1.127** (.180)	2.534** (.211)
R^2		.035	.013	.013	.013	
R^2 (within)	.005					.015
N	66,673	66,194	66,194	55,735	66,194	66,194

Note. These are equations in which the dependent variable is the level of distress measured by a GHQ score. The data are taken from British Household Panel Survey waves 2–5, 9, 11, and 14. Standard errors are in parentheses. The instrument is lagged income. Year dummies are included for all regressions. OLS = ordinary least squares; RE = random effects; IV = instrumental variables; FE = fixed effects.

$^+$ $p < .1$.
* $p < .05$.
** $p < .01$.

Table 5 presents FE estimates for each gender. Men suffer a significantly smaller blow from deaths than do women (with the exception of losing a partner, which seems to have a symmetrical impact on psychological distress for both men and women). This is consistent with some medical evidence that hospitalization rates for mental illness are higher, after the death of a child, among women (Li et al. 2005). When a father dies, for example, women here experience on average a worsening by 1.127 GHQ points; men experience a worsening by .534 points. The death of a child raises a woman's psychological distress by 2.169 GHQ points. A man's is raised by 1.315 points. The coefficient on income is not significantly different from zero, however.

It should be noted that, with the exception of the male/female divide, this paper has not greatly explored the case of disaggregated valuation of bereavement losses. Following the ideas of Sunstein (2004), there seems scope for a fuller analysis. Smith et al. (2005) conclude that wealth buffers the size of the decrease in happiness caused by a decline in health; it is possible that richer people are affected less by bereavement shocks, but Table A1 does not find empirical support for that. The sizes of possible payments for emotional damages are documented, in summary form, in Table 6.

A potential weakness of most of the regression equations estimated above is that income is arguably endogenously determined. This raises the standard identification problem: if happiness depends on income, and income is itself a function of happiness, then the parameter estimates are biased and inconsistent. To solve this, a valid instrument for income is needed. The use of lagged income is open to objections. Here we draw upon two instruments not used before. First, the British Household Panel Survey asks their interviewers to try to see the actual paycheck of the survey respondent. Where this is achieved, the information about income is likely to be more accurate. However, there is no reason to expect happiness to be affected by whether or not the interviewer sees the paycheck. Hence, we use this—a dummy variable for observation of the paycheck—as an instrument for income. Second, although income in the paper is deflated by a consumer price index, there is information in Britain on regional house prices. We employ this variable, lagged at $t - 1$, as a further instrument for income; one rationale is that high house prices eventually act to raise wages in a region.

We found that instrumented personal income then works strongly in a well-being equation. Table A2 gives the details. It shows that both instrumental variables enter positively, with well-determined standard

Table 5. Psychological Distress Regression Equations with Different Death Variables: Female and Male Subsamples

	Women		Men	
	Coefficient	SE	Coefficient	SE
Death father	1.127**	.166	.534**	.180
Death of mother	1.251**	.151	.380**	.148
Death of partner	2.743**	.230	2.188**	.287
Death of sibling	.476**	.189	−.178	.210
Death of child	2.169**	.342	1.315**	.436
Death of friend	.513**	.175	.091	.190
Personal and household characteristics:				
Age^2/100	.034**	.013	.023*	.012
Real household income per capita (£10,000s)	.009	.029	−.036	.026
Living as couple	.038	.086	−.213**	.079
Widowed	.625**	.125	.328**	.162
Divorced	.084	.115	−.047	.131
Separated	1.097**	.136	1.063**	.152
Single	.065	.113	−.051	.101
Unemployed	.838**	.103	.687**	.072
Retired	.009	.077	−.248**	.079
Family care	.148**	.061	.079	.248
Student	.165	.110	−.094	.105
A-level education	.022	.150	.036	.144
University education	.101	.143	.049	.133
Household size	.019	.027	.028	.024
Number of children:				
Ages 0–2	.114*	.067	.017	.062
Ages 3–4	.018	.064	−.084	.061
Ages 5–11	.125**	.040	−.083**	.039
Ages 12–15	.066	.046	−.006	.044
Ages 16–18	.096	.086	.081	.082
Home ownership	.093	.068	−.169**	.061
Constant	.972**	.392	.954**	.368
R^2 (within)	.019		.012	
N	43,258		36,374	

Note. These are equations in which the dependent variable is the level of distress measured by a GHQ score. The data are taken from British Household Panel Survey waves 2–5, 9, 11, and 14. Year dummies are included for both regressions.

$^+ p < .1$.

$^* p < .05$.

$^{**} p < .01$.

Table 6. Illustrative Valuations of Compensatory Damages in the First Year

Death	Amount per Annum
Partner	114–202
Child	89–140
Father	40–101
Mother	35–61
Friend	22–51
Sibling	16–32

Note. Data are from the GHQ-12 equation. Values are £10,000s per annum. Values are calculated from columns 3 and 5 (random effects results) of Table 4.

errors, in a log of personal income equation. An overidentification test suggests that the instruments are valid.

Table 7 thus reports the results of life satisfaction and mental distress regression equations in which the log level of real personal income is treated as an endogenous independent variable. The coefficients on the death variables are approximately as before. However, these instrumented estimates—particularly in columns 2, 4, and 6—produce much better defined coefficients on income. Moreover, instrumenting income increases the size of the estimated effect fivefold to 10-fold. In the life satisfaction equations in Table 7, for example, the coefficient on log income rises between columns 1 and 2. In the FE GHQ distress equations, instrumenting the income variable produces in column 6 a coefficient of $-.818$ with a standard error of .144. By contrast, without instrumenting the income coefficient is small. This suggests that the bias under ordinary least squares estimation is negative: happy people may work less hard to earn income, and in simple correlations where no correction for simultaneity is done, this can produce the illusion that money does not buy much happiness.

Calculating the size of necessary hedonic compensation per annum amounts once again gives, in this case using the GHQ equations from Table 7, for the average individual a set of amounts listed in Table 8. Despite the change in detailed method in Table 7, these numbers are not too different from those earlier in the paper.

Because the paper's aim is principally to lay out a method of analysis, we shall not here attempt to adjudicate between the compensation amounts calculated under different econometric specifications. Many economists, however, would be likely to put most reliance on equations in which person fixed effects were accounted for and in which the income variable was instrumented.

4. CONCLUSIONS

This paper studies a class of extreme negative shocks to utility—how people are affected by different kinds of deaths, and especially the death of a spouse, a child, or a parent. We are conscious that this is a complex, emotive area. By estimating mental well-being equations in a way that averages across the individuals in our sample, the paper draws five conclusions.

First, bereavement causes substantial mental distress. The rank order of emotional severity is (starting with the greatest) death of a spouse, death of a child, and death of a parent. Second, our data suggest that, in response to bereavement, women suffer larger decreases in happiness than do men. The death of a child, for example, here worsens women's mental well-being by 2.2 GHQ points, compared to 1.3 points for men.[12] Third, we find signs of hedonic adaptation to six kinds of bereavement (spouse, child, mother, father, sibling, and friend). Because of gaps in the collection of the deaths data, however, we lack enough consecutive years to allow us to study adaptation in a systematic way. This is an important arena for further inquiry. Fourth, the paper suggests that happiness equations could be used in a tort setting to calculate emotional damages.[13] Some illustrative compensation amounts are given. Using GHQ mental distress as the measure of well-being, the hedonic compensation amount in the first year for the death of a child might be on the order of £100,000 ($200,000). However, in our judgment more research is needed on other countries and data sets before courts can implement such methods. The paper's contribution is methodological;

12. These are large effects from bereavement—approximately equal in size to 1 standard deviation in measured well-being. They lie on a GHQ distress scale where the mean is approximately 2 and the range of possible levels of psychological well-being is between 0 and 12 points.

13. The paper does not attempt to contribute to ideas on deterrence, and, with some justification, a referee has criticized us for that. Issues of deterrence certainly matter, although Sunstein, Schkade, and Kahneman (2000) raise interesting difficulties with whether human beings actually want efficient deterrence. How deterrence and *restitutio in integrum* ought to interact—as discussed by Ireland (2001)—remains incompletely understood. It is likely that future work will have to tackle this.

Table 7. Well-Being Regression Equations with Death Variables and Personal Income: Further Instrumented Estimates

	Life Satisfaction Analysis				GHQ-12 Analysis	
	OLS	IV	RE	RE-IV	FE	FE-IV
Death of father	-.145 (.190)	-.108 (.213)	1.018** (.118)	1.016** (.156)	.892** (.128)	.935** (.162)
Death of mother	-.338* (.165)	-.168 (.174)	.888** (.107)	1.025** (.137)	.903** (.116)	.964** (.144)
Death of partner	-.809 (.537)	-1.642+ (.856)	2.829** (.273)	2.910** (.361)	2.748** (.308)	2.839** (.387)
Death of sibling	-.218 (.375)	-.133 (.453)	.407* (.187)	.086 (.237)	.313 (.208)	.093 (.251)
Death of child	-.130 (.242)	-.208 (.328)	2.228** (.333)	2.240** (.422)	2.441** (.361)	2.137** (.447)
Death of friend	.042 (.252)	.305* (.151)	.544** (.148)	.658** (.184)	.411** (.159)	.464* (.192)
Personal and household characteristics:						
Male	-.112** (.036)	-.385** (.059)	-.504** (.034)	.000 (.062)		
Age	-.094** (.011)	-.143** (.014)	.065** (.008)	.180** (.014)	.054 (.045)	.134* (.062)
Age²/100	.106** (.013)	.161** (.017)	-.077** (.010)	-.212** (.017)	-.064** (.017)	-.193** (.029)
Log of real personal income	.091** (.020)	.698** (.097)	-.017 (.013)	-1.159** (.092)	.018 (.017)	-.818** (.144)
Living as couple	-.142** (.049)	-.280** (.057)	.090* (.044)	.141 (.055)	-.048 (.062)	-.005 (.078)
Widowed	-.780** (.163)	-.771** (.163)	.693** (.103)	1.029** (.137)	.702** (.171)	1.018** (.220)
Divorced	-.770** (.077)	-.782** (.081)	.528** (.061)	.565** (.076)	-.013 (.093)	.143 (.117)
Separated	-.695** (.095)	-.810** (.116)	1.339** (.085)	1.597** (.112)	1.091** (.107)	1.472** (.136)
Single	-.603** (.062)	-.548** (.063)	.178** (.048)	.074 (.062)	.109 (.082)	.142 (.101)
Unemployed	-.540** (.099)	-.163 (.154)	.889** (.054)	.098 (.092)	.773** (.066)	.341** (.104)
Retired	-.006 (.087)	.246* (.096)	-.074 (.061)	-.540** (.083)	-.102 (.077)	-.444** (.107)
Family care	-.122 (.074)	.611** (.143)	.258** (.049)	-.958** (.110)	.174** (.062)	-.593** (.136)

Student	.167+	(.090)	.926**	(.166)	.166**	(.064)	−1.214**	(.135)	−.004	(.087)	−.876** (.176)
A-level education	.306**	(.052)	.241**	(.059)	−.211**	(.041)	−.025	(.055)	.118	(.112)	.176 (.139)
University education	.348**	(.052)	.085	(.067)	−.227**	(.042)	.208**	(.063)	.039	(.105)	.102 (.130)
Household size	.003	(.020)	.023	(.024)	−.018	(.014)	−.077**	(.020)	.014	(.020)	−.314** (.064)
Number of children:											
Ages 0–2	.079	(.050)	−.062	(.063)	.080*	(.040)	.191**	(.053)	.070	(.048)	.120* (.060)
Ages 3–4	−.014	(.060)	−.020	(.069)	−.011	(.040)	.002	(.051)	−.054	(.047)	−.103+ (.058)
Ages 5–11	−.076*	(.035)	−.112**	(.040)	−.056*	(.023)	−.005	(.030)	−.126**	(.030)	−.087* (.036)
Ages 12–15	−.051	(.040)	−.074+	(.044)	.066*	(.028)	.152**	(.036)	.013	(.034)	.046 (.043)
Ages 16–18	−.064	(.079)	−.157	(.096)	−.035	(.055)	.012	(.069)	−.023	(.064)	−.013 (.077)
Home ownership	.126*	(.051)	.272**	(.054)	−.221**	(.038)	−.265**	(.048)	−.084	(.054)	−.116+ (.065)
Constant	5.955**	(.269)	1.509+	(.781)	1.197**	(.201)	8.985**	(.677)	.550	(1.480)	
N	22,801		16,042		64,528		45,928		64,528		42,190

Note. The data are taken from British Household Panel Survey waves 9, 11, and 14 for life satisfaction regressions and include waves 2–5 for GHQ psychological distress regressions. Income is instrumented with a variable indicating whether the survey interviewer was shown the person's paycheck and the level of regional house prices. Standard errors are in parentheses. Round dummies are included for all regressions. OLS = ordinary least squares; IV = instrumental variables; RE = random effects; FE = fixed effects.

+ $p < .1$.
* $p < .05$.
** $p < .01$.

Table 8. Further Illustrative Compensation
Amounts in the First Year

Type of Death	RE	FE
Partner	110	312
Child	59	126
Mother	14	22
Father	14	21
Friend	8	8
Sibling	1	1

Notes: Values are implied per annum compensatory damages (in £10,000s) for different deaths, under GHQ random effects (RE) and fixed effects (FE) specifications.

we believe these ideas should, for the time being, be treated cautiously. Fifth, instrumenting the income variable raises its coefficient in well-being regression equations. This issue is of more than technical interest. The size of the parameter has a fundamental bearing on the appropriate level of compensation for hedonic harm.

Table A1. Psychological Distress Equations with the Death Variables Interacted with Income

	OLS		RE	
	Coefficient	SE	Coefficient	SE
Death of father	1.277**	.313	1.166**	.209
Death of mother	1.105**	.261	.989**	.191
Death of partner	3.277**	.571	3.114**	.412
Death of sibling	.611+	.353	.202	.331
Death of child	2.304**	.926	2.503**	.554
Death of friend	.744**	.241	.547**	.199
Real household income per capita (£10,000s)	−.149**	.022	−.098**	.017
Death of father × household income	−.127	.292	−.194	.182
Death of mother × household income	−.176	.216	−.130	.160
Death of partner × household income	−.195	.447	−.333	.364
Death of sibling × household income	−.176	.325	.206	.336
Death of child × household income	−.206	.664	−.293	.415
Death of friend × household income	.030	.107	−.006	.130
R^2	.035		.034	

Note. The data are from British Household Panel Survey waves 2–5, 9, 11, and 14. IV = instrumental variables; OLS = ordinary least squares; RE = random effects. Personal and household controls and year dummies are included for both regressions. $N = 66,077$.

$^+ p < .1$.

$^{**} p < .01$.

Table A2. Income Regression Equations: First-Stage Regression of Personal Income for Table 7

			Personal Income				
	Life Satisfaction IV		GHQ RE IV		GHQ FE IV		
Instruments	Coefficient	SE	Coefficient	SE	Coefficient	SE
Latest paycheck seen	.139**	.015	.115**	.011	.078**	.012
Early paycheck seen	.127***	.038	.095***	.028	.078**	.030
Not applicable	−.436***	.025	−.401***	.012	−.341**	.015
House price at $t − 1$	.048***	.012	.044**	.009	.043**	.012
Life event						
Death of father	−.021	.114	−.011	.043	−.019	.044
Death of mother	−.138+	.070	−.069+	.037	−.068+	.038
Death of partner	.152	.158	−.041	.098	−.027	.104
Death of sibling	−.130	.108	−.126+	.064	−.111+	.067
Death of child	−.356*	.149	−.211+	.115	−.254*	.119
Death of friend	.086	.107	.086+	.050	.104*	.051
Personal and household characteristics:						
Male	.498**	.016	.518**	.012		
Age	.087***	.005	.101**	.003	.100**	.016
Age²/100	−.096***	.006	−.115**	.004	−.138**	.005
Living as couple	.109***	.023	.088**	.015	.063**	.021
Widowed	.332***	.048	.393**	.036	.530**	.055
Divorced	.129***	.032	.138**	.021	.237**	.030
Separated	.120**	.043	.140**	.030	.209**	.036
Single	.006	.025	−.052**	.017	.045+	.027

Unemployed	−.485**	.051	−.350**	.021	−.202**	.024
Retired	−.092*	.046	−.114**	.022	−.148**	.026
Family care	−.783**	.045	−.687**	.019	−.537**	.023
Student	−1.035**	.073	−.911**	.024	−.768**	.031
A-level education	.057*	.023	.113**	.015	−.059	.037
University education	.300**	.023	.322**	.015	−.003	.035
Household size	−.079**	.010	−.066**	.005	−.413**	.007
Number of children:						
Ages 0–2	.208**	.025	.123**	.014	.063**	.016
Ages 3–4	.125**	.026	.045**	.014	−.028[+]	.015
Ages 5–11	.109**	.014	.052**	.008	.033**	.010
Ages 12–15	.083**	.019	.056**	.010	.057**	.011
Ages 16–18	−.008	.038	.012	.019	.018	.021
Home ownership	−.101**	.025	−.031*	.013	−.017	.018
Constant	7.259**	.121	6.826**	.068		
N	22,801	16,042	64,528	45,928	64,528	42,190

Note. These are instrumental variables (IV) equations used to identify the role of income in Table 7. Round dummies are included for all regressions. For the life satisfaction analysis, the partial $R2$ of excluded instruments = .045; the F-test of excluded instruments = $F(4; 11,408) = 130.59$; and the results of the overidentification test = 2.557 [significance level = .465]. For the GHQ fixed effects analysis, the partial $R2$ of excluded instruments = .021; the F-test of excluded instruments = $F(4; 30,991) = 168.87$; and the results of the overidentification test = 2.557 [significance level = .465]. RE = random effects.

[+] $p < .1$.
* $p < .05$.
** $p < .01$.

REFERENCES

Argyle, Michael. 2001. *The Psychology of Happiness.* London: Routledge.

Bagenstos, Samuel R., and Margo Schlanger. 2007. Hedonic Damages, Hedonic Adaptation, and Disability. *Vanderbilt Law Review* 60:745–97.

Ballas, Dimitris, and Danny Dorling. 2007. Measuring the Impact of Major Life Events upon Happiness. *International Journal of Epidemiology* 36:1244–52.

Blanchflower, David G., and Andrew J. Oswald. 2004. Well-Being over Time in Britain and the USA. *Journal of Public Economics* 88:1359–86.

Brickman, Phillip, Dan Coates, and Ronnie Janoff-Bulman. 1978. Lottery Winners and Accident Victims—Is Happiness Relative? *Journal of Personality and Social Psychology* 36:917–27.

Broman, Clifford L., Melissa L. Riba, and Merideth R. Trahan. 1996. Traumatic Events and Marital Well-Being. *Journal of Marriage and the Family* 58: 908–16.

Cardozo, Barbara L., Alfredo Vergara, Ferid Agani, and Carol A. Gotway. 2000. Mental Health, Social Functioning, and Attitudes of Kosovar Albanians following the War in Kosovo. *Journal of the American Medical Association* 284: 569–77.

Clark, Andrew E., Ed Diener, Yannis Georgellis, and Richard E. Lucas. 2004. Lags and Leads in Life Satisfaction: A Test of The Baseline Hypothesis. Working Paper No. 2003-14. DELTA, Paris.

Clark, Andrew E., Paul Frijters, and Michael A. Shields. 2006. Income and Happiness: Evidence, Explanations and Economic Implications. Working Paper No. 2006-24. Paris School of Economics, Paris.

Clark, Andrew E., and Andrew J. Oswald. 1994. Unhappiness and Unemployment. *Economic Journal* 104:648–59.

———. 2002. A Simple Statistical Method for Measuring How Life Events Affect Happiness. *International Journal of Epidemiology* 31:1139–44.

Cooter, R. 2003. Hand Rule Damages for Incompensable Losses. *San Diego Law Review* 40:1097–1121.

Diener, Ed, Eunkook M. Suh, Richard E. Lucas, and Herbert L. Smith. 1999. Subjective Well-Being: Three Decades of Progress. *Psychological Bulletin* 125: 276–302.

Di Tella, Rafael, Robert J. MacCulloch, and Andrew J. Oswald. 2001. Preferences over Inflation and Unemployment: Evidence from Surveys of Happiness. *American Economic Review* 91:335–41.

———. 2003. The Macroeconomics of Happiness. *Review of Economics and Statistics* 85:809–27.

Dolan, Paul, and Daniel Kahneman. 2008. Interpretations of Utility and Their Implications for the Valuation of Health. *Economic Journal* 118:215–34.

Easterlin, Richard A. 2003. Explaining Happiness. *Proceedings of the National Academy of Sciences* 100:11176–83.

Easterlin, Richard A., Sandra L. Reynolds, Olga Shemyakina, and Yasuhiko Saito. 2006. Do People Adapt Fully to Adverse Changes in Health? Working paper. University of Southern California, Department of Economics, Los Angeles.

Elliott, Catherine, and Frances Quinn. 2005. *Tort Law.* London: Pearson Education.

Ferrer-i-Carbonell, Ada, and Bernard M. S. van Praag. 2002. The Subjective Costs of Health Losses due to Chronic Diseases: An Alternative Model for Monetary Appraisal. *Health Economics* 11:709–22.

Frederick, Shane, and Goerge Loewenstein. 1999. Hedonic Adaptation. Pp. 302–29 in *Hedonic Psychology: Scientific Approaches to Enjoyment, Suffering, and Well-Being,* edited by Ed Diener, Norbert Schwarz, and Daniel Kahneman. New York: Russell Sage Foundation.

Frey, Bruno S., and Alois Stutzer. 2002. *Happiness and Economics.* Princeton, N.J.: Princeton University Press.

Fujita, Frank, and Ed Diener. 2005. Life Satisfaction Set Point: Stability and Change. *Journal of Personality and Social Psychology* 88:158–64.

Gardner, Jonathan, and Andrew J. Oswald. 2006. Do Divorcing Couples Become Happier by Breaking Up? *Journal of the Royal Statistical Society* 169:319–36.

———. 2007. Money and Mental Well-Being: A Longitudinal Study of Medium-Sized Lottery Wins. *Journal of Health Economics* 26:49–60.

Gilbert, Daniel T., Elizabeth C. Pinel, Timothy D. Wilson, Stephen J. Blumberg, and Thalia Wheatley. 1998. Immune Neglect: A Source of Durability Bias in Affective Forecasting. *Journal of Personality and Social Psychology* 75: 617–38.

Groot, Wim, Henriette M. van den Brink, and Erik Plug. 2004. Money for Health: The Equivalent Variation of Cardiovascular Diseases. *Health Economics* 13:859–72.

Hsee, Christopher K., and Reid Hastie. 2006. Decision and Experience: Why Don't We Choose What Makes Us Happy? *Trends in Cognitive Sciences* 10: 31–37.

Huang, Peter H., and Scott A. Moss. 2006. Implications of Happiness Research for Employment Law. Paper presented at the first annual Colloquium on Current Scholarship in Labor and Employment Law, Marquette, Wis., October 27–28.

Ireland, Thomas R. 2001. Hedonic Damages as Compensation: A Reply to Bruce. *Journal of Forensic Economics* 14:271–72.

Kahan, Dan M., and Martha C. Nussbaum. 1996. Two Conceptions of Emotion in Criminal Law. *Columbia Law Review* 96:269–374.

Kahneman, Daniel, Alan B. Krueger, David Schkade, Norbert Schwarz, and Arthur A. Stone. 2006. Would You Be Happier If You Were Richer? A Focusing Illusion. *Science* 312:1908–10.

Lehman, Darrin R., Christopher G. Davis, Anita DeLongis, Camille B. Wortman,

Susan Bluck, Denise R. Mandel, and John H. Ellard. 1993. Positive and Negative Life Changes following Bereavement, and Their Relations to Adjustment. *Journal of Social and Clinical Psychology* 12:90–112.

Li, Jiong, Thomas M. Laursen, Dorthe H. Precht, Jorn Olsen, and Preben B. Mortensen. 2005. Hospitalization for Mental Illness among Parents after the Death of a Child. *New England Journal of Medicine* 352:1190–96.

Lucas, Richard E., Andrew Clark, Ed Diener, and Yannis Georgellis. 2003. Re-examining Adaptation and the Setpoint Model of Happiness: Reactions to Changes in Marital Status. *Journal of Personality and Social Psychology* 84: 527–39.

Martikainen, Pekka, Jerome Adda, Jane E. Ferrie, George D. Smith, and Michael G. Marmot. 2003. Effects of Income and Wealth on GHQ Depression and Poor Self-Rated Health in White Collar Women and Men in the Whitehall II Study. *Journal of Epidemiology and Community Health* 57:718–23.

Menzel, Paul, Paul Dolan, Jeff Richardson, and Jan A. Olsen. 2002. The Role of Adaptation to Disability and Disease in Health State Valuation: A Preliminary Normative Analysis. *Social Science and Medicine* 55:2149–58.

Middleton, Warwick F., Beverley F. Raphael, Paul Burnett, and Nada Martinek. 1997. Psychological Distress and Bereavement. *Journal of Nervous and Mental Disease* 185:447–53.

Oswald, Andrew J. 1997. Happiness and Economic Performance. *Economic Journal* 107:1815–31.

Oswald, Andrew J., and Nattavudh Powdthavee. 2007. Obesity, Unhappiness, and the Challenge of Affluence: Theory and Evidence. *Economic Journal* 117: F441–54.

———. 2008. Does Happiness Adapt? A Longitudinal Study of Disability with Implications for Economists and Judges. *Journal of Public Economics* 92: 1061–77.

Pevalin, David J., and John Ermisch. 2004. Cohabiting Unions, Repartnering and Mental Health. *Psychological Medicine* 34:1553–59.

Posner, Eric A. 2001. Law and the Emotions. *Georgetown Law Journal* 89: 1977–2012.

Posner, Eric A., and Cass R. Sunstein. 2005. Dollars and Death. *University of Chicago Law Review* 72:537–98.

Powdthavee, Nattavudh. 2005. Unhappiness and Crime: Evidence from South Africa. *Economica* 72:531–47.

———. 2007. Are There Geographical Variations in the Psychological Costs of Unemployment in South Africa? *Social Indicators Research* 80:629–52.

———. 2008. Putting a Price Tag on Friends, Relatives, and Neighbours: Using Surveys of Life-Satisfaction to Value Social Relationships. *Journal of Socio-economics* 37:1459–80.

Rayo, Luis, and Gary S. Becker. 2007. Evolutionary Efficiency and Happiness. *Journal of Political Economy* 115:302–37.

Riis, Jason, George Loewenstein, Jonathan Baron, Christopher Jepson, Angela Fagerlin, and Peter A. Ubel. 2005. Ignorance of Hedonic Adaptation to Hemodialysis: A Study Using Ecological Momentary Assessment. *Journal of Experimental Psychology: General* 134:3–9.

Robinson, Kate L., John McBeth, and Gary J. MacFarlane. 2004. Psychological Distress and Premature Mortality in the General Population: A Prospective Study. *Annals of Epidemiology* 14:467–72.

Shields, Michael A., and Stephen Wheatley Price. 2005. Exploring the Economic and Social Determinants of Psychological Well-Being and Perceived Social Support in England. *Journal of the Royal Statistical Society: Series A* 168: 513–37.

Smith, Dylan M., Kenneth M. Langa, Mohammed U. Kabeto, and Peter A. Ubel. 2005. Health, Wealth and Happiness. *Psychological Science* 16:663–66.

Stevenson, Betsey, and Justin Wolfers. 2006. Bargaining in the Shadow of the Law: Divorce Laws and Family Distress. *Quarterly Journal of Economics* 121:267–88.

Sunstein, Cass R. 2004. Valuing Life: A Plea for Disaggregation. *Duke Law Journal* 54:385–445.

Sunstein, Cass R., David Schkade, and Daniel Kahneman. 2000. Do People Want Optimal Deterrence? *Journal of Legal Studies* 29:237–53.

Taylor, Marcia F., John Brice, Nick Buck, and Elaine Prentice-Lane. 2002. *British Household Panel Survey User Manual*. Colchester: University of Essex.

Tetlock, Philip E. 2003. Thinking the Unthinkable: Sacred Values and Taboo Cognitions. *Trends in Cognitive Sciences* 7:320–24.

Ubel, Peter A., George Loewenstein, and Christopher Jepson. 2005. Disability and Sunshine: Can Hedonic Predictions Be Improved by Drawing Attention to Focusing Illusions or Emotional Adaptation? *Journal of Experimental Psychology: Applied* 11:111–23.

van Praag, Bernard M. S., and Barbara E. Baarsma. 2005. Using Happiness Surveys to Value Intangibles: The Case of Airport Noise. *Economic Journal* 115: 224–46.

van Praag, Bernard M. S., and Ada Ferrer-i-Carbonell. 2004. *Happiness Quantified: A Satisfaction Calculus Approach*. Oxford: Oxford University Press.

Winkelmann, Liliana, and Rainer Winkelmann. 1998. Why Are the Unemployed So Unhappy? Evidence from Panel Data. *Economica* 65:1–15.

Happiness Research and Cost-Benefit Analysis

Matthew Adler and Eric A. Posner

ABSTRACT

A growing body of research on happiness or subjective well-being (SWB) shows, among other things, that people adapt to many injuries more rapidly than is commonly thought, fail to predict the degree of adaptation and hence overestimate the impact of those injuries on their SWB, and, similarly, enjoy small or moderate rather than significant changes in SWB in response to significant changes in income. Some researchers believe that these findings pose a challenge to cost-benefit analysis and argue that project evaluation decision procedures based on economic premises should be replaced with procedures that directly maximize SWB. This view turns out to be wrong or, at best, premature. Cost-benefit analysis remains a viable decision procedure. However, some of the findings in the happiness literature can be used to generate valuations for cost-benefit analysis where current approaches have proved inadequate.

1. INTRODUCTION

A new literature on happiness, the product of work of psychologists and economists, poses a significant challenge to traditional economics (see, for example, Adler [2006, p. 1886 n.31] for cites to some overviews of happiness surveys; see also Kahneman, Diener, and Schwarz 1999). Whereas economics assumes that people's choices advance their well-being, the happiness literature suggests that, in many settings, people make poor choices that undermine their happiness or subjective well-being (SWB). One important finding is that people adapt to both good and bad events but have trouble anticipating their own adaptation, with the result that they overestimate the benefits of good events and the

MATTHEW ADLER is the Leon Meltzer Professor of Law at the University of Pennsylvania Law School. ERIC A. POSNER is the Kirkland and Ellis Professor of Law at the University of Chicago Law School. Thanks to David Weisbach, other conference participants, and a referee for helpful comments and to Nathan Richardson for research assistance.

[*Journal of Legal Studies*, vol. XXXVII (June 2008)]

unpleasantness of bad events. The magnitude of this effect is contested, but if it is high enough, many verities of economics would seem to be called into question.

An important distinction, which we emphasize in this paper, is the distinction between well-being and SWB. An individual's well-being is determined by the satisfaction of her preferences—more precisely, by the attainment of those items that well-informed, rational, self-interested individuals would generally prefer (Adler and Posner 2006, pp. 35–52). Well-informed, rational individuals can have self-interested preferences for items other than their own happiness: for example, health, physical security, status in the community, or having a family. Still, SWB is surely an important component of well-being. If individuals are poor affective forecasters and in substantial measure prefer increased income as a means to increasing their happiness—overlooking the fact of affective adaptation—much conventional wisdom on macroeconomic and fiscal policy, taxes, government regulation, and development may be undermined (Layard 2005).

The happiness literature is mainly empirical, but researchers are beginning to focus on its normative implications. Some scholars argue that the basic premises of modern government regulation need to be rethought. If people's choices do not advance their happiness, and well-being is just SWB—a point that we dispute, but which happiness scholars often seem either to accept or at least not to vigorously question—then the basis of the market economy seems questionable. But nearly everyone shies away from the implications of this view, which is to replace the market economy with a system of pervasive government control, one that would prevent people from choosing and would instead force them to be happy.

The literature so far has gone in two more modest directions. First, some researchers have argued that ordinary means of project evaluation—such as cost-benefit analysis (CBA)—should continue to be used but that happiness measures should be employed to improve the monetary valuation of certain goods where market measures and contingent-valuation surveys produce unreliable results. The happiness literature is, in essence, used to improve measurement but not to reorient government policy. Second, some researchers have suggested that CBA might be replaced with an SWB-based procedure where aggregate happiness, rather than net monetized benefits, is used as the maximand. The difference between these two approaches is that the first works within the existing policy analysis framework while adding a tool for improving measurement, while the second overhauls the framework.

In this paper, we evaluate these and other normative implications of the happiness literature. We make two arguments. First, we argue that the happiness literature does not undermine CBA and similar conventional methods of project evaluation that rely on a money metric. The literature does not undermine the normative basis of CBA—does not even address it—and its empirical findings do not contradict the main empirical premises of CBA. Second, we argue that the main empirical results of the happiness literature do suggest ways in which CBA can be refined. In particular, certain preferences will need to be "laundered" to take account of problems of adaptation and affective forecasting.

We start off in Section 2 by describing the normative basis of CBA. In Section 3, we describe some of the basic facts about CBA, and in Section 4, we address and reject the argument that the happiness literature undermines CBA. In Section 5 we discuss the limited but important implications of the happiness literature for the way that CBA should be conducted.

2. WEAK WELFARISM AND COST-BENEFIT ANALYSIS

Normative debates about governmental policy analysis should begin with a moral view. This is not to say that legal provisions will perfectly mirror the moral bedrock. There is slippage between law and morality, for a host of reasons. But the ultimate justification for a legal requirement—in particular, for a legal requirement that governmental agencies employ some decision procedure, such as CBA—will be some moral framework.

Our framework, one we have discussed and defended at length elsewhere (Adler and Posner 2006, pp. 52–61), is "weak welfarism." Weak welfarism states that overall well-being is one of a possible plurality of fundamental moral considerations. In other words, it says that morality has the structure $\{W, F_1, \ldots, F_M\}$, where W is overall well-being and $M \geqslant 0$. Overall well-being and each F_i is a distinct moral factor or consideration. (On a moral theory as a series of distinct factors, see Kagan [1997]). The F_i might include distributive considerations or moral rights. Weak welfarism is not utilitarianism, which says that overall well-being is the sole moral consideration. Utilitarianism has the structure $\{W\}$. Nor is weak welfarism the same as welfarism in the standard sense, which eschews rights, intrinsic environmental values, or any other moral considerations that bring into play non-well-being information. Standard or "strong" welfarism has the structure $\{W_1, \ldots, W_N\}$, where each W_i is sensitive solely to facts about individual well-being.

The distinction between utilitarianism, strong welfarism, and our own view—weak welfarism—is not critical to this paper. Everything we say henceforth about the nature of well-being, the nature of CBA, and the implications of the SWB literature for CBA will be of relevance to utilitarians and strong welfarists. Still, the reader should understand that our own concern for well-being proceeds from a broader moral framework that also entertains nonwelfare considerations.

Because overall well-being is one element of weak welfarism, this moral framework requires a conception of well-being. What, exactly, is human welfare? What makes an individual life better or worse for that person? As we have noted elsewhere (Adler and Posner 2006, pp. 28–35), the philosophical literature on well-being offers three general candidates: objective-list accounts of well-being, preferentialist accounts, and mental-state accounts.

Objectivists point to goods such as friendship and social life, knowledge, health, accomplishment, and enjoyment. Martha Nussbaum (2000, pp. 78–80) is the most prominent contemporary philosopher working in this tradition and offers this list:

Life
Bodily health
Bodily integrity
Senses, imagination, and thought
Emotions
Practical reason
Affiliation (including the goods of both friendship and self-respect)
Play
Other species
Control over one's environment (including both political rights and
    property rights)

Outside philosophy, within various scholarly literatures such as public health or the literature on social indicators, there is a tradition of developing conceptions of the quality of life and corresponding metrics.[1]

---

1. For some reviews of this literature, see Cummins (1996) and Diener and Suh (1997). See also Alkire (2005, pp. 25–85), which reviews lists of aspects of human well-being from a number of different disciplines.

These conceptions are, in effect, objective-list accounts of human well-being or aspects thereof. An illustrative example is the World Health Organization's WHOQOL index (on the WHOQOL, see Adler 2006, pp. 1961–63). This was developed after a massive international effort, including focus groups in 15 countries where members of the general population were asked to develop a list of "the aspects of life that they considered contributed to its quality," and bears more than a passing resemblance to Nussbaum's list. The index, shown in Table 1, has 24 facets of quality of life, grouped into six domains.

A second family of accounts of well-being consists of preferentialist accounts. Preferentialists connect individual well-being to preference satisfaction. Economists traditionally equate well-being with the satisfaction of actual preferences—but this account is problematic, for a host of reasons. Actual preferences can be nonideal (consider the sadist's preference for pain infliction); actual preferences can be disinterested (if someone prefers an outcome on purely altruistic grounds, its occurrence does not benefit him); and actual preferences provide no obvious basis for interpersonal comparisons, which the construct of overall well-being requires. A better preferentialist view says something like the following: individual well-being consists in those things that individuals, with full information and deliberating rationally, contemplating the prospect of living different lives, converge in self-interestedly preferring.[2]

This view of well-being, full-information preferentialism, is our own view. Full-information preferentialism permits the "laundering" of non-ideal or disinterested preferences yet retains the basic attraction of preferentialist accounts of well-being: such accounts explain why individuals have reason to be motivated by their own well-being, something any decent account of well-being should do. Full-information preferentialism is the view of well-being that will structure our discussion of CBA.

The third family of accounts of well-being consists of mental-state accounts. Mental-state theorists claim that an individual's well-being is wholly a matter of her mental states. Jeremy Bentham argued that well-being reduces to pleasures and pains—to negative and positive affect,

---

2. The convergence requirement is needed to allow interpersonal comparisons. On this conception of well-being, see Adler and Posner (2006, pp. 35–52). Strictly speaking, the view of well-being we defend in Adler and Posner (2006) states that preferences must survive idealization, without taking a position as between full-information, objective-good, and other accounts of idealization. But we believe that the best account does appeal to full information or, equivalently, to objective goods understood just as those features of human lives that individuals want when they are fully informed.

Table 1. WHOQOL Index

Physical Domain	Psychological Domain	Independence Domain	Social Domain	Environment Domain	Spiritual Domain
Pain and discomfort	Positive feelings	Mobility	Personal relationships	Physical safety and security	Spirituality
Energy and fatigue	Thinking, learning, memory, and concentration	Activities of daily living	Social support	Home environment	
Sleep and rest	Self-esteem	Dependence on medications or treatments	Sexual activity	Financial resources	
	Body image and appearance	Working capacity		Health and social care (availability and quality)	
	Negative feelings			Opportunities for acquiring new information and skills	
				Participation in and new opportunities for recreation and leisure	
				Physical environment	
				Transport	

in the terminology of the SWB literature. Henry Sidgwick and John Stuart Mill argued that well-being reduces to the occurrence of preferred mental states. This view is broader than Bentham's because it allows that individuals might prefer mental states other than their own affects, such as a state of knowledge, contemplation, or awareness. But it still insists that nothing other than an individual's mental states can make a difference to her well-being.

We are persuaded by the arguments against mental-state views, beginning with Robert Nozick's (1974, pp. 42–45) famous "experience machine."[3] Any mental-state account, whatever the relevant mental state or states—pain, pleasure, happiness, emotion, belief—must say that two outcomes in which an individual's mental states are identical must be identically good for her. Experience machine hypotheticals undermine that basic premise. For example, an individual's well-being may depend upon her having a spouse who is actually faithful (not just one she believes to be), a career that is actually successful (not just one she is deluded into believing successful), or, for that matter, a happiness state that is authentic (in resting on true beliefs). Further, mental-state views face the difficulty of navigating the terrain between Bentham's narrow view, on the one hand, and Sidgwick's and Mill's expansive view, on the other. Surely human well-being is more than just pains and pleasures. But the Sidgwick/Mill position is also vulnerable: if we say that any mental state that an individual prefers (or prefers with full information) benefits him, why not recognize that an individual can prefer items other than his own mental states and allow those, too, to be welfare relevant?

These weaknesses of the mental-state accounts have been fully rehearsed elsewhere, both in the philosophical literature and in our own work, and we will not belabor them here. The arguments are not knockdown. They do not show that it is illogical or essentially confused to adopt a mental-state view of well-being. The proponent of SWB-based policy analysis might, without incoherence, embrace the position that well-being does reduce to pains, pleasures, happiness states, states of life satisfaction, or other mental states. What is problematic, we think, is for the proponent of SWB-based policy analysis to embrace that position without normative argument. Most of the existing literature on SWB is purely empirical. That literature, written by psychologists and economists, is important and illuminating, helping to lay bare the causal de-

---

3. Citations to overviews of the philosophical literature, where the arguments against mental-state theories are reviewed, are furnished in Adler and Posner (2006, p. 196 n.9).

terminants of individual SWB. But the scholar who wishes to take a position about the appropriate structure of law and policy and its appropriate sensitivity to SWB cannot do so on purely empirical grounds. She must engage in normative argument—and, specifically, confront the large body of normative scholarship that argues against reducing well-being to mental states.[4]

To add to the confusion, some scholars in the SWB literature use the term "well-being" as a synonym for happiness or SWB (subjective well-being). Diener and Seligman, for example, define "well-being" as "peoples' positive evaluation of their lives, includ[ing] positive emotion, engagement, satisfaction, and meaning" (Diener and Seligman 2004, p. 1). This is unfortunate because it precludes the possibility of even having a normative debate about whether well-being reduces to happiness or SWB. Well-being, conceptually, is a matter of how an individual's life goes for her (Sumner 1996, p. 20). This is conceptually distinct from some feature of an individual's mental states, such as her "positive evaluation of her life," her sense of satisfaction, her overall affect, or anything else. At the end of the day, we may conclude—after normative argument—that well-being reduces to SWB. But to define them as equivalent at the outset just cuts short this debate by definitional fiat.

Our conclusion, after engaging the normative issues, is to adopt a full-information preferentialist rather than a mental-state view of well-being. One way to understand the difference is that full-information preferentialism allows both the individual's mental states and non-mental facts (such as facts about his body, or about the external world) to affect his well-being. A view of well-being that held that pains, pleasures, and happiness were irrelevant to well-being would be absurd. Full-information preferentialism says that good mental states are one component of well-being, among others. In particular, various mental states are a positive or negative component of well-being just insofar as self-interested individuals, with full information, generally prefer or disprefer them.

So what, exactly, are the sources of well-being, given full-information preferentialism? One bit of evidence comes from the objectivist literature on well-being. We believe (Adler and Posner 2006, pp. 51–52; Adler 2000, pp. 297–300) that there is substantial overlap between full-

---

4. Some subjective well-being (SWB) scholars explicitly argue that happiness is the sole morally relevant item (Layard 2005 pp. 111–25). Others refrain from making that claim (Kahneman 2000, p. 691; Kahneman and Sugden 2005, p. 176).

information preferentialism and objectivism, in the following sense: the best and most plausible lists of objective welfare goods, such as the WHOQOL or Nussbaum's list, are plausible precisely because they list the items that, it seems, people with good information end up self-interestedly preferring.

A second bit of evidence comes from the survey literature. Surveys whereby individuals are asked about their goals and preferences for their own lives would be helpful in specifying full-information preferentialism. Most surveys that touch on well-being take a different format—in particular quality-adjusted life-years (QALY), contingent-valuation, and SWB surveys, as discussed in Adler (2006)—but there are a few surveys of this sort that have been undertaken (see the surveys cited in Cummins 1996, pp. 304–5; Ryff 1989; King and Napa 1998; Diener and Scollon 2003). For example, Hadley Cantril (1965), in his seminal survey work that helped galvanize SWB research, not only asked respondents an early quantitative life satisfaction question but also asked them for open-ended answers to a question about personal aspirations and a question about personal fears. The personal aspirations question was, "All of us want certain things out of life. When you think about what really matters in your own life, what are your wishes and hopes for the future?" (p. 23).[5] The personal fears question was, "Now, taking the other side of the picture, what are your fears and worries about the future?" (p. 23). On the basis of 3,000 (!) preliminary interviews, he developed 34 categories of answers to the personal-aspirations question and 33 categories for the personal-fears question.[6] The answers to the final U.S. questionnaire fell into the following categories shown in Table 2, in descending order (Cantril 1965, p. 35).

There are, obviously, many differences in the details of Nussbaum's list, the WHOQOL, and Cantril's list. There would be yet more differences if we were to look at all the lists of objective welfare goods compiled by philosophers, all the quality-of-life frameworks compiled by public health or social indicator researchers such as those who developed the WHOQOL, and all the lists of personal concerns developed by survey

5. Unfortunately, the question then asks: "In other words, if you imagine your future in the best possible light, what would your life look like then, if you are to be happy?" So it veers from a question about the content of the respondent's self-interested preferences to a question about the causes of the respondent's happiness. Still, the answers to Cantril's questionnaire provide some initial evidence about the content of individual's self-interested preferences. More work of this sort, with unambiguous questions, needs to be undertaken.

6. A fuller description of the categories is provided in Cantril (1965, pp. 329–33).

Table 2. Categories of Answers to Cantril (1965) Questionnaire

Personal Aspirations	% Respondents	Personal Fears	% Respondents
Own health	40	Own health	40
Decent standard of living	33	Family health	25
Children	29	War	21
Housing	24	Inadequate standard of living	18
Happy family	18	Children	12
Family health	16	No fears	12
Leisure time	11	Unemployment	10
Keep status quo	11	Dependency	9
Old age	10	Family responsibilities	5
Peace	9	Unhappy family	5
Resolution of religious problems	8	Loneliness	5
Working conditions	7	Deterioration in standard of living	5
Family responsibility	7		
To be accepted	6		
An improved standard of living	5		
Employment	5		
Attain emotional maturity	5		
Modern conveniences	5		

researchers who have posed questions similar to Cantril's. For our purposes here, however, all these sources of evidence about the content of fully informed preferences confirm the critical point that people can and do prefer more than their own mental states. It is this point—not the precise list of mental and nonmental items that advance fully informed preferences, or the precise balance between the two—that will drive our analysis of the challenges that the SWB literature poses to CBA.

Consider, for example, Nussbaum's list. The list does include various aspects of SWB. Nussbaum lists "[b]eing able to have pleasurable experiences, and to avoid . . . pain" as an aspect of her "senses, imagination, and thought" category. And she lists "[n]ot having one's emotional development blighted by overwhelming fear and anxiety" as an aspect of her "emotions" category. But Nussbaum's list also includes items such as physical health, physical security, employment, affiliation with friends and family, and status in the community (Nussbaum 2000). These items are not mentalistic or wholly mentalistic. They depend, at least in part, on the individual's physical state or on facts in the world outside the individuals' mind and body, and thus cannot be captured by an SWB measure (however internally complex). An individual whose limbs or organs are diseased—where the concept of disease is defined by the functioning of average humans, or by evolutionary considerations, or by the consensus of experts, that is, doctors—is in a state of imperfect health, even if she is happy in that state. Someone subject to more frequent physical assaults is less secure, even if those assaults affect her SWB not a whit. The researcher who dedicates her life to science has made a genuine accomplishment if she discovers some novel and important truths, regardless of whether that discovery improves her mood. The dedicated parent has succeeded if her children's lives improve because of her efforts, whether or not the effort or that improvement make her happier. The individual who is treated as a second-class citizen, for example, in a system of apartheid or gender discrimination, is deprived of what Nussbaum calls "the social bases of self-respect and non-humiliation" even if she is happy with her second-class status—a point underscored by Amartya Sen's (1987, p. 45) famous example of the downtrodden, but happy, housewife.

For purposes of this paper, individual health and safety furnish a particularly important instance of the point that well-being consists in part of nonmental items. Much of our regulatory apparatus is focused on reducing health and safety risks; the monetary valuation of these risks is a large part of governmental CBA, and the tort system, in compensating for physical harms, is also centrally concerned with such valuation. It is plausible that individuals with full information would prefer not to suffer diseases or accidents on nonhedonic grounds—as a matter of their physical integrity—and not merely on hedonic grounds. A number of papers in this volume make essentially this point (Ubel and Loewenstein 2008; Sunstein 2008; see also Bagenstos and Schlanger 2007). Because individuals hedonically adapt to many physical setbacks, including serious conditions such as paraplegia or the loss of limbs, purely hedonic compensation for tortious wrongdoing causing physical injuries, and purely hedonic compensating variations (CVs) for health and safety losses as a matter of CBA, might be counterintuitively small. But because physical integrity is itself (plausibly) something that people with full information prefer, physical integrity itself is (plausibly) a concern of CBA and the tort system, above and beyond the hedonic losses (large or small) that flow from physical injury.

The clever proponent of SWB-based policy analysis might, at this juncture, respond that preferences for health and other nonmental items can be "translated" into a mentalistic framework by reconstructing them as preferences for beliefs. Rather than say that the individual prefers to have the use of limbs, let us say that she prefers to believe that she has the use of her limbs. Rather than say that the individual prefers to have her children lead good lives, let us say that she prefers to believe that her children lead good lives. Rather than say that she prefers not to be treated as a second-class citizen, let us say that she prefers to believe that she is not treated as a second-class citizen. This "translation" might not be true to the preferences—that is the point of Nozick's experience machine. But would it not be good enough for government work? In particular, would there be systematic differences between the policies chosen by a partly nonmentalistic CBA that took an individual's preferences regarding her own body, or third parties, at face value—as preferences for nonmental items—and a CBA that translated those as preferences regarding the individual's beliefs about her body and about third parties?

It is not clear whether there would be systematic differences between these two sorts of CBA. (Whether there would be depends on whether individuals form beliefs that tend to deviate from the true state of the world in one direction—for example, whether individuals tend to believe that they are healthier than they really are.) If the two variants do deviate, that shows that the mentalistic translation of partly nonmentalistic CBA is problematic as a policy matter. If the two variants do not deviate, then that simply shows that there are certain variants of purely mentalistic policy analysis that are coextensive with partly nonmentalistic CBA—not that the partly nonmentalistic CBA that we favor should be abandoned or altered.

In any event, this belief based translation of preferences for health and other nonmental items is of purely theoretical interest. The SWB scales that have been generally used by SWB researchers—the life satisfaction and happiness scales—as well as the scale of momentary experience favored by Kahneman, Wakker, and Sarin (1997) and Kahneman (1999, 2000) are not simply measures of the extent to which an individual believes her preferences to be satisfied. Rather, they are—to a substantial extent—influenced by the individual's mood and affect (see Schwarz and Strack 1999).[7] Happiness is, in common parlance, largely a matter of mood and affect. And a question such as "how satisfied are you with your life" is naturally understood as asking, in part, about how strong the respondent's feeling of satisfaction with his life is—not just about his (possibly affectless) judgment about the extent to which his self-interested preferences are satisfied.

To sum up: Our position is that overall well-being has moral relevance, under the rubric of weak welfarism, and that full-information preferentialism is the most attractive account of well-being. On this account, it is very plausible to think that individual well-being depends, in part, on the individual's mood and affect and other aspects of her mental state. But it is also very plausible to think that an individual's well-being depends on her physical integrity, her physical security, her children's well-being, whether she belongs to a group that is legally or socially subordinated, and other items that are not mental states—and, in particular, are distinct from the individual's mood and affect.

3. COST-BENEFIT ANALYSIS

The traditional view sees CBA as a mirror for Kaldor-Hicks efficiency. We have defended a different view (Adler and Posner 2006). First, Kaldor-Hicks efficiency has zero moral relevance. A policy is Kaldor-

7. Indeed, a standard understanding among SWB researchers is that it encompasses mood, not just judgments of life quality. As Diener and Suh (1997, p. 200) note, "Subjective well-being consists of three interrelated components: life satisfaction, pleasant affect, and unpleasant affect. Affect refers to pleasant and unpleasant moods and emotions, whereas life satisfaction refers to a cognitive sense of satisfaction with life."

Hicks efficient if the winners could, potentially, compensate the losers. But either this potential compensation would actually occur, for example, via a very well functioning tax system—in which event the policy is a genuine Pareto improvement over the status quo, and the Kaldor-Hicks criterion is otiose—or the potential compensation would not occur, in which case the mere unattained potential for a Pareto improvement furnishes no moral basis for choosing a policy that, in fact, would harm some.

Second, CBA is a rough and administrable proxy for overall well-being. Overall well-being is a fundamental moral criterion; CBA is not. In particular, because of the variable marginal utility of money, a policy can have positive net monetized benefits but reduce overall well-being or vice versa. In general, however, CBA overlaps with overall well-being sufficiently well, and is sufficiently easily monitored by the president, the Congress, the judiciary, and the citizenry, to be one component of the appropriate decision procedure for administrative agencies in a wide range of choice situations.[8]

This, in the smallest of nutshells, is our revisionary framework for CBA—one that embeds it within weak welfarism and links it to overall well-being. But what, exactly, is CBA? To be clear, by CBA we mean monetized CBA: the sum of CVs' test. Take a set of possible policy choices, including the status quo choice of inaction. In the simplest case, each choice maps for sure onto one outcome. So the choice situation becomes $\{O_1, O_2, \ldots, O_m\}$, where O_1 is the status quo outcome. Consider some other outcome, O_i, and some individual P_j. P_j's CV for O_i—taking O_1 as baseline—is the amount of money, added to or subtracted from P_j's holdings in O_i, that would make her just as well off as in O_1. Designate this as $CV_{i,j}$. The net benefits of O_i are $\sum_{j=1}^{N} CV_{i,j}$, where N is the population size. The CBA rule says to pick the outcome with the greatest net benefits.

In a more realistic case, the policymaker will be unsure which outcome results from a given policy choice. Formally, the choice situation becomes $\{A_1, A_2, \ldots, A_m\}$, where each A_i is a lottery over outcomes and $CV_{i,j}$ is a function of the lottery of outcomes associated with A_1 plus the lottery associated with A_i. Because this redefinition of the CV to accommodate lotteries is orthogonal to the issues at stake in this paper,

---

8. We say "one component" because CBA is not a superprocedure that serves to track all the factors potentially of relevance to weak welfarists but rather the decision procedure justified in light of overall well-being (see Adler and Posner 2006, pp. 154–58).

our analysis will focus on CVs for outcomes rather than for lotteries. That simplification is meant to make the discussion less cumbersome. A fuller (and more cumbersome) analysis would reach the same result.

Compensating variations are a money metric of change in well-being. The idea is to measure the difference in well-being for some individual P, as between some baseline outcome O and some alternative outcome O^* by asking about the hypothetical monetary increment to P's holdings, in O^*, that equilibrates the change in well-being. In addition, the following features of CVs, all relevant to the implications of the SWB literature for CBA, bear noting:

Compensating Variations Are a Generic Tool. Cost-benefit analysis can, and is, used to evaluate policies that affect a range of nonmarket goods, not simply policies that change the structure of markets. P's CV is the change in his money holdings in O^* that just counterbalances his welfare difference between O and O^*. Although the CV itself is a change in P's money endowment, the difference between O and O^* need not be. The difference may be that P is healthier in O^* than in O, that he has access to different public goods, that there are changes to the well-being of P's friends or family, and so forth.

Compensating Variations Assume That Money Is Instrumentally, Not Intrinsically, Beneficial. Money is not intrinsically beneficial. To put this in the language of economics, money is an intermediate good, not a final good. An increment in P's income increases P's well-being because P can spend the money in various ways—on consumption goods, health care services, education, travel, and so forth. And CBA does not suppose otherwise. P's CV for O^* is not the change in P's income that makes him just as well off as in O, holding everything else constant in O^*. Rather, the CV is determined by imagining that P's income in O^* is slowly increased or decreased and that P's pattern of expenditure in O^* varies as well, until we reach a point where P is just as well off as in O.

Compensating Variations Hold Constant the Social Background in the Policy Outcome. While the CV is determined by varying P's expenditures in the policy outcome O^*, the social background in O^*—the price vector, the incomes of other individuals, and other such background characteristics—is held constant. We imagine hypothetical changes in P's income in O^* and P's expenditures in O^*, holding constant social background in O^*, until we reach the point where P's well-being in O^*, with these changes, is equal to his well-being in O.

There are several subtle points here that are easy to misunderstand. First, O and O^* themselves can vary in terms of general social facts.

Prices may be different in O^* and in O. Everyone's income may be higher in O^* than in O. But the technique CBA uses to measure the change in overall welfare, moving from O to O^*, is to sum individuals' CVs—where each individual's CV is, in turn, determined by holding constant general social facts in O^* and imagining hypothetical changes just to that individual's income and expenditure.

A closely related point is that the utility of money, in the context of determining a CV, is boosted by relative-income effects. A hypothetical change to an individual's income, holding the social background constant, changes both her absolute and her relative income. In principle, a CV is the change to P's income in O^* that would make her just as well off as in O, given all the effects on well-being (absolute and relative) that would occur if P's income were changed in O^* without anyone else's income changing. So (a point we return to below) even if well-being reduces to SWB, and the linkage between money and SWB is solely a matter of relative—not absolute—effects, the extreme claim that CVs are undefined because money does not change SWB would be untrue.

Compensating Variations Can Be Estimated Using Surveys as Well as Revealed Preference Evidence. Market prices and other behavioral information are one standard source of evidence for CVs. But so-called contingent-valuation surveys are also widely used to estimate CVs. Economists are sometimes skeptical about such surveys. This position might reflect a universal skepticism about the utility of any survey data—a deeply problematic position, and not one that anyone who is interested in the sources of SWB can sustain. (The SWB literature is, after all, built on happiness and life satisfaction surveys.) Or it might reflect a specific skepticism about the contingent-valuation format. But most of the anomalies with this format involve "nonuse" values: stated preferences for items, such as the improvement of distant ecosystems or the preservation of endangered species, that do not affect the respondents' well-being. There is no reason to dismiss the utility of well-conducted contingent-valuation surveys regarding health, recreation, psychological states, or other items with respect to which individuals have substantial self-regarding preferences (see generally Adler 2006).

Compensating Variations Can Be Laundered. Our prior work on CBA emphasizes that agencies can "launder" CVs, as warranted by the full-information preferentialist account of well-being (see Adler and Posner 2006, pp. 124–53; see also Adler 2006, pp. 1904–35). In other words, they can screen out disinterested preferences, poorly informed preferences, or preferences that are distorted by irrationality. Consider that the "utility" numbers representing P's well-being in outcomes O and O^*, $v(O)$ and $v(O^*)$, are numbers representing the preferences of a fully informed and rational observer contemplating the prospect of stepping into P's shoes in O and O^*.[9] These numbers are possibly quite different from the utility numbers representing P's actual preferences as between O and O^*, $u(O)$ and $u(O^*)$. Because CBA is a proxy for overall well-being, P's CV should (putting aside considerations of administrability) be adjusted to approximate the difference $v(O^*) - v(O)$ rather than reflect $u(O^*) - u(O)$.

In practice, agencies actually do launder CVs, at least to some extent (Adler and Posner 2006, pp. 126–33). They (implicitly) screen out disinterested preferences, except in the area of environmental law. Agencies often attempt to compensate for informational failures, for example, by using contingent-valuation surveys that provide respondents with information or by characterizing the goods in certain ways (for example, describing a pollution-reducing policy in terms of its ultimate visibility and health impacts rather than its regulatory language or the changes in tonnage of pollutants emitted). Agencies also sometime compensate for irrationality (such as a departure from expected utility theory) by debiasing survey respondents.

To be sure, the precise extent to which agencies should launder preferences in determining CVs raises difficult issues of balancing the accuracy of CBA against decision costs and ease of monitoring. But some degree of laundering is, we believe, optimal. We return to this issue below.

4. DOES THE SUBJECTIVE WELL-BEING LITERATURE UNDERMINE COST-BENEFIT ANALYSIS?

The literature on SWB calls into question the connection between money and SWB. Let us distinguish between two possible claims, which we shall examine in turn. The Extreme Claim says that money generally makes no difference to an individual's SWB. The Moderate Claim says that money generally makes little difference to an individual's SWB.

Why might these claims undercut CBA? On our account of well-

9. Given our full-information preferentialist account of well-being, utility numbers—representing interpersonally comparable welfare levels—are naturally defined with reference to the preferences of a fully informed observer contemplating the prospect of living different lives (see Adler and Posner 2006, pp. 47–51).

being—full-information preferentialism—SWB is one component of well-being, along with nonmental items. If SWB were irrelevant to well-being, research undercutting the link between money and SWB would be irrelevant to CBA. But, because well-being is partly constituted by SWB, such research has the potential to undermine CBA. Whether it does is what we consider here.

Our conclusions will be as follows. First, the Extreme Claim is false. Second, the Moderate Claim may be true, but the relevant question for CBA is not whether money's effect on SWB is large or small. Rather, the relevant question is one of variable marginal utility. If, because of differential adaptation or differential affective forecasting ability, the money/well-being nexus varies across individuals or goods, CBA may, in theory, deviate from overall well-being. It is not clear whether these are real or theoretical issues, and, in any event, they can be mitigated by the techniques that we shall discuss in Section 5: laundering preferences and incorporating information about SWB-based CVs.

4.1. The Extreme Claim: Money Generally Makes No Difference to Individual Subjective Well-Being

Some of the literature on SWB seems to advance the Extreme Claim. "Many surveys of the field . . . conclude that the connection between money and [SWB] is slight or non-existent" (Gardner and Oswald 2007, pp. 49–50). The Extreme Claim is supported by the famous Brickman lottery study (Brickman et al. 1978) and, seemingly, by studies that find no change in average SWB in various countries despite large income growth. This evidence will be discussed in a moment.

It might be thought that the Extreme Claim is a straw man, which no SWB scholar actually endorses. At most, SWB scholars claim that money has a very small impact on well-being. For purposes of CBA, however, there is a "cliff effect" here: the Extreme Claim threatens to wholly undermine CBA, while CBA is quite viable if money has a very small but positive impact on well-being, as long as marginal utility is not too variable. It is therefore worth distinguishing between the Extreme Claim and the Moderate Claim and discussing in some detail why the Extreme Claim is untrue.

Why does the Extreme Claim pose a radical threat to CBA? Assume that expenditures of money make no difference to P's well-being at all. Then P's CV for outcome O^*, as against status quo outcome O, would just be undefined (except in the limiting case where P is equally well off in both worlds). If P is better off in O^* than in O, no reduction in P's income and expenditures in O^* will suffice to reduce his welfare to the level he attains in O. If P is worse off in O^* than in O, then no increase in P's income and expenditures will suffice to increase his well-being to the level he attains in O. With even one undefined term, the sum of CVs formula becomes undefined and gives no guidance at all in choosing policies. Of course, we could salvage the formula by dropping occasional undefined terms—but if the Extreme Claim means that individuals generally have undefined CVs, the bona fides of CBA as a proxy for overall welfare would be devastated.[10]

Fortunately, it is not the case that individuals generally have undefined CVs. To begin, the SWB literature does not call into question the connection between money and the nonmental items that appear on Nussbaum's (2000) list, the WHOQOL, or similar lists of objective goods or the elements of quality of life (using these, once more, as defeasible evidence of what fully informed individuals would self-interestedly prefer).[11] Consider Nussbaum's list. Money can be used to purchase pharmaceuticals, medical care, healthier foods, leisure time for exercise, and other items that extend life (the "life" good) and improve health ("bodily health"). Wealthier individuals can live in safer neighborhoods and purchase better security devices or services ("bodily integrity"). Money can be used to fund an education ("senses, imagination, and thought," "practical reason"). Money helps to advance the good of friendship ("affiliation") by funding the leisure time to spend with friends and the costs of traveling to be near them and, in the case of the special friendship institutionalized in marriage, by reducing the financial stresses that can cause divorce. It hugely promotes the good of family ("affiliation") on the assumption of parent-child utility interdependence (if increments to

10. If money has no impact on well-being, then observed willingness-to-pay and willingness-to-accept amounts might exist, but appropriately laundered CVs would be undefined. The same is true if money has no impact on SWB and well-being and SWB are equivalent.

11. The focus of the literature on "affective forecasting" is on individuals' failures to understand how to improve their SWB, not on their failure to understand how to improve their position with respect to the nonmental items on these lists of objective goods or the elements of quality of life (on affective forecasting, see Kahneman and Sugden 2005). Analogous failures may, to some extent, affect individual pursuit of nonmental well-being, but the evidence suggests that increased income does in fact tend to improve individuals' nonmental well-being (see Diener and Biswas-Diener 2002, p. 121). Finally, there is no doubt that money can be used to improve individual attainments on a list such as that in Nussbaum (2000) or the WHOQOL. Thus, as further discussed below, even if certain individuals do not actually employ increased income to improve their well-being (nonmental and/or mental), their "laundered" CVs would still be well defined.

the child's well-being increase the parent's). There are many ways in which parents can use money to improve the well-being of their children—most obviously, by providing for their basic needs and then furnishing them an excellent education. Under the heading of "affiliation," Nussbaum also lists "[h]aving the social bases of self-respect and non-humiliation." In a materialistic society, increases in income bolster the "social bases of self-respect."

Even if the Extreme Claim were true and money had no impact on SWB, CVs would still be well defined as long as money has an impact on the nonmental sources of well-being. Imagine that P is at a different well-being level in O* than in O (because of variation in either his mental states, his nonmental states, or both). Assume, further, that changes to P's income in O* have no effect on his SWB in O*. As long as changes to P's income in O* affect his attainments with respect to the nonmental sources of well-being, sufficiently to equilibrate the well-being difference between O* and O, P's CV will be defined.

In any event, the Extreme Claim is false. Money may not have a large impact on SWB—that is a point we will consider in a moment—but it generally has some positive impact. The Extreme Claim is undercut by cross-sectional studies, which consistently demonstrate that individuals with higher incomes tend to have greater SWB. As Easterlin (2001, p. 468) notes, "[I]n every representative national survey ever done a significant positive bivariate relationship between happiness and income has been found." Nor does the relationship hold only in the lower stretches of the income distribution. "[T]he supposed attenuation at higher income levels of the happiness-income relation does not occur when happiness is regressed on log income, rather than absolute income" (Easterlin 2001, p. 468; see also Diener and Biswas-Diener 2002, p. 129). The strength of the correlation is in dispute. Robert Frank (2005, p. 67), analyzing 1980s data from the U.S., concludes, "When we plot average happiness versus average income for clusters of people in a given country at a given time, rich people are in fact a lot happier than poor people. It's actually an astonishingly large difference. There's no single change you can imagine that would make your life improve on the happiness scale as much as to move from the bottom 5 percent on the income scale to the top 5 percent."

Diener and Biswas-Diener (2002, pp. 122–24, 126), reviewing nine studies from different nations, conclude that there is a more modest correlation between income and SWB (ranging from .13 to .24). The correlation appears to become stronger when a particular measure of

SWB (so-called affect balance) is used.[12] In any event, the Diener and Biswas-Diener (2002) review of the cross-sectional literature undercuts the claim that money has no impact on SWB.[13]

A different group of studies attempts to correlate changes in an individual's SWB with changes in her income (for citations of these studies, see Diener and Biswas-Diener 2002, pp. 131–34). An important issue here is controlling for unobserved characteristics that might cause both increased income and less SWB. (For example, it may be that materialistic individuals have a disposition that both impels them to make more money and makes them less happy than nonmaterialistic individuals. It does not follow that increasing an individual's income, holding constant her disposition for materialism, will make her less happy!) Although Brickman et al.'s (1978) famous lottery study found that lottery winners were no happier than controls, the most recent lottery study reaches a different conclusion. Using data from the British Household Panel Survey, Gardner and Oswald (2007) looked at changes in SWB among medium-sized lottery winners (above £1,000), as compared to smaller winners and those who did not win, using the General Health Questionnaire (GHQ) score as a measure of SWB. The study concludes,

> When compared to two control groups—one with no wins and the other with small wins—the paper demonstrates that these medium-size winners go on to have significantly better psychological health. After 2 years, their mental wellbeing compared to before the lottery win has improved by approximately 1.4 GHQ points on a 36-point scale. . . . To provide a better feel for the size of the units, . . . it [can be noted] that the worst thing observable in standard data sets is—perhaps as might be expected—the impact . . . of being widowed. That rare and traumatic event is associated with a worsening in people's mental wellbeing of, on an average, approximately five GHQ points. Such a calculation suggests that 1.4 points, the estimated consequence of a medium-sized lottery win . . . is economically significant and not merely statistically significant. (Gardner and Oswald 2007, p. 48)

What, then, is the evidence supporting the Extreme Claim? Perhaps the strongest evidence comes from within-country studies that find no

---

12. The authors looked at 11 studies altogether, but two were from cities or villages in India and generated much higher correlations.

13. Another important piece of evidence undercutting the Extreme Claim consists of international comparisons that show a strong correlation between per capita income and average SWB (see Diener and Biwas-Diener 2002, pp. 136–39).

change in average SWB despite large income growth. For example, Japan's per capita gross domestic product increased fivefold between 1958 and 1987, with virtually no change in average SWB (Diener and Biswas-Diener 2002, pp. 139–40). Diener and Oishi (2000, pp. 202–3) examine 15 nations during the period 1965–90 and find a mean SWB slope of virtually zero despite substantial average economic growth rates, in the neighborhood of 2 or 3 percent.[14]

A real difficulty with these studies is the possibility of scale recalibration (see Ubel and Loewenstein 2008). If the mapping from the numbers on a happiness or life satisfaction scale to mental states is not fixed but rather varies with national prosperity, then an increase in prosperity might produce a positive change in individuals' average mental states but a compensating shift downward in the scale. (Imagine that an individual's understanding of the scale is, in part, a function of her expectations with respect to her own SWB and that these expectations increase with general prosperity.)

Another way to understand this point is in terms of the debate about whether the effect of income on SWB is solely a matter of relative income or whether absolute income makes a difference too. The relative-income-only position is controversial, and we are skeptical that it is true (Frank 2005). The within-country studies seem to support the relative-income-only position. When everyone's income increases, no one's relative income changes, and therefore average SWB does not increase at all—or so the story goes. However, the studies are also consistent with the proposition that absolute income does have an effect on SWB but that this effect is counterbalanced by scale recalibration as a country's income increases over time.

In any event, even if the relative-income-only position is true and absolute income has no effect on SWB, that fact would not—in turn—imply the Extreme Claim. Remember the crucial point that an individual's CV is determined by making hypothetical changes to her income and expenditure, holding constant the social background. The marginal utility of money in producing SWB, in the context of determining CVs, is the sum of the marginal utility that derives from the absolute contribution of expenditure to SWB and the marginal utility that derives from

14. For reasons of data availability, these were all developed countries; there is some evidence that the slope of SWB has been larger in poor countries. See Diener and Oishi (2000, p. 204) and Hagerty and Veenhoven (2003).

relative-income effects. Even if the first term is zero (and that is controversial), the second term is not.

A final point is that even if the Extreme Claim is true in some unusual cases—even if there are individuals whose SWB would remain neutral or decrease with more income—any difficulty this might create for the existence of CVs can be resolved by laundering the preferences. Imagine that P is quite irrational in using money for his own benefit, both with respect to SWB and with respect to the nonmental components of well-being. (For example, P cares about his SWB, his health, and his children's lives but is a poor affective forecaster, health forecaster, and parent and fritters away his income on material comforts that do not improve his attainment with respect to these components of well-being at all.) There is a policy that leads to outcome O^*, which makes P worse off than in the status quo outcome O. We are trying to identify P's CV for O^*, which is in turn a rough metric of $v(O^*) - v(O)$—where $v()$ is the utility of a well-informed and debiased (or unbiased) observer contemplating the prospect of living P's life in O and O^*. If we try to determine how much money would equilibrate the welfare difference between O and O^*, as that money would be expended by P, the answer is no amount. But we might instead produce a laundered CV by asking, how much money would equilibrate the welfare difference between O and O^*, as that money would be expended by a well-informed and debiased adviser who cared about P's interests? There are many things that a well-informed and debiased adviser could do with increased income to improve P's SWB or his attainments with respect to the nonmental components of well-being.[15]

To sum up: The SWB literature does not undermine CBA by implying that CVs do not exist. First, even if the Extreme Claim is true, CVs will be defined as long as money increases attainments with respect to the nonmental components of well-being. Second, the Extreme Claim is false: money does generally improve individual SWB to some extent.

---

15. With respect to SWB, the literature suggests in particular that SWB is correlated with the following items, all of which money is helpful in producing: mental health; avoiding certain physical health states, such as severe or progressive diseases; marriage and relationships; leisure; social status; and the satisfaction of material goals (which improves SWB at least to some extent). See generally Argyle (1999), Diener and Biswas-Diener (2002), Diener et al. (1999), and Furnham and Argyle (1998). Note also that, even if SWB is purely dispositional, money can increase an individual's lifetime SWB by increasing his longevity (see Veenhoven 2005). This is a relevant point because overall well-being is, strictly, overall lifetime well-being, and CVs are therefore money amounts that would equilibrate policy-induced changes in individuals' lifetime well-being.

Third, in unusual cases where individuals are sufficiently irrational or poorly informed that increases to their income would not, in fact, increase their well-being, well-defined CVs can be constructed by laundering out the irrationality and poor information.

Although our analysis in this section has focused on CBA, it should be noted that the proposition that money has no impact on well-being would not merely explode CBA by leading to undefined CVs. It would also have radical implications for other practices even more central to the legal system than CBA, such as judicial damage awards in tort and contract cases, antitrust law, and progressive taxation. The compensatory rationale for awards would evaporate. No amount of money would help repair any loss of well-being the plaintiff may have suffered. The deterrence rationale for awards would also evaporate, at least with respect to activities causing pecuniary losses. (If less money does not mean less well-being, then why worry about deterring activities causing pecuniary losses?) The upshot would be that damages in contract law would disappear entirely, tort damages would be limited to personal injury torts rather than property torts, and our current understanding of how to set tort damages as a matter of optimal deterrence (which assumes that money payments increase the plaintiff's well-being and reduce the defendant's) would need to be radically changed.

Antitrust law would also need to be repealed. The modern justification for these laws is that firms with excessive market power will charge excessive prices and engage in other costly practices that harm consumers. If money makes no difference to well-being, then higher prices do not, in fact, harm consumers. The justification for progressive taxation would also evaporate. That justification is the diminishing marginal utility of money. If money, instead, has zero (and therefore constant) marginal utility, there is no gain in overall welfare when money is transferred from higher to lower income citizens. Perhaps we might say that money has zero marginal utility above a low threshold—the poverty line. But this would imply that tax-and-transfer systems that succeed equally in redressing poverty but differ in other ways (for example, in their transfers between the rich or super rich and the middle class) are identical as a matter of overall welfare. Similar points can be made about environmental regulation, which is partly justified by its reduction of medical expenses; market regulation, which is usually justified by the wealth-reducing impact of natural monopolies; and many other areas of the law.

4.2. Money Makes Little Difference to an Individual's Subjective Well-Being

Even though the Extreme Claim is false, and CBA is a coherent decision procedure—because CVs are generally well defined—the question remains whether CBA is a good decision procedure. If money has a positive but small effect on SWB, perhaps CBA is not the best way for governmental agencies to determine whether policies increase overall well-being.

In estimating the effect of money on SWB, it is important to bear in mind a point that has already been stressed: money's connection to SWB is instrumental, not intrinsic. Money produces SWB indirectly, by causing changes in individual attainments with respect to various nonmonetary determinants of SWB, such as need satisfaction, status, or the consumption of desired goods. Multivariate studies that control for some of these determinants will therefore tend to underestimate the impact of money on SWB (see Dolan and Peasgood 2006, p. 11). In a complete study that controlled for both money and every other possible determinant of SWB, we would expect the coefficient on income to be zero. And, in less complete studies, controlling for some of the variables on the causal pathways from money to SWB can produce misleading results. For example, the income coefficient in a study that controls for both money and health status would fail to capture the positive influence of income on SWB via health improvements (see also Smith et al. 2005). (Money can fund health care interventions to cure or mitigate physical disease, thus improving health measured in a purely physical sense, and it can alleviate the functional detriments of disease, thus improving health measured in a functional sense, as QALY and other measures often do.) The income coefficient in a study that controls for both money and physical location would fail to capture the positive influence of income on SWB via the individual's relocation to a safer or more pleasant environment. The income coefficient in a study that controls for both money and marital status would fail to capture the fact that increased income partly enhances SWB by improving marital prospects—by making the individual more desirable to prospective mates who care about the spouse's income and/or status and by mitigating the financial stresses that lead to divorce.[16]

---

16. To be sure, there are some changes to an individual's SWB that might flow from changing her income but are ruled out in the context of determining the CV. What exactly these are depends on how, exactly, the CV is defined. Precisely what thought experiment does the construct of a CV involve? Do we imagine that the individual uses changes in her

However, it may well be the case that effect of income on SWB, properly determined, is still small. The jury is still out on this issue.[17] In any event, it is incorrect to think that the utility of CBA as a decision procedure hinges on this issue. Even if the connection between money and SWB is small, that itself would not undermine CBA if the marginal utility of money across individuals was constant. To see this in a simple way, imagine that individuals care just about SWB, and money translates into SWB at a very low rate that is constant across persons. Then CVs would be a perfect metric of project effects.

A possible problem would arise only if the effect of money on SWB varies by type of person. Such a pattern could arise because of (1) differential adaptation, that is, differential SWB benefits of money for different people, or (2) differential affective forecasting, that is, differential ability to predict the effect of money on SWB. To see the first possibility, imagine that the winners from a particular project adapt more quickly to money than the losers and that we elicit CVs for the project by a project-specific contingent-valuation survey. The project is a dam, and the winners enjoy lower electricity bills while the losers suffer from higher tax payments. If the winners, for whatever reason, adapt to their greater wealth more rapidly than the losers adapt to their reduced wealth, then the winners' CVs will exaggerate their SWB gain from the dam relative to the losers' SWB loss.

To see the second possibility, consider a project to reduce noise, where the costs will be reduced consumption. Individuals are good at predicting the effect of noise on their SWB but not so good at predicting the effect of consumption (they tend to overestimate its effect). Compensating variations elicited from a contingent-valuation survey would accurately reflect the SWB gain from the reduction in noise but exaggerate the SWB loss from the reduction in consumption.

With respect to the problem of differential adaptation, some of the literature lends itself to the interpretation that people with some money adapt to additional income relatively quickly, whereas the very poor do not adapt to additional income but enjoy significant SWB increases (for

---

income to change her expenditures on private goods and services, holding fixed her marital status? Or is her marital status also allowed to vary?

17. For studies showing that the coefficient is small, see, for example, Blanchflower and Oswald (2004, p. 1373), Oswald and Powdthavee (2006), and Clark and Oswald (2002, p. 1139). For arguments that the coefficient is large, see Frank (2005, p. 67), Gardner and Oswald (2007), and Cummins (2000). It may well be that the effect of income on SWB is large in some contexts and not others, may vary with wealth, and so forth. At this point, there seems to be a fair amount of confusion and disagreement.

example, Di Tella et al. 2007). But relatively few people of the latter sort live in the United States—they are mainly found in developing countries—and in any event the benefits and costs of most projects cut across income groups. Other types of differential adaptation might exist, but so far there is no evidence for them.

The problem of differential affective forecasting is more serious. The SWB literature does suggest that people not only commit affective forecasting errors in an absolute sense but particularly overestimate the effect of certain goods—material goods, in particular—on SWB. However, differential affective forecasting can be handled by the techniques that we will consider in Section 5.

5. SUBJECTIVE WELL-BEING AND NEW APPROACHES TO POLICY ANALYSIS

The case for CBA is a comparative case: the question is always whether another decision procedure would better advance overall well-being. The literature on SWB has not, however, developed a decision procedure based on SWB that is comparable to CBA. Instead of developing such a decision procedure, the happiness literature has for the most part focused on how its empirical findings can be used to justify broad-gauged interventions in public policy or to tweak the methodology of CBA. In this section, we first discuss how a possible SWB-based decision procedure might work and the problems with it. Then we address how SWB research could be used to improve CBA.

5.1. A Decision Procedure Based on Subjective Well-Being

We have not found a detailed description and defense of an SWB-based decision procedure in the literature, but there are a number of hints. Dolan and Peasgood (2006, p. 8), for example, suggest that the cost of a project should not be measured in terms of money, but in terms of a "resource-based compensating variation," by which they mean that "the household would be given another non-market good, V, up to the level at which it just compensates for" the nonmarket good produced by the project. However, they do not explain how this process would work. Which nonmarket good would be used? In order to evaluate projects, one needs a common metric. Kahneman and Sugden (2005) argue, in an article with the promising title "Experienced Utility as a Standard of Policy Evaluation," that valuations should be based on the moment-by-moment affective states of people; however, they do not in fact propose a standard for evaluating projects.[18]

Without guidance in the literature, we can only provide some conjectures about how such a metric could be developed. One possible approach, which we will call the intuitive approach, involves using the insights of the happiness literature to guide agencies in a rough, intuitive way. Consider, for example, the finding in the literature that people gain SWB from a reduction in commuting times. One could imagine an agency using this finding to justify new projects to improve transportation infrastructure. The problem is that an agency needs to be able to take account of the costs of these projects as well as the benefits. These costs can be put in monetary terms, of course, but it is not clear how they would be weighed against the benefits, which are described in terms of an SWB scale. Would a project that reduces average commute times from 1 hour to 30 minutes for 10,000 commuters be justified if it costs $100 million? $20 million? The intuitive approach does not provide sufficient guidance to agencies.

A more rigorous approach would translate the monetary cost into SWB units, so that a common metric can be used to evaluate a project. Suppose that a transportation project costs $100 million, which in turn amounts to an annual $100 loss for each of 1 million taxpayers. Survey instruments can then be used to translate this $100 per person loss into an SWB unit loss. Suppose that the project increases the average happiness of commuters by .2 on a 10-point scale, while reducing the average happiness of taxpayers by .01. One could imagine multiplying .2 by 10,000 to obtain an aggregate gain of 2,000, while multiplying .01 by 1 million to obtain an aggregate loss of 10,000: therefore, the project reduces rather than increases aggregate happiness.

However, nearly every step of this analysis is open to criticism. First, it is doubtful that one can obtain reliable, fine-grained valuations of the impacts of projects on SWB. Second, the comparison of SWB levels across persons is problematic. If one person moves from level 7 to level 6 in terms of his self-rated happiness or life satisfaction, and another person improves from 2 to 2.5. can we say with confidence that the second person gains less SWB than the first person loses? The question

---

18. Dolan and White (2007) have suggestions along similar lines. Frey and Stutzer (2002, pp. 175–79) discuss a range of possibilities, including tax policy and constitutional reform, at a high level of abstraction. Kahneman et al. (2004) advocate "national well-being accounts," which would guide policy instead of gross domestic product; see also Diener and Seligman (2004) and Veenhoven (1996).

is whether the numerical scales used in SWB surveys correspond to a true, interpersonally comparable scale of happiness.[19] Third, the notion of aggregation is troubling as well. If one person moves from 5 to 4.8 and 100 people move from 6 to 6.01, does the project increase aggregate SWB? To be sure, some of these problems are characteristic of conventional CBA; however, they have not yet received similar full theoretical scrutiny. At a minimum, an SWB-based procedure will not escape many of the puzzles that continue to trouble CBA analysts.

Another difficulty can be seen in proposals for using SWB to determine the proper level of compensation in tort cases (for example, Oswald and Powdthavee 2006). Suppose that an injured victim sues the wrongdoer and obtains damages. The injury causes the victim's SWB level to decline from 5 to 4.8 for a period of 6 months. What is the proper level of damages? Note that judicial awards typically occur after a lengthy delay; here we will assume that the award is made at the conclusion of the 6-month period. Thus, the problem for the court is to compensate a person whose happiness level is back up to 5, for a 6-month period during which his happiness level was depressed by .2. One might argue that the award should equal the amount of money that would cause a .2 increase in the level of happiness for a person who has a happiness level of 4.8 for a period of 6 months. However, the effect of such an award would be to enrich a person who has a happiness level of 5. The sum of money necessary to raise a person from 4.8 to 5 is not necessarily the same (and is likely to be lower than) the sum of money necessary to raise a person from 5 to 5.2. But the main problem is that it is not clear that raising a person from 5 to 5.2 really compensates him for being reduced from 5 to 4.8.

In the absence of a coherent and adequately defended SWB-based decision procedure, the choice comes down to the intuitive approach and a modified version of CBA. In the next section, we endorse the latter.

5.2. Improving Cost-Benefit Analysis

As we have discussed elsewhere, the optimal version of CBA does not rely exclusively on CVs based on actual preferences. Agencies often "launder" preferences, and this practice is justified whenever actual preferences do not reflect overall well-being (Adler and Posner 2006, pp.

19. Kahneman hopes to circumvent the standard happiness or life satisfaction scales and believes that his approach yields an interpersonally comparable scale of SWB (Kahneman 2000, p. 684).

125–43). Preferences do not reflect overall well-being when cognitive biases cause people to make poor choices. The happiness literature focuses on one such cognitive bias: affective forecasting. People often fail to appreciate the impact of a positive or negative event on their SWB. They often think that monetary gains and losses will have a greater impact than they actually do. They also think that physical injuries will reduce their SWB more than these injuries actually do, and they think that mental and emotional harms will reduce their SWB less than those injuries actually do. These phenomena provide a strong case for laundering preferences when two conditions are met: (1) when fully informed preferences include enhancing SWB in a particular setting and (2) when affective forecasting prevents actual preferences from approximating these fully informed preferences.

As an example, suppose that people who live near an airport, or think about moving near that airport, would enjoy higher SWB if airplane noise were reduced. If they have low CVs for reducing airplane noise, these CVs may be accurate or inaccurate. They are inaccurate if the individuals would, with full information, strongly prefer not to endure the noise because it reduces their SWB. However, the individuals fail to predict the effect of the noise on their SWB, and thus their actual CVs are low. Or imagine that people who engage in dangerous activities or take dangerous jobs have high CVs for avoiding disabilities but, with full information, would have lower CVs because the disabilities neither significantly lower hedonic affect nor interfere with important preferences. However, the individuals wrongly predict high rather than low negative effects. In both these cases, it may be appropriate for agencies to launder the actual preferences and use CVs based on estimated fully informed preferences instead.

5.2.1. Compensating Variations Based on Subjective Well-Being.

Let us start with two sophisticated efforts in the literature to incorporate the happiness research into otherwise conventional economic analysis.[20] The first example involves project evaluation, while the second involves the determination of damages in legal actions, but the themes are the same.

Van Praag and Baarsma (2005) use an SWB-based approach to monetize the cost of noise pollution for those living near an airport. Their motivation is not affective forecasting but the assumption that housing prices do not adjust fully to the SWB-reducing effect of noise because

20. For other examples, see Welsch (2002, 2006), Frey et al. (2007), Rehdanz and Maddison (2005), and Clark and Oswald (2002).

of rigidities in the housing market caused by legal regulation. Thus, they implicitly assume that people's preferences and SWB are aligned; but for the rigidities, people would choose where to live by balancing the cost of noise against the various hedonic benefits of locating near the airport, and the price of housing would reflect its benefit for the marginal buyer in terms of SWB and other sources of preference satisfaction. Van Praag and Baarsma estimate an equation where people's self-reported SWB level is a function of subjectively perceived aircraft noise (determined through surveys of people living near the airport), income, and various controls. The regression results allow them to determine how much extra money must be given to a person so that his level of happiness remains constant despite an increase in the noise level. This study provides an example of using an SWB-based methodology to value a nonmarket good where contingent-valuation studies are deemed suspect and market-based studies are undermined by market rigidities.

Oswald and Powdthavee (2006) use a similar methodology for determining how to value disabilities.[21] Conventionally, courts implicitly value disabilities as the sum of medical costs, lost income, and pain and suffering, with the latter determined in an ad hoc fashion. Economists would normally estimate the cost of disability for the purpose of project evaluation by using market studies (how much do people spend on disability insurance) or, possibly, contingent-valuation surveys that asked people how much they would be willing to pay to avoid a disability. The findings in the happiness literature cast doubt on these approaches. Of course, an ad hoc approach is not satisfactory. And market studies and contingent-valuation surveys presuppose that people accurately anticipate their disutility from disability; in fact, people systematically overestimate the disutility because they underestimate their ability to adapt over time. At the same time, monetary awards based on lost income or pain and suffering may have little effect on the disabled person's happiness because money is relatively unproductive of happiness. Oswald and Powdthavee (2006) adjust for these cross-cutting effects—that people overestimate the SWB loss from disability but that money compensates for lost happiness only poorly—in a manner similar to that of van Praag and Baarsma (2005). Regression equations using life satisfaction surveys for the disabled and nondisabled, income, and controls, can be

---

21. See also Oswald and Powdthavee (2008), which uses the analysis for compensating relatives for the deaths of relatives.

used to determine the sum of money necessary to make a disable person just as happy as a nondisabled person.

Although these authors' focus differs from ours, their methods illustrate how the happiness research can be used in CBA. Van Praag and Baarsma (2005) assume that people's CV to avoid noise does not actually reflect the effect of noise on their SWB. They justify this assumption by reference to market rigidities, but one could also point to problems of affective forecasting: people who buy houses near airports, or fail to sell them, do not anticipate the effect of noise (or quiet) on their SWB. To be sure, contingent-valuation methods could be employed as well, but these are imperfect (even putting aside the problem, discussed earlier, of nonuse value). Oswald and Powdthavee (2006) rely on the affective forecasting story. If either of these assumptions are correct, the SWB approach provides a reasonable alternative to market-based or contingent-valuation evidence of the value of noise abatement measures—as long as, in this context, people's fully informed preferences are substantially for SWB.

The latter point is a crucial assumption. For the SWB approach to be an adequate alternative, it must be the case that, in this setting, SWB contributes to overall well-being—that is, people's fully informed preferences are to maximize SWB. If people live near airports so that they can easily travel, and they travel in order to satisfy a particular ambition not related to their own SWB, they may well care relatively little about their SWB. If fully informed people engage in actions that risk disability—such as mountaineering, for example—because they think that the risky activities are more important than being happy, then again the SWB impact of disability might have less impact on their well-being than the happiness studies assume.

In sum, the case for using SWB-based survey results to monetize goods for the purpose of CBA depends on an empirical assumption. The more closely linked SWB and people's fully informed preferences are, the stronger the case for using SWB-based survey results.

5.2.2. A Note on the Hedonic Treadmill.

As mentioned, one strand of the SWB literature suggests that the link between money and SWB is substantially, even exclusively, a matter of relative income. A related idea is that increasing someone's monetary holdings has negative third-party effects. The gainer's increased SWB comes at the cost of other people's lost SWB. People seek status, and they obtain status through greater consumption, but in doing so, they lower the status of others. In this way, greater wealth creates negative externalities: everyone is trapped on a "hedonic treadmill."

Researchers of SWB cite evidence for this effect as yet another reason for abandoning CBA and its reliance on monetary valuations in favor of an SWB-based approach that avoids reliance on monetary valuations. The evidence is that although SWB rises with income for individuals, it does not rise, or does not rise much, with the average income of groups such as the citizens of a nation.[22] The evidence is incorporated into normative analyses, such as that of Oswald and Powdthavee (2006), that assume that money is not highly productive of SWB in the aggregate (because income gains to one person can result in SWB losses for others) and thus that a greater amount of money needs to be used to compensate for certain SWB-reducing injuries than might otherwise be thought.

However, the claim that the hedonic treadmill undermines CBA, or that it provides an additional reason for preferring SWB-based procedures, rests on a misunderstanding. The status competition idea is consistent with the empirical and normative premises of CBA. If the idea is correct, it means that people have a preference for consuming goods that others cannot afford. In acting pursuant to this preference, an individual both increases his own utility and decreases the utility of others. In this way, status-based consumption is no different from other activities that create negative externalities. Just as manufacturing creates pollution that hurts third parties, so does conspicuous consumption create status costs for third parties.

The hedonic-treadmill problem might justify taxation of luxury goods, redistribution of wealth, or other projects that suppress conspicuous consumption, but it does not undermine CBA. A critical point is that CBA itself is a general methodology for valuing policies—both policies to create nonmarket goods and policies to increase consumption—rather than a substantive set of policy recommendations. Cost-benefit analysis uses the construct of a CV to value policies but is neutral on the question whether the best policy is to increase consumption or undertake some other policy. Cost-benefit analysis can arrive at positive valuations for policies to promote nonmarket goods.[23] And CBA, in principle, can arrive at a zero or negative valuation of policies to promote consumption. If increasing P's consumption has a negative externality

22. See the studies of change in SWB within countries over time discussed in Section 4.

23. This is particularly true if conventional methods for laundering preferences plus the SWB-based methods discussed above are used to counteract affective-forecasting errors and other cognitive mistakes.

on Q, then adding Q's negative CV for the policy to P's positive CV may yield a zero or even negative valuation.

In actual practice, consumption externalities are not typically incorporated in CBA, and we are not convinced that it makes sense to change the practice, given the incremental administrative costs of a fuller CBA (compare Frank & Sunstein 2001; on administrative cost and CBA, see Adler and Posner [2006, pp. 62–88]). In sum, SWB studies provide additional evidence for the theory that conspicuous consumption causes negative externalities, but the hedonic-treadmill theory has no particular implication for CBA.

5.2.3. Cost-Benefit Analysis with Valuations Based on Subjective Well-Being.
Let us briefly describe how CBA would work, as adjusted to reflect the happiness research. An agency considers a project that produces winners and losers. Consider, for example, a dam that reduces the cost of electricity but interferes with recreational use of a river. The reduction in the cost of electricity is a straightforward monetary gain for electricity users that can easily be treated as aggregated CVs. On the cost side, the agency needs to estimate the loss to the losers. A contingent-valuation survey might well result in exaggerated CVs: because of defects in hedonic forecasting, individuals underestimate their ability to adapt and thus overestimate their CV to maintain the status quo. However, the survey could also reflect something different: the view that the dam would interfere with an important choice, wholly apart from its hedonic effect. If this is so, the CV to maintain the status quo might not be exaggerated.

A parallel SWB analysis could provide a useful corrective. Suppose that surveys revealed that people with close access to a river for recreational use are slightly happier than those who do not. The happiness difference can then be converted to a monetary amount. This monetary amount corrects for the problem of affective forecasting but also reflects only the hedonic effect of the project and not its effect on preferences or choices.

If the numbers are similar, then the agency can probably safely conclude that they are reliable. People correctly forecast how loss of access to a river affects their well-being, and in doing so they focus on the hedonic aspect of their well-being. If the numbers diverge, then there are two possible explanations. One is hedonic forecasting error; the other is divergence between well-being and SWB. In such a case, the agency will need to use its judgment and choose a number within the range. It is possible that more refined survey instruments can tease out the relative contribution of the two factors, but further research would be necessary to establish this.

5.3. Cost-Benefit Analysis if Subjective Well-Being Were the Exclusive Social Maximand

We argued in Section 2 that SWB is not the exclusive social maximand; weak welfarism provides a better normative goal for government. However, it is worth noting that even if SWB maximization were the appropriate goal, CBA might still be an appropriate decision procedure. There are two separate reasons for this.

First, an SWB-promoting government might use CBA as part of a two-step procedure for advancing SWB. In step 1, CBA approves projects that enhance social wealth; in step 2, the government taxes and spends its way toward greater SWB. Suppose that people strive to satisfy preferences rather than maximize their SWB. Thus, as noted above, a dam that passes CBA makes people wealthier but not happier. Nonetheless, the dam could be justified on SWB grounds. The reason is that if people are wealthier, they can be taxed more; and if they can be taxed more, then the government has more revenue to spend on SWB-maximizing projects. For example, the government could use the extra revenue to improve health care, which results in SWB-increasing happiness and longevity.

This argument is analogous to the argument made by Shavell and Kaplow (2000) that a government that cares about redistribution should regulate efficiently and use taxes and transfers rather than issue inefficient but distributively attractive regulations. Here the argument is that a government that cares about maximizing SWB should maximize revenue using efficient regulations and taxation and then use the revenue to choose SWB-enhancing projects. As long as SWB-promoting projects are properly monetized, taking account that a lot of money is necessary to buy just a little SWB, CBA can be used for SWB-promoting ends.

Second, a government that sought to advance SWB would still need a decision procedure that allowed it to compare projects using a common metric. Again, the use of the money metric is not inconsistent with policy oriented toward maximizing aggregate SWB. As long as SWB gains and losses are properly transformed into dollars, projects' SWB effects, and their monetary costs and benefits, can be properly evaluated.

Of course, one could produce an alternative procedure that avoided dollars and instead used SWB units as the common metric. Then the dollar effects of projects would be transformed into SWB units rather than vice versa. There is no reason in principle why such an alternative would not be adequate in a world where the government advances SWB alone, but, as we have seen, researchers have not yet come up with a plausible SWB-based decision procedure.

6. CONCLUSION

The happiness literature does not undermine CBA—at least, not yet. The implicit normative claim in much of that literature—that government should maximize aggregate SWB and nothing else—is implausible and should be rejected. The government should advance a measure of well-being based on the satisfaction of fully informed preferences. Subjective well-being is one of the items that individuals with full information prefer in their own lives, but not the only item.

The empirical results of the SWB literature pose a more serious challenge to CBA. If money does not advance well-being because of affective forecasting and similar problems, the case for CBA is significantly weakened. However, the literature does not establish the Extreme Claim that money has no impact on SWB. A fortiori, because well-being does not reduce to SWB, the literature does not establish the proposition that money has no impact on well-being. The literature's findings with respect to adaptation and status competition have no particular implications for CBA. Its findings with respect to affective forecasting imply that, in some cases, it will be necessary to launder preferences for CBA purposes. This might involve informing or debiasing people before asking for valuations in contingent-valuation studies or using the results of SWB studies when CVs are, because of affective forecasting problems, unreliable. Finally, the literature in some ways strengthens the case for CVs by showing that SWB data can be used to value nonmarket goods where contingent-valuation studies have been unsuccessful.

Proposals to depart from CBA entirely and use an SWB-based procedure have not received adequate theoretical justification. Workable proposals (other than intuitive balancing, which gives too much discretion to agencies) have not been specified and, more fundamentally, the proposals all ignore that SWB is only one part of well-being.

REFERENCES

Adler, Matthew D. 2000. Beyond Efficiency and Procedure: A Welfarist Theory of Regulation. *Florida State University Law Review* 28:241–338.

Adler, Matthew D. 2006. Welfare Polls: A Synthesis. *New York University Law Review* 81:1875–1970.

Adler, Matthew D., and Eric A. Posner. 2006. *New Foundations of Cost-Benefit Analysis.* Cambridge, Mass.: Harvard University Press.

Alkire, Sabina. 2005. *Valuing Freedoms: Sen's Capability Approach and Poverty Reduction.* New York: Oxford University Press.

Argyle, Michael. 1999. Causes and Correlates of Happiness. Pp. 353–73 in *Well Being: The Foundations of Hedonic Psychology,* edited by Daniel Kahneman, Ed Diener, and Norbert Schwarz. New York: Russell Sage Foundation.

Bagenstos, Samuel R., and Margo Schlanger. 2007. Hedonic Damages, Hedonic Adaptation, and Disability. *Vanderbilt Law Review* 60:745–800.

Blanchflower, David, and Andrew Oswald. 2004. Well-Being over Time in Britain and the USA. *Journal of Public Economics* 88:1359–86.

Brickman, Philip, Dan Coates, and Ronnie Janoff-Bulman. 1978. Lottery Winners and Accident Victims: Is Happiness Relative? *Journal of Personality and Social Psychology* 36:917–27.

Cantril, Hadley. 1965. *The Pattern of Human Concerns.* Piscataway, N.J.: Rutgers University Press.

Clark, Andrew E., and Andrew J. Oswald. 2002. A Simple Statistical Method for Measuring How Life Events Affect Happiness. *International Journal of Epidemiology* 31:1139–44.

Cummins, Robert A. 1996. The Domains of Life Satisfaction: An Attempt to Order Chaos. *Social Indicators Research* 38:303–28.

———. 2000. Personal Income and Subjective Well-Being: A Review. *Journal of Happiness Studies* 1:133–58.

Diener, Ed, and Robert Biswas-Diener. 2002. Will Money Increase Subjective Well-Being? A Literature Review and Guide to Needed Research. *Social Indicators Research* 57:119–69.

Diener, Ed, and S. Oishi. 2000. Money and Happiness: Income and Subjective Well-Being across Nations. Pp. 185–218 in *Culture and Subjective Well-Being,* edited by E. Diener & E. M. Suh. Cambridge, Mass.: MIT Press.

Diener, Ed, and Christie Scollon. 2003. Subjective Well-Being Is Desirable, But Not the Summum Bonum. Unpublished manuscript. University of Minnesota Workshop on Well-Being, Minneapolis.

Diener, Ed, and Martin E. P. Seligman. 2004. Beyond Money: Toward an Economy of Well-Being. *Psychological Science in the Public Interest* 5:1–31.

Diener, Ed, and Eunkook M. Suh. 1997. Measuring Quality of Life: Economic, Social, and Subjective Indicators. *Social Indicators Research* 40:189–216.

Diener, Ed, Eunkook M. Suh, Richard E. Lucas, and Heidi L. Smith. 1999.

Subjective Well-Being: Three Decades of Progress. *Psychological Bulletin* 125: 276–302.

Di Tella, Rafael, John Haisken–De New, and Robert MacCulloch. 2007. Happiness Adaptation to Income and to Status in an Individual Panel. Working Paper No. 13159. National Bureau of Economic Research. Cambridge, Mass.

Dolan, Paul, and Tess Peasgood. 2006. Valuing Non-market Goods: Does Subjective Well-Being Offer a Viable Alternative to Contingent Valuation? Unpublished manuscript. Imperial College London, Tanaka Business School, London.

Dolan, P., and M. P. White. 2007. How Can Measures of Subjective Well-Being Be Used to Inform Public Policy? *Perspectives on Psychological Science* 2: 71–85.

Easterlin, Richard A. 2001. Income and Happiness: Towards a Unified Theory. *Economic Journal* 111:465–84.

Frank, Robert. 2005. Does Absolute Income Matter? Pp. 65–91 in *Economics and Happiness: Framing the Analysis,* edited by Luigino Bruni and Pier Luigi Porta. Oxford: Oxford University Press.

Frank, Robert H., and Cass R. Sunstein. 2001. Cost-Benefit Analysis and Relative Position. *University of Chicago Law Review* 68:323–74.

Frey, Bruno S., Simon Luechinger, and Alois Stutzer. 2007. Calculating Tragedy: Assessing the Costs of Terrorism. *Journal of Economic Surveys* 21:1–24.

Frey, Bruno S., and Alois Stutzer. 2002. *Happiness and Economics: How the Economy and Institutions Affect Human Well-Being.* Princeton, N.J.: Princeton University Press.

Furnham, Adrian, and Michael Argyle. 1998. *The Psychology of Money.* New York: Routledge.

Gardner, Jonathan, and Andrew J. Oswald. 2007. Money and Mental Well-Being: A Longitudinal Study of Medium-Sized Lottery Wins. *Journal of Health Economics* 26:49–60.

Hagerty, Michael R. and Ruut Veenhoven. 2003. Wealth and Happiness Revisited: Growing National Income *Does* Go with Greater Happiness. *Social Indicators Research* 64:1–27.

Kagan, Shelly. 1997. *Normative Ethics.* Boulder, Colo.: Westview.

Kahneman, Daniel. 1999. Objective Happiness. Pp. 3–25 in *Well Being: The Foundations of Hedonic Psychology,* edited by Daniel Kahneman, Ed Diener, and Norbert Schwarz. New York: Russell Sage Foundation.

———. 2000. Experienced Utility and Objective Happiness: A Moment Based Approach. Pp. 673–92 in *Choices, Values, and Frames,* edited by Daniel Kahneman and Amos Tversky. Cambridge: Cambridge University Press.

Kahneman, Daniel, Ed Diener, and Norbert Schwarz, eds. 1999. *Well Being: The Foundations of Hedonic Psychology.* New York: Russell Sage Foundation.

Kahneman, Daniel, Alan B. Krueger, David Schkade, Norbert Schwartz, and

Arthur Stone. 2004. Toward National Well-Being Accounts. *AEA Papers and Proceedings* 94:429–34.

Kahneman, Daniel, and Robert Sugden. 2005. Experienced Utility as a Standard of Policy Evaluation. *Environmental and Resource Economics* 32:161–81.

Kahneman, Daniel, Peter P. Wakker, and Rakesh Sarin. 1997. Back to Bentham? Explorations of Experienced Utility. *Quarterly Journal of Economics* 112: 375–405.

King, Laura A., and Christie K. Napa. 1998. What Makes a Life Good? *Journal of Personality and Social Psychology* 75:156–65.

Layard, Richard. 2005. *Happiness: Lessons from a New Science*. New York: Penguin Press.

Nozick, Robert. 1974. *Anarchy, State and Utopia*. New York: Basic Books.

Nussbaum, Martha C. 2000. *Women and Human Development*. Cambridge: Cambridge University Press.

Oswald, Andrew J., and Nattavudh Powdthavee. 2006. Does Happiness Adapt? A Longitudinal Study of Disability with Implications for Economists and Judges. Discussion Paper No. 2208. Institute for the Study of Labor, Bonn.

———. 2008. Death, Happiness, and the Calculation of Hedonic Damages. *Journal of Legal Studies* 37:S217–S251.

Rehdanz, Katrin, and David Maddison. 2005. Climate and Happiness. *Ecological Economics* 52:111–25.

Ryff, Carol D. 1989. In the Eye of the Beholder: Views of Psychological Well-Being among Middle-Aged and Older Adults. *Psychology and Aging* 4: 195–210.

Schwarz, Norbert, and Fritz Strack. 1999. Reports of Subjective Well-Being: Judgemental Processes and Their Methodological Implications. Pp. 61–84 in *Well Being: The Foundations of Hedonic Psychology*, edited by Daniel Kahneman, Ed Diener, and Norbert Schwarz. New York: Russell Sage Foundation.

Sen, Amartya. 1987. *On Ethics and Economics*. Oxford: Blackwell.

Shavell, Steven, and Louis Kaplow. 2000. Should Legal Rules Favor the Poor? Clarifying the Role of Legal Rules and the Income Tax in Redistributing Income. *Journal of Legal Studies* 29:821–35.

Smith, Dylan M., Kenneth M. Langa, Mohammed U. Kabeto, and Peter A. Ubel. 2005. Health, Wealth, and Happiness: Financial Resources Buffer Subjective Well-Being After the Onset of a Disability. *Psychological Science* 16:663–66.

Sumner, L. W. 1996. *Welfare, Happiness, and Ethics*. Oxford: Clarendon Press.

Sunstein, Cass. 2008. Illusory Losses. *Journal of Legal Studies* 37:S157–S194.

Ubel, Peter A., and George Loewenstein. 2008. Pain and Suffering Awards: They Shouldn't Be (Just) about Pain and Suffering. *Journal of Legal Studies* 37: S195–S216.

van Praag, M. S. Bernard, and Barbara E. Baarsma. 2005. Using Happiness

Surveys to Value Intangibles: The Case of Airport Noise. *Economic Journal* 115:224–46.

Veenhoven, Ruut. 1996. Happy Life-Expectancy. *Social Indicators Research* 39: 1–58.

Veenhoven, Ruut. 2005. Apparent Quality-of-Life in Nations: How Long and Happy People Live. *Social Indicators Research* 71:61–86.

Welsch, Heinz. 2002. Preferences over Prosperity and Pollution: Environmental Valuation based on Happiness Surveys. *Kyklos* 55:473–95.

Welsch, Heinz. 2006. Environment and Happiness: Valuation of Air Pollution Using Life Satisfaction Data. *Ecological Economics* 58:801–13.

What Does Happiness Research Tell Us About Taxation?

David A. Weisbach

ABSTRACT

This paper analyzes the consequences of happiness research for taxation. It focuses on the finding that happiness depends on status as well as income, examining how adding status concerns to standard optimal tax models changes the results. It then compares the empirical findings of the happiness literature to see whether they provide the type of data needed to parameterize the models, arguing that the models need different types of data than most happiness studies emphasize. The paper also looks at Robert Frank's arguments for a progressive consumption tax based on the findings of the happiness research. It finds that these claims are not supported by the current models or empirical data. Finally, the paper considers a number of other potential implications of happiness research for taxation, including marriage penalties or bonuses, special tax rates for the disabled, and age-dependent taxation.

Happiness research has the potential to change our views about taxation, possibly significantly. Standard tax models assume a very simple utility function that is uniform across all individuals, increases in consumption, and decreases in work effort. Individuals vary only in their ability to earn income. Happiness research shows that reported levels of happiness (which I will take here to mean utility) are complex functions of many different variables. Utilities may be interdependent because of status concerns. Utility may be time dependent in that individuals may adapt to income levels or disabilities and may vary systematically by age. Very low work effort such as unemployment may reduce happiness, even

DAVID A. WEISBACH is the Walter J. Blum Professor at the University of Chicago Law School. I thank participants at the University of Chicago Law School conference Legal Implications of the New Research on Happiness and the Harvard Law School colloquium Current Research in Taxation and an anonymous referee for comments.

[*Journal of Legal Studies*, vol. XXXVII (June 2008)]

holding consumption constant. A more complex view of utility functions will lead to different conclusions on the design of the tax system. This has long been noticed, and a number of models incorporate some of these ideas, particularly those related to status.

The question this paper will address is whether the findings of happiness research to date, taking them as valid, tell us what we need to know to be confident making tax policy recommendations. The more casual literature, such as the many books by Robert Frank, suggest that the findings of the happiness literature imply a number of concrete results, such as higher tax rates overall, lower tax rates on savings, and, sometimes, a more progressive tax system. I will argue here that we do not yet know enough to make recommendations to change the tax system on the basis of the happiness literature. There are many different ways to incorporate the findings into formal models, each with different implications. Moreover, we do not yet have the relevant data needed to set the parameters of existing models, even if we were to agree that one of them is the best approach. In short, happiness research is not yet at the point that it can determine which modeling strategies are best and how to set the parameters.

Two caveats are in order. First, I am taking happiness research as valid and as measuring utility. There are significant issues in both regards, issues that have been widely discussed in the literature. It is not my comparative advantage to evaluate these issues. If the research does not validly measure utility, its implications for taxation will be more limited. To explore the question of its implications for taxation, I will assume that the research is at least potentially relevant.[1]

Second, I am asking whether there is empirical support for including the findings of the happiness research in tax calculations. Most tax theory, however, is based on limited empirical support, and simplifying assumptions are often made to make the problem mathematically tractable rather than because they are supported by the data. It is no more valid to assume a standard utility function (that is, only consumption and labor effort effect utility) than it is to assume a more complex utility

---

1. There are a variety of objections to the happiness literature. For example, because the literature relies on self-reports, scaling is a problem. For example, consider asking children in various grades how tall they are. Children will naturally scale their answers to the appropriate height given their age. If this scaling effect is not taken into account, we might conclude that height does not change as children grow older. See Kaplow (2008, chap. 5D) for a discussion. There are also serious questions of whether happiness reflects utility.

function that reflects the tentative findings of happiness research. That is, asking for empirical support for including happiness information but not for what are currently more standard models arguably unfairly stacks the deck.

A standard response is to use Occam's razor to argue for a higher standard of proof on models that add complexity to the utility function, but this is not my reason for subjecting the happiness research to scrutiny. Instead, my goal here is to be constructive. We need to understand the best way to incorporate new research into standard models and to understand the empirical parameters relevant to the revised models. Because of the complexity of the optimal tax models, we are unlikely to get definitive results from the happiness literature. There are few if any strong results even in standard optimal tax work, and it is not reasonable to demand such a level of proof from the happiness literature. Nevertheless, understanding the various modeling strategies and the relevant empirical parameters can help direct future research.

The focus of this paper is on relative income and status effects, which is where the majority of the research on happiness and taxation has been focused. Section 1 of this paper will provide some very brief background on tax theory, background that is necessary for considering how happiness research might change the standard learning. Section 2 considers how status concerns might affect marginal tax rates on labor income. There are a number of papers modeling tax rates given status concerns. Section 2 will try to show what drives these models and what information is needed to specify the utility function. I will then briefly discuss what the literature on happiness tells us about these aspects of utility functions. Section 2 will also examine claims made by Robert Frank about how status concerns affect the optimal tax structure, claims that to some extent are distinct from those related to optimal tax rates. Section 3 offers a grab bag of other possible implications of happiness research for tax policy, including the effect of taxation on marriage and whether or how the tax system should take disability into account. The list is merely suggestive, and I do not examine any of the possibilities in any detail.

1. A VERY BRIEF PRIMER ON TAX POLICY[2]

The now standard approach to taxation (including negative taxation or transfers), due to Mirrlees (1971), is to view taxation as a problem of information. Individuals are assumed to vary by their ability to earn income, which is assumed to be private information. The government wants to redistribute from those with high ability to those with low ability either because the social welfare function is concave or because marginal utility is declining in income. With complete information, the government could assign higher unavoidable taxes to those with higher ability and, thereby, redistribute from those with high ability to those with low ability. The Second Welfare Theorem would apply, and we could achieve a first-best result.

If ability is private information, however, the government cannot simply assign high taxes to high ability individuals because it cannot tell who has high ability. Instead, it must rely on observable signals of ability, usually taken to be labor income. The central problem is that individuals can avoid taxes on labor income by working less. We can think of someone with high ability working less as the individual masquerading as someone with low ability to get the advantage of the tax rates that apply to the low-ability individual.

The optimization problem is to maximize a function of utilities subject to a resource constraint (total consumption has to equal total income) and an incentive constraint (to prevent masquerading). The incentive constraint is that an individual of a given ability cannot prefer to earn the income of someone with lower ability by working less. Solving this maximization is mathematically complex, and the first-order conditions, in their general form, are hard to interpret. It is common to use numerical simulations to get a sense of the resulting tax schedule.

A simplifying assumption often used to understand the first-order conditions is to assume that utility is quasi-linear in consumption, so utility can be expressed as $u = c + v(l)$, where c is consumption and l is labor effort. The major effect of this assumption is to remove income effects. Using this assumption, Diamond (1998) showed that the marginal tax rate at any given income level is based on three effects: (*a*) labor supply elasticity—the higher the labor supply elasticity, the lower the tax rate; (*b*) a measure of the social cost of taking a dollar

---

2. For extensive reviews of the literature, see Kaplow (2008), Stiglitz (1987), and Tuomala (1990).

away from everyone above that income level; and (*c*) a measure of the relative size of the populations at that ability level and above it.

To understand how these factors affect tax rates, Saez (2001), following Stiglitz (1987), suggested the following thought experiment. Suppose that tax rates are set optimally and we consider a small increase in the marginal tax rate at some income level, such as between $50,000 and $50,001. Individuals at that level will face a higher marginal tax rate, which will distort their work effect, as measured by labor supply elasticity. Individuals above that level will not face a change in marginal rates, so their work effort remains the same (there is no income effect). They have less income, however, because of the higher rate they pay at the $50,000 level. The second factor measures the social cost of lowering their income. The final factor is the ratio of the size of the two effects.

The first-order conditions become considerably more difficult to interpret in general cases because of income effects and because labor supply elasticity can vary with ability. The quasi-linear case, however, is restrictive because it eliminates declining marginal utility of consumption (utility is linear in consumption), which is an important motivation for redistribution.

The focus of the following discussion is on how happiness-informed utility functions change the conclusions about taxation. It is worth, therefore, making several notes about the utility functions and assumptions used in the standard analysis. First, some individuals will not work in this model. Utility is assumed to be a nondecreasing function of consumption and leisure. Nothing else matters. High rates on low-income individuals may be desirable because the cost of their lost work effort is low and the high rates are inframarginal for everyone else. These high rates may cause low-income individuals to have zero labor effort, but as long as there are sufficient transfers, they are better off not working. It is not clear, however, whether individuals not working is equivalent to commonly used notions of unemployment because individuals will choose not to work while unemployment normally refers to individuals seeking work who cannot find it. This difference may be important in applying the findings of happiness research on unemployment.

Second, utilities are independent of one another, which rules out status concerns as well as altruism. In particular, individuals care only about their own consumption and leisure. Third, individuals are assumed to be identical to one another other than with respect to innate ability to produce income (which is assumed to vary by a known distribution).

This means that there is no heterogeneity other than with respect to income.

One consequence of assuming no heterogeneity is that, subject to exceptions not relevant here, the government should tax only labor income (or, equivalently, consumption). Individuals vary only in this dimension, and therefore, taxing other attributes can serve only as a bad proxy for directly taxing labor income. Thus, for example, taxing capital income as a proxy for taxing individuals with high ability (as is commonly suggested by those supporting a conventional income tax) does not make sense absent heterogeneity. Replacing such a tax with a direct tax on labor income leaves the distributive effects and effects on labor the same while reducing the distortions in savings patterns.[3] Introducing heterogeneity significantly complicates the picture because it may be desirable to tax items other than labor income. Models with more than one dimension of difference among individuals, however, are in their infancy, and because of mathematical difficulties, it is not clear when general propositions will be available. Heterogeneity will be relevant later in the discussion of adaptation to disability—before discussing how adaptation affects taxation, we need to have an understanding of how heterogeneity, say, because of disability, affects taxation.

The assumption that the government cannot observe anything other than income means that the government will not, in the standard analysis, attempt to tax ability directly. As discussed below, most models of status and taxation continue this tradition by assuming that the government cannot directly tax status-seeking activities and instead must adjust the income tax as a proxy. Frank (1985b, 2000) rejects this assumption, arguing that we can identify status-seeking activity. For example, he argues that consumption of expensive watches or large houses is a form of status seeking and that the tax system can be designed to weigh more heavily on purchases of these items.

2. TAXATION AND STATUS

The observation that status matters to individuals goes back at least to Adam Smith's ([1759] 2002) *The Theory of Moral Sentiments*. Status

---

3. An exception would be if taxing capital income can reduce the distortions caused by labor income taxation because capital income is a complement to leisure. This possibility is generally regarded as unlikely, and similar considerations may lead to a subsidy rather than a tax on capital income.

has been the subject of numerous of studies since then, with such figures as John Stuart Mill, Arthur Pigou, Milton Freidman and Leonard Savage, and Gary Becker contributing to the literature (for a summary of the literature, see McAdams 1992). Proposals for taxing status consumption have been traced back to John Rae (1834). The intuition is that improving one's status imposes a cost on others, at least if status comes in fixed supply—we cannot all have the highest income or be the best looking, the smartest, or whatever it is that confers status. Status seeking creates negative externalities because gains in one's status reduce someone else's. Taxing status-seeking activities, therefore, might be welfare enhancing much like any other Pigouvian tax. Frank (2000, pp. 152–53) compares the problem to an individual standing up in a stadium to see better. Each individual separately gains by standing, but if everyone stands, everyone is worse off—they cannot see any better, and they have to stand instead of sit (and in Frank's story, they stand on the seats, straining their heads until someone falls off).[4] Status competition might make everyone work too hard or consume goods they otherwise would prefer not to consume, but at the end of the day, there is no overall gain in status.[5]

This simple intuition does not tell us very much about the likely effects of status on the tax rate schedule. For example, it might imply that average rates are higher, but it does not say anything about progressivity. Increasing progressivity would move everyone closer together on the income scale. This might decrease status competition, because the gains from competition are smaller—it would be harder to separate yourself from the group. On the other hand, a more progressive tax might increase status competition: if you are closer to beating someone in a status race, you might try harder.[6] In general, to understand the effect of status on tax rates, we need to know precisely how status affects utility and labor effort, such as whether utility gains and losses from status are increasing or decreasing with differences from the reference income.

4. The stadium analogy was used by Oswald (1997). The referee reported that the analogy may date to much earlier literature. I have not been able to locate its origin.

5. There is a question of whether relative preferences, such as envy, should count in social welfare calculations. For a discussion, see Kaplow and Shavell (2002, pp. 418–31). Regardless of one's views on this issue generally, it would be difficult ignore relative preferences because (1) the data show that relative preferences are common if not predominant and (2) they may be significant effects on behavior. I will take the view here that relative preferences should generally be considered.

6. See, for example, Hopkins and Kornienko (2004), who find this type of result in a game-theoretic model of status competition.

Given the possibilities, we can imagine status considerations leading to either a more progressive tax system or a less progressive tax system. More careful modeling is necessary to determine precisely how these factors or others enter the optimal tax formula. The question for this section is how status has been (or can be) incorporated into the optimal tax models and whether the empirical research on status effects gives us the relevant information.

Although numerous papers discuss taxing status consumption, only a handful embed the analysis in an optimal tax framework: Boskin and Sheshinski (1978), Oswald (1983), Tuomala (1990), Ireland (1998, 2001), Allgood (2006), and Beath and FitzRoy (2007).[7] Each of these authors models status differently. To keep the discussion manageable, I will focus on two papers, Oswald (1983) and Ireland (2001).

2.1. The Models

Oswald takes the standard utility function (utility is a function of consumption and leisure) and adds a concern for the consumption of others, measured by a comparison function. Thus, in standard models, utility is equal to $u_n(c, l)$, where c is a vector of consumption goods, l is leisure, and n represents the ability type or wage rate of the individual distributed according to some density function. To allow for individuals to compare themselves to others, Oswald adds a comparison function α to the utility function, now represented as $u_n(c, l, \alpha)$. The comparison function α is the weighted sum of the consumption of all other individuals in society, with weights $\omega(n)$ potentially varying by type. If all individuals are weighted equally, the comparison function measures average consumption. In this case, the individual compares his consumption to the average consumption of all other individuals. If the individual is envious, he is made worse off as average consumption goes up; if the individual is altruistic, he is made better off as average consumption goes up. Alternatively, the consumption of the rich or the poor could be weighted more heavily so that the individual would compare himself more to the rich or the poor, respectively. Depending on the sign of α as consumption changes, it can represent either altruism (utility goes up as others' consumption increases) or envy (utility goes down as others' consumption increases).

---

7. Outside of the optimal tax framework, major papers on taxation and status include the many papers by Frank as well as Hopkins and Kornienko (2004). Abel (2005) considers the effect of relative consumption concerns on taxation in a growth model.

A key to this model (and all other models of status) is that individuals compare themselves to the consumption of others, not utility—conspicuous leisure does not confer status. Moreover, there are no particular status goods, which means that overall income or consumption is what confers status. We might call this model of status the big fish/small pond theory of status. Holding income constant but moving to a place where comparison income is lower improves welfare. Moving, however, is not easy within the model: all individuals subject to taxation are required by the model to have the same comparison group. If the tax is a national tax, the comparison group is necessarily the nation. That is, contrary to Frank (1985a), individuals within Oswald's world cannot choose their pond.[8]

One implication of using this model of status is that redistribution does not necessarily improve (or change at all) how status affects utility. For example, suppose that status is based on average consumption, and we perfectly equalized all incomes. Those whose status goes up would have increased utility, and those whose status goes down would have decreased utility. Depending on the distribution of individuals and exactly how the comparison function enters utility, overall status effects may be higher, lower, or unchanged. Also, if we, say, destroyed $1 billion of Bill Gates's fortune, everyone's (but Gates's) utility would go up because average income would go down. Depending on how strongly status matters and how social weights are computed, overall social welfare might even go up because of this destruction of wealth. Giving the same $1 billion to the poor, however, would leave average income unchanged but move the poor closer to the middle. The effect on social welfare is indeterminate and would depend on the factors just mentioned.

This status-based utility function is then run through the optimal tax analysis. As in the standard case, the optimization problem is to maximize a function of utilities subject to a resource constraint and an incentive constraint. The results are similar except that the status term in the utility function leads to an extra constraint in the optimization and a corresponding first-order condition with respect to α. As in the more general case, income effects make interpretation difficult, although it is clear that the additional term alters the general formula, and many of

8. This feature is not unique to Oswald's model. In virtually all of the literature, both empirical and theoretical, the reference group is imposed on individuals. Falk and Knell (2004) is an exception.

the basic results of optimal taxation change. To get some intuitions, Oswald makes two simplifying assumptions. First, he considers only the case where the comparison is average income. Second, he considers the case where envy (or altruism) has no effect on consumption decisions or labor effort. Instead, it merely reduces utility. (Technically, it is additively separable in status.)

This latter assumption is not trivial. It abandons the stadium theory of status competition because the effect of status on work effort is eliminated. Because status has no effect on work effort, the change in the tax function due to status is also unrelated to work effort. In effect, status in this model is merely a taste for everyone else being worse off. It is a model of pure envy (or altruism) rather than status competition. This should be controversial. It is one thing to ask everyone in the stadium to sit down. It is another to give weight to a preference that others be worse off.[9]

With these assumptions, Oswald is able to derive a very simple term for the effect of envy or altruism on tax rates. In particular, suppose that average income goes up by a dollar (because taxes are reduced by a dollar), and consider the effect on utility of each individual (assuming the individual's income, however, is constant). The sum of these effects across the whole population determines the cost of lowering taxes by a margin.[10] For example, if individuals are generally envious, their utility goes down as average income goes up (holding their income constant). Lowering taxes increases average income and, therefore, lowers utility, all else equal. Thus, if individuals are generally envious, marginal tax rates should be higher than otherwise.

To know more about the marginal tax schedule, however, we need to know how the marginal benefit or cost from changes in comparison group income changes with income: the shape of the marginal utility from status for each type of individual n. For example, we need to know how having status affects those with twice average income compared to how it affects those with three times average or one-half average income. If everyone compares themselves to the average, we would want to know, for example, whether status benefits decline with distance from the average or increase with distance.

9. Tuomala (1990) is able to generalize the paper to allow envy to have behavioral effects, but the generalized form of his conditions does not allow easy interpretation.

10. In particular, the shadow price of envy (or altruism) is equal to (minus) the sum of the effects on marginal utility of changes in average income, or $\phi = -\int u_a f(n) dn$, where u_α is marginal effect of utility from envy or altruism.

Ireland (2001, 1998) models status concerns differently. He starts with a standard utility function where individuals maximize a function of consumption and leisure. He then assumes that individuals care about how others perceive them. Others, however, can observe only particular types of visible status consumption, *s,* such as fancier than necessary automobiles. Others observe this status consumption and use this signal to infer utility. The individual giving the signal knows this and gets utility from their inferences. Status consumption is nonvaluable other than as a signal to others. It may be closely related to valuable consumption— it may involve an automobile for example, but it is the portion beyond the optimal amount that is consumed solely for signaling purposes. Ireland sets overall utility equal to a weighted average of own consumption and the benefits of status consumption. Thus, using notation similar to that used above, an individual of type *n* weighs own consumption by $1 - \alpha$ and status by α, maximizing

$$z(n) = (1 - \alpha)U(c, l) + \alpha U(v(s^*), l^*),$$

where *s* is status consumption, $v(s^*)$ is the total consumption others assume he has when they observe *s,* and l^* is the corresponding amount of leisure or work. The asterisks symbolize the amounts others impute when they observe *s.* Ireland considers only the case where the signal separates types and then shows that signaling and utility increase with ability types (higher-ability individuals signal more and have higher utility). A key fact to note is that status in this model is not zero sum. Status is merely perceived utility, which can increase for everyone.

Ireland runs this utility function through an optimal tax analysis based on Diamond (1998) and, making the same simplification of utility being quasi-linear in consumption, gets a similar expression for marginal tax rates given by Diamond. Recall that Diamond's expression had three terms: the marginal tax rate at an income level *n* was based on (*a*) the effect on labor effort of a small increase in the tax rate at that income level, (*b*) the social cost of taking a dollar away from everyone above that income level, and (*c*) a measure of the relative size of these effects. The only difference in Ireland's expression is in the *b* term, which measures the social cost of taking a dollar away from everyone above a given income level. In Ireland's model, only the "normal" or "own" utility matters in this calculation.

For example, suppose that we are computing the tax rate for individuals at some level *n*. If μ^n is the average of marginal social weights on people of type higher than *n*, the Diamond expression would be

$1 - \mu^n$. When we add status signaling, the expression is $1 - (1 - \alpha)\mu^n$, where α is the status weight and $1 - \alpha$ is "own" weight in the utility function. We only count the own utility cost of taking a dollar away from higher-type individuals. Thus, the more high-income individuals are concerned about status, the less we weigh their welfare and the more we are willing to impose high average rates on them.[11]

To illustrate, assume the government is utilitarian (along with Ireland's assumption that preferences are quasi-linear in consumption). Without status, the optimal marginal tax rate would be zero. No redistribution would be desirable because marginal utility does not decline with income (quasi-linear preferences) and the government does not otherwise care about inequality (utilitarianism). Mathematically, the second factor would be zero. With status, however, this factor is a function of α and is not equal to zero. If caring about status is constant (so that α, and therefore this factor, is constant) and labor supply elasticity is constant, tax rates would depend on the distribution of ability types.[12] The tax rate at a given level n would depend on the number of individuals with ability types above that level.

The reason for nonzero marginal tax rates in the status case but not in the normal case is that taxes make it cheaper to signal status, thereby reducing wasteful status consumption. That is, the primary driver of the model is signaling costs rather than Frank-like standing on the seats in a stadium. Status seeking is not zero sum in the model. Consuming a status good is very much like consuming any other good in that it increases utility and also in that there are no particular external effects. The difference between status consumption and other consumption is that status consumption increases utility indirectly by signaling to others, and it is others' esteem that increases utility. We can tax the signal and not necessarily reduce its benefits. In fact, the reason for positive tax rates in this simplified case is to make status signaling cheaper. In effect, the tax system is trying to enhance rather than reduce status differen-

11. Ireland's equations imply higher average rates on high-ability types because the status enters through the second term. This term, recall, measures the cost of taking a dollar away from everyone of higher type by raising marginal rates at type n. This might result in higher marginal rates at high income levels, but it depends on the distribution of types and labor supply elasticities. Ireland (2001) offers simulations to illustrate.

12. Ireland uses a Pareto distribution as an example to illustrate relative effects of status. With this distribution, marginal rates would be constant as well.

tiation.[13] Note that unlike in the Oswald model, there can be labor supply effects of status seeking, which are reduced through taxation. Thus, we might think of the Ireland model as the half-stadium model. There are labor supply effects, but status is not zero sum.

The key information about status in the Ireland model, similar to that needed for the Oswald model, is the distribution of $\alpha'(n)$: how preferences for status vary across the population. Ireland illustrates this in several examples. In one example, he compares a society with five types in a Pareto distribution and a constant elasticity of labor supply with and without a constant status parameter (α) equal to 25 percent. Taxes are uniformly higher, but the marginal rate schedule is flatter. We get less progressivity because of status concerns. The reason the schedule is flatter relates to the comment above that higher marginal tax rates on low-ability types reduce signaling costs for high-ability types. On the other hand, if α increases with type, the tax schedule is both higher and steeper than in the case where status does not matter. Thus, the distribution of α' is critical.

As noted, there are a number of other models of status and taxation, but at this point, we can ask whether the empirical happiness research can provide the information needed by these models (and whether the models are supported by the information we have). In both cases, the key information is how status matters for different individuals in the population.

2.2. The Evidence

The empirical evidence for status starts with the Easterlin paradox (Easterlin 1974, 1995; for a survey of the literature, see Clark, Frijters, and Shields 2006). The paradox is that there is a positive relationship between income and happiness within a country for different individuals at a given period of time, but once a country has reached some minimum level of wealth, there is a very small relationship between overall wealth in a country and happiness (both across countries and within a country over time). One way to reconcile the data is to assume that happiness is relative: increasing income within a society improves status and, therefore, happiness, but changing the overall wealth of society does nothing for status rankings within the country and, therefore, does not affect

---

13. A similar effect can be seen in Hopkins and Kornienko (2004). These authors consider only a corrective or Pigouvian tax rather than a complete optimal income tax, but their corrective tax has the similar feature of reducing signaling costs by high earners.

happiness. Although the Easterlin paradox suggests that status matters, it does not provide any direct evidence. Moreover, the Easterlin paradox is too broad based and crude to give us the information needed to solve the optimal tax problem. Instead, we must look at more direct evidence.

There are a large number of studies on this topic. Veenhoven (2007) lists 1,300 articles on happiness and status—and I cannot do justice to them all. Clark, Frijters, and Shields (2006) provides a recent survey. I consider here the recent studies by Ferrer-i-Carbonell (2005), Luttmer (2005), and Vendrik and Woltjer (2007).

Luttmer (2005) examines how reported well-being correlates with neighborhood income. He uses the National Survey of Families and Households from 1987–88 and 1992–94 that included a question on well-being. He is able to construct panel data for about 10,000 individuals living in more than 550 separate areas. He matches these data with information about local earnings. To get local earnings, he estimates information from the Public Use Microdata Areas (PUMAs) with Current Population Survey data on national earnings by industry, occupation, and year.[14] In simple regressions on the data, he finds a coefficient of .20 on the log of own household income and a coefficient of −.17 on the average log of predicted household income in one's locality. Thus, relative income matters approximately as much as own income: a dollar of increased income increases happiness about the same amount as a dollar reduction in average income in a neighborhood. The finding is robust to a variety of controls and highly significant. In a specification that hints at some of the information required by the optimal tax models, he examines how local earnings affect happiness for households above and below the local median. He finds almost identical effects: wealthier and poorer families respond identically to a change in predicted local earnings.

Luttmer imposes PUMAs as the comparison group. It would be nice to know how this affects the results and whether the neighborhood is the right comparison. In unreported regressions, he says that he finds that within a neighborhood, individuals compare themselves to smaller subgroups, in his specification, college educated or not. Further examination of this issue would likely be helpful because neighborhoods as

---

14. Public Use Microdata Areas range in size from about 127,000 to 144,000. Using predicted local earnings opens up the possibility that individuals whose income falls relative to predictions are not doing well in their careers and that utility drops for this reason rather than merely because they compare themselves to others. That is, predicted earnings might act as information.

comparison groups raise the "right pond" issue. If neighbors are the comparison group, comparison groups are endogenous because you can choose where to live. If individuals know about the comparison income effect, however, we might expect sorting to take advantage of this. Thus, a wealthy person might live in a poor neighborhood to increase his subjective well-being. The effect of such sorting on overall happiness, if it were to happen, would be unclear, but it is also contrary to the casual observation that individuals sort into neighborhoods by wealth, not against wealth. Luttmer cites Loewenstein, O'Donoghue, and Rabin (2003) for the claim that individuals make forecasting errors when choosing neighborhoods, although these authors only casually suggest this possibility and do not provide evidence for it. An alternative explanation is that reference groups are not endogenous—they are the type of individuals you compare yourself to and would be even if you did not choose to live near them. Therefore, there is no cost to sorting into neighborhoods by wealth. The neighborhood effect is simply picking up the fact that comparison groups and neighborhoods coincide.

Ferrer-i-Carbonell (2005) uses panel data from the German Socio-Economic Panel to estimate an equation in which subjective well-being is a function of own income, a comparison, and a set of controls. The sample includes about 16,000 individuals from the former East and West Germany during the years 1992–97. She tests three comparisons: average income of the reference group, the difference between the log of own income and the log of the average reference group income, and an asymmetric measure in which being below the average of reference group income matters more than being above. The reference group is one of 50 different groups, categorized by education level (five categories), age bracket (10-year windows), and whether the individual lives in the former East or West Germany.

Like Luttmer (and other studies), she finds that reference group income matters. Moreover, like Luttmer, she finds roughly similar coefficients for own income and reference group income (of opposite signs). For example, if own income and reference group income go up by the same amount, subjective well-being stays roughly constant. The asymmetric test is interesting for the optimal tax analysis because it might help us understand how status effects vary across the population. Unfortunately, the data seem inconclusive: she finds some evidence for asymmetry in the West German sample but not for the East German sample.

The most recent paper that measures relative preferences is Vendrik and Woltjer (2007). Although not concerned with taxation, these authors are the first, to my knowledge, to attempt to address the shape of the utility function with respect to status, which is the information needed to determine how status affects tax rates. They use the same data set used by Ferrer-i-Carbonell (2005), but for the years 1984–2001 and focused on West German individuals. The data include 16,000 individuals who were in the panel during that entire time period, each of whom was asked how satisfied they were with their life, all things considered. To test for curvature, they estimate a power function where a variable gives an estimate of the curvature.[15] They use a similar set of reference groups and controls as Ferrer-i-Carbonell (2005).

Contrary to the suggestions in Luttmer and Ferrer-i-Carbonell, Vendrik and Woltjer find that utility is concave in relative income. That is, the marginal improvement in happiness declines as one's income goes up relative to average reference group income. The benefit from being above the average in a reference group declines as one gets further above. The cost of being below, however, increases as one gets further below. This result holds significantly for income below the average of the reference group but is significant only under some specifications for income above the average.

This result is highly suggestive of the information needed to determine optimal tax rates. Although difficult to trace in particular models, an intuition is that status gains from moving low-ability individuals up exceed the status losses from moving high-ability individuals down, so taxes should be more progressive than otherwise. Status concerns might provide an additional reason for progressivity. Nevertheless, the conclusions may depend on the particular model. For example, in Ireland's model, we might interpret the Vendrik and Woltjer results as suggesting that $\alpha' < 0$. Correspondingly, tax rates would be less progressive because of status to reduce the costs of signaling.

A basic problem with interpreting the results, however, is that reports of happiness may themselves reflect concavity. That is, we can measure the curvature of happiness reports, but we do not know how the shape of the reports relates to actual happiness. For example, individuals may be reluctant to report extremely high levels of happiness and instead reduce their happiness scores, on a relative basis, as their happiness

15. Specifically, their relative income component of the utility function is $[(Y/Y_r)^{1-\rho} - 1]/(1 - \rho)$, where Y is own income and Y_r is reference income weighted by a relative income factor and separated for income above and below the average to allow for different effects of status if an individual is above or below the average.

increases. Curvature of the reports may reflect the reporting function rather than actual happiness (see Oswald [2005] for a discussion of this point).

Vendrik and Woltjer discuss this problem extensively. They address it by running their regressions under various possible translations of the happiness reports. Their extreme case is where someone with the highest possible happiness, a score of 10, reports a score of 8 while someone with a "true" score of 7 accurately reports a 7. They still find concavity in relative income. They conclude, therefore, that their result reflects more than merely concavity in reporting.

While important, this is only a first step because to determine how status affects tax rates, we have to know the actual curvature. Indeed, given that we may have to rely on happiness reports and that we cannot know the curvature of the reporting function, we may not be able to refine the Vendrik and Woltjer data significantly, if at all.[16] Estimates of the sort done in this study may be as close as we can get.

There are a number of other studies as well as problems inherent to all of the studies.[17] We can at this point, however, ask what we get out

16. McBride (2001) finds the opposite, that relative income matters more for the wealthy, but McBride's paper has a number of problems that make it less convincing, including a very small number of observations.

17. Clark and Oswald (1996) look at British data on job satisfaction and find a negative relationship between reference group income and job satisfaction. Blanchflower and Oswald (2004) look at U.S. General Social Survey data by state and over time. Their paper is not focused on relative income—it is a general study of the determinants of happiness. They find, for example, that the overall trend has been negative for the United States and that work and marital status have large and well-defined effects. They test the relative income hypothesis by examining how the ratio of an individual's income to state per capita income affects happiness. They find a positive coefficient. McBride (2001) uses General Social Survey data (only 324 observations) to estimate well-being as function of log income plus log(past standard of living) plus log(cohort income). The reference group is individuals within a 10-year age group. Individuals with incomes above $75,000 are excluded on the theory that if there are relative income effects at moderate or low income levels, this is sufficient. He finds negative effects of cohort income on happiness. He finds some interesting results: absolute income seems to matter more for low-income individuals and relative income more for high-income individuals. These finds are suggestive of data required by the optimal tax models. Unfortunately, his data are crude—subjective well-being is in only three categories—his sample size is very small, and he does not have data for income above $75,000, which makes the study suggestive but in need of further confirmation. Clark, Frijters, and Shields (2006) list some endemic problems with the empirical estimates of relative preferences. For example, most studies impute a reference group instead of allowing the individuals to make this selection. In addition, they do not take into account that reference groups might be endogenous and chosen to maximize long-run utility. (For example, an individual might choose a high-achieving reference group, making him unhappy today, but with the benefit of inducing harder work and happiness in the long run. Would

of the empirical literature. Almost every paper, including all three reviewed here, finds that relative income matters. Moreover, relative income seems to be close to a zero-sum game. Thus, if both an individual's income and the reference group's income goes up, subjective well-being seems to stay constant. This means that there is little support for the Ireland (1998, 2001) formulation of status, which was not zero sum. The Vendrik and Woltjer study also supports a claim that happiness is concave in relative income, but, as noted, we cannot measure the degree of concavity without knowing the happiness reporting function—how true happiness relates to happiness reports.

Frank's stadium analogy suggests that what we need to know is what happens if reference group income declines but leisure increases because the goal of a tax based on status is in part to reduce the work externality. No study gives this information. The existing studies measure a change in subjective well-being when reference group income changes, but we do not know why this is occurring. If reference group income goes up (but own income does not), this could be because the reference group has increased hours at work or increased earnings per hour. Without knowing which, we cannot sort out the effect of a tax. That is, an increased labor tax will make people work less and earn less. Showing that subjective well-being goes up when the reference group earns less might not show that it would go up if the reference group also works less.

Before turning to Frank's proposals on taxation and status, there are two final comments on optimal taxation. First, a prediction of those arguing for status taxation is that higher labor income tax rates should, up to a point, increase overall happiness. I do not know of any study that has attempted to measure this. Although one can imagine many complications, we should be able to compare data such as those used by Easterlin to labor tax rates in those countries to see whether higher taxes do indeed increase happiness.

Second, to understand the effect of taxing status, we need a better understanding of why status concerns arise. They might be an evolutionary detritus akin to an appendix. They might, however, continue to serve a useful function, such as sorting or providing incentives. For

you rather go to a school with a bunch of smart people who will inspire you to learn more or with a bunch of mediocre people who will give you immediate status benefits?) For an exception, see Falk and Knell (2004). In addition to the problems listed by Clark, Frijters, and Shields, reference group earnings might be information about performance instead of creating envy.

example, there is a literature arguing that rank order tournaments are, in certain circumstances, efficient (Bolton and Dewatripont 2005). Rank order status concerns might provide similar incentives. Before concluding that taxing status is desirable, we should know more about why it arises.

2.3. Frank's Status Taxation Proposals

Robert Frank has been very prominent in thinking about the link between status seeking and taxation. His proposal, however, is distinct from the optimal labor income tax discussed above. Although never outlined in detail, Frank (1985a, 1985b, 1997, 2000, 2005a, 2005b) has argued in several papers and books for a progressive consumption tax because of status concerns. The question for this section is how Frank's arguments relate to the optimal taxation arguments given above.

The optimal taxation literature models a tax on labor income, while Frank argues for a tax on consumption. The two, however, are closely related and, in basic cases, identical. The reason is that leaving aside bequests and gifts (neither of which is an apparent concern here), labor income and consumption have the same present value: you can only spend what you earn. This means that taxes on labor income and consumption also tend to have the same present value and, therefore, impose the same burden.

To illustrate, suppose that an individual earns labor income y in period 0 and can consume it in either of two periods, period 0 or period 1. If the individual waits until period 1, he invests it at rate r. If C_i is consumption in period i, we know that

$$y = C_0 + C_1/(1 + r).$$

If we impose a tax on consumption at rate t, labor income must equal the present value of consumption inclusive of the tax. Therefore,

$$y = C_0(1 + t) + C_1(1 + t)/(1 + r).$$

If we divide by $(1 + t)$, we see that a tax on consumption is equivalent to reducing labor income by $1/(1 + t)$, which is equivalent to a tax rate of $t/(1 + t)$ on labor income. This identity used a flat rate tax t, but the same holds for progressive taxes on labor income. In particular, if an individual faces some tax rate on labor income, this tax rate is equivalent to tax at flat rate on his consumption, even if other individuals face other labor income tax rates. (As will be discussed below, the reverse is not quite true: a progressive tax on consumption need not translate into a particular labor income tax rate.)

There are two relevant differences between Frank's arguments and the optimal income tax arguments.[18] First, Frank argues that holding labor income constant, individuals in status races will consume too early and save too little. The idea is that spending is observable while savings is not, so individuals concerned with status will spend too much. On this basis, he argues that we should shift from the current income tax, which burdens savings as well as labor, to a consumption tax.

The optimal income tax models take for granted that we should tax labor income and not the return to savings. They are models of labor income taxes, not conventional capital income taxes. In addition, there are good reasons, independent of status concerns, for taxing only consumption or labor and not savings (see Bankman and Weisbach 2006). Nevertheless, the optimal income tax models generally do not have savings (or even time), so they do not consider whether status concerns reduce savings and, if so, whether the tax system should be modified as a result. Frank argues for lower taxes on savings, so if we otherwise believe the tax on savings should be zero, perhaps we should have a savings subsidy.

A difficulty with this argument is that it treats savings like any other good. Suppose that there are two goods, apples and oranges, and consumption of apples is an observable signal of status and the consumption of oranges is not. We might expect individuals to consume more apples than otherwise. In Frank's world, savings is like the orange—a good the consumption of which is unobservable and, therefore, underutilized. Savings, however, is just future consumption: it is like two apples in the future, not like the orange. Consuming more today to win a status race means consuming less in the future and losing the status race in the future. Frank has to be arguing that status competition distorts discount rates because individuals would have to be willing to give up future status for current status. This could be true, but as far as I know, there is no empirical support for this. None of the studies reviewed above say anything about discount rates. It does not seem implausible, and I am

18. There are a number of other differences between a progressive, individual-level consumption tax and a labor income tax. For example, as Summers (1981) points out, the timing of government revenue flows is different in the two systems. There are also administrative differences. With a labor income tax, employers could withhold taxes, while a withholding system would be difficult to incorporate into a progressive consumption tax. Although labor taxes are used throughout the world, no country currently uses a progressive consumption tax of the sort Frank proposes. None of these differences are directly relevant to the discussion.

not aware of a study that rejects the claim (or that even addresses it), but it is not yet supported by evidence. We do not know, therefore, whether status considerations argue for a lower tax or even a subsidy on savings.

The second relevant difference between a progressive consumption tax and a labor income tax is that if the rate on consumption is progressive within a given period, lumpy consumption is taxed at a higher rate than level consumption. To illustrate, compare a person who spends $100 each period to a person who spends $200 every other period with the same overall total. Suppose that we impose a progressive consumption tax with a 0 percent tax rate on the first $100 consumed each period and a 20 percent tax rate on everything above $100. The first individual would owe no tax. The second individual, with the same overall consumption but with a lumpier pattern, would pay $20 of tax every other period. Lumpy consumption, by pushing individuals into higher tax brackets, is taxed at a higher rate than level consumption. It is for this very reason that Vickrey (1947) proposed an averaging scheme to complement progressive taxation: income averaging prevents this effect.

To support Frank's proposal separately from the findings of the optimal income tax literature, it would have to be the case that lumpy consumption is particularly related to status and that it is desirable to tax lumpy consumption at higher rates than level consumption.[19] As far as I know, however, there are no data supporting a claim that status concerns lead to lumpy consumption. None of the studies are able to pinpoint how comparisons are made and whether big splurges create more status than constant, everyday spending. Perhaps big splurges are more visible and, therefore, create more status, but this is merely an assertion, not something yet supported by the literature. Frank often cites the Easterlin data for the claim that preferences are relative, but these data say nothing about lumpy as compared to smooth consumption.

Moreover, whether something counts as lumpy depends on the accounting system. Durable goods, such as houses, cars, and watches, all frequent targets of Frank, are often counted as lumpy because their purchase is made all at once. Because they are durable, however, they

·

19. The statement in the text is relative to the optimal income tax models. Frank also wants to change the current income tax, which imposes a burden on savings, to a consumption tax. This change is taken for granted in the optimal income tax models because they are models of a labor income tax. There are, however, very good independent reasons for shifting to a consumption tax.

actually offer consumption over a period of time. One can alternatively buy a durable good or rent it. A progressive consumption tax would likely treat buying it as lumpy and tax it at a high rate but treat renting it as smooth, taxing it a low rate. The lumpiness of these goods, however, is simply an arbitrary construct of accounting rather than anything fundamental. Moreover, it is hard to see how owning a fancy car compared to leasing it changes its status-enhancing properties.

To summarize, there are two claims that Frank makes that are distinctive from the optimal tax literature reviewed above. The first is that status concerns change discount rates, causing individuals to care more about status today than in the future. Although possible, there is not yet any evidence to support this claim. The second is that status concerns lead to lumpy consumption, as conventionally measured by tax systems. There is also, to my knowledge, no evidence to support this claim, particularly because tax systems' measurements of lumpiness are arbitrary. Without these distinctive elements of Frank's proposals, the analysis of taxation and status reverts to the discussion of optimal taxation considered above.

3. ADDITIONAL TAX CONSIDERATIONS AND CONCLUSION

There are a number of other ways the happiness literature might change basic tax results. This section considers some of the possibilities, including the effects of taxation on marriage and how the tax system should take disability into account.

3.1. Marriage

A standard problem in taxation is how to reconcile a system of graduated rates with household sharing by married and unmarried individuals. The tax system cannot be neutral with respect to the choice to marry or remain single (or with respect to who within a marriage earns income) while maintaining increasing marginal rates (Bittker 1975). Tax systems with increasing marginal rates generally must choose between marriage penalties or marriage bonuses.

The happiness literature shows a large effect on well-being from marriage. For example, Blanchflower and Oswald (2004) calculate that being married translates to the equivalent of an extra $100,000 of income per year. Marriage increases happiness consistently around the world (Stack and Eshleman 1998), and attempts to isolate causality show that at least some of the effects are that people are happier because they marry, not that happier people marry (Stutzer and Frey 2006).[20]

The effect of these data on the tax treatment of marriage, however, is unclear. The key reason is that the data do not tell us how marriage affects the marginal utility of income, which is a central variable in determining the proper tax treatment. We can imagine marriage alternatively increasing or reducing the marginal utility of income regardless of its effect on absolute levels of utility. Moreover, we also have to know how marriage rates respond to tax rates (not particularly a happiness-related issue) and whether marriages that are based on incentives to marry or stay married actually make people happier. (Imagine, for example, if everyone were forced to marry. It is possible that the marriages might make people happier, but it is possible that they would not.)

To illustrate the complexities, consider a very simple model of marriage based on Kaplow (1996). He considers as a base case a model where there are three individuals, two married adults and a third, unmarried adult. The individuals do not respond to incentives; taxation is merely redistributive. If everyone got equal shares of a fixed pot (no incentives), the unmarried individual would get one-third of the resources and the married couple would get the rest. The married individuals, Kaplow assumes, may share the resources given to them unequally, and the government cannot observe the allocation of resources internal to the marriage.

The first-order conditions set the marginal utility of a dollar equal for each of the individuals. Consider allocating an additional dollar to the married couple. Because of unequal sharing within the marriage, there are two offsetting effects. Some fraction of the additional dollar goes to the individual who is getting more than his or her share of family income. If marginal utility of income declines or the social welfare function is curved, this fraction of the dollar is not well spent because it goes to the individual with a lower marginal utility of income or higher utility overall. On the other hand, the remaining fraction of the dollar goes to the individual with a smaller share, and this may be desirable. Whether to allocate more to the married couple depends on both the sharing ratio and how much we care about giving a fraction of a dollar to the worse-off individual (the one who gets less of the married couple's resources) compared with giving the rest to the better-off individual.

---

20. The literature on marriage and happiness is extensive. For a partial list of cites, see Stutzer and Frey (2006).

The key factors in the model are the marginal utility of income of married and unmarried individuals and the curvature of the utility (and social welfare) function. Knowing that married people are happier (and even possibly that marriage makes people happier) does not give us this information. Moreover, more complex models of marriage have more subtle effects. (See the additional considerations raised in Kaplow [2008, chap. 12].) For example, married couples may have economies of scale that unmarried individuals do not enjoy.

It is clear that the data on happiness and marriage have the potential to provide important information regarding the proper tax treatment of marriage. It is also clear, however, that the effects are likely to be subtle and complex and that current studies showing that marriage increases happiness do not yet give us the necessary information.

3.2. Disability

Another important issue raised by the happiness literature for the tax and transfer system is the idea that individuals may adapt to circumstances. The most striking version of this claim is that individuals with severe disabilities, such as tetrapalegia, are just as happy as healthy individuals. Although the data do not support this precise claim, they do show significant adaptation to disability. The question is how these data affect disability policy.

Since Diamond and Mirrlees (1978), it has been standard in the economics literature to model disability as a wage rate of zero but not otherwise affecting an individual. The planner's problem is to provide insurance against the risk of having a zero wage rate at some time in the future while reducing the moral hazard problems created by offering the insurance. This model of disability is not very helpful in the present context because we need to examine the distinctive element that disability has in happiness. Disability has to be thought of as affecting individuals more generally. We want to compare an individual with a disability to an individual with the same wage rate without a disability and determine how they should be taxed. That is, we have to expand the optimal tax theory to allow individuals to vary in two dimensions: wage rate and disability.

This problem, of differences among individuals other than wages, was noted by Mirrlees (1976), but in the 30 years since then, modeling has remained its infancy. The key problem is that if individuals vary in more than one unobservable dimension, incentive constraints may no longer bind in a single direction, which makes the model impossible to solve in any general form. As illustrated above, even in the single-dimension case, simplifying assumptions are often used to help interpret the results. Adding a second dimension compounds the difficulty significantly.

The most straightforward way to simplify the problem is to assume that disability is observable. This will be true of some but not all disabilities. (Even with a given medical diagnosis, however, individuals may vary dramatically, so observing many disabilities may be difficult.) If disability is observable, the standard optimal tax results hold because we can divide the population into categories. Within each category, individuals would be the same except with respect to their earning ability, and we can apply the optimal tax results to each category. The overall tax schedule across categories would be linked by a common shadow price of revenue (Kaplow 2006; Boadway and Pestieau 2003).[21]

This simplification means that we can determine the treatment of the disabled by examining how disability affects the parameters in the optimal tax formula. Recall that the optimal rate at some income level n is based on three factors, labor supply elasticity, the social value of taking away money from individuals at higher income levels, and the relative size of the relevant populations.

In the disability context, the key factor is in the social value or cost of taking money away from individuals at a higher income level. To understand this, we need to know two factors to determine this: the social welfare weights on individuals and their change in utility when they lose a dollar. That is, we need to know $W'(u)u_c$, where $W(u)$ is the social weighting of an individual and u_c is their marginal utility from consumption. We need to add up these terms for all individuals with income above n.[22]

Determining $W'(u)$ depends on philosophical theories and not empirical facts about happiness, so there is little to say about it here. We also need to know the level of utility and marginal utility of disabled and nondisabled individuals of a given income. That is, we need to know

21. Kaplow (2006) briefly discusses the case where the second dimension of difference (here disability) is not observable. He characterizes the solution as imposing commodity taxes with effects that roughly mimic the case where disability is observable.

22. In the continuous case, for a tax rate on a type-n individual, we get $B = [\int_n^\infty (1 - W'(u)u_c/\lambda)dF(n)]/[1 - F(n)]$ following Diamond's (1998) notion of labeling the relevant term B. The division of $W'(u)u_c$ by λ converts the social costs to dollars. It is the λ term that links the tax schedules of the different types of individuals.

how disability affects individuals. The happiness research may have a lot to say about this.

There is a cottage industry examining the effect of disability on subjective well-being, originating with the well-known study by Brickman, Coate, and Janoff-Bulman (1978). The overwhelming majority of these report only changes in subjective well-being, not controlled for any differences among individuals and, in particular, not controlled for income. A typical example is Dijkers (1997), which is a meta-analysis of 22 studies but does not provide any significant controls.[23]

There are a handful of studies that begin to give us the data we need. Smith et al. (2005) compare changes in subjective well-being due to a disability for individuals with higher and lower than median wealth (within the sample). They find that the wealthier half of their sample experienced a smaller decline in subjective well-being than the poorer half. They conclude that wealth has a larger effect on subjective well-being at the onset of disability than it does more generally. This would mean that disability increases the marginal utility of wealth.

Oswald and Powdthavee (2006) look at the British Household Panel Survey from 1996–2002 and examine how complete disability (meaning inability to work) affects well-being, measured on a scale from 1 to 7. A significant and new aspect of the study is that their data allow them to do a panel study, while prior work tends to be cross-sectional. Moreover, their study uses a much larger data set than prior studies. The raw data show the disabled to be less happy: the nondisabled have an average of well-being score of 5.3, while the disabled have a score of 4.3. The authors then run a time series analysis, which shows some but not full recovery. Controls for gender, age, and education do not significantly change the results. They then control for income and find similar effects. Although they do not run the regression, their data should allow them to compute the interaction of disability and income and, therefore, the marginal effect of income on reported well-being for the disabled and the nondisabled.[24]

A problem with the Oswald and Powdthavee study is that at their measured onset of disability, individuals already have a significantly lower happiness score than individuals who never experience a disability.

---

23. A problem with all of these studies for determining social policy toward the disabled is that they ask happiness questions with the existing institutions in place.

24. Note that there is a separate issue of whether data on marginal happiness scores tell us anything about marginal utility. The problem is that there might be some nonlinear translation of happiness reports to actual happiness.

At the onset of the disability, their well-being goes down from this lower starting point and then recovers somewhat, at most up to the lower starting point. For example, an individual who never experiences a disability reports a happiness score of 5.3. An individual who experiences a disability starts at 4.2 prior to the onset, goes down to 3.9 immediately after the onset, and then recovers to almost 4.1. As compared to the predisability number, the recovery is significant. The lower starting point, however, suggests that the disability began prior to the reported time or that, for some reason, those who are likely to become disabled are unhappy for some other reason. If we compare the fully recovered well-being to the well-being of the nondisabled (on the assumption that if we could correctly measure the onset of disability, the individuals would start at the nondisabled level), recovery is not even close to complete, even for the less seriously disabled.

These studies remain preliminary. Moreover, we have a wealth of data on the income, consumption, and employment of the disabled, and it would be nice to be able to reconcile these data with the well-being data. For example, we know that disability makes it much less likely that an individual is employed and that unemployment leads to a significant decline in subjective well-being. If disability does not lead to a significant decline in well-being, however, the reports seem inconsistent.

3.3. Additional Issues

Taxing Status Goods. The literature examined so far makes the assumption that we cannot directly tax status-seeking activities. If status seeking simply involves earning more labor income, then the labor income tax directly taxes the activity, but if status seeking involves consumption of particular goods, adjusting the labor income tax only indirectly addresses the problem. Adjusting the labor income tax is justified on the grounds that which goods act as status goods is highly contingent. If we try to tax them, we make them more expensive, and the goods that are used to signal status will shift.[25]

Ireland (1994) suggests taxing status goods but does not address what

---

25. Ng (1987) suggests that some goods, so-called diamond goods, are valued for their value. If taxed, individuals will consume a lower quantity of the good but spend the same total amount. He uses the example of a diamond. He suggests that an individual who wants to spend $1,000 on a diamond will spend the same $1,000 whether this buys one carat or half a carat. As Ng carefully points out, diamond goods are not the same as status goods because diamond goods can be consumed privately and status goods may not have the "valued for value" feature of diamond goods.

these goods might be or whether they could feasibly be taxed. In a recent paper, Blumkin and Sadka (2007) suggest that charitable donations are status goods. Although charitable donations have a positive externality (they help the recipient as well as provide utility to the donor) and, therefore, might be subsidized, if they are status goods, we might want to tax them. Whether the net result is a tax or a subsidy depends on the parameters.

Frank (2000) suggests large homes, fancy automobiles, and mechanical watches as status goods. Observers of social behavior note many others. (Ireland [1994] recounts a story about a brand of basketball shoes in high demand among the urban poor.) We do not, however, understand how these arise and the extent to which they can shift if taxed.

Unemployment. Standard models of optimal taxation are not particularly concerned about unemployment. Unemployment is simply labor supply of zero. Holding income constant (say, through transfers), utility goes up as labor supply goes down, even to zero. Consider a high marginal rate on a low-ability person. If the person reduces work effort, say, to zero, there is little lost productivity. The high rate at the low end of the income scale, however, is inframarginal to a large number of individuals. Therefore, high marginal rates on low incomes may be desirable.[26]

The happiness literature generally finds a large negative effect on subjective well-being from (involuntary) unemployment, controlling for income. For example, Clark and Oswald (1994, p. 655) find that "joblessness depressed well-being more than any other single characteristic (including important negative ones such as divorce and separation)." This suggests that the standard utility function used in the optimal tax literature might not accurately reflect utility when labor supply is low. I do not know of any models of taxation that attempt to include these effects in utility functions, but if the data are correct about the effect of unemployment, incorporating these effects may change the results significantly.

Age-Based Taxation. There have been some suggestions that taxes should be age based (Kremer 2005). The argument is that by separating individuals by age, we can take better advantage of the parameters in the optimal tax equation. In particular, labor supply of the young might be

---

26. This is to be distinguished from average rates. Average rates could be low or negative because the poor may receive transfers.

very elastic, while the labor supply of the middle-aged might be very inelastic. Moreover, distribution of wage rates is likely to be different for the young than for the middle-aged or old. If the young have a higher percentage of individuals with low wages, high rates on low wages distort more for the young than for others. Kremer (2005) suggests that, all else equal, taxes should be lower for the young than for the middle-aged.

The happiness literature, however, suggests that individuals are least happy in middle age. If this is true, the distributional consequences of imposing higher taxes in middle age may not be desirable. We would be making unhappy people more unhappy. Theorizing about age-based taxation is in its infancy, so we do not yet understand the full effects. Nevertheless, the happiness literature should be relevant to future learning in this area.

4. CONCLUSION

It is clear that the findings of happiness research have the potential to change tax policy. The research is interesting by itself, but if one of the goals of the research is to have policy implications—to find out how to make individuals happier—the key message of this paper is that the research must line up better with the normative models.

REFERENCES

Abel, Andrew B. 2005. Optimal Taxation When Consumers Have Endogenous Benchmark Levels of Consumption. *Review of Economic Studies* 72:21–42.

Allgood, Sam. 2006. The Marginal Costs and Benefits of Redistributing Income and the Willingness to Pay for Status. *Journal of Public Economic Theory* 8:357–77.

Bankman, Joseph, and David A. Weisbach. 2006. The Superiority of an Ideal Consumption Tax over an Ideal Income Tax. *Stanford Law Review* 58:1413–56.

Beath, John, and Felix FitzRoy. 2007. Status, Happiness, and Relative Income. Discussion Paper No. 2658. IZA, Bonn.

Bittker, Boris I. 1975. Federal Income Taxation and the Family. *Stanford Law Review* 27:1389–1463.

Blanchflower, David G., and Andrew J. Oswald. 2004. Well-Being over Time in Britain and the USA. *Journal of Public Economics* 88:1359–86.

Blumkin, Tomer, and Efraim Sadka. 2007. On the Desirability of Taxing Charitable Contributions. Working Paper No. 1900. CESifo, Munich.

Boadway, Robin, and Pierre Pestieau. 2003. Indirect Taxation and Redistribution: The Scope of the Atkinson-Stliglitz Theorem. Pp. 387–403 in *Economics for an Imperfect World*, edited by Richard Arnott, Bruce Greenwald, Ravi Kanbur, and Barry Nalebuff. Cambridge, Mass.: MIT Press.

Bolton, Patrick, and Mathias Dewatripont. 2005. *Contract Theory*. Cambridge, Mass.: MIT Press.

Boskin, Michael J., and Eytan Sheshinski. 1978. Optimal Redistributive Taxation When Individual Welfare Depends upon Relative Income. *Quarterly Journal of Economics* 92:589–601.

Brickman, Philip, Dan Coate, and Ronnie Janoff-Bulman. 1978. Lottery Winners and Accident Victims: Is Happiness Relative? *Journal of Personality and Social Psychology* 36:917–27.

Clark, Andrew E., Paul Frijters, and Michael A. Shields. 2006. Income and Happiness: Evidence, Explanations and Economic Implications. Working Paper No. 2006-24. Jourdan Sciences Economiques, Paris.

Clark, Andrew E., and Andrew J. Oswald. 1994. Unhappiness and Unemployment. *Economic Journal* 104:648–59.

———. 1996. Satisfaction and Comparison Income. *Journal of Public Economics* 61:359–81.

Diamond, Peter A. 1998. Optimal Income: An Example with a U-Shaped Pattern of Optimal Marginal Tax Rates. *American Economic Review* 88:83–95.

Diamond, P. A., and J. A. Mirrlees. 1978. A Model of Social Insurance with Variable Retirement. *Journal of Public Economics* 10:295–336.

Dijkers, Marcel. 1997. Quality of Life after Spinal Cord Injury: A Meta Analysis of the Effects of Disablement Components. *Spinal Cord* 35:829–40.

Easterlin, Richard. 1974. Does Economic Growth Improve the Human Lot? Pp. 89–125 in *Nations and Households in Economic Growth: Essays in Honour of Moses Abramovitz*, edited by Paul A. David and Melvin W. Reder. New York: Academic Press.

———. 1995. Will Raising the Incomes of All Increase the Happiness of All? *Journal of Economic Behavior and Organization* 27:35–47.

Falk, Armin, and Markus Knell. 2004. Choosing the Joneses: Endogenous Goals and Reference Standards. *Scandinavian Journal of Economics* 106:417–35.

Ferrer-i-Carbonell, Ada. 2005. Income and Well-Being: An Empiral Analysis of the Comparison Income Effect. *Journal of Public Economics* 89:997–1019.

Frank, Robert H. 1985a. *Choosing the Right Pond*. New York: Oxford University Press.

———. 1985b. The Demand for Unobservable and Other Nonpositional Goods. *American Economic Review* 75:101–16.

———. 1997. The Frame of Reference as a Public Good. *Economic Journal* 107: 1832–47.

———. 2000. *Luxury Fever*. New York: Free Press.

———. 2005a. Positional Externalities Cause Large and Preventable Welfare Losses. *AEA Papers and Proceedings* 95:137–41.

———. 2005b. Progressive Consumption Taxation as a Remedy for the U.S. Savings Shortfall. *Economists' Voice* 2:1–10.

Hopkins, Ed, and Tatiana Kornienko. 2004. Running to Keep in the Same Place: Consumer Choice as a Game of Status. *American Economic Review* 94: 1085–1107.

Ireland, Norman J. 1998. Status-Seeking, Income Taxation and Efficiency. *Journal of Public Economics* 70:99–113.

———. 1994. On Limiting the Market for Status Signals. *Journal of Public Economics* 53:91–110.

———. 2001. Optimal Income Tax in the Presence of Status Effects. *Journal of Public Economics* 81:193–212.

Kaplow, Louis. 1996. Optimal Distribution and the Family. *Scandinavian Journal of Economics* 98:75–92.

———. 2006. Optimal Policy with Heterogeneous Preferences. Working Paper No. w14170. National Bureau of Economic Research, Cambridge, Mass.

———. 2008. *The Theory of Taxation and Public Economics*. Princeton, N.J.: Princeton University Press.

Kaplow, Louis, and Steven Shavell. 2002. *Fairness versus Welfare*. Cambridge, Mass.: Harvard University Press.

Kremer, Michael. 2005. Should Taxes Be Independent of Age? Working paper. Harvard University, Department of Economics, Cambridge, Mass.

Loewenstein, George, Ted O'Donoghue, and Matthew Rabin. 2003. Projection Bias in Predicting Future Utility. *Quarterly Journal of Economics* 118: 1209–48.

Luttmer, Erzo F. 2005. Neighbors as Negatives: Relative Earnings and Well-Being. *Quarterly Journal of Economics* 120:963–1001.

McAdams, Richard H. 1992. Relative Preferences. *Yale Law Journal* 102:1–104.

McBride, Michael. 2001. Relative-Income Effects on Subjective Well-Being in the Cross-Section. *Journal of Economics Behavior and Organization* 45: 251–78.

Mirrlees, James A. 1971. An Exploration in the Theory of Optimal Income Taxes. *Review of Economics Studies* 38:175–208.

———. 1976. Optimal Tax Theory. *Journal of Public Economics* 6:327–58.

Ng, Yew-Kwang. 1987. Diamonds Are a Government's Best Friend: Burden-Free Taxes on Goods Valued for the Values. *American Economic Review* 77: 186–91.

Oswald, Andrew J. 1983. Altruism, Jealousy and the Theory of Optimal Non-linear Taxation. *Journal of Public Economics* 20:77–87.

———. 1997. Happiness and Economic Performance. *Economic Journal* 107: 1815–31.

————. 2005. On the Common Claim That Happiness Equations Demonstrate Diminishing Marginal Utility of Income. Discussion Paper No. 1781. IZA, Bonn.

Oswald, Andrew J., and Nattavudh Powdthavee. 2006. Does Happiness Adapt? A Longitudinal Study of Disability with Implications for Economists and Judges. Discussion Paper No. 2208. IZA, Bonn. http://ssrn.com/=921040.

Rae, John. 1834. *Statement of Some New Principles on the Subject of Political Economy.* Boston: Hillard, Gray.

Saez, Emmanuel. 2001. Using Elasticities to Derive Optimal Income Tax Rates. *Review of Economic Studies* 68:205–30.

Smith, Adam. [1759] 2002. *The Theory of Moral Sentiments.* Reprint, New York: Cambridge University Press.

Smith, Dylan M., Kenneth M. Langa, Mohammed U. Kabeto, and Peter A. Ubel. 2005. Health, Wealth and Happiness. *Psychological Science* 16:663–66.

Stack, Steven, and J. Ross Eshleman. 1998. Marital Status and Happiness: A 17-Nation Study. *Journal of Marriage and the Family* 60:527–37.

Stiglitz, Joseph. 1987. Pareto Efficient and Optimal Taxation and the New New Welfare Economics. Pp. 991–1042 in vol. 2 of *Handbook of Public Economics*, edited by Alan J. Auerbach and Martin Feldstein. Amsterdam: Elsevier.

Stutzer, Alois, and Bruno S. Frey. 2006. Does Marriage Make People Happy or Do Happy People Get Married? *Journal of Socio-Economics* 35:326–47.

Summers, Larry H. 1981. Taxation and Capital Accumulation in a Life Cycle Growth Model. *American Economic Review* 71:533–54.

Tuomala, Matti. 1990. *Optimal Income Tax and Redistribution.* Oxford: Clarendon Press.

Veenhoven, R. 2007. World Database of Happiness. Erasmus University, Rotterdam. http://worlddatabaseofhappiness.eur.nl.

Vendrik, Maarten C. M., and Geert B. Woltjer. 2007. Happiness and Loss Aversion: Is Utility Concave or Convex in Relative Income? *Journal of Public Economics* 91:1423–48.

Vickrey, William. 1947. *Agenda for Progressive Taxation.* New York: Ronald Press.

The Effect of Crime on Life Satisfaction

Mark A. Cohen

ABSTRACT

Crime often ranks at the top of public concern, and a majority of the public report they sometimes worry about crime. Yet we know little about crime's impact on day-to-day quality of life. This paper provides new evidence on crime's effect on life satisfaction using a combination of victimization and subjective survey data. I find that county-level crime rates and perceived neighborhood safety have little impact on overall life satisfaction. In contrast, the effect of a home burglary on life satisfaction is quite large—nearly as much as moving from excellent health to good health. In monetary terms, I estimate a compensating income equivalent of nearly $85,000 for a home burglary. Thus, while being burglarized has a large and significant effect on a victim's overall life satisfaction, neither county-level crime rates nor neighborhood safety appear to have very large effects on daily life satisfaction for the average American.

1. INTRODUCTION

Crime often ranks at the top of the public's concerns in surveys conducted in the United States. For example, a recent survey in the Minneapolis/St. Paul metropolitan area found crime to be the number one

MARK A. COHEN is Vice President for Research, Resources for the Future; the Justin Potter Professor of Competitive Enterprise, Owen Graduate School of Management, Vanderbilt University; and a fellow at the Center for Criminal Justice Economics and Psychology, University of York. This study was supported by a grant from the National Institute of Justice through the Institute for Law and Justice. Additional support is acknowledged from the Dean's Fund for Summer Research, Owen Graduate School of Management, Vanderbilt University, and the Leverhulme Trust. I am grateful for the valuable research assistance provided by Barnali Basak and Suman Seth. Additional comments and suggestions on early drafts of this research were received from Paul Dolan, Simon Moore, an anonymous referee, and participants at seminars at the University of Cardiff and the University of York. The views expressed are solely those of the author and do not represent the sponsoring agencies or those who have provided comments in any manner.

[*Journal of Legal Studies*, vol. XXXVII (June 2008)]

concern among residents (Kollodge 2007). In New York State, crime was second only to taxes when survey respondents were asked "In your opinion, what do you think is the single most important issue facing your community as a whole?" (Blakely 2007). In addition, a large majority of the public routinely reports worrying about crime. For example, in a nationally representative random sample survey of the public, 25.3 percent responded that they worry "a lot" and 53.9 percent worry "some" when asked "How much do you personally worry about a loved one becoming a victim of a crime?" (Cohen, Rust, and Steen 2002; Cohen et al. 2004). Yet these open-ended surveys are of only limited value in helping us understand the relative impact of crime on quality of life.

This paper provides new evidence using a combination of objective crime risk data and responses to subjective evaluations about quality of life. In particular, I combine local crime rates and subjective evaluations of neighborhood safety with measures of life satisfaction to determine the impact of community crime rates on quality of life. I also examine the effect of actual victimization on life satisfaction.

Section 2 reviews the literature on life satisfaction and crime. Section 3 describes the data used in this study. Section 4 describes the underlying theory and empirical methods, while the main results are in Section 5. Concluding remarks are reserved for Section 6.

2. REVIEW OF LITERATURE

There is growing interest among economists in evaluating public surveys of subjective well-being in order to determine which factors have the most significant impact on the public's quality of life (see Kahneman and Krueger 2006; Di Tella and MacCulloch 2006). Examples of research that have used life satisfaction (or happiness) surveys include the conditions under which higher income produces happiness (Easterlin 2001), the effect of marriage and sex on happiness (Blanchflower and Oswald 2004), and the impact of noise on life satisfaction (van Praag and Baarsma 2005).

Recent evidence suggests that life satisfaction can be measured with a reasonable degree of reliability—sufficient to be able to compare means over time or across jurisdictions, especially in large samples (Krueger and Schkade 2007). More important, as done in this paper, life satisfaction studies can be analyzed using multiple regression analysis to understand the factors that affect happiness in a large population. While we might not be able to compare two individuals directly (for example, is someone who rates his level of life satisfaction a 7 really happier than someone who rates himself a 6?), we can ask how individual life satisfaction changes at the margin when life events change. Further, despite commonly held beliefs that responses to such questions are affected by the mood of the individuals at the time of the survey and not by their overall well-being, evidence suggests otherwise. For example, Eid and Diener (2004) estimated that mood effects could explain only about 1.7 percent of the variability of life satisfaction responses.

A few studies have begun to explore the effect of crime on life satisfaction. Michalos and Zumbo (2000) studied quality of life in Prince George, British Columbia. They found that victims of crime reported slightly lower measures of overall life satisfaction (5.4 versus 5.6 on a seven-point scale), although victims reported much larger differences in other satisfaction scores such as the quality of their neighborhood. In a multiple regression analysis explaining overall life satisfaction, crime-related variables were able to explain only about 7 percent of the variation in scores—although they were able to explain 38 percent of the variation in overall neighborhood satisfaction.

Powdthavee (2005) analyzed a 1997 survey of 30,000 households in South Africa—about 2,000 of whom reported a burglary, robbery, house-breaking, or murder in their household in the prior 12 months. The life satisfaction question was also based on households, with the question being "Taking everything into account, how satisfied is this household with the way it lives these days?" Households who were victimized reported a life satisfaction level .265 point lower on a five-point scale (3.660 versus 3.395). Powdthavee (2005, table 4) added to the analysis the objectively reported crime rate in the region where the individual household was located and found significant differences in life satisfaction levels by regional crime rate. However, when comparing the magnitude of the individual and the regional crime rates, he found that it would take a regional crime rate more than 35 times the average to be equivalent to a life satisfaction score reported by an actual victim.

While life satisfaction surveys do not ask respondents for monetary valuations, they usually obtain information about an individual's (or household's) income. Assuming that respondents are rational utility maximizers, they will trade off various aspects of "happiness" in exchange for money. Thus, one can empirically trace out indifference curves and measure the amount of additional income, for example, that would be required to make an individual just as well off if she had to accept the risk of one additional crime. These life satisfaction surveys may be used in part to place monetary values on crime. They may serve as an alternative to other survey approaches to valuing crime such as directly asking respondents how much they are willing to pay for crime reduction programs (for example, Cohen et al. 2004; Cohen 2005, 2007) or attaching monetary estimates to health-based quality-adjusted life-year measures for criminal victimization (for example, Dolan et al. 2005).

Moore (2006) has used this approach to estimate monetary values associated with living in a high-crime area. Moore (2006) analyzed the 2002 European Social Survey (ESS)—a survey administered to over 30,000 individuals in 22 countries. The question of interest in the ESS asked respondents to rank on an 11-point scale from "extremely unhappy" to "extremely happy" their assessment of the question "Taking all things together, how happy would you say you are?" The survey also used a four-point scale from "very unsafe" to "very safe" for a question on neighborhood safety, "How safe do you—or would you—feel walking alone in this area after dark?" Using multiple regression analysis, Moore obtained an estimate that moving from "very unsafe" to "very safe" is equivalent to an additional income of 13,538 euros—about $20,000 based on 2000 exchange rates.

Di Tella and MacCulloch (2005) compared life satisfaction in 12 Organisation for Economic Co-operation and Development countries and the United States from 1975 to 1997. They included aggregate measures such as income, unemployment, inequality, hours worked, inflation, life expectancy, divorce rate, pollution, and the violent crime rate (measured by the number of serious assaults per 100,000 residents). In multiple regression analyses, violent crime was found to be negatively associated with life satisfaction. For example, they noted that "the rise in violent crime from 242 to 388 assaults per 100,000 people in the United States (that is, a 60 percent rise) during our sample period would be equivalent to a drop of approximately 3.5 percent in *GDP per Capita*" (Di Tella and MacCulloch 2005, p. 19). Although the authors did not take the next step in valuing crime, a rough calculation based on their study would value an aggravated assault at about $550,000 in 2000 dollars—nearly eight times the amount of a serious assault estimated using the willingness-to-pay approach in Cohen et al. (2004).[1] However,

1. Per capita gross domestic product (GDP) ranged from $7,604 to $30,458 over this time period. A 3.5 percent reduction in GDP in 1975 would thus amount to $266 per

this estimate is statistically significant at only $p < .10$; hence the 95 percent confidence interval would range from approximately zero to $1.1 million. Note the differences in methodology between the two studies. Cohen et al. (2004) specifically asked respondents to value decreases in assault. In contrast, Di Tella and MacCulloch (2005) included assault rates in a multiple regression analysis. While they included many country-specific amenities such as pollution, life expectancy, and income inequality, it is quite possible that the crime measure in Di Tella and MacCulloch (2005) serves as a proxy for other crimes (for example, burglary, theft, murder) and social ills such as drugs, loss of social cohesion, and inner-city strife. Thus, because of missing-variable bias, it might not be appropriate to attribute this entire figure to serious assaults alone—but instead as a measure of crime and social disarray in general.

3. DATA

In this study, I collected all 7 years of data from the U.S. General Social Survey (GSS; Davis, Smith, and Marsden 1972–2004) when life satisfaction data are available—1993, 1994, 1996, 1998, 2000, 2002, and 2004. The GSS is administered to approximately 2,800 individuals annually. The relevant question on the survey asks, "Taken all together, how would you say things are these days—would you say that you are very happy, pretty happy, or not too happy?" Following convention, "not too happy" was coded to be "1," "happy" to be "2," and "very happy" to be "3." These data were combined with county-level identifiers so that I know the year and county of the respondent and can augment the GSS data with other county-level data.[2] Overall, the data include 111 different counties, ranging from one to 474 observations

capita. An increase in serious assaults from 388 to 242 per 100,000 represents an increase in the risk of serious assaults of .146 percent. Dividing $266 by .00146 results in an estimate of $182,000 per serious assault. Updating this to 2000 dollars using the consumer price index would result in an estimate of approximately $580,000. Using the hourly wage rate growth from 1975 to 2000 as the inflator would yield an estimate of approximately $550,000.

2. These data are not included in the publicly available General Social Survey (GSS) data set. However, upon request, for a fee, the National Opinion Research Center at the University of Chicago (the GSS research team) will provide that information subject to confidentiality provisions so that individuals are not identified and the geocode designations are not shared with others. These data are available at the level of the primary sampling unit, which means they will identify either a metropolitan area or a nonmetropolitan county, depending upon the population. Because of availability of information for the remaining portion of this project, I converted these into county-level identifiers.

each (with a median of 82 observations per county). Each year a new sample is drawn; thus there are virtually no repeated respondents. Table 1 lists the main variables collected as part of this study. The mean "happiness" score is 2.18. While I have 14,944 cases with subjective happiness scores, this number declines depending upon which variables are included. Nevertheless, there are no significant differences in the means of these variables regardless of which sample is used—that is, there is no apparent selection bias in the various samples reported throughout the paper.

I am interested in three different potential measures of crime. First, violent crime rates are measured from offenses known to police at the county level from the FBI's Uniform Crime Reports (UCR) (Federal Bureau of Investigation 1993–2004; Fox 1976–99).[3] County-level crime rates are available for 14,318 individuals.

Second, respondents are sometimes (but not always) asked, "Is there any area right around here—that is, within a mile—where you would be afraid to walk alone at night?" Out of the 9,954 respondents who were asked that question, about 40.3 percent responded "yes." Once again, those who respond "yes" are expected to have a lower level of well-being, ceteris paribus.

Third, during some years, respondents were asked if they had been the victim of a robbery or burglary during the previous year.[4] These individual victimization events should have an effect on well-being. As shown in Table 1, I have data on burglary and robbery for 3,082 respondents. The reported burglary rate is 4.7 percent, while the robbery rate is 3.2 percent. The GSS reported burglary rate is reasonably close

---

3. I also collected Uniform Crime Report (UCR) data on property crimes reported to police and UCR arrest data for other crimes such as vandalism and drug offenses. I did not include these in the reported results because they are highly correlated with violent crime rates (as were individual crime types within the violent or property crime categories). Thus, in this paper, I report only on violent crime rates—murder, rape, and robbery, which was the best fit.

4. Between 1993 and 1996, respondents were asked about robbery and burglary, "During the last year that is, between last March and now did anyone break into or somehow illegally get into your (apartment/home)?" and "During the last year, did anyone take something directly from you by using force—such as a stickup, mugging, or threat?" Similar questions were asked in 2004, "Next, did any of the following criminal or legal events occur to you since (current month), 2003: (1) A robbery (for example, a mugging or stickup), and (2) Your home burglarized or broken into." While an additional question in 2004 asked about physical assaults (for example, being beaten up, hit, or attacked with a weapon), the sample size is too small to rely upon (for example, only 37 assaults, fewer when the sample is restricted to only cases where all variables are available).

to the National Crime Victims Survey (NCVS) victimization rate. For example, the NCVS victimization rate for household burglary was 4.5 percent (or 5.4 percent if attempted burglaries are included) in 1994 (Perkins and Klaus 1996) and 2.5 percent (or 3.0 percent if attempts are included) in 2004 (Catalano 2005). While the GSS and NCVS rates differ somewhat, so do their definitions. For example, burglary in NCVS would include illegal entry into a garage or shed on someone's property as well as into a hotel room if members of that household were staying at a hotel. It would also include attempted burglaries, but the GSS definition appears to include attempts as well. Thus, the NCVS burglary definition is slightly more expansive. One reason why the GSS rate might be higher, however, is that, because of recall bias, respondents might respond affirmatively to the victimization question even if the event occurred more than 1 year prior to the survey. This telescoping problem is largely overcome in the NCVS through careful survey design in which respondents are interviewed every 6 months and the first interview is thrown out of the sample. On balance, however, the NCVS and GSS burglary estimates are relatively close.

However, the GSS reported robbery rate is significantly higher than that in the NCVS. Compared to the 3.2 percent reported in GSS, the NCVS robbery rate is only .37 percent for individuals 12 or older (or .61 percent if attempted robberies are included) in 1994 and .12 percent (or .2 percent if attempts are included) in 2004 (Catalano 2005). Despite these large differences, the two definitions appear quite similar, as both involve the use or threat of force. Even if I were to include purse snatching and pickpocketing, the NCVS victimization rate would still be considerably less than 1 percent. Additional factors, however, tend to bias the GSS figures downward. First, the GSS definition of robbery does not appear to include attempted robberies. Second, the GSS includes only respondents age 18 or older, and the NCVS includes individuals 12 and older. Restricting robberies to those who are 18 or older reduces the rate of robbery further in NCVS, since 12–17-year-olds have considerably higher robbery rates than the rest of the population. It is not clear why the GSS reported robbery rate is so much higher than that in the NCVS. However, one possibility is that GSS respondents included incidents that NCVS would classify as "theft"—that is, the taking of property without force. For example, including purse snatching, pickpocketing, and thefts over $250 would bring the NCVS victimization rates in line with the GSS robbery rate. Given the fact that NCVS interviewers ask open-ended questions about victimizations and classify the events

Table 1. Subjective Life Satisfaction (Happiness) in the United States, 1993–2004: Description of Variables

Variable	Source and Definition	Cases	Mean	Min	Max
Life satisfaction	GSS	14,944	2.18	1	3
Crime measures:					
Violent crime rate (per 1,000)	UCR; offenses known to police for murder, rape, robbery, and aggravated assault		5.79	0	36.73
Unsafe neighborhood	GSS	14,318	.403	0	1
Burglary victim	GSS	9,954	.047	0	1
Robbery victim	GSS	3,082	.032	0	1
Demographics:	GSS	3,082			
Age	GSS	14,944	45.768	18	99
Household income (2000$)	GSS	13,197	$32,500	$294	$141,038
Work (full time, unemployed, retired, student, housewife)	GSS	14,944	.543, .028, .138, .030, .114	0	1
Status (married, widowed, divorced, separated)	GSS; excluded category is never married and represents 23.1% of sample	14,944	.483, .094, .155, .037	0	1
Single parent	GSS; adult with child < 18 not living with spouse	14,944	.129	0	1

Variable	Source / description	N	Mean	Min	Max
Education (less than high school, high school, less than college, college graduate)	GSS; excluded category is graduate degree and represents 8% of sample	14,944	.155, .534, .068, .163	0	1
Female	GSS	14,944	.558	0	1
Black	GSS	14,944	.137	0	1
Health (excellent, fair, poor)	GSS; remaining 41.2% indicated good health	14,944	.241, .134, .037		
County-level region (Northeast, South, West)	GSS	14,944	.194, .360, .203	0	1
Urban (top 100 SMSAs), Rural	Census; excluded categories are surburban and other urban (cities with population >10,000 but not in top 100 SMSAs)		.241, .100		
Pollution noncompliance	EPA	14,944	.108	0	1
Income equality	Census; ratio of % household income < $15,000 to % household income > $100,000	14,944	2.05	.115	15.7
Homeownership	Census; % owner occupied	14,944	.662	.195	.873

Note. SMSA: standard metropolitan statistical area. GSS: Davis, Smith, and Marsden (1972–2004). UCR: Federal Bureau of Investigation (1993–2004), Fox (1976–99); Census: U.S. Department of Commerce (2000); EPA = Designation of Areas for Air Quality Planning Purposes (40 C.F.R. pt. 81).

into crime types themselves, while the GSS has respondents directly respond to a question about whether they were robbed, this explanation is plausible. It also suggests that the typical robbery in GSS is not as severe as it is in the NCVS and is more akin to petty theft for the vast majority of reported robberies.

Additional demographic variables of individual respondents were collected from the GSS, including household income, age, gender, race, education, and work and marital status. From the county-level matching process, I could identify crime rates from the UCR, relative income from census data (U.S. Department of Commerce 2000), as well as county-level data on population density (for example, rural versus urban), income equity (the ratio of households with incomes under $15,000 compared to those over $100,000), home ownership rates, and pollution.[5] I include these county-level variables because I expect some correlation between the county-level crime rates and other amenities. For example, I expect less crime in areas with a high percentage of home ownership and more crime in highly urbanized areas. However, I also expect there may be an independent effect of urbanization on life satisfaction. Thus, leaving these county-level amenities out of the regression could result in omitted-variable bias.

4. THEORY AND EMPIRICAL APPROACH

Since the approach I follow is well developed elsewhere (and reviewed in Section 2), I only briefly recap my theory and empirical approach. Life satisfaction (or happiness) is assumed to be a proxy for individual utility. As such, I assume that individual utility can be captured by the following equation:

$$U = f(\text{INCOME, CRIME, IND, COUNTY}),$$

where INCOME is household income; CRIME is individual-level objective and subjective risks of victimization, including county-level risk of victimization, perceived neighborhood safety, and actual victimization; IND is individual characteristics (marital status, employment,

5. Following Chay and Greenstone (2005), I identified whether each county was in compliance with total suspended particulates (TSP) levels of pollution. These data are taken from Designation of Areas for Air Quality Planning Purposes, 56 Fed. Reg. 56,694 (November 6, 1991) (codified at 40 C.F.R. pt. 81). In addition, I coded nonattainment for sulfur dioxide, carbon monoxide, ozone, and nitrogen oxide. Since none of these pollution measures were significant, I report only TSP in my regressions.

health, and so on); and COUNTY is county-level amenities other than crime. While I do not observe either utility or its proxy (a life satisfaction score) directly, the GSS survey provides the individual's assessment of life satisfaction in one of three categories, "not too happy," "happy," and "very happy." Thus, I estimate the underlying life satisfaction score using an ordered probit model:

$$\Pr(\text{LIFESATIS}_{ijt} = 1) = \Pr(\beta_1 \text{INCOME}_{it} + \beta_2 \text{CRIME}_{ijt}$$
$$+ \beta_3 \text{IND}_{it} + \beta_4 \text{COUNTY}_{jt} + u_{ijt} \leqslant 1),$$

$$\Pr(\text{LIFESATIS}_{ijt} = 2) = \Pr(1 < \beta_1 \text{INCOME}_{it} + \beta_2 \text{CRIME}_{ijt}$$
$$+ \beta_3 \text{IND}_{it} + \beta_4 \text{COUNTY}_{jt} + u_{ijt} \leqslant 2),$$

and

$$\Pr(\text{LIFESATIS}_{ijt} = 3) = \Pr(2 < \beta_1 \text{INCOME}_{it} + \beta_2 \text{CRIME}_{ijt}$$
$$+ \beta_3 \text{IND}_{it} + \beta_4 \text{COUNTY}_{jt} + u_{ijt} \leqslant 3),$$

where i, j, and t refer to individuals, counties, and years, respectively, and u_{ijt} is assumed to be normally distributed. Note that income and individual-level variables are dimensioned by person and year, while county-level variables vary by county and year.

The coefficient on INCOME is expected to be positive, while the CRIME coefficients should be negative. The first crime variable measures the county-level risk of victimization. This is an objective measure that reflects a relatively wide geographic area (the best I could obtain given data limitations) that would generally encompass where individuals live, work, and shop. Of course, some individuals are at very low risk of victimization, while others have a higher than average risk even within the same county. Thus, I include a second crime variable to capture the subjective assessment of how safe the individual feels in his or her neighborhood. Presumably, being safe in one's neighborhood will affect daily life satisfaction more than being safe elsewhere in the county. I also include a crime variable based on actual victimization for the small percentage of individuals who are asked about victimization on the survey. Finally, I include COUNTY variables for other noncrime characteristics (for example, pollution, poverty) as well as time-dimensioned county dummies to account for both county and time fixed effects. Following Moulton (1990), I estimate the ordered probit using clustered robust standard errors to account for the fact that the survey is clustered by county.

In addition to estimating the coefficients on the CRIME variables, I am interested in understanding their economic significance. For example, I would want to know what it means if I found that a 10 percent increase in crime rate reduces life satisfaction by 2 percent. Following Clark and Oswald (2002) and Moore (2006), I calculate the compensating income variation needed to maintain life satisfaction (utility) while varying crime rates to determine the marginal value of crime.

5. EMPIRICAL RESULTS

5.1. Relationship between Crime and Life Satisfaction

Table 2 reports univariate comparisons of life satisfaction scores for the key variables of interest. Respondents who report living in an unsafe area also report significantly lower life satisfaction scores (2.115) than do those who live in safe areas (2.229). This difference of .114 is significant at $p < .01$. Significant decreases in life satisfaction were also found for individuals who were victimized by burglaries—a reduction of .222 (2.181 versus 1.959, $p < .01$)—and robbery—a reduction of .134 points (2.175 versus 2.041, $p < .05$). Interestingly, these reductions in life satisfaction are close to the .20 reduction found by Michalos and Zumbo (2000) and the .265 point reduction found by Powdthavee (2005) when comparing the happiness of all crime victims (combined) to those who have not been victims of crime (although they were measured on seven- and five-point scales, respectively).

Table 3 examines where victims live. As shown, both robbery and burglary victims are more likely than nonvictims to report living within a mile of an area that is unsafe to walk at night. For example, 3.6 percent of residents who reportedly live in safe areas were burglarized, compared to 6.1 percent of those who reportedly live in unsafe areas.

Table 4 reports on ordered probit regressions using the complete data set including key variables such as crime rates and household income.[6]

6. Note that throughout this paper, I use an ordered probit model. While some authors in the life satisfaction literature use ordered logit models instead, there appears to be no consistency in this literature. According to Wooldridge (2001), since probit assumes a cumulative normal distribution and logit assumes a binomial, the ordered probit is more appropriate when the underlying latent variable is quantitative, while the logit would be appropriate for categories. Viewing happiness as a state of being on a continuum, I choose

Table 2. Comparison of Life Satisfaction Scores by Area Safety and Victimization

	Average Score	Mean Difference	95% Confidence Interval of Difference	Cases
Unsafe:				
0	2.229**			5,941
1	2.115**	.114	.089–.139	4,013
Burglary:				
0	2.181**			2,936
1	1.959**	.222	.118–.326	146
Robbery:				
0	2.175*			2,984
1	2.041*	.134	.008–.260	98

$* p < .05.$
$** p < .01.$

The sign and magnitude of the coefficients of demographic variables are consistent with those found by previous authors. For example, life satisfaction is decreasing in age, but at a decreasing rate (hence the inclusion of an age-squared term as others have used). Work and marital status also have significant effects on life satisfaction. Both higher real income and higher relative income are also positive.

The key variable of interest in Table 4 is the county-level violent crime rate. I show three ordered probit models—first, with violent crime being the only county-level variable. Second, I add county-level variables, while the final column includes county-level variables and time-trended county fixed effects. As expected, the magnitude of the violent crime coefficient decreases when the other county-level variables are included (from $-.010$ to $-.006$), and the significance level also decreases (from $p < .001$ to $p < .105$).[7] This is similar to the finding of Di Tella and MacCulloch (2005), who examine crime rates at the country level and find only marginal significance of crime rates on life satisfaction.

the ordered probit. As most authors find, there is little difference in the estimates when using the ordered logit or the ordered probit. I do find, however, that the magnitude of the coefficients on crime are generally larger using the logit—hence my approach is conservative. Since the GSS is based on a random sample of locations (not individuals), all reported levels of statistical significance are based on clustered standard errors. I also estimated these regressions using ordinary least squares. Although not reported here (and available upon request from the author), I find no substantive differences in the signs or significance levels of coefficients.

7. Note that while the county-level variables are correlated, the correlation coefficients generally range from .2 to .4; none are over .5.

Table 3. Crime Rates by Perceived Area Safety

	Safe Area		Unsafe Area		
	N	%	N	%	Significance[a]
Burglary:					
0	1,506	96.4	1,012	93.9	.002
1	56	3.6	66	6.1	
Robbery:					
0	1,530	97.9	1,036	96.1	.005
1	32	2.0	42	3.9	

[a] Analysis of variance.

Table 5 reports on a restricted set of data where the question about neighborhood safety was available. First, I note that while the sample size is smaller than Table 4, there are virtually no differences in any of the mean values of the variables or in the distribution of counties represented in the two data sets. The first column reproduces the second column of Table 4 using this smaller data set but an identical regression model. While there are no important differences in the size of the coefficients when comparing this with the larger data set, and the coefficient for the violent crime rate is reduced slightly from −.006 to −.005, the significance level is reduced from $p < .012$ to $p < .113$. The second and third columns report data on the variable of interest in Table 5—whether or not the respondent reportedly lives in an unsafe neighborhood. Whether or not I control for county-level trends, this variable has a negative and highly significant coefficient in both models ($p < .001$), which indicates that individuals who live within a mile of an area where they would feel unsafe walking alone at night have lower levels of life satisfaction, all else equal. The variable for county-level violent crime rate is still negative in Table 5, but it is not statistically significant.

Table 6 reports the results of similar regressions using all observations where actual burglary and robbery data were available. Once again, the mean values of the variables in this restricted sample are virtually identical to those in the larger samples (although the years are now restricted to 1993, 1994, and 2004). The first column of Table 6 replicates the middle column of Table 5 using the sample of 2,260 and once again indicates that most coefficients are unchanged. One important difference, however, is the coefficient on the variable for unsafe neighborhood, which is now of smaller magnitude (−.047 versus −.106) and no longer statistically significant ($p < .469$ versus $p < .000$). The coefficient on the burglary variable in the next two columns is always negative and significant ($p < .05$), while the variables for violent crime rate and unsafe area remain statistically insignificant. Surprisingly, the robbery variable is not significant. However, recall that the GSS robbery rate appears to be five to 10 times higher than NCVS victimization rates. The fact that robbery did not affect life satisfaction is consistent with the hypothesis that GSS respondents who indicate that they were robbed were often responding to minor incidents such as having their pockets picked or even larceny.

The fact that statistical significance of the variables for violent crime rate and unsafe area decreases with the sample size is not necessarily surprising, as larger samples reduce variability and increase significance levels, all else equal. More important is the question of the economic significance of these variables—a subject to which I turn next.

5.2. Interpretation of Regression Coefficients

Coefficients in an ordered probit regression are not easily interpretable, and thus one cannot directly compare the magnitude of the coefficients. However, sensitivity analysis can be conducted to assess the effect that changing any of the independent variables has on the life satisfaction score. This is shown in Table 7 for our key variables of interest. At the mean violent crime rate of 5.75 per 1,000 residents, the expected life satisfaction score is 2.173. An increase or decrease in the violent crime rate of 10 percent changes the expected life satisfaction score by only .002 (about .09 percent of the mean score of 2.173). Doubling the violent crime rate from 5.75 to 11.5 decreases life satisfaction by .017—a decrease of .8 percent. As shown in the third column, however, the 95 percent confidence interval on these estimated changes in life satisfaction crosses over zero, as the significance level on this coefficient is only $p < .105$. The effect of moving from an area perceived to be safe to an unsafe area reduces life satisfaction by .060 (a reduction in life satisfaction of about 2.3 percent from the base of 2.226 when living in a safe area). Thus, perceived neighborhood safety has a much larger effect on life satisfaction than does the objective county-level crime rate. Not surprisingly, an actual criminal event has an even more significant effect on life satisfaction. The expected reduction in life satisfaction from a burglary is .173 from a base of 2.151—a decrease of 8.0 percent, which is more than three times the effect of moving from a safe to unsafe area.

To put these numbers into perspective, the survey asks respondents to assess their health using a four-point ordinal scale with the responses

Table 4. Ordered Probit Regressions: Full Sample

	Mean	Excluding County-Level Variables		Excluding County Trends		Including County Trends	
		Coefficient	p-Value	Coefficient	p-Value	Coefficient	p-Value
Violent crime	5.752	−.010	.000	−.006	.012	−.006	.105
Age	44.938	−.016	.000	−.016	.000	−.016	.000
Age^2	2,297	.0002	.000	.0002	.000	.0002	.000
ln(Real income)	9.974	.062	.001	.077	.000	.083	.000
Relative income	.828	.051	.047	.034	.222	.031	.299
Full-time	.563	.065	.043	.063	.051	.062	.067
Unemployed	.028	−.274	.000	−.265	.000	−.267	.000
Retired	.126	.158	.002	.155	.002	.162	.000
Student	.028	.127	.062	.139	.041	.132	.002
Housewife	.107	.099	.016	.096	.023	.096	.062
Married	.488	.422	.000	.409	.000	.403	.026
Widowed	.082	−.167	.001	−.176	.001	−.187	.000
Divorced	.159	−.099	.011	−.104	.008	−.110	.005
Separated	.038	−.256	.000	−.260	.000	−.266	.000
Single parent	.131	−.045	.221	−.053	.151	−.055	.146
Less than high school	.143	−.075	.098	−.089	.053	−.100	.033
High school graduate	.533	−.085	.026	−.096	.012	−.099	.011

Less than college	.069	−.040	.355	−.050	.252	−.053	.252
College graduate	.171	−.010	.819	−.013	.771	−.023	.599
Female	.548	.056	.011	.058	.008	.056	.012
Black	.135	−.104	.008	−.091	.024	−.102	.011
Northeast	.194	−.062	.091	−.047	.216	−.152	.004
South	.356	.075	.009	.066	.027	.007	.878
West	.217	−.044	.108	−.028	.369	−.069	.237
Excellent health	.243	0.394	.000	.394	.000	.392	.000
Fair health	.131	−.391	.000	−.393	.000	−.410	.000
Poor health	.036	−.655	.000	−.658	.000	−.675	.000
TSP (pollution)	.111			.018	.716	.069	.401
Urban	.247			−.069	.012	−.053	.125
Rural	.083			−.086	.055	−.024	.738
Income equity	1.882			.024	.002	.020	.145
Homeownership	.661			.154	.225	.168	.315
Trend	5.828	.007	.056	.007	.039	: :	: :
County trends included?			No		No		Yes
Cut point = 1		−.710		−.442		−.468	
Cut point = 2		1.169		1.439		1.436	
Pseudo-R^2			.0803		.0813		.0910

Note. The dependent variable is life satisfaction. Significance levels are based on clustered standard errors. $N = 12{,}632$.

Table 5. Ordered Probit Regressions: Including Question on Area Safety

	Mean	Replication of Table 4		Excluding County Trends		Including County Trends	
		Coefficient	p-Value	Coefficient	p-Value	Coefficient	p-Value
Violent crime	5.752	−.005	.113	−.004	.217	−.007	.157
Unsafe area	.403	. . .	. . .	−.106	.000	−.120	.000
Age	44.983	−.012	.008	−.012	.008	−.012	.008
Age²	2,301	.0002	.001	.0002	.001	.0002	.001
ln(Real income)	9.968	.058	.023	.055	.031	.063	.018
Relative income	.822	.047	.177	.045	.194	.035	.358
Full-time	.563	.086	.031	.084	.035	.085	.041
Unemployed	.029	−.255	.001	−.260	.001	−.277	.001
Retired	.127	.202	.001	.203	.001	.211	.001
Student	.028	.142	.164	.142	.165	.129	.232
Housewife	.108	.151	.004	.149	.005	.146	.006
Married	.486	.364	.000	.360	.000	.353	.000
Widowed	.082	−.241	.000	−.243	.000	−.270	.000
Divorced	.161	−.136	.007	−.137	.007	−.156	.003
Separated	.038	−.269	.001	−.273	.000	−.290	.000
Single parent	.133	−.073	.150	−.076	.134	−.083	.107
Less than high school	.147	−.115	.066	−.115	.065	−.135	.035
High school graduate	.529	−.148	.004	−.147	.004	−.157	.003

Less than college	.068	-.126	.034	-.122	.040	-.126	.045
College graduate	.169	-.078	.206	-.077	.209	-.102	.097
Female	.542	.061	.038	.089	.002	.097	.001
Black	.136	-.138	.002	-.142	.002	-.159	.001
Northeast	.192	-.095	.033	-.095	.032	-.270	.000
South	.358	.010	.768	.016	.641	-.144	.018
West	.217	-.090	.028	-.086	.036	-.221	.005
Excellent health	.307	.413	.000	.408	.000	.405	.000
Fair health	.167	-.402	.000	-.400	.000	-.421	.000
Poor health	.045	-.646	.000	-.642	.000	-.672	.000
TSP (pollution)	.111	.072	.254	.074	.242	.102	.332
Urban	.247	-.090	.001	-.075	.006	-.078	.027
Rural	.082	-.053	.332	-.060	.278	-.012	.895
Income equity	1.888	.022	.025	.022	.022	.020	.281
Homeownership	.661	.080	.615	.071	.657	-.171	.452
Trend	5.834	.013	.003	.012	.007		
County trends included?			No		No		Yes
Cut point = 1		-.616		-.674		-.981	
Cut point = 2		1.245		1.192		.920	
Pseudo-R^2			.0908		.0917		.1065

Note. The dependent variable is life satisfaction. Significance levels are based on clustered standard errors. $N = 8,444$.

Table 6. Ordered Probit Regressions: Including Individual Victimization

	Mean	Replication of Table 5		Including Only Violent Crime		Including County-Level Variables	
		Coefficient	p-Value	Coefficient	p-Value	Coefficient	p-Value
Violent crime	5.698	−.004	.645	−.004	.689	−.017	.115
Unsafe area	.407	−.047	.467	−.042	.521	−.065	.327
Burglary victim	.046	. . .	. . .	−.310	.017	−.351	.010
Robbery victim	.027	. . .	. . .	.022	.885	.070	.655
Age	45.253	−.014	.119	−.015	.114	−.015	.117
Age^2	2,324	.0002	.038	.0002	.037	.0002	.020
ln(Real income)	10.010	.092	.031	.091	.033	.111	.008
Relative Income	.898	.107	.026	.105	.030	.084	.079
Full-time	.549	.072	.317	.058	.422	.089	.244
Unemployed	.033	−.090	.536	−.094	.510	−.069	.659
Retired	.131	.189	.137	.181	.151	.145	.267
Student	.029	.113	.471	.098	.529	.086	.603
Housewife	.112	.184	.058	.176	.068	.183	.068
Married	.522	.135	.057	.130	.068	.120	.131
Widowed	.076	−.377	.009	−.392	.007	−.376	.014
Divorced	.154	−.203	.030	−.213	.024	−.248	.011
Separated	.034	−.430	.002	−.435	.001	−.454	.001

Single parent	.114	−.046	.613	−.033	.718	−.051	.578
Less than high school	.149	−.046	.693	−.050	.666	−.072	.565
High school graduate	.537	−.078	.385	−.076	.395	−.112	.251
Less than college	.062	−.093	.411	−.098	.386	−.078	.556
College graduate	.160	−.021	.858	−.016	.891	−.072	.567
Female	.553	.130	.018	.124	.028	.122	.034
Black	.127	−.230	.011	−.226	.013	−.186	.075
Northeast	.178	−.173	.033	−.166	.039	−.303	.008
South	.372	.007	.916	.009	.889	−.098	.246
West	.215	−.084	.174	−.076	.218	−.273	.011
Excellent health	.295	.403	.000	.399	.000	.388	.000
Fair health	.173	−.434	.000	−.436	.000	−.474	.000
Poor health	.042	−.561	.000	−.538	.000	−.584	.000
TSP (pollution)	.101	−.034	.772	−.047	.689	.161	.375
Urban	.226	−.022	.760	−.015	.830	.104	.208
Rural	.095	−.127	.286	−.126	.306	.018	.894
Income equity	1.975	.029	.194	.031	.172	.031	.258
Homeownership	.662	.442	.215	.454	.196	.307	.534
Trend	5.207	.008	.122	.008	.142		
County trends included?			No		No		Yes
Cut point = 1		−.102		−.133		−.246	
Cut point = 2		1.785		1.758		1.712	
Pseudo-R^2			.0892		.0908		.1202

Note. The dependent variable is life satisfaction. Significance levels are based on clustered standard errors. $N = 2{,}260$.

Table 7. Sensitivity Analysis: Effect of Crime Variables on Life Satisfaction

	Score	Change in Score from Base Case		Compensating Income ($)	
		Mean	95% Confidence Interval	Mean	95% Confidence Interval
Violent crime:					
−100% (0)	2.191	−.017	{−.037, .003}	−4,054	{−7,655, 918}
−75% (1.44)	2.186	−.013	{−.027, .003}	−3,118	{−6,045, 685}
−25% (4.31)	2.178	−.004	{−.009, .001}	−1,098	{−2,250, 227}
−10% (5.18)	2.175	−.002	{−.004, .000}	−443	{−923, 90}
Mean (5.75)	2.173	· · ·		· · ·	
+10% (6.32)	2.172	.002	{.000, .004}	449	{−89, 961}
+25% (7.19)	2.169	.004	{−.001, .009}	1,154	{−224, 2,510}
+75% (10.06)	2.160	.013	{−.003, .027}	3,649	{−663, 8,429}
+100% (11.5)	2.156	.017	{−.003, .037}	5,003	{−880, 11,931}
+200% (17.25)	2.139	.035	{−.007, .073}	11,182	{−1,724, 30,538}
Unsafe area:					
0	2.226	· · ·		· · ·	
1	2.165	.060	{.030, .091}	34,322	{12,745, 69,488}
Burglary:					
0	2.151	· · ·		· · ·	
1	1.977	.173	{.042, .304}	83,772	{10,354, 322,261}
Health:					
Excellent	2.327	−.190	{−.254, −.125}	−18,226	{−19,992, 15,018}
Good	2.138	· · ·		· · ·	
Fair	1.903	.234	{.169, .298}	161,060	{80,090, 304,370}
Poor	1.849	.288	{.142, .433}	276,624	{57,511, 1,082,080}

Note. Violent crime is estimated from Table 4, unsafe area from Table 5, and burglary and health from Table 6. All estimates are based on the full ordered probit models (the columns including country trends).

"poor," "fair," "good," and "excellent." In Table 6, going from good health to fair health reduces life satisfaction by .234 from a base of 2.138—a reduction in life satisfaction of 10.9 percent. Moving from good to fair health is also a significant change in health status. For example, Kaplan and Camacho (1983) estimated that those who assessed their health status as fair had a 163 percent relative risk of mortality in the following 9 years compared to someone who assessed their health to be good.[8] Thus, a burglary is only slightly less harmful to life satisfaction than moving from good to fair health. On the other hand, moving from good to poor health (which in Kaplan and Camacho [1983] implies a 259 percent higher relative risk of mortality) is about 66 percent more harmful to life satisfaction than is a burglary incident (.288 versus .173).

While the estimates in this paper suggest that being burglarized has nearly the impact that moving from good to fair health has on life satisfaction, I do not know if this comparison is transitory or permanent. While the survey questions are asked at one point in time, it is likely that someone in fair health will remain so for a long time and, as indicated above, will have a higher likelihood of mortality over time. Thus, it is possible that currently being in a worse health state has a longer lasting impact on life satisfaction than being burglarized within the past 12 months. However, there is also evidence that criminal victimization may affect individuals over the long term. While this is especially true for victims of violent crime (see, for example, Kilpatrick et al. 1992), there is also evidence suggesting longer-term implications for victims of property crime. For example, Dugan (1999) found that burglary victims were more likely to move from their homes—something that is costly in terms of both dollars and presumably social relationships. In addition, there is evidence that houses victimized by a burglary have significantly higher chances of being burglarized again than does the average home (see, for example, Farrell 1995). Thus, being burglarized might indeed have long-term implications for quality of life. However, the extent to which these effects are short term versus long term is beyond the scope

---

8. Self-assessed measures of health have long been validated as having predictive power for both physician assessments and long-term morbidity and mortality. While I am unaware of any narrative description of what it typically means to move from one health state to another, one study following up on mortality over a 9-year period following self-assessed health found the age-adjusted relative mortality risk of being in fair health was 1.63 compared to good health. Thus, those in fair health were 63 percent more likely to die within 9 years than were those in good health. These figures are computed from table 2 of Kaplan and Camacho (1983).

of this paper, as the data do not provide us with any information to answer that question.

5.3. Economic Significance of Regression Coefficients

As mentioned earlier, Moore (2006) estimated the compensating income required to maintain constant utility (as measured by the life satisfaction score) while moving from a safe to an unsafe neighborhood. Using the same methodology, I can convert the regression coefficients in Tables 4–6 into estimates of compensating income for both my crime and health measures. These are shown in the last column of Table 7. In the case of the county-level crime rate, living in a county with a 10 percent higher violent crime rate would require an estimated $449 in annual compensation to maintain the same level of life satisfaction. Of course, as shown in Table 4, the coefficient on the county-level crime rate is not statistically significant at the conventional 5 percent level ($p < .105$). Thus, the 95 percent confidence interval for this change ranges from −$89 to $961 in compensation; while I can compute a compensating income variation for living in a county with a relatively high violent crime rate, I cannot with confidence state that this is any different than zero.[9] Even doubling the violent crime rate would require only $5,003 (−$880 to $11,931) in compensating household income annually. Despite their lack of statistical significance, the point estimates are instructive if only for their relative magnitude. In comparison, Cohen et al. (2004) utilized a stated-preference survey to estimate the public's willingness to pay for reduced crime. The average willingness to pay for a 10 percent reduction in murder was estimated to be $146 per household in 2000, while the average was $126 for rape, $121 for assaults, and $110 for armed robbery. Assuming I can combine these figures (that is, ignoring income effects), the willingness to pay for a 10 percent reduction in violent crime is thus estimated to be $503—nearly identical to the point estimate of $449 shown in Table 7.

On the basis of the regression coefficient in Table 5, moving from a safe to an unsafe neighborhood would require $34,322 in annual com-

9. While the valuation of compensating income has been derived from the coefficient estimate in Table 4, similar estimates can be made from Tables 5 and 6 using the smaller samples. In Table 5, the regression coefficient of −.007 corresponds to a point estimate of $688 (95 percent confidence interval between −$249 and $1,616), while in Table 6, the coefficient of −.017 results in an estimate of $1,070 (−$238 to $2,551). While somewhat larger, they all cross zero, and the point estimates are within the bounds of all other confidence intervals.

pensation (ranging from $12,745 to $69,488 based on the 95 percent confidence interval) for the average household. Note that this is also very similar to the estimated $20,000 value based on the ESS in Moore (2006). Although not shown in Table 7, I can compute the income compensation from the smaller sample in Table 6. Controlling for actual victimization, the coefficient estimate on the variable for unsafe neighborhood increases from $-.120$ (Table 5) to $-.065$ (Table 6). The corresponding compensation value decreases to $7,447 (ranging from $-$5,594 to $30,912) and is no longer significantly different from zero. Thus, this smaller sample calls into question whether, at the margin, households require compensating income to live in an unsafe area. Perhaps this is not surprising given the fact that there is evidence that housing prices and rents are lower in high-crime areas (see, for example, Thaler 1978; Hoehn, Berger, and Blomquist 1987)—individuals might largely be compensated through the housing market, and thus at the margin those who live in unsafe areas are no less happy than those who live in (more costly) safer areas.

Finally, the compensating income for a burglary is $83,772. While this is considerably higher than any previous estimates of the "cost" of a burglary, the 95 percent confidence interval ($10,354–$322,261) is relatively large given the small number of burglaries in the sample (104 out of 2,260). Cohen et al. (2004) estimated the willingness to pay to reduce burglary to be $29,000 per victimization—a figure that is also within the 95 percent confidence interval reported in Table 7.

To put these figures into perspective and to validate the results I obtain from this sample, I can compare the compensating incomes for crime to those of varying health states. For example, going from good health to fair health would require annual compensation of $161,060 to maintain life satisfaction, while moving from good health to poor health would require $276,624 in annual compensation. These figures are two to three times the amount of compensating income for a burglary. In comparison, Clark and Oswald (2002) estimate the value in the United Kingdom of moving from excellent to good health to be £12,000 per month, and moving from excellent to fair health to be £41,000 in 1992. On the basis of the exchange rate at the time, these are equivalent to annual values of $280,000 and $960,000, respectively—values that are in line with the value of health found in this study.

6. CONCLUDING REMARKS

This paper reports on an attempt to disentangle the effect of crime on life satisfaction. Using survey results from over 12,000 individuals between 1993 and 2004, I find evidence that individuals in high-crime areas are relatively less satisfied with life than those who live in low-crime counties—even after controlling for other county amenities such as population density, home ownership, and pollution. Once I control for perceived neighborhood safety, recent experiences with crime, and county-level fixed effects, however, this finding is no longer statistically significant at conventional levels ($p < .105$). Regardless of the statistical significance, the effect of the crime rate on life satisfaction is relatively small. For example, decreasing the violent crime rate by 10 percent from its mean improves life satisfaction by only about .002 on a 3.0 scale—the equivalent of no more than a few hundred dollars annually if I monetize this figure. In the most extreme comparison, the difference between the expected life satisfaction score for someone living in an area where the risk of violent crime is about 1.4 per 1,000 (about the 10th percentile of counties) versus 17.25 per 1,000 (about the 95th percentile) is only .047 on a 3.0 scale. In contrast, the difference between someone who is in good health versus excellent health is .190, and the difference between good health and poor health is .288. Put differently, changing health status is between four and six times as important for life satisfaction as moving from the safest to the least safe county in the United States.

Perceived neighborhood safety is relatively more important than county-level crime rates. Living within a mile of an area perceived to be unsafe reduces life satisfaction by .060 relative to not living that close to an unsafe area. However, controlling for actual victimization in a smaller sample once again reduces the significance level of this finding to $p < .10$, which calls into question the strength of the results. One reason we might not observe any reduction in life satisfaction for those who live in unsafe neighborhoods is the fact that these same individuals are already compensated for this higher risk of victimization through lower housing and rental prices. Thus, higher disposable income might offset the effect of less safety. In addition, it is likely that people self-select into neighborhoods on the basis of both their personal preferences and their financial constraints. Thus, people who are willing to bear more risk will live in riskier neighborhoods and enjoy other amenities (for example, being closer to the city center) in exchange. Related to this is the fact that individuals adapt in their avoidance and prevention behaviors. Thus, by installing burglar alarms, people will fear crime less even though they live in less safe neighborhoods. All of these reasons are plausible explanations for the finding that living in an unsafe neighborhood ultimately has little effect on daily life satisfaction for the majority of Americans.

The most significant finding is the effect of criminal victimization. Burglary victims report a life satisfaction score that is .173 lower than those who had not been burglarized in the previous 12 months—a magnitude comparable to moving from excellent to good health. Put in dollar terms, I estimate the compensating income value for a household burglary to be $83,772 (ranging from $10,353 to $322,261 based on a 95 percent confidence interval)—a figure that compares to the most recent willingness-to-pay estimates of $29,000 per victimization.

Despite the apparent salience of crime in open-ended opinion polls, I find that crime is able to explain only a small portion of the variation in individual well-being. It is one thing to ask the public about what they believe to be the most important policy issues facing their community but quite another to ask them about the most important issues they personally face in their daily lives. Thus, despite the fact that crime rates very high in terms of community-level issues, it does not appear to be a major factor affecting day-to-day life satisfaction for the majority of the U.S. population.

REFERENCES

Blakely, Robin M. 2007. Community Issues in New York State: What's Important? *Rural New York Minute.* http://cardi.cce.cornell.edu/images/UserFiles/July_2007.pdf.

Blanchflower, David G., and Andrew J. Oswald. 2004. Money, Sex and Happiness: An Empirical Study. *Scandinavian Journal of Economics* 106: 393–415.

Catalano, Shannan M. 2005. *Criminal Victimization, 2004.* Bureau of Justice Statistics National Crime Victimization Survey. Report No. NCJ 210674. Washington, D.C.: U.S. Department of Justice.

Chay, Kenneth Y., and Michael Greenstone. 2005. Does Air Quality Matter? Evidence from the Housing Market. *Journal of Political Economy* 113: 376–424.

Clark, Andrew E., and Andrew J. Oswald. 2002. A Simple Statistical Method for Measuring How Life Events Affect Happiness. *International Journal of Epidemiology* 31:1139–44.

Cohen, Mark A. 2005. *The Costs of Crime and Justice*. New York: Routledge.

———. 2007. Valuing Crime Control Benefits Using Stated Preference Approaches. Vanderbilt Law and Economics Research Paper No. 08–09. Vanderbilt University, Owen Graduate School of Management, Nashville. http://ssrn.com/abstract = 10910456.

Cohen, Mark A., Roland T. Rust, and Sara Steen. 2002. *Measuring Public Perception of Appropriate Prison Sentences*. Report to the National Institute of Justice. NCJ No. 199365. Washington, D.C.: U.S. Department of Justice. http://www.ncjrs.org/pdffiles1/nij/grants/199365.pdf.

Cohen, Mark A., Roland Rust, Sara Steen, and Simon Tidd. 2004. Willingness-to-Pay for Crime Control Programs. *Criminology* 42:86–106.

Davis, James A., Tom W. Smith, and Peter V. Marsden. 1972–2004. General Social Surveys (computer file). ICPSR No. 4295. Ann Arbor, Mich.: Inter-university Consortium for Political and Social Research.

Di Tella, Rafael, and Robert MacCulloch. 2006. Some Uses of Happiness Data in Economics. *Journal of Economic Perspectives* 20:25–46.

———. 2005. Gross National Happiness as an Answer to the Easterlin Paradox? Working paper. Harvard Business School, Boston. http://ssrn.com/abstract = 707405.

Dolan, Paul, Graham Loomes, Tessa Peasgood, and Aki Tsuchiya. 2005. Estimating the Intangible Victim Costs of Violent Crime. *British Journal of Criminology* 45:958–76.

Dugan, Laura. 1999. The Effect of Criminal Victimization on a Household's Moving Decision. *Criminology* 37:903–930.

Easterlin, Richard A. 2001. Income and Happiness: Towards a Unified Theory. *Economic Journal* 111:465–84.

Eid, Michael, and Ed Diener. 2004. Global Judgments of Subjective Well-Being: Situational Variability and Long-Term Stability. *Social Indicators Research* 65:245–63.

Farrell, Graham. 1995. Preventing Repeat Victimization. Pp. 469–534 in *Building a Safer Society: Strategic Approaches to Crime Prevention,* edited by Michel Tonry and David Farrington. Chicago: University of Chicago Press.

Federal Bureau of Investigation. 1993–2004. Uniform Crime Reports, County Level Arrest and Offenses (computer file). ICPSR No. 8703. Ann Arbor, Mich.: Inter-university Consortium for Political and Social Research.

Fox, James Alan. 1976–1999. Uniform Crime Reports, Supplementary Homicide Reports (computer file). ICPSR No. 3180. Ann Arbor, Mich.: Inter-university Consortium for Political and Social Research.

Hoehn, John P., Mark C. Berger, and Glenn C. Blomquist. 1987. A Hedonic Model of Interregional Wages, Rents, and Amenity Values. *Journal of Regional Science* 27:605–20.

Kahneman, Daniel, and Alan B. Krueger. 2006. Developments in the Measurement of Subjective Well-Being. *Journal of Economic Perspectives* 20:3–24.

Kaplan, George A., and Terry Camacho. 1983. Perceived Health and Mortality: A Nine-Year Follow-up of the Human Population Laboratory Cohort. *American Journal of Epidemiology* 117:292–304.

Kilpatrick, Dean G., Christine N. Edmunds, and Anne Seymour. 1992. *Rape in America: A Report to the Nation.* Arlington, Va.: National Victim Center.

Kollodge, Bonnie. 2007. Crime, Transportation Top Problems for Region. News release. St. Paul, Minn.: Metropolitan Council. February 5. http://www.metrocouncil.org/news/2007/news_561.htm.

Krueger, Alan B., and David Schkade. 2007. The Reliability of Subjective Well-Being Measures. IZA Discussion Paper No. 2724. Institute for the Study of Labor, Bonn. http://ssrn.com/abstract = 982115.

Michalos, Alex C., and Bruno D. Zumbo. 2000. Criminal Victimization and the Quality of Life. *Social Indicators Research* 50:245–95.

Moore, Simon Christopher. 2006. The Value of Reducing Fear: An Analysis Using the European Social Survey. *Applied Economics* 38:115–17.

Moulton, Brent R. 1990. An Illustration of a Pitfall in Estimating the Effects of Aggregate Variables on Micro Units. *Review of Economics and Statistics* 72: 334–38.

Perkins, Craig, and Patsy Klaus. 1996. *Criminal Victimization, 1994.* Bureau of Justice Statistics National Crime Victimization Survey. Bulletin No. NCJ 158022. Washington, D.C.: U.S. Department of Justice.

Powdthavee, Nattavudh. 2005. Unhappiness and Crime: Evidence from South Africa. *Economica* 72:531–47.

Thaler, Richard. 1978. A Note on the Value of Crime Control: Evidence from the Property Market. *Journal of Urban Economics* 5:137–45.

U.S. Department of Commerce. 2000. Bureau of Census. Census of Population and Housing (computer file). ICPSR No. 13402. Ann Arbor, Mich.: Inter-university Consortium for Political and Social Research.

van Praag, Bernard M. S., and Barbara Baarsma. 2005. Using Happiness Surveys to Value Intangibles: The Case of Airport Noise. *Economic Journal* 115: 224–46.

Wooldridge, Jeffrey M. 2001. *Econometric Analysis of Cross Section and Panel Data.* Cambridge, Mass.: MIT Press.

Index

adaptation, hedonic: adaptation-resistant consumption, 117–120, 125–129; altruistic and moral motives in, 207; capabilities, 206; defined, 99–100, 198–199; emotional and experiential variety in, 206; lacks in measuring of, 205; myth of "Making Whole," 207; preferences *versus* happiness, 202–205; reality of, 199–202; set point theory, 221–222; taxation and, 316–319
Americans with Disabilities Act of 1990, 38
Apology (Socrates), 91
Aristotle: on negative emotions, 94; on pleasure, 84–85
Autobiography (Mill), 107, 108

Bentham, Jeremy: on happiness, 82; Mill on, 83; pain-pleasure seeking, 2, 95–99, 102; philosophers on, 83–84; on well-being, 257–259
Benthamism, 100, 102, 103
bereavement and happiness: concepts in, 222–223; conclusions, 241–244; discussion, 217–222; econometric studies in, 223–224; philosophers on, 94–95; psychological distress and income, 245; survey results in, 226–241; surveys of mental well-being, 225–226
Brave New World (Huxley), 190
British Household Panel Survey (BHPS), 6–10, 224–228, 231, 238

capability damages, 175–181. *See also* disabilities; hedonic losses, legal judgments for
Central Human Capabilities, 110–111
"Character of the Happy Warrior" (Wordsworth), 89, 108–110
Cicero, 94, 102
Civil Rights Act of 1964, 37–38
Clark, Candace, 98
communitas, 140–141
compassion for others, 95–97
compensatory damages. *See* bereavement

and happiness; hedonic losses, legal judgments for
consumption: adaptation-resistant, 117–120, 125–129; inequality and, 36–37; inherently evaluable, 120–125; variables, 120–125
Cornwell, David (John le Carré), 101, 103
cost-benefit analysis and happiness research: author's views of, 256–266; compensating variations as metric of change in, 267–269; conclusion, 288; discussion, 253–255, 265–269; hedonic-treadmill problem and, 284–286; literature on subjective well-being (SWB) and, 269–279; SWB and policy analysis, 279–288; weak welfarism and, 255–265
crime and life satisfaction: conclusion, 350–351; discussion, 325–326; economic significance of regression coefficients, 348–349; interpretation of regression coefficients, 339–348; life satisfaction and, 336–339; literature review, 326–329; National Crime Victims Survey (NCVS), 331–334, 339; relationship between, 336–339; theory and empirical approach, 334–336; U.S. General Social Survey (GSS) data, 329–334; Uniform Crime Reports (UCR), 330

dancing, 136, 140–141. *See also* movement and joy
Darwin, Charles, 137
Dawkins, Richard, 138
death, alleviating pain in, 107. *See also* bereavement and happiness; hedonic losses
disabilities: British Household Panel Survey, 318–319; compensation for, 175–181, 282–284; hedonic measures' misses, 205–207; juries' task in, 211–213; money amount determination, 210–211; physical integrity and, 264; ranking injuries, 208–210; scale recalibration with, 200–202; taxation and, 316–319; time trade-off (TTO) method, 202–203; valuing

pain and suffering, 191–197, 207–213, 283–284. *See also* adaptation, hedonic; hedonic losses, legal judgments for
diversity and happiness, 37–38, 151–152. *See also* General Social Survey (GSS)
Dolan, Paul, 5–26, 104
Durkheim, Emile, 135–136, 140

Easterlin, Richard, 2, 123, 272; Easterlin paradox, 123
economy, stimulating to increase happiness, 125–129
Elster, Jon, 99
Emile (Rousseau), 97–98
emotional harm. *See* bereavement and happiness; hedonic losses, legal judgments for
emotions, positive, 92–95
European Social Survey (ESS), 328

Family and Medical Leave Act of 1993, 38
fascism, 148
Frank, Robert, 311–314
free-rider problems, 138–139
Frontiers of Justice (Nussbaum), 104

General Health Questionnaire (GHQ), 7, 273
General Social Survey (GSS): aggregate trends in happiness in, 38–51; correcting for question order effects in, 74–77
group activity as technique of ecstasy, 139–143, 149–150
group selection, 137–139

happiness: Allardt on, 89–90; approach, 1–2; Aristotle on, 88–89; assessing trends in, 51–57; Bentham on, 82; decline in inequality of, 67–74; defined by philosophers, 88–92; determinants of, 15; and disabilities, 173; distinction in, 117; emotions, positive, 92–95; General Social Survey (GSS), 38–39; health and, 137–139, 173, 175–181; hedonic adaptation, 99–100, 116, 316–319; marriage and, 15, 56, 135, 165, 172; moment-by-moment measures of, 178, 188–189; movement and, 139–143, 149–150; multilevel selection and, 137–139; Prichard on, 89; trends in, 38–51; U.S. trends, 41; and unemployment, 320. *See also* life satisfaction
happiness and philosophy: adaptation, 99–100; aggregation across persons, 103–104; happiness, defined, 88–92; life

choices and actions, 100–103; life satisfaction questions, 86–88; objective-list approach, 104–106; pain-pleasure questions, 95–99; philosophers' definitions of pleasure, 80–86; positive emotions, 92–95; subjective states analysis, 106–108
happiness, increasing sustainability of: discussion, 125–129; hedonomic approach to, 115–117; promoting adaptation-resistant consumption, 117–119; promoting inherently evaluable consumption, 120–125; race and, 54
happiness inequality, trends in U.S., 36–38
happiness measures: global questions and, 200; scale recalibration, 200–202. *See also specific surveys and indices*
Harsanyi, John, 11, 21, 96–97
Having, Loving, Being (Allardt), 89–90
health and happiness: disabilities, 173; natural selection, 137–139; pain and suffering, 175–181. *See also* death, alleviating pain in; pain and suffering, valuing
hedonic adaptation. *See* adaptation, hedonic
hedonic damages, 158
hedonic losses, legal judgments for: adaptation, 169–170; adaptation neglect and hedonic forecasting errors, 165–166; capability damages, 175–181; determining damages in, 210–211; doctrine of damages, 159–161; enduring *versus* illusory losses, 166–168; establishing guidelines for, 184–186; establishing monetary equivalents, 159–161; failure to focus, 170–172; failures of affective forecasting, 168–169; hedonic measures' misses, 205–208; juries' hedonic judgment errors, 173–175; meaning and, 190; measuring, 161–163; relative economic position and, 183–190; resilience and measurement, 164–165; translating into money, 182–184; willingness to accept, 161–163; willingness to pay, 161–163, 186–187
hedonic-treadmill problem, 284–286
hedonomic approach, 115–117
hive hypothesis: activities that enable, 139–143; differing from fascism, 147; early psychologists and, 143–145; evolutionarily informed methods, 137–139; movement and joy as cohesiveness measure, 139–143; policy implications of, 147–152; transcending the self, 145–147
hive psychology and public policy, 149–152

Hume, John, 101, 103
Huxley, Aldous, 190

income inequality, 36–38
income and life satisfaction as well-being measurement: conceptual appropriateness of measure, 14–16; empirical usefulness of measure, 19–22; validity of measurement, 16–19
income as proxy for well-being, 6
Index of Economic Well-Being, 6
inequality of happiness: aggregate trends in happiness, 38–51; assessing trends, 51–57; changes to General Social Survey, 74–77; discussion, 67–74; education and, 36; findings, 33–35; general approach to, 57–66; trends in, 36–38
Ireland, Thomas R., 303–305

James, William, 147
juries, 157–158, 173–175

Kahneman, Daniel, 81–82, 86–87
Kindlon, Dan, 98

law: civil damages guidelines, 184–186; compensatory damages in U.K., 218–220; deregulation of the family, 38; equality of opportunity, 37–38; juries, 157–158, 173–175; personal injury tort suits, 207–213
leisure inequality, 37
life satisfaction: and crime, 325–329, 336–339; German romanticists and, 87–88; Kahneman on, 86–87; measurement, 21–22; theory and empirical approach for, 334–336
lives, value of individual, 100–103

marriage: deregulation of the family, 38; as determinant of happiness, 15, 56, 135, 165, 172; surveys on happiness, 39; taxation and, 314–316
Mill, John Stuart: depression of, 106–107; last words, 87; on sex equality, 96–97; qualitative states of happiness, 85
Misery and Company (Clark), 98
movement and joy, 139–143, 149–150

National Crime Victims Survey (NCVS), 331–334, 339
natural selection and the human mind, 137, 147
Nietzsche, Friedrich, 81, 87–89

Nineteen Eighty-Four (Orwell), 99
Nozick, Robert, 16, 86, 100, 259
Nussbaum, Martha C.: defense of list, 104–106; objective-list accounts of, 256–257, 260–261, 263

objective-list approach, 104–106
Olavson, Tim, 142–143
Orwell, George, 99
Oswald, Andrew J., 300–302

pain and suffering, valuing: discussion, 191–197; hedonic adaptation, 198–202; hedonic measures' misses, 205–207; patient interviews, 202–205; proposal for, 207–213; time trade-off (TTO) method, 202–203; valuation, 207–213
pain-pleasure seeking, 95–99, 102
Pareto, Vilfredo, 13, 266, 305
Peasgood, Tessa, 5–26, 279–280
personal injury tort suits, 207–213
Philebus (Plato), 84
philosophical views of happiness. *See* happiness and philosophy; *specific philosophers and authors*
Pleasure and Desire (Gosling), 85
Positive Psychology (Seligman), 102
Prichard, Henry, 89–90
public policy and well-being measures: appropriateness criteria, 11–12; British Household Panel Survey (BHPS), 6–11; capabilities list (Nussbaum), 104, 110–111; determining well-being, 5–11; empirical usefulness of criteria, 13–14; hive psychology and, 149–152; income as measure of preference satisfaction, 14–22; issues in, 23–26; SWB and policy analysis, 259–260, 264, 279–288; validity criteria, 12–13
The Purpose Driven Life (Warren), 146

Raising Cain (Kindlon and Thompson), 98
relatedness hypotheses, 135–136
religion and well-being, 136, 139, 142
Rhetoric (Aristotle), 93
Rousseau, Jean-Jacques, 97–99

The Selfish Gene (Dawkins), 138
Seligman, Martin: on positive emotions, 92, 94–95, 98–99; "positive psychology" movement, 82; on well-being, 260
Sen, Amartya, 99, 263
Smith, Adam, 298–299
Smith, Tom, 75–76

Spencer, Herbert, 143
status-seeking activities, taxation of: competition and, 299–300; Frank's status taxation proposals, 311–314; literature on, 319–320
The Subjection of Women (Mill), 96–97
subjective evaluation, 6
subjective well-being (SWB): cost-benefit analysis (CBA) and, 286–288; compensating variations based on, 282–282; discussion, 253–255; decision procedure based on, 279–281; Extreme Claim and, 269–276; money and, 277–279; policy analysis and, 259–260, 264, 279–281; sources of, 260–264; usefulness of scales on, 265. *See also* well-being

taxation: age-based, 320 321; basics of tax policy, 296–298; disability and, 316–319; evidence for models, 305–311; Frank's status proposals, 311–314; happiness research and, 293–295; issues in, 319–321; marriage and, 314–316; models for, 300–305; status and, 298–300; status goods and, 319–320; unemployment and, 320
The Theory of Moral Sentiments (Smith), 298–299
Thompson, Michael, 98
Turner, Victor, 140–141

U.S. General Social Survey: aggregate trends in happiness, 38–51; crime data and, 329–334; happiness inequality, 54–57
Ubel, Peter A., 195–213
Uniform Crime Reports (UCR), 330
Utilitarianism (Mill), 85

The Varieties of Religious Experience (James), 147

weak welfarism and cost-benefit analysis, 255–256
wealth and happiness: Easterlin paradox, 2; income as measure of preference satisfaction, 14–22; income as proxy for well-being, 6; international increases in, 187–188; SWB (subjective well-being) literature and, 269–279; trends in income inequality, 36–38, 116, 187–188, 271–276
well-being: age and, 7; children and, 9; commuting and, 10; cost-benefit analysis, compensating variations in, 267–269; definitions of, 260; degrees and, 8; determining, 5–11; group-level improvements, 149–150; income as proxy, 6, 10–11; measurements of, 6–8; mental-state accounts, 257–259; objective-list accounts of, 256–257, 260–261, 263; preferentialist accounts, 257, 260; sports and, 145; surveys of, 257, 258, 261–263; World Health Organization Quality of Life (WHOQOL) index, 257–258, 261, 262–263, 271. *See also* subjective well-being (SWB); public policy and well-being measures
White, Mathew P., 104, 106–108
WHOQOL (World Health Organization Quality of Life) index, 257–258, 261, 262–263, 271
Williams, Bernard, 103
Williams, George, 137–138
willingness to accept (WTA), 161–163
willingness to pay (WTP): happiness and, 186–187; as measure of benefit in cost-benefit analysis, 10; measuring, 161–163
Women and Human Development (Nussbaum), 104–106
Wordsworth, William: "Character of the Happy Warrior," 108–110; on happiness, 89; on valuable activities, 97